SAGE was founded in 1965 by Sara Miller McCune to support the dissemination of usable knowledge by publishing innovative and high-quality research and teaching content. Today, we publish over 900 journals, including those of more than 400 learned societies, more than 800 new books per year, and a growing range of library products including archives, data, case studies, reports, and video. SAGE remains majority-owned by our founder, and after Sara's lifetime will become owned by a charitable trust that secures our continued independence.

Los Angeles | London | New Delhi | Singapore | Washington DC | Melbourne

THE BELT and ROAD INITIATIVE

THE BELT and ROAD INITIATIVE

Opportunities and Challenges of a Chinese Economic Ambition

EDITED BY

**DAVID DE CREMER
BRUCE McKERN
JACK McGUIRE**

Los Angeles | London | New Delhi
Singapore | Washington DC | Melbourne

Copyright © David De Cremer, Bruce McKern and Jack McGuire, 2020

All rights reserved. No part of this book may be reproduced or utilized in any form or by any means, electronic or mechanical, including photocopying, recording or by any information storage or retrieval system, without permission in writing from the publisher.

First published in 2020 by

SAGE Publications India Pvt Ltd
B1/I-1 Mohan Cooperative Industrial Area
Mathura Road, New Delhi 110 044, India
www.sagepub.in

SAGE Publications Inc
2455 Teller Road
Thousand Oaks, California 91320, USA

SAGE Publications Ltd
1 Oliver's Yard, 55 City Road
London EC1Y 1SP, United Kingdom

SAGE Publications Asia-Pacific Pte Ltd
18 Cross Street #10-10/11/12
China Square Central
Singapore 048423

Published by Vivek Mehra for SAGE Publications India Pvt Ltd. Typeset in 10.5/13 pt Bembo by Fidus Design Pvt Ltd, Chandigarh.

Library of Congress Control Number: 2019954530

ISBN: 978-93-5328-792-4 (HB)

SAGE Team: Rajesh Dey, Syed Husain Naqvi, Indra Kumar Mishra and Kanika Mathur

*My daughter Hannah—a source of happiness and hope.
Jess Zhang—an inspiring and loving beacon of light.
—David De Cremer*

*My friends in China who showed me that ambition and
dedication can build a better society.
—Bruce McKern*

*My mum, June. You generously supported my first trip to China
and opened up the world to me.
—Jack McGuire*

Thank you for choosing a SAGE product!
If you have any comment, observation or feedback,
I would like to personally hear from you.

Please write to me at **contactceo@sagepub.in**

Vivek Mehra, Managing Director and CEO, SAGE India.

Bulk Sales

SAGE India offers special discounts
for purchase of books in bulk.
We also make available special imprints
and excerpts from our books on demand.

For orders and enquiries, write to us at

Marketing Department
SAGE Publications India Pvt Ltd
B1/I-1, Mohan Cooperative Industrial Area
Mathura Road, Post Bag 7
New Delhi 110044, India

E-mail us at **marketing@sagepub.in**

Subscribe to our mailing list
Write to **marketing@sagepub.in**

This book is also available as an e-book.

Contents

Part I. Why a Focus on the Belt and Road Initiative?

Chapter 1   An Academic Approach to the Belt and Road Initiative   3
David De Cremer, Bruce McKern and Jack McGuire

Part II. On the Significance of the Belt and Road Initiative

Chapter 2   The Belt and Road Initiative: Views from the Chinese Side and the European Side   9
Ying Zhang

Chapter 3   Implementing the Belt and Road Initiative: Competing Priorities   27
Bruce McKern

Part III. Belt and Road Initiative at the Societal and Country Level

Chapter 4   The Belt and Road Initiative: A Pathway to World Leadership?   61
Stefanie Weil and Dora Munteanu

Chapter 5   Soft Infrastructures and the Belt and Road Initiative   92
Bala Ramasamy, Matthew Yeung, Yann Duval and Chorthip Utoktham

Chapter 6   The Belt and Road Initiative and Sino-Russo-Japanese Relations   111
Nikolay Murashkin

Chapter 7   China's Infrastructure Investment in Africa   137
Saite Lu

Chapter 8	Urban Development along the Belt and Road: A Case Study of North Africa	157
	Chuchu Zhang and Chaowei Xiao	
Chapter 9	Developing Effective Cross-Cultural Negotiations: The Case of the 'Belt and Road Initiative' for Turkey and China	179
	Mustafa Gokhan Bitmis and Jack McGuire	
Chapter 10	China on the Arabian Sea: A Risk Assessment	203
	Michael Tai	

Part IV. Managing the Business Dynamics of the Belt and Road Initiative

Chapter 11	Realizing the Potential of the Belt and Road Initiative: What Role for M&A?	221
	Peter J. Williamson	
Chapter 12	Globalizing Innovation Ecosystem, Entrepreneurs and the Digital Silk Road	236
	Mark J. Greeven	
Chapter 13	'One Belt, One Road': Risk Assessment and Chinese Investment	258
	Chaowei Xiao and Chuchu Zhang	
Chapter 14	RMB Internationalization in Relation to the Belt and Road Initiative	276
	Yimin Zhang and Qinli Zhu	
Chapter 15	On the Leadership Challenges for China in the Belt and Road Initiative	300
	David De Cremer	
Chapter 16	How Will the Belt and Road Initiative Be Financed?	319
	Simon Taylor	
Chapter 17	Promoting the Belt and Road Initiative: A Strategic Marketing Approach	344
	Eden Yin	
Chapter 18	Central Asia and the Belt and Road Initiative	365
	Richard Pomfret	

| *About the Editors and Contributors* | 387 |
| *Index* | 396 |

PART I

Why a Focus on the Belt and Road Initiative?

Chapter 1

An Academic Approach to the Belt and Road Initiative

David De Cremer, Bruce McKern and Jack McGuire

In 2013, while on official visits to Kazakhstan and Indonesia, President Xi Jinping first proposed the One Belt One Road (OBOR) Initiative (now called the Belt and Road Initiative, or BRI), with the aim of revitalizing transport, infrastructure and trade links along the ancient Silk Road routes and boosting China's role on the international stage. The BRI is likely the most significant development in global economics in many years, as it promotes investments of trillions of dollars in infrastructure across Asia, Europe and Africa. This region includes more than half the world's population, inhabiting low-income countries as well as fast-growing economies, including Indonesia, India, Vietnam and Pakistan.

The initiative is a visionary Chinese programme whose goal is to maintain an open world economic system and achieve diversified yet inclusive and sustainable development in a region of the world where development is sorely needed. In light of this ambition, BRI is also referred to as the 'Chinese Marshall Plan'. It has indeed a focus on achieving increased prosperity in a vast region, with a major leadership role for China, while at the same time being open to all developing countries and providing stimulus for those with a slowing economy.

However, critics say that BRI is in essence nothing more or less than a brilliant marketing campaign to justify the extensive Chinese investments that are currently happening around the world. In light of this ambitious plan, which also has a clear focus on tackling China's slowing growth via global investments and trade, inside and outside of China, the BRI has become a symbol of a more assertive China that has the potential and ambition to reshape the world both politically and economically.

One thing not to forget, however, is that BRI is basically a revival of an old idea. Indeed, the Silk Road was deployed at a time when China's Han Dynasty (206 BCE–220 CE) engaged in expansion efforts in the direction of the West. Networks were built and ran throughout today's Central Asian countries, such as Afghanistan and Kazakhstan, as well as India and Pakistan. Thus, in the past, China has already been the epicentre of globalization ambitions, making BRI today an old idea in a new format. Because BRI business involves more than 120 countries, a complex and potentially high-conflict situation could easily emerge. How to navigate this maze of national ambitions and rivalries?

Until now, China has primarily adopted an approach in which it is essential first to establish state-agreed cross-border policies to unlock 'soft' barriers to BRI. Trade and investment agreements are the most visible, and probably most powerful, means of spurring flows of economic factors across borders, and China has focused primarily on achieving those first.

It is important to note, however, that although the programme set out under the umbrella term of 'BRI' is intended to create prosperity for the participating countries and contribute to a prosperous future of globalization, deep scepticism remains. For instance, Europe wants to have greater assurance of reciprocal market access and is instituting tougher screening of Chinese investments within the EU. Claude Juncker made clear that the EU is very much willing to do business with China, but added immediately that this desire to engage in business relationships does not mean that the EU is 'naïve'. Instead, the EU seems very careful about China's implicitly assumed economic opportunism. In a similar vein, the UK has mentioned several times that they are a 'natural partner' for China and its BRI, but at the same time has refused to give its full backing. Furthermore, the BRI is currently also facing allegations that the economic project is a scheme to entrap poor nations into debt, which has led China to commit to actions to make BRI sustainable and lower the debt risk. Finally, the trade war currently going on between China and the USA has also fuelled perceptions about BRI that are negative and portray China's behaviour as predatory. All of these challenges and pushbacks mean that China is realizing that it needs to be more transparent and display an increased sense of accountability to deal with the concerns raised by Asian, European, American and African countries. Reconciling all these different interests will test China's diplomatic skills to the utmost.

This diversity of interests and perceptions of BRI has resulted in misunderstandings, feelings of irritation and frustration, and a hesitant, even distrusting, attitude towards what to make of BRI and how to assess its true potential. An important goal of the book now lying in front of you is therefore to bring a wide variety of academic perspectives together to illuminate the different facets of the BRI. In doing so, our goal is to provide a deeper understanding and a corresponding logic to analyse the potential opportunities and challenges China and its collaborators are, and will be, facing. Especially since President Xi Jinping has put his personal stamp and authority on the BRI, by having written this initiative as policy into the Party's Constitution at the 19th National Congress of the Communist Party of China in October 2017, we need to put more effort into understanding what this policy means for this ambitious project in a global setting where China will continue to play a more important role. Why do we need more academic-driven analysis to understand this initiative? First, BRI will influence significantly the whole world economy in the short- and long-term future. Second, given that the project aims to promote greater communication and cooperation between the East and the West, a deeper analysis is required of the BRI that is not influenced by politics or specific ideologies. Regrettably, much of the commentary about BRI has taken the form of opinion, often driven by political viewpoint. Therefore, an academic perspective based on knowledge generation and critical assessment and promoting the well-being of society must be central to exploring and reflecting on the potential and challenges of the BRI.

Providing an academic perspective entails an effort to make claims about BRI by means of rigorous inquiry, which is documented and elaborated upon by peer review. To that end, each chapter in this book was reviewed, feedback was provided to authors and revisions made, placing a strong emphasis on logical reasoning and accuracy, to resolve contradictions. This approach we believe is needed in analysing BRI as an economic project with many goals, and which will have effects across many different domains of business and society. Therefore, in the present book, we have brought together scholars with diverse backgrounds to articulate their differing perspectives, with the aim of providing divergent yet authoritative views on BRI.

The origin of this book project dates back to 29 September 2017, when the then KPMG chaired professor in management studies at the University of Cambridge, Dr David De Cremer, and Royal Society Fellow Dr Xiang Zhang launched an international platform in Cambridge to bring scholars and business representatives together with a shared interest in BRI.[1] The launch of this international platform brought together an international group of scholars for a roundtable discussion on the meaning of BRI, the goals underlying the economic initiative and the implications for both the East and the West. The outcomes of this roundtable meeting held in Cambridge provided the initial input to this book. We hope that you will enjoy reading and consider the various chapters as an important contribution to understanding the challenges and opportunities of an ambitious Chinese economic initiative with profound global implications.

---

[1] see http://www.chinadaily.com.cn/china/2017-09/30/content_32674950.htm

PART II

On the Significance of the Belt and Road Initiative

Chapter 2

The Belt and Road Initiative
Views from the Chinese Side and the European Side

Ying Zhang

Although the Belt and Road Initiative (BRI) has been acknowledged as a cross-continent project being expected to benefit both sides of the world (the Western and the Eastern), the tension and misunderstanding, instead, are still in dominance, particularly for practitioners. This chapter would propose solutions from both theoretical and practical perspectives. The motivation, and hope, is to offer certain insights and implications to the readers in order to facilitate the progress of rethinking about our shared traits—pursuing common goals by acknowledging differences.

INTRODUCTION

Deeply rooted in the ancient Eurasian Silk Road, developed over thousands of years ago, and lately revisited by the Chinese President Xi Jinping in 2013 in the period of China's economic transition, the BRI, also named the New Silk Road and One Belt One Road, has been seemingly widely accepted as an initiative to facilitate cross-continent trade, geo-economic integration and global prosperity. However, with regard to this idea, since its emergence, it has been interpreted variously, mainly in two directions: aptly reflecting what China has been challenged with in terms of domestically slowing down economic growth and boldly projecting the growing influence of China onto the global landscape with an alternative international geo-economic relationship approach. This initiative has also elicited three kinds of mixed reflexes or concerns: respect and/or awe; enthusiasm and/or paranoia (toward its proposer—China—as a provider of a visionary idea to the world); and it raises the question of whether this idea (i.e., BRI) is an altruistic game changer for the world, or if it is just another plot from an egotistically motivated superpower to further its self-interest.

The concern comes with a reason, similar to the pursuit of the Trans-Pacific Partnership (TPP) by other superpowers (such as the United States of America) that was lauded as well as criticized. Some thought of it as a beacon of world trade, giving the economies of the Pacific Rim their well-deserved trading club; while others saw it as just another instrument to align the Pacific Rim allies in an exclusive club of economic cooperation. With the unexpected withdrawal of the USA from the TPP under the Trump administration, the general attention has shifted to the other forward-looking initiative of the BRI, and China has ultimately been catapulted into the position as a thought leader to build a new world order. This position draws the eyes of the entire world to discuss the BRI offered by China and of course, expose China to the risk of losing its ordinary charm vis-à-vis the ordinary onlooker.

The current wave of reaction to the BRI is mixed, with enthusiasm to the BRI from some countries and criticism and worries from others. In three years, the BRI framework projects have taken place across the Eurasian continent from mid-2013; the lines have been shifting as disappointment has become a reality. Typically, many countries of the world started as supportive towards the BRI platform, as they see tangible advantages both in the short and long term, while others continue to beat the drum against this change. There are also some torn between believing in the benefits of a new vision and fearing its ramifications that they cannot fully grasp. Their wait-and-see attitude is a linchpin.

As an important financial arm of the BRI, the Asian Infrastructure Investment Bank (AIIB)[1] has been widely accepted and operated. Over the years, comments about the role of AIIB and the 'special

---

[1] AIIB is commonly labelled as a 'crowd-funded and crowd-owned' project.

connection' with BRI projects have been diverse, with clear categories emerging depending on whether profit is measured by economic or social axes. As AIIB is structurally considered to be more like a cooperative, it would make sense that the BRI, as its investment target platform, is not only jointly owned but also the one requiring shared commitment (including design, plan, investment and execution). However, this so far is hard to foresee from the European side. Europeans worry about the consequences of AIIB as a possible future financial order in the future (similar to the World Bank), and the BRI as an arm for the logistics and trade of new rule, with Europeans not participating in shared ownership.

There are always multiple interpretations from and towards different layers, regarding an initiative. To face the change of the world and to build a harmonious global society, each participant, theoretically, needs to carefully take into consideration the facts of the past, seriously see through the phenomena of the current, and ethically plan for the future by taking account of the influence of technology and geo-social-economics. The future is the future for all communities, not only for a particular member or a specific club. Therefore, the BRI, as a cross-continent platform with the vision of facilitating common prosperity, should be authentically treated as a jointly owned instrument to nurture our future society with the nature of an equality-based socio-economic environment.

THEORETICAL BACKGROUND: EQUALITY AND UNIVERSAL VALUE

In the past centuries, especially after the Second World, a polarized world was composed of capitalism-oriented (including market, state and social capitalism) and communist-ruled nations. Equality, usually in the eyes of economists and politicians, relates to equal economic income and opportunities. During the early and middle decades of the 20th century, the Western world achieved reduced inequality on these two pillars dramatically, even without commonly shared visions between different classes. The economy in the West, following the two industrial revolutions, had achieved fast growth and per capita growth kept at the highest level (Cooper, 2018). Opportunities were called to be equal, echoed particularly by education, social welfare and gradually equal access to the job market by the blue and white collars. The instrument to facilitate such equality was not others but something that most of the social capitalist countries still conduct today—social insurance, minimum wage, welfare framework, progressive income tax and equal access to education.

There are three causes (conditions) in that period driving equality. First, the fear of social and political turmoil from the West had been existing, if the western world did not conduct proper reform. This fear derived directly from the continuous threat from the opponent ruled by communists' alliances of the Soviet Union back to that era. Second, the impact of two World Wars on people and nations pushing the world to seek for the peace and equality in wealth. Third, the rise of the revolutionary belief in favouring collective force, destiny and prosperity. However, since the 1980s, when Soviet Union's alliances started collapsing, these three factors, drawing from the side of competition between two ideologies (capitalism and communism) as well as fear (to be disrupted by the other side), started to become self-disruptive. This disruption process later on exaggerated the growth of the concept of a rather exclusive ideological norm (determined by winners), favouring economic return and economic equality seemingly driven by capitalism, free-market principles and democracy. Such equality achieved by the West cannot be completely claimed as equality if associated with its central merit—the social dimension. Sociologically, equality has the merit of identifying and respecting the difference in commonality among people, organizations and national regimes. Running vastly on the track to harvest as much short-term economic returns as possible with discrimination (including discriminating up and discriminating down) to particular groups is not called equality because depriving one group of opportunities to enrich the other cannot be the way to reach economic and even social equality broadly. Therefore, being of a singularity, in the sense of identifying uniqueness and applying such unique value to the communities and others via reciprocal relationships, is the core of equality. The question then becomes, with the rule of capitalism, where does equality emerge from?[2]

Since the two biggest geo-economic-political shocks (from two World Wars and the collapse of the Former Soviet Union), the phenomena aforementioned (in the last paragraph) has been retained in

---

[2] It means inequality and insecurity are the default offspring (i.e., Muller 2013)

the current world order. Prosperity, similar to all other good things (e.g., people are happier, more democratic and less likely to go to war with one another; see Treverton 2017), form the basis of what humans are expecting/hoping but paradoxically conflicts with what the behaviour of humans seems to dictate (i.e., behavioural discrimination to the alternative ideologies). Such a conflict between expectation and action facilitates the dark side of individualism (promoted by liberty and democracy) to be selfish and discriminative, instead of appreciating singularity. Singularity is different from individualism; it calls for the uniqueness, the unique value of uniqueness to a broader community. Singularity considers human's universal values[3] as an aggregate value to achieve, such as power, achievement, hedonism, stimulation, self-direction, universalism, benevolence, tradition, conformity and security (Schwartz and Bilsky 1987). From this angle, the BRI (with its goal to reach a shared prosperity) can be a practice to use singularity to achieve equality and bring universal values to the global community in terms of achievement (bringing up capability, influence and intelligence for each region), hedonism (bringing in pleasure and happiness for people), universalism (developing more equality and peace, unifying with nature, harmony between each other), benevolence (being honest, forgiving, and responsibility to each other), tradition (respect, humility, moderation) and security (stability of social order, reciprocation of favours).

Specifically, within these 10 universal values, power (reflected by social status and prestige, control or dominance over people and resources and the motivation underpinning some values) plays a very critical role in guiding the other 9 universal values. If power cannot be treated appropriately (in this sense, it means that power mainly serves economic-driven aims, like in the economic return driven system), its effect will emerge to exaggerate the attainment and preservation of a dominant position within the more general social system for specific groups (Schwartz 2012). And such an exaggerating effect feeds inequality, strengthens discrimination and accentuates individualism, killing

---

[3] Universal Values have following two ways to be understood: the value that everyone finds valuable and the value that everyone has reason to believe it has value.

the other nine universal values (at the community level) and disregarding the value of singularity.

THE PARADOX IN THE BRI

The BRI, originally named as One Belt One Road initiative (from October 2013 to mid-2016), inspired by China's ancient 'Silk Road' back from Tang/Song Dynasty, is the latest Chinese international strategy, at both China's national and corporate levels. This strategy is structured to build up (stronger) connections and cooperation among Eurasian countries via the Belt and Road Connections (the belt refers to the land-based economic belt, and road refers to the ocean-going Maritime Silk Road). In the past few years until the end of 2017, the BRI, since the first stage of focusing on infrastructure investment, construction, railway and highway, automobile, power grid, and iron and steel, has become one of the biggest infrastructure investments in human history. In total, it spans across 68 states, 40 per cent of world GDP, and around 65 per cent of the world population in 2017 (Ramasamy et al. 2017).

With a very abstract vision, the BRI has structured six different economic corridors.[4] Viewing the BRI's day-to-day map progression, the signal sent to and received by China is that the BRI is not merely a Eurasian project but also a project starting to involve Oceania and Africa. The fast development of the BRI, in contrast to the TPP and Transatlantic Trade and Investment Partnership, has filled the rest of the world with widely varied responses over time.

---

[4] New Eurasian Land Bridge, from Western China to Western Russia through Kazakhstan.
China–Mongolia–Russia Corridor, running from Northern China to Eastern Russia
China–Central Asia–West Asia Corridor, running from Western China to Turkey
China–Indochina Peninsula Corridor, running from Southern China to Singapore
China–Myanmar–Bangladesh–India Corridor, running from Southern China to Myanmar
China–Pakistan Corridor, from South-Western China to Pakistan

In general, there are mainly two responses about the BRI at present: (a) the BRI is considered to be a strategy that the Chinese (government) are using to transfer China's domestic economic overcapacity to the overseas market and (b) the BRI is created by the Chinese side as an alternative international geopolitical approach to deal with the complex global geopolitical environment. It explains that an economic relationship (such as via investment and collaboration) with players from neighbouring countries could strengthen the mutual understanding between China and other countries and therefore release the potential macro-level tensions (i.e., geopolitical) at different times. These two responses are not independent but integrated as a paradoxical emotion proffered by the rest of the world. The BRI has elicited respect and awe, while simultaneously provoking enthusiasm and paranoia.

Such a paradoxical response from the rest of the world is not surprising, but the reason for such a paradox does have an association with an Inept Systematic Intelligence (ISI) that most countries have held. This ISI is primarily determined by one of the universal values mentioned before—power. An existing power does not usually accept a new rising power (which might hold alternative regimes and beliefs). The relationship between the existing power and the rising power is similar to the paradoxical relationship between the entrepreneurs and existing firms in the process of creative destruction (Schumpeter 1994, 82–83), whereby entrepreneurs constitute the disruptive force that sustains economic growth; however, they also challenge the value of established companies and labourers (Sidak and Teece 2009). This applies to China, as one of the current economic powers, and the BRI project they are initiating. The BRI has caused enormous doubt for many Western countries. There doubt is derived from a fear that China, with its economic power, aims to destroy the existing world power structure and the existing world order, because China, with its breakthrough economic growth record (for the continuous three decades) and alternative regime of domestic power system (a country governed by a single party, named as dictatorship), is equipped to do so. Regarding this, China has always denied in both words and action.

PROPOSITIONS DERIVED FROM THE BRI PRACTICE

Regarding the two different responses to the BRI, one view believes that the BRI is a beacon of world trade, giving the economies of the Pacific Rim their well-deserved trading club. This view is often held by two types of countries [noted here as C1 and C2]: nation C1 depicts the countries whose GDP depends heavily on international trade and overseas market such as the United Kingdom and the Netherlands; nation C2 depicts the ones that need to economically catch up in the short-term (such as many eastern European countries, Poland and Lithuania). These two group of countries, similar to innovative firms and latecomer firms at a corporate level, are usually (pro)active in attempts to understand and participate in the BRI-related projects. The BRI in this case is more likely to be interpreted as an opportunity rather than a threat.

The other view, on the side of either being against or having a strategy of wait-and-see-then-react, is held by those who are part of the current global geopolitical–economic power and act in the centre of the present world order (such as France, the UK, Germany, the USA, Japan, etc.) [Here noted as C3]. This group of countries is reluctant to accept new initiatives by others, similar to those incumbent firms that cannot easily open doors to newcomers into the market because of the effect of creative destruction in disrupting the existed order built by them. With this view, the BRI, initiated by an economic follower, could be seen as an alternative instrument to align its Pacific Rim allies to an alternative exclusive club of economic cooperation.

The Complexity of the BRI Network

The Chinese side of the story claims that the BRI is a global strategy, with a vision to bring shared prosperity to the global population. Regarding its structure, the BRI is a multilateral network. If taking China as the node of network centrality (initiator) with other network nodes, the principal characteristic of the BRI network is its high level of heterogeneity (of countries). These countries, in another dimension, can be north countries and south countries (noted as NC and SC; rich and poor, in other words). With regard to China's positioning in the

BRI network, China stays in-between currently: between the rich and poor (in terms of GDP per capita), between C2 and post-C2[5] (measured by China's fast growth of GDP in the past few decades and ranked as the second largest economic country in the world), and between C1 and C3[6] (measured by China's export in goods and service in GDP, i.e., 17.58% in 2017, compared to 86.46% of the Netherlands in 2017). This complexity of China's position brings difficulties for other network players in understanding the purpose and action of China in such an initiative, and second, it generates hardship in progressing the BRI at an aggregated level. Thus the first proposition.

Proposition 1. The BRI will not be easily understood and executed, because of the high degree of heterogeneity of BRI associated countries and the complexity of the BRI's initiator in its eco-social positioning (C1, C2, and C3).

To analyse the BRI network complexity, the BRI network players need to be clustered by their geo–economic–positioning natures (C1, C2 or C3) as mentioned previously. The reason is to reduce the cognitive gap in understanding and to improve the efficiency in the execution of the BRI projects in different regions. In the countries denoted as C1 and C2, the BRI has slowly switched from a giant multilateral project to numerous bilateral projects via merger and acquisitions or greenfield investments by Chinese corporates.

In addition to clusters, the complexity of the BRI network implies that working with partners should be on the order of one by one (country), if partners are not from the same cluster. Strategically, it is efficient to do so in that it improves China's bargaining power and significantly reduces the level of heterogeneity[7] in the existing complex geopolitics relationship, if, as what is stated at the beginning of this chapter to consider the BRI as a shared property, the BRI can be a

---

[5] Due to China's dual development pattern between China's East and West, Urban and Rural.

[6] Due to China as the frontier players in the 4th Industrial Revolution and positioning as an economic power.

[7] In such case means several quality and/or content in social norms, customs, regulations, etc.

cooperatively governed institution where China should share the ownership, responsibility, actions and consequences with others. Thus, the format of cooperative (in game theory) can be delivered in many scenarios. First, with a very limited number of members (for example working one by one with the BRI members), the reduced heterogeneity[8] can induce the emergence of cooperatives (as governance structure) as long as one party in such a cooperative would actively play like a champion (China, as the initiator and network centrality, in this case, is considered to be proactive). Therefore, this brings us to Proposition 2.

> *Proposition 2.* The one-to-one cooperative model can be effective (emerged) if China (as the network node in the BRI centrality) works with countries with a lower level of heterogeneity (for example, in South Asia and Central Asia).

The European Union embraces a high-level of complexity in its members' various economic development levels, investment demands and geopolitical relationships with China. To this case, using strategies such as Proposition 2 will not be effective, because it will be against the EU's collective vision and internal agreements, laws and norms. If abstractly simulating in a game[9] (without the reality that there are no coordinators between EU and China on the BRI project), we can come to a third proposition in light of this case.

> *Proposition 3.* If there is no outsider (a third party) as a coordinator to manage the complex group, the governance of a cooperative (for the BRI) will not emerge in a top-down approach.

The reality is, by far, that the BRI hasn't set up any central coordinating groups/committees composed by both the Chinese side and the European side. First, the BRI hasn't been legitimatized by the major countries in the EU and the EU commission from the top. Second,

---

[8] Because it is impossible for two members with same nature, reducing heterogeneity to a medium level is already satisfying.

[9] Due to the limitation of the space, I will not elaborate the simulation. The abstracted simulation can be referred to the Chapter 2 of my PhD student Anna Petruchenya's (2018) thesis.

due to a lack of legacy from the top, the BRI has left a big space for entrepreneurs from both sides to collaborate freely. From the eyes of Europeans, however, the bottom-up collaboration is hardly planned by the top and systematically controlled by the top. The propositions[10] are therefore as follows.

> *Proposition 4.1.* Emerging from a bottom-up approach, entrepreneurs from both sides will search for partners with similarity, with a medium or lower level of heterogeneity.
>
> *Proposition 4.2.* Such collaborations will not be bonded to outsiders in the same way as in a top-down approach. Outsiders (project managers or coordinators) in the scenarios with an entrepreneurs' bottom-up approach will show a high value. Business is constructed in a manner of 'either take it or leave it' with selfish outsiders.

As proposed above, working at a high level of heterogeneity within EU, the emergence of a cooperative appears rather difficult, if without outsiders (official coordinator in between). Under such a circumstance, opportunities are therefore given to a bottom-up approach involving entrepreneurial cooperation between the two sides (and it does happen); however, the freedom of doing reciprocal business is still significantly restrained by the underdeveloped bilateral or multilateral higher-level agreements. One key executive (anonymous) from a BRI-related project from the European side stated, 'The transparent and open talk between Europe and China is missing. Europe should talk to China in one mouth, rather than in 10 mouths'. Another said, 'In order to build shared destiny, we need to start talking ... to a business, there are no worries in logistics, but the local government has worries about the political influence of China'. Also, due to many organizations using the BRI as a title to act as a fake broker rather than an officially appointed coordinator, many BRI-associated European entrepreneurs have raised doubts about the credibility of the BRI. Common questions usually mentioned at the EU or state-level roundtables by European business players are, for example, 'Is there a list or database of what

---

[10] The simulation will not be shown here. If interested, please refer to Anna Petruchenya (2018).

BRI-associated firms and projects are?' 'Can I trust this list?' 'Is there signed approval, the guarantee of quality?' 'What about BRI people and organizations?' 'Who owns the BRI? Shared ownership or China itself?'

To think of the possible solutions (together with the propositions mentioned above), supposing in the future that coordinators at different levels can be either voted (bottom-up) or appointed (top-down) by both sides, by applying the game-playing simulation (Petruchenya 2018, Ch. 2), a possible solution for bringing about an efficient cooperative for the BRI between EU and China can be as follows: An outsider (coordinator or coordinating committee participated by both the EU and China sides) needs to be arranged and (a) if its value is high to the BRI attended members, a top-down approached cooperation will be efficient and (b) if its value is low, a bottom-up approached benevolent outsider (such as an NGO) can be compelling.

ISSUES OF THE BRI PARADOX

In the past five years, the BRI projects on land and maritime have exhibited a paradox at various levels. For the Chinese side, the paradox is mainly presented on the execution nerve between localization and globalization. For the European side, towards the BRI, a paradox exists as well, mostly at the cognitive level. The paradox here exists between the EU, state and enterprise levels, in addition to the way various understandings of the BRI have emerged and treatment of the BRI as an opportunity or threat.

First, Chinese firms' international progress, before and after the BRI, has always been one of the strong drivers of China's economic growth. Since the early 1980s, internationalization of Chinese organizations had gone through from the mode of international trade (from a little to a massive quantity) to collaboration with inward foreign investment and to outward Chinese investment (including massive global merger and acquisitions, i.e., Zhang 2014). Throughout this progress, the major issue regarding Chinese movement into the global market, particularly in host countries, is its insufficient adaptation to locals' (invested countries) norms, rituals and conduct of business, although it has indeed delivered much positive impact to locals, by bringing in infrastructure, technology, capital and job positions. This is highly in contrast to Chinese firms in adapting to foreign investment in the territory of China.

There are a number of reasons for why this occurs. First, there is a considerable distance between the Chinese and the West in project management and dynamic capabilities (i.e., Zhang et al., 2015; Zhang, 2017)). This applies to the Chinese firms that are shorted in international Chinese talents (who can bridge the East and West easily). Second, in terms of ownership, there are reasons expressed by Chinese corporates as to why a dilemma exist. The dilemma can be explained through dual drives (sometimes on the same direction, sometimes with the opposite directions): (a) drives from the dual markets (domestic and international) and (b) drives from the dual shareholder(s) (governments for state-owned and private investors for private firms).

In principle, the drive from the market requires firms to respond to the local markets effectively by adapting to local rituals, regulations, norms and conduct of business. The drive from the solo shareholder, however, determines that they have to mainly follow their shareholders' orders,[11] acting as an executor rather than an entrepreneurial entity. This is a big dilemma for managers and executives in the local/host market because concerning corporate governance and the source of investment capital, an intervention from the home state is the default. For the sake of job security, anyone would not dare to risk themselves to move against an upper order.

For private firms, even if they have an investment in BRI projects, ineptness in localization is also a big issue that has been seen in recent years. This is majorly due to the lack of knowledge and experience in internationalization,[12] the limited access to international information, and the shortage of capital and cash flow compared to the state-owned firms.

---

[11] Sometimes it might not be rational or just for a propaganda's purpose.
[12] Even though those Chinese private firms had experience in collaborating with non-Chinese firms in China.

Therefore, an interesting phenomena emerges: The progress of Chinese firms' internationalization is composed of two stages (P1 and P2, referring to Figure 2.1 in terms of rows): the first stage of internationalization (collaborating with international firms in China's domestic market, noted as the stage P1—the two grids in the upper row in Figure 2.1) and the second stage when Chinese firms go abroad, doing business in the international market in the host countries (noted as P2—the two grids at the bottom in Figure 2.1). Regarding both columns, the left column depicts China (home) territory relative to the Chinese; while the right column depicts the non-Chinese (host) territory relative to the Chinese. To elaborate, Chinese firms adaptation in the past few decades into an international arena (from international trade to collaboration with inward foreign investment, noted in the stage P1, and to Chinese outward investment noted in the stage P2), the extent of Chinese firms' adaptation to locals in the stage P1 appears more significant than that is shown in the stage P2.

To further elaborate, P1 and P2 have an independently dependable relationship. P1 is a sufficient by not necessary condition of P2. In the case for Chinese who have experience from both P1 and P2, cognitive bias is natural to be generated because one may learn internationalization from the P1 stage and likely to apply what is learned in P1 to P2.

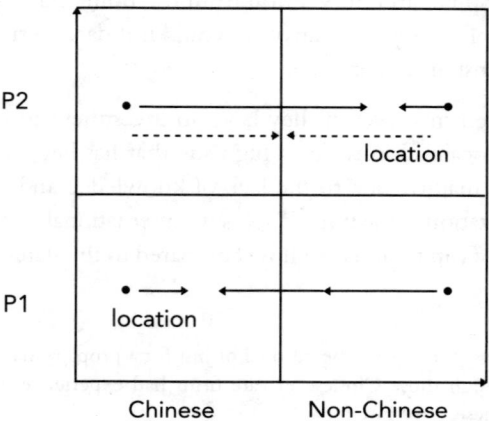

Figure 2.1 *Stages of Chinese Internationalization*

Although P1 and P2 may share the similar types of participants (for example, Chinese may deal with the same Western firms in China and abroad), however, the approach to deal with partners (for the Chinese side) may not be the same. To be more efficient in both P1 and P2, Chinese, for example, must adapt to the foreign cognition and behaviour quicker and faster than that of locals. For example, in the stage P1 when foreign firms do business in China (the solid line starting from the left to the right), the foreign side has to adapt much faster to the local (see the solid line extending to the bottom-left grid) than that of Chinese adapting to foreign (in China). With the same logic, when Chinese firms step into a foreign territory, doing business with them, in the stage P2, they need to adapt faster than the locals (the upper right grid) in the local territory (see the solid line extending into the upper-right grid). However, due to the inertia developed in the P1 stage as mentioned previously, the Chinese partners did not develop their adaptation sufficiently (see the dotted lines in the figure representing what Chinese firms have been practicing in the P2 scenario), whereas in this case, the locals must make more effort to adapt (including understanding and compromising to the Chinese side).

Although European entrepreneurs are very entrepreneurial and likely to approach the BRI associated projects in a bottom–up way (as mentioned in the last section), under the circumstance where macro-level understanding is lacking, their opinions at the micro level are mainly filled with worries. For instance, practitioners entail a list of comments such as (anonymous) the following:

> 'Chinese businesses are coming to your land; they should operate in the way that is operated here and not in the Chinese way'.

> 'And when Chinese money in invested in Eastern Europe, a railroad was built with Chinese Financing, so they also were obligated to use Chinese contractors and this is completely against the European Law'.

> 'From the Chinese perspective, I understand China has its ports and wants to direct their ships to their own ports, to manage the whole chain. But that's the Chinese way. Our way of business is always to specialize in something you are the best in and leave smoothers in the whole chain to other partners who are best in this part … then everyone can specialize and protect his/her part and the cooperation'.

'I am fine that the Chinese want to export their overcapacity, but can I export my stuff to China? Can I establish my factories in Shenzhen or Suzhou, or Qingdao (port) (as what the Chinese are doing here)? It is not allowed! ... If you want to do something in Europe, then you also need to open your market'.

Regarding Chinese firms' adaptation in Europe and correspondence from local entrepreneurs and stakeholders to Chinese behaviour, there are also some promising examples (though in modest proportion) in dealing with the paradox of localization and globalization. One Chinese multinational high-tech firm, globalized for 20 years in the overseas market, described their strategy, 'When we do globalization, we have to balance with localization ... and we believe the very fundamental part is to build one open, fair and transparent management system ... We also decide our strategy based on our own business ... We have our five-year plan'. Such a mindset and behaviour should be the role model for ordinary Chinese firms conducting business overseas.

CONCLUSION

With the significant positive historical evidence of China's Silk Road, back from thousands of years ago, the BRI would have to play an essential role in connecting each corner of the world by facilitating shared prosperity for the 21st century. Despite bias and different views towards the progress of cooperation between the member states, the BRI, with its vision for the goodness of global population, should not be displaced.

In addition to setting up high-level discussions and agreements in a top-down approach, I propose that entrepreneurs (at a corporate and enterprise level) from both sides should be given enough space to collaborate in a bottom-up approach. Both sides should arrange coordinating committees to facilitate the BRI progress (building up a database, executing management of the BRI agenda and work plan among the BRI related countries, proposing the BRI rules and regulations, finding solutions to existing crippling problems, eliminating an overall defensive and competitive mentality, and creating a cooperative foundation for the future agenda). The BRI's progress should not rest only on the shoulder of a single country and a single government, but should be on the shoulders of all participants, from the businesses, research institutes, education centres and individuals. By combining everyone's joint efforts, the BRI's aim to set up an inclusively equality-oriented prosperous community can be realized. But something we need to always bear in mind is that difference is the source of challenges, disputes and problems, while simultaneously also ironically the driver of opportunities, collaborations and solutions. To deal with a paradox of opportunity and threat, a paradox in the process of globalization and localization, each of us is required to continuously believe in human-kind's universal values and the principle of singularity. Behaviour-wise, each of us must pay collective intelligence and courage and apply hard work as a strongly bonded team.

REFERENCES

Cooper, Richard N. 2018. 'Global Trends: Paradox of Progress/World on the Move: Consumption Patterns in an Equal Global Economy'. *Foreign Affairs* 96 (3): 156.

Muller, Jerry Z. 2013. 'Capitalism and Inequality'. *Foreign Affairs* 92 (2).

Petruchenya, A. 2018. 'Essay of Cooperative'. PhD thesis series, Erasmus Research Institute of Management.

Ramasamy, B., M. Yeung, C. Utoktham, and Y. Duval. 2017. 'Trade and Trade Facilitation along the Belt and Road Initiative Corridors'. ARTNeT Working Paper Series, Bangkok, United Nations ESCAP.

Schumpeter, Joseph A. 1994 [1942]. *Capitalism, Socialism, and Democracy*. London: Routledge.

Schwartz, S. H. 2012. 'An Overview of the Schwartz Theory of Basic Values'. *Online Readings in Psychology and Culture* 2 (1): 11.

Schwartz, S. H., and W. Bilsky. 1987. 'Toward a Universal Psychological Structure of Human Values'. *Journal of Personality and Social Psychology* 53 (3): 550–562.

Sidak, J. Gregory, and David J. Teece. 2009. 'Dynamic Competition in Antitrust Law'. *Journal of Competition Law & Economics* 5 (4): 581–631.

Treverton, G. 2017. 'Global Trends: Paradox of Progress'. NIC/DNI, Washington.

Zhang, Ying, C. Marquis, S. Filippov, and M. van der Steen. 2015. 'The Challenges and Enhancing Opportunities for Global Project Management: Evidence from Chinese and Dutch Cross-Cultural Project Management'. Harvard Business School Working Paper 15–063, Harvard Business School.

Zhang, Ying. 2014. 'Catching-Up by Chinese Multinational Firms Using Network Strategies'. In *Successes and Challenges of Emerging Economy Multinationals*, edited by M. Marinov and S. Marinova. UK: Palgrave Macmillan.

———. 2017. 'The Belt and Road Initiative and its Influence on East–West Cooperation'. *European's World*, 16 November.

Chapter 3

Implementing the Belt and Road Initiative*
Competing Priorities

Bruce McKern

THE BELT AND ROAD INITIATIVE AND COMPETING PRIORITIES

Introduction

According to the Asian Development Bank (ADB 2017), developing countries in Asia (excluding China) need to invest $8.8 trillion on new infrastructure between 2016 and 2030. So there is little doubt that the One Belt One Road Initiative (hereinafter referred to as the Belt and Road Initiative or BRI) addresses a highly important need. BRI also has ambitious goals for China's economic and geopolitical influence in the central Asian region, the security of its energy supplies and the land and sea routes between China, Central Asia, Europe and Africa. There is also a so-called eastern Pacific 'East Wing' encompassing Latin America.

The initiative is also providing stimulus to China's external trade at a time when the economy is shifting away from exports towards internal

---

* This chapter is based in a part on McKern (2018).

consumption, and China's growth rate has been slowing to around 6.4 per cent per annum. At the same time, the country has been under serious pressure from the United States of America to reduce its trade surplus. By mid-2019, the agreement had not been reached, and further tariffs were imposed on both sides. If agreement is reached between the USA and China, it seems probable that the two parties will set up administrative bodies to monitor protective actions on either side and drop most of the tariffs imposed in 2018 and 2019.

Whatever the outcome, China's global current account surplus has already fallen considerably. In 2018, it had dropped to $49 billion (0.4% of GDP), compared with its peak of $421 billion 10 years before (Qinqin and Wei 2019). Severe restrictions on China's trade with the USA would have deleterious effects on its economy, and implementing the BRI as fully as possible would therefore be all the more important, to help maintain its trade among the Central and South Asian countries and further west. It would no doubt force China to seek further expansion of the BRI, as it has already done towards Europe, Africa and Latin America. The investment needed will be one of the competing priorities that will pose challenges for China's investment beyond its borders.

This chapter considers the scope of the BRI, the investment and other pressures on China's foreign and domestic priorities over the coming years, and the attitudes of other countries. Its focus is on the overall investment needs rather than how they will be financed, together with the international issues concerning its implementation. Chapter 16 of this book by Professor Simon Taylor provides a detailed examination of China's capacity to finance the BRI. Taylor notes that the overall cost has not been officially specified, but he quotes estimates ranging from $1 trillion (Hurley, Morris, and Portelance 2018) to $8 trillion (Balding 2017). In this chapter, for the purposes of assessing the competing demands for capital and in view of the pressures on China's trade outlined above, we adopt an estimate of $4 trillion for the required BRI investment, an allegedly official figure (*The Economist* 2016), and add to that other pressing investment needs that China will need to balance against BRI.

Poverty Reduction: A High Priority

China faces challenges on many fronts, including an ageing population and shrinking workforce (despite a population approaching 1.4 billion people), domestic environmental and health concerns, and growing global protectionism. Despite China's remarkable success in reducing poverty over the last 30 years, inequality remains a matter of high priority. President Xi in December 2017 vowed to eradicate poverty by 2020 among the remaining 16.6 million people acknowledged to be living below the extreme poverty line. Mr Xi repeated this goal at the second session of the 13th National People's Congress (NPC) in March 2019.[1] Extreme poverty was defined at 95 cents a day (¥2,300 or $340 per year in 2010 prices). Adjusted for inflation, the goal would be around ¥3,000 or $880 per year at 2016 prices (EIU 2018). In what follows, we make a rough estimate of the capital investment needed to eradicate poverty in China.

Between 2013 and 2017, the number of people in rural areas living in poverty as defined above fell, according to the *South China Morning Post*, from 98.9 million in 2013 to 43.35 million, a reduction of 55.6 million (Zhuang 2017). Over this period, the central government's budget for poverty alleviation totalled ¥282 billion or $44 billion, and it had increased each year, reaching ¥85 billion in 2017.

In 2018, the number below the poverty was reported by the National Bureau of Statistics as having fallen to 16.6 million from a level of 30.5 million in 2017, a lower figure for 2017 than reported earlier.[2] This amounted to a reduction by 13.9 million people of those in poverty between 2017 and 2018. The average annual income of the 13.9 million increased from ¥9,377 ($1,400)—already above the

---

[1] https://news.cgtn.com/news/3d3d414f3463544d33457a6333566d54/index.html
People with an annual income lower than ¥2,300 ($340) per year, based on 2010 prices, were defined as living below the poverty line in China.

[2] National Bureau of Statistics of China, Statistical Communiqué of the People's Republic of China on the 2018 National Economic and Social Development, 28 February 2019.

poverty line—to ¥10,371 ($1,548). Therefore, the increase in annual income was $148 per person. The improvement in total income for this group of 13.9 million people would have been $2.06 billion per annum.

What capital would have been invested to effect this improvement? In 2018, the Ministry of Finance of the PRC announced that the government would spend ¥106 billion ($16.7 billion) on poverty reduction in 2018 (Xinhuanet 2018). Assuming this was fully spent to assist the 13.9 million people, this would have amounted to an investment of $1,200 per person. That implies an incremental capital–output ratio of 8:1, somewhat higher than the average for China but not unreasonable (OECD 2018).[3] The increase in incomes may have been aided by other forms of assistance, including local and provincial government budgets and the central government's 'mass entrepreneurship and innovation' programme to stimulate local businesses.[4] But this estimate gives some idea of the funds needed for poverty alleviation.

What would be needed to bring the remaining 16.6 million up to the poverty line? Accepting the above assumptions and ignoring inflation, to eradicate extreme poverty completely by 2020 would require an expenditure of a further $1,200 per person, or $19.9 billion in 2019, some 20 per cent more than spent in 2018. Given the strong emphasis given by the central government to this important objective, we can assume that the needed funds will be allocated.

However, there are many people in the Chinese middle class who are still poor by world standards. The World Bank estimates that in 2018 there were 373 million people in China living below the 'upper middle income' threshold of $5.50 per day or $2,000 per year (World Bank 2019a).[5] What investment would be needed to bring that vast

---

[3] China's overall incremental capital–output ratio has increased to around 6:5 in 2018, but we assume it would be higher for poverty reduction interventions, which may be more difficult as the percentage diminishes.

[4] Also, there is some inconsistency between the figures quoted by the *South China Morning Post* and the National Bureau of Statistics. Also, the Bureau's data implies that the 13.9 million assisted in 2018 were already above the poverty line.

[5] Average per capita income in China was $8,800 at current prices in 2017.

population to $8,800, the current average Chinese income per year? We can make a guess at what would be needed. Assuming, optimistically, that the average income of this group is already equal to the threshold of $2,000 per year, and the same incremental capital–output ratio of 8:1, an increase of $6,800 per person per annum (46 times the increase per person in 2018) would require an investment of $54,400 per person. For 373 million people, the total would amount to $20,291 billion, almost twice China's GDP in 2017.

To achieve this more challenging goal of becoming a 'moderately prosperous society', investment resources of this magnitude will be needed over time, perhaps over 10 years. These investments in people will of course add to GDP and be financed by government budgets that would increase as GDP grows, but this option implies a large claim on resources of perhaps $2 trillion per annum over 10 years. For the purposes of the analysis in this chapter, we assume that these funds will be found from regular government budgets, and they will not be included in the estimates of competing priorities. However, given the importance of the goal, some demands might have to take lower priority.

Priorities and Policy Approach

The previous section outlined the broad problems facing the Chinese economy over the next 10 or so years, with the discussion focused on poverty alleviation. But, of equal concern is dealing with the shrinking workforce, the shift to increased consumption and declining savings; becoming more efficient in the use of resources; and creating a strongly competitive and innovative economy in an uncertain global environment.

China's policy approach to these and related problems includes three broad economic initiatives:

- Increasing productivity in private business and state-owned enterprises (SOEs), with an increased emphasis on innovation and new technologies
- Regional integration within China to create more efficient urban agglomerations

- Deeper foreign engagement beyond existing trade patterns, including the BRI

We examine each of these solutions in turn in order to draw implications for the BRI over the next five years.

INCREASING PRODUCTIVITY THROUGH INNOVATION
China's Innovation Ecosystem

China has nearly exhausted the growth achievable in the past by the classic development strategy of shifting under-employed labour from the countryside to more productive use in the cities, in combination with the investment of capital garnered from high domestic savings. At the same time, the workforce is shrinking and becoming more expensive. Increasing workforce productivity is seen as a necessary solution. Consequently, in each of its five-year plans for many years, increasing productivity through innovation has been emphasized as a key focus of China's development policies. Since the opening-up after 1980, China has succeeded in building an innovation ecosystem from the ground up. It has invested growing government budgets in establishing an infrastructure of government science and technology parks, industrial zones, research institutions and universities, and these have been accompanied by over 1,600 foreign R&D centres set up by multinational corporations (Yip and McKern 2016). This direct emphasis on innovation has been accompanied by a vast expansion of the national transport, telecommunications and logistics infrastructure, which facilitate the efficiency of the economy.

This investment in hard infrastructure has been supported by 'soft' policies to encourage private enterprises and SOEs to invest in R&D. Led by the government budget allocations, China's gross expenditure on R&D (GERD) has increased steadily, in absolute terms and as a percentage of GDP, and, in 2017, it reached 2.1 per cent of GDP, slightly above the average for the EU as a whole (World Bank 2019b). The value was ¥1.76 trillion or $262 billion at current prices.[6] The government

---

[6] All monetary figures are in current prices and exchange rates, not at purchasing power parity.

share of GERD, although growing in absolute terms, has fallen relative to that of business (down to some 23% of the total in 2017) but government has consistently been the exemplar and proponent of innovation.

While China's overall GERD to GDP ratio is lower than that of the USA, which was 2.74 per cent ($468 billion),[7] China intends for R&D to reach 2.5 per cent of GDP by 2020. There are questions about the comparability of the figures, due to accounting differences and the definition of R&D expenditure, which in China includes science communications, administration, scientific exchanges and cooperation, but there is no doubt that the country has vastly increased its R&D spending and is continuing to do so.

This investment is reaping rewards in technological capacity and measures of innovative success. China's publications in top scientific and technological journals now lead the world in many important domains. Its total scientific publications in 2016 were 426,000, whereas those of the USA were 409,000 (NSF 2018). It was No. 1 in engineering, chemistry and geoscience and No. 2 in computer science, agricultural science, mathematics and physics[8] and a leader in several scientific and technical sub-domains.

In another indicator of innovative output, China is the world leader in the number of innovation patent applications each year, with some 1.3 million filings in 2016 to the China National Intellectual Property Administration (CNIPA), formerly the State Intellectual Property Office, and that was more than twice the number for the USA. But this figure is misleading: 65 per cent of these applications were for 'utility' patents or design patents, compared with 35 per cent for invention patents, which require greater proof of originality. And of the total patents granted (about 50% of the total applications), only19 per cent were invention patents; the granted patents were only a quarter of the invention patent applications (Center for Strategic and International Studies 2019). Nevertheless, the growth in innovation patents is impressive.

---

[7] OECD data, available at https://data.oecd.org/rd/gross-domestic-spending-on-r-d.htm

[8] Author's calculation from NSF (2018).

Another indicator is the number of patent applications submitted through the Patent Cooperation Treaty (PCT) process.[9] Chinese applicants for patents using the PCT process accounted for 20 per cent of global applications in 2017, compared with 23 per cent for the USA and 19.8 per cent for Japan (WIPO 2018). Some of China's corporations are world leaders in PCT patent applications: Huawei and ZTE were No.1 and No. 2 respectively among the top patent PCT filers and BOE Technology Group was No. 7. China's best companies are highly active in patenting their research and are indicative of the rapid strides China has made in its innovative capabilities in recent years.

The central importance of innovation has been further emphasized in related initiatives such as the 'Made in China 2025' plan, and it was reiterated by President Xi at the World Economic Forum in January 2017. The government's target for R&D spending to reach 2.5 per cent of GDP by 2020 implies a doubling of expenditure from the 2017 annual level of $254 billion per year to some $500 billion by next year. However, there are suggestions that China might not be able to achieve that increase. A senior official of a committee of the NCP was quoted as saying that China might spend $100 billion less than it had budgeted (Trivedi 2018). Allowing for a lower target of $400 billion per annum, over the next five years, we can expect this expenditure to cost at least $2,000 billion and to increase further as GDP grows. Achieving this would require further hard decisions regarding expenditure priorities, which could reduce the funds available for BRI.

DEEPER FOREIGN ENGAGEMENT

The second component of China's solution to the problems outlined above—deeper foreign engagement—is evolving in three directions. The first part is of course the BRI, with emphasis on infrastructure

---

[9] The PCT process facilitates the filing of patent applications in multiple countries by making a single application that conforms to standardized requirements in any one of the 148 PCT contracting states, or directly with the WIPO. Approximately 10 per cent of worldwide patent applications are filed through the PCT process, which is recognized as a more rigorous process than filing through one national body.

development in Western China and Central Asia, and funded by Chinese policy banks, the Asian Infrastructure Investment Bank (AIIB; funded at $100 billion) and China's Silk Road Fund of $40 billion (backed by China Investment Corporation, the country's sovereign wealth fund). We discuss the BRI commitments at the end of the chapter.

The second element in foreign engagement is the outward expansion of Chinese firms and the third is the creation of free trade zones (FTZs) at strategic locations on the mainland.

Outward Expansion of Chinese Firms

Chinese companies' innovative capabilities evolved through three phases, of which the latest phase is outward foreign direct investment (FDI) into the markets of the developed world (Yip and McKern 2016). This shift has become possible as a result of the world-class innovation capabilities in manufacturing and technology that Chinese private firms have developed over the years, coupled with domestic earnings and loans from China's banks.

The outward expansion of Chinese companies was encouraged by the government's 'Go Global' policy. Outward FDI (OFDI) by Chinese firms is not a new phenomenon: SOEs and private companies have been seeking and investing in natural resources, mainly energy and power (33%), metals (12%), transport (10%) and real estate (9%) for many years.[10] Much of this has been in developing countries, although natural resources in the USA, Australia and Canada have also been acquired. As a result, OFDI by Chinese enterprises increased rapidly from some $10 billion in 2005 to a peak of $177 billion in 2017, although in 2018 there was a drop in investment in North America and Europe due to Chinese restrictions and greater foreign scrutiny of Chinese projects.

What is different in the last 10 years is that the focus of Chinese private firms has shifted towards the consumer-oriented and technologically

---

[10] Calculated from sector data in Table 3.2, Scissors (2019).

sophisticated markets of the developed countries. The motivation has been to seek brand names, markets, management skills and whatever technologies may be lacking in their R&D portfolios. Firms have used acquisitions or greenfield investments, depending on the capabilities they have developed in the domestic market.

A consequence of this third phase is that emerging Chinese multinationals are less inclined to invest in infrastructure and resource projects in developing Central Asia. Also, OFDI has been under greater scrutiny inside China in recent years, and certain kinds of investments regarded as non-essential or frivolous have been stopped. It may be that OFDI may be capped at around $175 billion per year for some time (Scissors 2018). As we see below, this will have implications for private investments in the BRI.

Free Trade Zones

There is also a third element, which is a push to strengthen exports by setting up FTZs around the coast and inland where they can contribute to the BRI.

China has had for many years a network of thousands of industrial parks and development zones.[11] The most significant are known by the abbreviations ETDZ (Economic and Technological Development Zone), EPZ (Export Processing Zone), HIDZ (High-Tech Industrial Development Zone) and the more recent FTZ.

The FTZs represent an intensification of efforts to facilitate exports and imports through elimination of bureaucratic administration and tariff controls and attraction of foreign firms. The changes include streamlined customs procedures for companies inside FTZs, with bonded warehouses; simplified company registration processes, especially for foreign invested companies, which enjoy a more welcome market entry environment; and more lenient foreign exchange regulations, allowing businesses inside FTZs easier conversion of currencies. They are an 'experiment' similar in purpose to others that China has

---

[11] It is said that only 1,250 zones have received official approval from the State Council or provincial governments.

engaged in since the market opening, to implement market-oriented reforms in a controlled manner.[12]

These FTZs are relatively new.[13] Expansion of the Shanghai FTZ was approved in 2013, and it now has four sub-zones. The FTZs improved administration and facilitation have perhaps been part of the reason that FDI into China has remained quite strong, reaching a record $135 billion in 2018 (MOFCOM 2019).

During the more than four years of the FTZ initiative, the 11 zones have attracted many companies, both domestic and foreign, to set up inside them. These are shown in Figure 3.1 below. The infrastructure investment made by the government is not known, but, as of 2019, companies that had registered to operate in the zones had registered capital amounting to ¥8.5 trillion or $1.35 trillion (Table 3.1). Registered capital, of course, is not the actual funds invested; rather, it is the maximum commitment of shareholders to invest, so it greatly exaggerates the capital already spent, or likely to be spent in the near future. For example, the Hainan zone has attracted ¥424 billion ($64 billion) in registered capital of firms intending to establish there, but little of those funds have yet been spent. The figures do demonstrate, however, a strong confirmation of companies' interest in the FTZs.

In addition to the FTZs, there are many industrial and high-tech zones across China, as mentioned above. As the country implements projects such as the 'Made in China 2025' programme, there will be no doubt further government investment in these areas as well. For example, in Shanghai, the Shanghai Lingang Economic Development (Group) Co. Ltd is a large investment company owned by the Shanghai Municipal Government with a registered capital of ¥6.37 billion ($1 billion) and assets under management of ¥58.7 billion ($9.5 billion) in 2014. It was established to coordinate the development of 14 existing industrial parks and technology centres within greater Shanghai. It aims

---

[12] The advice of Chen Xiaoming, Managing Partner of Sino-Euro Capital Management, Shanghai, for explanation of these procedures in FTZs as well as data on the capital of investing companies is gratefully acknowledged.

[13] The Waigaoqiao FTZ, which is part of the Bonded Area of the Shanghai FTZ, was established in 1990.

38 | The Belt and Road Initiative

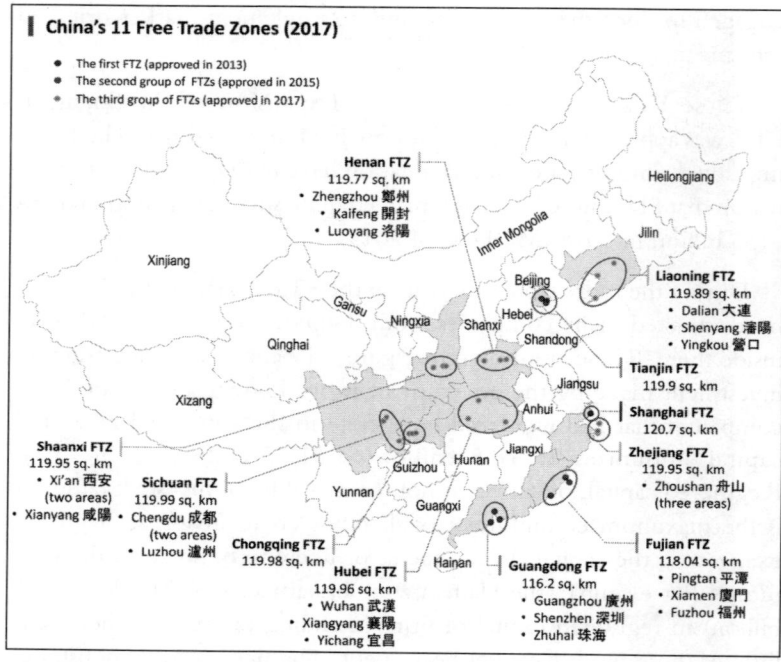

Figure 3.1 *China's Free Trade Zones*

Source: Fung Business Intelligence, Fast Facts of the Guangdong -Hong Kong-Macau Greater Bay Area, May 2017 (Permission by Fung Business Intelligence to reproduce this diagram is gratefully acknowledged.)

to provide a stronger focus for advanced manufacturing initiatives, including the 'Made in China 2025' programme. The Lingang Group has been carrying out several renovation projects, for example, in the long-established Caohejing Hi-Tech Park, as well as development of a new industrial park, the Shanghai Lingang Industrial Area.

The Shanghai Lingang Industrial Area, located on the coast southeast of Shanghai, is an industrial and high-technology park covering an area of 250 km². Most of the space has already been allocated to companies, research centres, incubators and factory buildings, which are available for low-cost rental or free use. Lingang includes residential estates offering affordable apartments and has well planned amenities, local transport, schools and parkland to attract educated professionals into what is becoming a new high-tech city.

Table 3.1 Corporate registered Investment in the Free Trade Zones

FTZ Series	Name	Date	New Corporate Registered Capital & Time Period	New Corporate Investment RMB bn	New Corporate Investment USD bn	Av. Exch rate* RMB/$
1	Shanghai	9/29/2013	Total investment:$73 billion in the first two years	449	73	6.15
2	Guangdong	4/20/2014	Total investment:RMB 3 trillion in 2016	3000	487	6.16
2	Tianjin	4/20/2014	Total investment:RMB 1.1 trillion in the first three years	1100	179	6.16
2	Fujian	4/20/2014	Total investment:RMB 1.5 trillion in the first four years	1500	244	6.16
3	Liaoning	8/31/2016	Total investment:RMB 643 billion in the first two years	643	97	6.65
3	Zhejiang	8/31/2016	Total investment:RMB 158 billion in the first year	158	24	6.65
3	Henan	8/31/2016	Total investment:RMB 442 billion in the first year	442	66	6.65
3	Hubei	8/31/2016	Total investment:RMB 91 billion in the first year	91	14	6.65

(Table 3.1 continued)

(Table 3.1 continued)

FTZ Series	Name	Date	New Corporate Registered Capital & Time Period	New Corporate Investment		Av. Exch rate*
				RMB bn	USD bn	RMB/$
3	Chongqing	8/31/2016	Total investment: RMB 231 billion in the first two years	231	35	6.65
3	Sichuan	8/31/2016	Total investment: RMB 310 billion in the first year	310	47	6.65
3	Sanxi	8/31/2016	Total investment: RMB 602 billion in the first two years	602	91	6.65
	Total to 2016		(Excluding Hainan)	¥ 8,526	$1,355	–
4	Hainan	10/16/2018	Phase 1 Plan: RMB 23 billion;			
			Phase 2 Plan: RMB 260 billion;			
			Phase 3 Plan: RMB 141 billion;	424	64	6.63
	Total		(Including Hainan)	¥ 8950	$1,419	

Source: Chen Xiaoming, Sino-Euro Capital Management, Shanghai, May 2019
Notes: Corporate registered investment is the registered capital of companies newly establishing in the FTZs. It is not capital spent
*Exchange rates source: 2010–2019 Macrotrends LLC

In 2014, the total revenue of the companies in the Lingang Group's industrial parks reached ¥537 billion ($87 billion) and their industrial output value was ¥150 billion ($24 billion).[14] These figures are indicative of the government's commitment to creating high-tech zones and achieving economic growth.

Expanding and completing China's FTZs and high-tech zones, particularly in the interior provinces, will require further investment by the government, although the major component will be from the corporations set up there. It is unlikely that these initiatives will be slowed due to their importance to future trade and to the 'Made in China 2025' programme. As the government financial commitment for these important programmes is not known, we have not included any estimate for these initiatives in the analysis of this chapter.

REGIONAL INTEGRATION

The third element is regional integration, through creating agglomerations of cities and rural areas. These agglomerations are intended to strengthen productivity by speeding transport and commuting, creating and connecting industry clusters, technology parks and innovation regions, and improving the quality of life. The rationale is that clusters in the USA such as Silicon Valley have much higher per capita incomes and shares of national GDP than regions that lack an innovation ecosystem. This also holds true for China, where clusters such as special export zones and industrial parks contribute over 20 per cent of national GDP, 60 per cent of exports and a disproportionate share of employment. Recognizing this, many provinces are attempting to strengthen their clusters and there are now 19 agglomeration initiatives under way or planned (Figure 3.2).

Jing-Jin-Ji

A prime example is the Jing-Jin-Ji initiative for the Beijing-Tianjin-Hebei region (which includes the Xiong'an New Area south of Beijing,

---

[14] Author's meeting with executives of Shanghai Lingang Economic Development (Group), 14–15 December 2016.

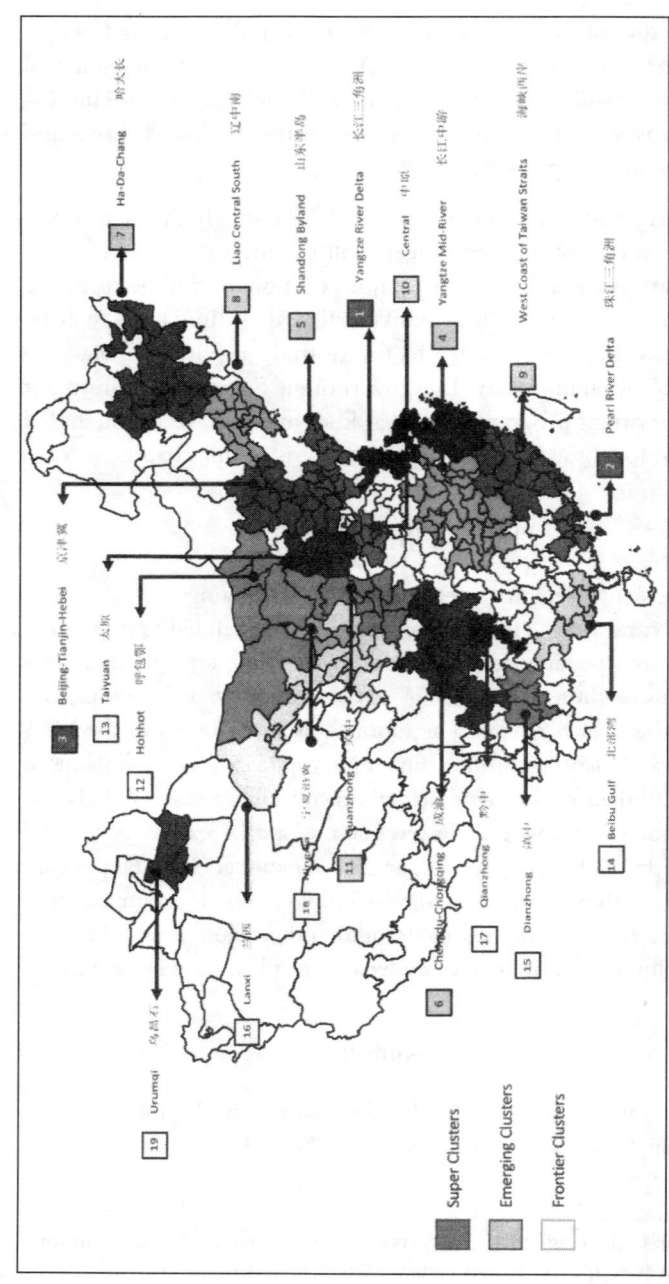

Figure 3.2 *Planned City Agglomerations in China, 2014*

Source: Frontier Strategy Group (now DuckerFrontier), 2014. Permission by DuckerFrontier to reproduce the diagram is gratefully acknowledged.

spanning three counties in Hebei Province and intended to absorb non-governmental activities from Beijing). The Jing-Jin-Ji region of 130 million people is equal in area to New England in the USA and accounts for 10 per cent of China's GDP, or ¥7.46 trillion, in 2017. Eleven cities in Hebei province will be linked with Beijing and Tianjin by a high-speed rail network and new highways, and the central government has already earmarked $36 billion to build 700 miles of rail within three years.

The scheme aims to revitalize Tianjin as a centre for advanced manufacturing and shipping. Beijing is shifting out factories and will concentrate on its role as the nation's capital and its administrative, political and cultural centre, while Hebei province will focus on clean manufacturing and wholesale trading. The average annual income of Hebei's 75 million people in 2017 was ¥48,000 ($7,200). This was 40 per cent of the average income of Beijing's 21.5 million people, which was ¥141,000 ($21,300) in 2018 (China.org.cn 2019), so improving Hebei incomes will require substantial investment. To bring the average income of Hebei residents to the national average of $8,800 (an increase of $1,600 per year per person) would imply an increased total income of $120 billion for the province's population, and an overall investment of $960 billion.[15] To reach the average Beijing income would of course require much more.

Considerable investment has already taken place in the region. Investments in the Binhai New Area of Tianjin since 2015 have included projects with a contracted value of over ¥392 billion ($57 billion), and, in Tianjin as a whole, they have totalled an estimated $235 billion (Xinhuanet 2019).[16] In Hebei Province, investment from outside including from Beijing and Tianjin is said to have been $660 billion over five years (Xinhuanet 2019).[17] Therefore, for the Jing-Jin-Ji agglomeration as a whole investment over the last five years or so has amounted to some $660–950 billion, from a mixture of public and private sources.

---

[15] Assuming the capital–output ratio of 8:0 used in the earlier part of this chapter.

[16] The source cites investment of $94 billion for Tianjin, which is says is 40 per cent of the total.

[17] The source cites investment of $264 billion for Hebei, which it says is half of the total over five years.

This total excludes recent new investment in Beijing itself. Assuming that further investment in fast rail, highways and infrastructure will continue at this pace, it would be reasonable to expect the further capital need for the region to be of the order of $100 billion to $200 billion per year over five years.

The Greater Bay Area

A second example of planned agglomeration is the 'Greater Bay Area' plan (originally called the Pan Pearl River Delta or '9 + 2' plan and abbreviated here to 'GBA'), which aims to integrate the major cities of the Pearl River Delta (Hong Kong, Macau, Shenzhen and Guangzhou) and seven other regional cities through fast transport connections and infrastructure. This ambitious concept was announced in 2017 and details were released by the State Council in February of 2019 (State Council 2019).

The GBA plan goes far beyond the provision of improved transport and infrastructure (KPMG 2019). It differentiates the future roles of the four major cities in the region and will provide them with the necessary economic and social infrastructure to support their roles as well as help improve living conditions in the countryside and the less advanced towns. It will integrate industry, work and knowledge creation in the region, with changes to the rules applying to citizens of Hong Kong, Macau and mainland China. An important emphasis will be advanced R&D and innovation. For example, a government-backed ¥100 billion ($14.8 billion) private equity fund was launched in Hong Kong in 2018 to support high-tech industries in the GBA (Wei and Jia 2018).

The goal of the GBA is to create an integrated megalopolis which will be more significant than the regional agglomerations of San Francisco, New York or Tokyo. It is seen by the PRC's government as an important component of the BRI (State Council 2019). Hong Kong and Macau are already free trade economies with long experience of trading worldwide, whereas the FTZs are catching up. The port cities can provide access to foreign markets not only for the Pearl River Delta but also for the land-locked provinces of Guizhou, Jiangxi, Hunan, and Guangxi and perhaps even beyond to Yunnan, Hainan and Fujian (which has an FTZ).

The GBA region, already a major economic force, is home to 70 million people and accounts for 12 per cent of China's GDP and 37 per cent of the country's total exports. The investment will be substantial: for example, the recently opened 36km Hong Kong–Zhuhai–Macau sea bridge, the first notable part of the new transport system, cost $20 billion. The high-speed train from Hong Kong to Shenzhen and Guangzhou, which began its services in 2018, is another piece of the network and costs $11 billion.

Despite the high incomes of the four key cities, incomes in the countryside of Guangdong are much lower, while nearby Guizhou Province is one of the poorest in China. It is expected that the poverty alleviation programme will help these neighbouring provinces over time and there will perhaps be spillovers from the richer parts of the Pearl River Delta. In Chapter 8 of the State Council's report, there is emphasis on improving the living conditions in the region, including health, elderly care, education, environment, culture and employment. Enabling citizens to gain these benefits from the GBA initiative will require additional investment. Given the more extensive transport connections, infrastructure and institutions to be constructed in the GBA project, and the planned betterment of living conditions for the less well-off, a further $500 billion to $1 trillion investment over five years could be expected.

Yangtze River Delta

A third agglomeration, even more economically powerful, is the Yangtze River Delta (YRD) cluster around Shanghai–Suzhou–Nanjing–Hangzhou. The region includes Shanghai plus three provinces, six major cities and a population of 160 million, and it contributes 20 per cent of China's GDP. An example of the bold forward planning in the region was the construction of the Yangshan Deep-Water Port in 2005, established on two islands in Hangzhou Bay and connected to the mainland via the 32.5km Donghai Bridge. The bridge cost ¥11.6 billion to build ($1.7 billion) while the overall cost of the port is expected to be $12 billion by 2025.

Much more is planned for this large region and significantly more investment will be needed to achieve its goals, perhaps $100 billion per year.

What happens in these three regions, already contributing 40 per cent of China's GDP, will have a profound impact on China's overall growth. They will require large investments. In addition, eight 'emerging clusters' and a further eight 'frontier clusters' are intended, all of which will need specific infrastructure investments.

Summarizing the estimates above, over the next five years, Jing-Jin-Ji may cost as much as $500 billion–$1,000 billion, as there are big disparities between Beijing and Hebei Province. The GBA will probably cost $500 billion and the YRD a further $500 billion. With the other cluster initiatives planned, it would not be surprising if over $600 billion would be needed per year or some $3 trillion over five years. These figures are not official costings; rather, they are the author's educated guesses. However, they lend support to the view that important initiatives are likely to compete with the BRI for both attention and funding. We turn now to this question.

DEMANDS OF BRI
China's Outward FDI

In evaluating the investment needs of the BRI, it is important to distinguish between direct investment and construction. Direct investment (as distinct from portfolio investment) means the provision of finance and management, together with the continuing ownership of the assets created. Construction is a service activity by (mainly) Chinese firms[18] to build assets that are owned and financed by others, although construction firms may provide some financing and take some equity in specific projects. We consider FDI first.

Data collected for China's outward direct investment by the American Enterprise Institute (AEI) and published in its China Global Investment Tracker (AEI 2018) separate these two categories of China's outward expansion and also tracks the specifically BRI-related components. AEI's data differ slightly from the data published by China's

---

[18] A total of 86 per cent of BRI construction projects use Chinese contractors.

Table 3.2 Largest 10 Recipients of China FDI (2005–2018, USD Billion)

Country	Investment 2005–2018
USA	180
Australia	94
UK	81
Switzerland	61
Brazil	57
Canada	54
Germany	41
Singapore	33
Russia	29
France	25
Total all nations	1,138

Source: Scissors (2019), AEI (2018).

Ministry of Commerce (MOFCOM).[19] There is not a great difference between the two totals (although individual years differ), but AEI believes its figures are more accurate than MOFCOM's. AEI's data includes, in a public database, details of some 1,400 individual foreign investments at a cost of $1.9 trillion as well as 1,500 construction projects costing $780 billion.

The AEI data show the top 10 countries that have been recipients of China's overall FDI over the period 2005–2018 (Table 3.2). The major recipients over this period are clearly developed economies, led by the United States of America. Natural resource investments have been important in the early years of China's OFDI, and they continue to be important; however, in recent years, Chinese companies have also been investing in industrial, consumer and services sectors in the

---

[19] For example, the total accumulated outward investment from 2005 until 2018 is estimated by AEI at $1,138 billion (Table 3.2) whereas MOFCOM's estimate is $1,154 billion.

developed countries. Also, the pattern in relation to BRI is quite different, as explained below.

The total annual outflows dropped sharply between 2017 and 2018 to $106 billion (AEI 2018),[20] but BRI activity was little changed from the previous year. Part of the drop can be explained by greater official scrutiny of OFDI flows in recent years, banning non-essential foreign acquisitions. It is thought that OFDI may be capped at around $175 billion for some time (Scissors 2018), perhaps signalling constraints due to the range of investment demands described in this chapter.

China's OFDI and Construction in BRI Countries

How much of this outward direct investment was for the BRI? The AEI data show that over the five-year period since BRI was established in 2014, China's direct investment in BRI has amounted to $148 billion or 22 per cent of its total FDI outflow of $669 billion during that same period (Scissors 2018). Another $255 billion has been spent on BRI construction projects in that period. What is interesting is that, among the recipients of the OFDI of $148 billion, relatively developed BRI countries were among the top 10 over the five-year period (Table 3.3). These were Singapore, Malaysia, Russia, Israel and South Korea. Important as China's FDI is to BRI countries, there is a clear preference among Chinese firms for developed countries as hosts (Li, Luo and De Vita 2018), where the markets are more mature, the risk lower and acquisition opportunities more common. The pattern is quite different for construction activity, as we see below.

A second conclusion is that, relative to the potential total cost of BRI ($4 trillion), the $148 billion investment so far by Chinese companies has been modest. Adding in the $256 billion spent on construction projects, mainly funded by loans, brings the total outlay from China to some $404 billion. Of course, this bold initiative got under way only in 2014, and it is understandable that private firms would take time to evaluate opportunities, so the pace of spending will probably pick up. But

---

[20] $120 billion as estimated by MOFCOM.

Table 3.3 Largest 10 BRI Recipients of Chinese FDI (2014–2018, USD Billion)

Country	Value
Singapore	24.3
Malaysia	13.2
Russian Federation	9.9
Israel	9.8
India	9.0
Indonesia	8.7
South Korea	8.1
Pakistan	7.6
UAE	5.6
Laos	4.7
Total all BRI	148

Source: Joy-Pérez and Scissors (2018), from AEI (2019)

spending probably needs to grow to some $400–$500 billion per year in order to reach the target in 10 years.

Private companies have difficulty in raising funds and support to invest in risky environments, and they contributed only 28 per cent of the total BRI investment (Joy-Pérez and Scissors 2018). SOEs have longer experience in building infrastructure and handling risk with government backing, and they have been the main investors in the BRI countries, largely in energy (38% of the total) and transport (12.5%).

In summary, private companies invested 28 per cent of the part of China's FDI that went into BRI during its first five years, and that part was 22 per cent of China's total OFDI. In other words, private FDI in BRI represented only 6.2 per cent of the country's total OFDI during the early years of BRI.

The priorities have been quite different for construction expenditure. Among the 126 countries of the BRI signed up to date, the value of construction performed has been $255 billion. The distinguishing feature is that the major recipients have been developing countries, led by Pakistan, Bangladesh, Egypt, Malaysia, Indonesia, Russia, Laos and Iran. Saudi Arabia is also an important recipient, as a node in the BRI pathway into Africa. Chinese SOEs are also by far the actors in BRI construction projects, with only 4 per cent of the construction activities being undertaken by private firms (Joy-Pérez and Scissors 2018). The major role both for investing and for undertaking construction projects in BRI has been shouldered by SOEs.

As early as mid-2016, it was announced that there were 900 BRI deals under way, worth $890 billion (*The Economist* 2016). While these figures are high compared with the data later provided by MOFCOM and AEI, discussed in the preceding section, they probably included a number of infrastructure projects under way before BRI was announced, as Chinese investment in the region predates the announcement of BRI.

CONCLUSION

According to the ADB (2017), developing Asia needs to invest $1.6 trillion a year on new infrastructure, or $22.6 trillion from 2016 to 2030. A total of 61 per cent of this will be for China, so the rest of the 45 countries in Asia will need some $8.8 trillion, or $630 billion per year.[21] It is clear that BRI addresses an important development need for a region that encompasses 4.4 billion of the earth's people.

China's estimated $4 trillion of BRI infrastructure investment will account for a significant part of the need as well as building infrastructure beyond Asia. Despite the breath-taking magnitude of the undertaking, a number of BRI projects have been completed, including ports, pipelines, railroads and highways, tangible reminders of the Silk Road of antiquity. BRI projects are providing revenue for Chinese state-owned construction, engineering and equipment companies, and this has helped protect them from slower growth in domestic capital spending. They

---

[21] The ADB investment estimates use a detailed country-by-country and sector-by-sector methodology. The figures quoted here do not include ADB's estimate for climate change mitigation, which adds $3.6 trillion to the total or $1.4 trillion to the BRI region needs. Also, the ADB estimates do not cover BRI countries in Europe, Africa or Latin America.

have demonstrated China's ability to complete visionary projects in difficult environments and provide growing security for the nation's energy supply and trade routes.

OBSTACLES TO BRI

In spite of this outward success, the BRI has generated concern among some developed countries, whose interest ranges from puzzlement to indifference, envy or opposition. The USA is concerned about what is seen as a shift in the world economic and political order, an extension of China's already important role in East and Southeast Asia. The postwar period of US centrality in the leadership of Europe and Asia appears to be challenged, and changing rapidly. From the Pacific through Central Asia to Africa and the heart of Europe, a new Asia–Eastern Europe bloc seems to be emerging, led by China. The USA has not engaged in the BRI and has raised a number of concerns about its aims and long-term viability. Some observers argue on the other hand that 'the United States does not have to choose between securing its global position and supporting economic growth in Asia: selectively backing the B&R would help achieve both goals' (Luft 2016). Some US allies have adopted a similarly cautious approach, as described in other chapters of this book. The EU has been diffident about the arrival of a new power on its doorstep. In Eastern Europe, for example, China is building roads, railways and bridges, including projects linking Serbia with Hungary from the Chinese-operated port of Piraeus (Areddy 2018). These developments, welcomed for the most part by the host nations, have provoked some concerns in Brussels.

Countries directly affected by BRI were initially enthusiastic. Later, geopolitical relations between China and South Asia, in particular Pakistan and India, became more salient. While India was an investor when China established the AIIB, it has not been a partner in BRI,[22] whereas Pakistan has large projects under way. India is concerned at China's relations with some of its neighbours and the security implications of the China–Pakistan Economic Corridor in particular. This $46

---

[22] However, India became the largest borrower from the AIIB in June 2018.

billion 2,000km land corridor between Pakistan and Kashgar in Xinjiang will shorten China's route to the Middle East by some 11,000km, but it will pass through contested areas of Kashmir.

There is also a mistaken view that existing multilateral institutions could better provide the financing to undertake these projects without any need for China to take the lead. However, it would in fact not be possible for those institutions to undertake any significant part of the BRI enterprise, due to their existing commitments, high risk aversion and slow evaluation processes (Bataineh, Bennon, and Fukuyama 2018). The multilateral banks are already stretched to deal with the range of needs they are asked to fund to the extent that today they could not fund more than 10 per cent of Asia's needs (Luft 2016).

The World Bank's IBRD has adopted increasingly risk-averse positions towards investment in infrastructure projects in developing countries, placing stringent requirements on borrowers to satisfy developed world attitudes about social welfare, environment and related perspectives. An example was the US government's support in 2013 for a ban on World Bank funding for new coal-fired power plants. As a result, the Bank's investments in infrastructure have declined from $25 billion per year in the 1980s and 1990s to $16.6 billion between 2000 and 2009 (Bataineh et al. 2018).

By contrast, Chinese lending institutions have both the support and the impetus of their government to lend and can be less concerned about the risk issues. Not surprisingly, Chinese construction firms, financed by Chinese banks, account for three quarters of infrastructure projects in the developing world. As a consequence, the loan portfolio in 2016 of the two major Chinese policy banks, China Development Bank and the Export–Import Bank of China, was 3.5 times the combined loans of the six major international development banks.[23]

---

[23] These were the International Bank for Reconstruction and Development, the European Bank for Reconstruction and Development, the ADB, the African Development Bank, the Inter-American Development Bank, and the International Finance Corporation (Bataineh et al. 2018).

Another concern is among some of the countries that are hosting investment and construction projects. A number of BRI countries have poor sovereign debt ratings and worry about being saddled with debt they cannot service and losing control of important infrastructure. Some ambitious projects have been stalled or delayed due to problems of implementation and host government problems in servicing the loans. In some such cases, China has forgiven debt in exchange for equity and control of the infrastructure, leading to accusations of a 'debt-trap'. Indebtedness has also led to negative reactions from local communities (Small 2018). Countries that face default on sovereign debt obligations may have no alternative but to turn to the IMF for help.

According to a report in 2018, 32 per cent of the infrastructure projects in the South and Southeast Asia region have been stalled due to problems of practicality or financial viability (Greer 2018). For example, an analysis of three new Indian Ocean ports being developed for shipping along the Maritime Silk Road raises doubts about their commercial soundness. The analysis concludes that inadequate transport connections to the hinterland, as well as competition from existing ports, makes it unlikely that they can be competitive (Funaiole and Hillman 2018). However, the ports have an important strategic purpose, as the report acknowledges, which may be sufficient justification, and China is responding by building necessary connecting infrastructure.

Opposition also reflects the difficulties non-Chinese investors and contractors face to gain a foothold in the BRI region and to participate in major projects there. A number of foreign firms have in fact been successful,[24] mainly by providing materials, services and equipment as suppliers to Chinese firms, which are the prime contractors for most projects. As noted earlier, Chinese companies have the most experience in undertaking large projects, and they have the advantage of access to financing, so they are strong competitors. But only 18 per cent of BRI projects involve foreign companies. Foreign firms might engage directly through joint ventures, if assurances regarding risk were forthcoming.

---

[24] These include GE, Caterpillar, Honeywell, Fluor, Citigroup, ABB, DHL, Linde, BASF and Maersk Group.

The Investment Dilemma

Another question about the BRI is the extent to which it can benefit from China's outward FDI flow, which reached $177 billion in 2017, falling back to $106 billion in 2018 (AEI 2018). There are some contradictions here. On the one hand, the government has been encouraging outward investment into the developed Western markets. On the other hand, it wants Chinese companies to invest in New Silk Road projects. For China's emerging MNCs, BRI means accepting a developing country risk, whereas given their current drive to acquire brands, knowhow and market positions, they prefer to invest in Europe and North America.

Rough estimates of the additional demands on China's financial system for important priorities beyond BRI over the next five years are made in this chapter. Summarizing the investment required for the major initiatives described above, China could be facing annual investment of $300 billion a year for regional clusters, $175 billion a year for OFDI and some $400 billion a year for R&D (of which three quarters typically comes from business and one quarter from the government). The total needs amount to some $875 billion per year, on top of $400 billion a year for BRI. The estimate ignores the further investment needed for the expansion of FTZs or high-tech parks, to alleviate poverty, or to raise nation-wide incomes to the average.

The funds will come from varied sources—some from annual budgets, some from SOEs or private firms and some from bank lending—but they will amount to a heavy demand for China to fund from its own resources. This will not be an impossible demand on foreign exchange reserves, as a large part of the expenditures will be denominated in Chinese yuan. Much of the equipment, construction materials and labour will come from China. And China's foreign exchange reserves of $3 trillion are adequate to fund the foreign expenditures. The issue is the amount of investment required, given the competing priorities.

China has for years invested a high proportion of its income, and, in 2017, its gross fixed capital formation was 44.6 per cent of GDP ($5.45 trillion of its $12.2 trillion economy). But capital investment, both public and private, has many purposes, including maintaining the existing stock and supporting domestic growth. Also, savings will decline as consumption rises, and the government budget has many competing demands, of which capital investment is only one.

Likewise, as noted, China's emerging multinationals cannot be relied on to fill the gap without turning away from their expansion into the developed world. And their OFDI is likely to be limited to under $200 billion per year. Financing with debt will also put a strain on the New Silk Road Fund (with $40 billion funding), the AIIB (with $100 billion of capital), China's policy banks and the domestic banking system.

The financing question is examined by Simon Taylor in Chapter 17 of this book, and he concludes that a BRI investment of $300–$400 billion per year could be handled, but that demands beyond that would stress China's financial capacity. Adding the initiatives outlined in this chapter, if they are additional claims on China's budget on top of large debt burdens, would necessitate some difficult trade-offs.

How China will resolve these competing priorities is unclear, but China has often surprised the world by dealing creatively with difficulties and is determined to make a success of one of the boldest initiatives of our times. Although there have been challenges for gathering widespread international support for BRI, there may be an opportunity for foreign firms to take a stronger role in the Central Asian region. Many of their governments surely wish to do so, as demonstrated by the widespread support for the AIIB.

China could benefit from attracting foreign investment to BRI as a means of bringing to the region not only technology and equipment but also foreign capital and expertise, and reducing the pressure to compromise its domestic initiatives. The way forward might be an innovative collaboration between private companies from China, the USA, Japan and the EU to share the opportunities and risks in this endeavour, potentially so valuable to a large share of the world's people.

It may be feasible to enlist developed world corporations in a limited but more collaborative approach to Asian development. A starting point could be to experiment in a limited number of specific projects based on the interests of the parties, jointly undertaken, with agreed governance and accountability processes, and avoiding strongly politicized projects.

There would be a need for an agreed framework negotiated between participants at the government level. In the present state of great power relations, such collaboration is not readily foreseeable, but, if and when current tensions get resolved, perhaps the parties might accept that their national interests could be better served by cooperation.

REFERENCES

ADB. 2017. *Meeting Asia's Infrastructure Needs*. Mandaluyong City, Philippines: Asian Development Bank.

AEI. 2018. *China Global Investment Tracker*. American Enterprise Institute and Heritage Foundation. http://www.aei.org/china-global-investment-tracker/

Areddy, James T. 2018. 'Trophy Infrastructure, Troublesome Debt: China Makes Inroads in Europe'. *The Wall Street Journal*, November 5.

Balding, Chris. 2017. 'Can China Afford its Belt and Road?' *Bloomberg*, May 17. https://www.bloomberg.com/view/articles/2017-05-17/can-china-afford-its-belt-and-road

Bataineh, Bushra, Michael Bennon, and Francis Fukuyama. 2018. 'Beijing's Building Boom: How the West Surrendered Global Infrastructure Development to China'. *Foreign Affairs*, May 21.

Center for Strategic and International Studies. 2019. 'Are Patents Indicative of Chinese Innovation?' China Power Project.China.org.cn. 2019. 'Beijing's Per Capita GDP Exceeds US$20,000 in 2018'. March 9. http://www.china.org.cn/business/2019-03/09/content_74550976.htm

EIU. 2018. 'China's Plan to Eliminate Poverty by 2020'. *The Economist*, January 5. http://country.eiu.com/article.aspx?articleid=536285437&Country=China&topic=Economy

Funaiole, Matthew, and Jonathan Hillman. 2018. 'China's Maritime Silk Road Initiative: Economic Drivers and Challenges'. Centre for Strategic and International Studies.

Greer, Tanner. 2018. 'One Belt, One Road, One Big Mistake'. *Foreign Policy*, December 6. https://chinapower.csis.org/patents/#1460666584560-f68fb2cc-8f39

Hurley, John, Scott Morris, and Gailyn Portelance. 2018. 'Examining the Debt Implications of the Belt and Road Initiative from a Policy Perspective'. Center for Global Development Policy Paper, Washington, DC. https://www.cgdev.org/publication/examining-debt-implications-belt-and-roadinitiative-policy-perspective

Joy-Pérez, Cecilia, and Derek Scissors. 2018. 'Be Wary of Spending on the Belt and Road'. AEI.

KPMG. 2019. 'Greater Bay Area Update'. KPMG Huazhen LLP, February 19. https://home.kpmg/cn/en/home/insights/2019/02/gba-outline-development-plan.html

Li, Chengchun, Yun Luo, and Glauco De Vita. 2018. 'Institutional Difference and Outward FDI: Evidence from China'. *Empirical Economics* 1–26. doi:10.1007/s00181-018-1564-y

Luft, Gal. 2016. 'China's Infrastructure Play: Why Washington Should Accept the New Silk Road'. *Foreign Affairs* 95 (5). https://www.foreignaffairs.com/articles/asia/china-s-infrastructure-play

McKern, Bruce. 2018. 'Attracting Foreign Funding to Build the BRI Would Be a Capital Idea'. *East Asia Forum*, April 13.

MOFCOM. 2019. 'MOFCOM Department of Foreign Investment Administration Comments on China's Absorption of Foreign Investment in January–December 2018'. http://english.mofcom.gov.cn/article/newsrelease/policyreleasing/201901/20190102827255.shtml

NSF. 2018. 'Research Publications'. In *Science and Engineering Indicators 2018*. National Science Board. https://nsf.gov/statistics/2018/nsb20181/report/sections/overview/research-publications

OECD. 2013. *Economic Outlook for Southeast Asia, China and India 2014: Beyond the Middle-Income Trap*. OECD Publishing.

Qinqin, Peng, and Han Wei. 2019. 'China's Current Account Surplus Touches Record Low'. *Caixin Global*, February 19. https://www.caixinglobal.com/2019-02-19/chinas-current-account-surplus-touches-record-low-101381025.html

Scissors, Derek. 2018. 'China's Global Investment: Neither the US nor Belt and Road'. AEI.

Scissors, Derek. 2019. 'Chinese Investment: State-Owned Enterprises Stop Globalizing, for the Moment'. AEI, January 17.

Shah, Fahad. 2015. 'A Costly Corridor: How China and Pakistan Could Remake Asia. *Foreign Affairs*, December 3. https://www.foreignaffairs.com/articles/asia/2015-12-03/costly-corridor

Small, Andrew. 2018. 'The Backlash to Belt and Road: A South Asian Battle Over Chinese Economic Power'. *Foreign Affairs*, February 16. https://www.foreignaffairs.com/articles/china/2018-02-16/backlash-belt-and-road

State Council. 2019. 'Outline Development Plan for the Guangdong-Hong Kong-Macao Greater Bay Area'. State Council of the PRC, February 25. http://chinainnovationfunding.eu/dt_testimonials/outline-development-plan-for-the-guangdong-hong-kong-macao-greater-bay-area/

The Economist. 2016. 'Our Bulldozers, Our Rules'. *The Economist*, July 2.

Trivedi, Anjani. 2018. 'China's Made in 2025 Plan is a Paper Tiger'. *Bloomberg Opinion*, December 16. https://www.bloomberg.com/opinion/articles/2018-12-16/china-s-made-in-2025-industrial-ambitions-are-a-paper-tiger

Wei, Yiyang, and Denise Jia. 2018. 'China Launches $14.8 Billion Greater Bay Area Development Fund'. *Caixin*, December 14.

WIPO. 2018. *Patent Cooperation Treaty Yearly Review 2018*. Geneva: World Intellectual Property Office.

World Bank. 2019a. 'World Bank in China: Overview'. IBRD and IDA. https://www.worldbank.org/en/country/china/overview

World Bank. 2019b. 'Data Bank, World Development Indicators'. https://databank.worldbank.org/data/reports.aspx?source=2&series=GB.XPD.RSDV.GD.ZS&country = #

Xinhuanet. 2018. 'China Continues Largest Poverty Alleviation Campaign in History'. *Xinhuanet*, March 5. http://www.xinhuanet.com/english/2018-03/05/c_137018278.htm

Xinhuanet. 2019. '"Jing-Jin-Ji": China's Regional City Cluster Takes Shape, 2018'. *Xinhuanet*, February 26. http://www.china.org.cn/china/2019-02/26/content_74505201.htm

Yip, George S., and Bruce McKern. 2016. *China's Next Strategic Advantage: From Imitation to Innovation*. Boston MA: MIT Press.

Zhuang Pinghui. 2017. 'Five Things to Know about China's Huge Anti-Poverty Drive'. *South China Morning Post*, September 6.

PART III

Belt and Road Initiative at the Societal and Country Level

Chapter 4

The Belt and Road Initiative
A Pathway to World Leadership?

Stefanie Weil and Dora Munteanu

INTRODUCTION

China's leadership is promoting its Belt and Road Initiative (BRI) as a 'grand strategy' that can challenge US hegemony (Rolland 2017). It is using the BRI as a vehicle in its attempt to claim leadership in the international system (Economy 2018). Its desire for leadership is not unrealistic especially when considering that US political and economic power is eroding while China's capabilities are rising (Kirshner 2014). As such the costs for China to shape the international order are declining while its incentives are increasing (Gilpin 1981). Indeed, China's leadership has committed itself to an ambitious project, which gives it the potential to reconstruct the current economic and political landscape. Some scholars argue that the world will witness a strong Chinese prominence on the issue of globalization (Brown 2017a). Others claim that China is simply re-emerging from its historical dominant position as a leading political, cultural, economic and military power (Duggan 2014). As such, the BRI is not purely grounded on economic motivation given its political agenda of a long-term ambition to recover from its past glory and challenge the international system (Gan and Mao 2016; Rolland 2017).

China's re-emergence as a global power undoubtedly has already influenced the current liberal world order. China aims to portray a positive image through the BRI yet it remains an illiberal state (Economy 2018). Nevertheless, the consequences of China's BRI, for example, the Asian Infrastructure Investment Bank (AIIB), pose questions to an order that the US has created and influenced since the Second World War.

US–China relations have always been difficult not just since the Trump administration. The nature of their relationship is influenced by China's worldview, its ideas and interests on the international system (Braumoeller 2012). Ever since the establishment of the People's Republic in 1949, relations between the two states have been constrained. China was caught in the ideological capitalist versus communist battle and even fought a proxy war with the USA in Korea. In the same vein, the other main cold war conflict of the USA, Vietnam, was another attempt to restrain China from spreading communism and thus threaten the 'free world'. Albeit the rapprochement of China–US relations in the early 1970s, relations between the two States remained difficult. The USA was facing a dilemma with China's opening reform in the late 1970s. On the one hand, it had difficulties adjusting to a rising China that started to be engaged in the international sphere, while, on the other hand, access to China's domestic markets provided opportunities for US businesses. Rapprochement was accompanied by distrust. China has multiple reasons to remain suspicious towards the USA, such as the latter's support for Taiwan, US intervention in Kosovo in 1999 and the US military attack against Iraq without a mandate of the US Security Council in 2003 (Foot and Walter 2011). Most crucially, China argues that the USA poses a threat to its communist political system, while the USA perceives a capitalist economy with a one-party system as dangerous because it offers alternatives to the US narrative that only liberal democracy ensures wealth and power (Friedberg 2011).

Thus, it is not surprising that the USA is questioning China's motivations behind the BRI. When Xi Jinping unveiled the BRI in 2013, he also announced the establishment of a new Chinese-led multilateral organization, the AIIB. The USA reacted with scepticism. It puts pressure on other states not to join the AIIB and promoted the narrative that the AIIB would not comply with international standards (Gan and Mao 2016; Rolland 2017).

In this chapter, we will aim to provide an answer to this question by moving beyond the classical liberal/realist debate. The liberal international order is a system that promotes economic liberalism and political freedom, as guided by international institutions. For the past 70 years, the international system has been guided by multilateral institutions that embody values, norms and laws that monitor the international community. These norms and values particularly emphasize free markets based on a democratic system (De Graaff and Van Apeldoorn 2018). In the framework of the BRI, China invests in countries with low economic security and poor political institutions and transparency. In contrast to loans from established global institutions such as the International Monetary Fund (IMF), Chinese loans are not based on conditionality, a main pillar of the rule-based international system. Conditionality refers to preconditions to receive a loan from institutions such as the IMF, where governments are requested to implement certain economic policies to improve their economic situation. Typically, states are asked to reduce governmental spending to curtail inflation as a pre-condition to receive the loan. Borrowing countries often perceive these policy constraints as illegitimate and harmful for their economies (Foot and Walter 2011).

However, before Xi's presidency, China applied Deng's approach to foreign policy of keeping a low international profile. China has seen itself as a major ambassador of the developing world, the voice of the emerging powers in the global governance system. With Xi's presidency, this image is changing; moving away from being merely an advocate of the developing world towards being the 'saviour' of the rules-based liberal system. In one manifestation of this approach, under the umbrella of the BRI, China actively invests in emerging and developed nations alike. While the Trump administration is challenging ideas it once promoted, China is actively promoting its commitment to a liberal world order. As one vehicle to promote its foreign policy approach of economic liberalism, the BRI has already shown influence on the global order. The question of China's influence on the global order has been highly debated among scholars (Breslin 2013; Brown 2017a, 2017b; Harnisch et al. 2016; Kennedy 2017; McNally and Gruin 2017; Nordin and Weissmann 2018; Nye 2016; Wang and Song 2016). While realists argue that China is not in the position to peacefully challenge the USA (Mearsheimer 2010; Morgenthau 1978; Waltz 2001), liberalists draw a more optimistic picture (Fukuyama 2006; Ikenberry 2009, 2011; Keohane and Nye 1974, 1989, 2000; Moravcsik 1997; Nye and Keohane 1971). These two approaches to unravel China's leadership are highly valuable, yet they are not able to capture all facets of potential leadership. Thus, in this chapter, we aim to introduce a distinct approach to investigate the question of whether the BRI can be a successful vehicle to challenge the current liberal order. We argue that in order to understand the BRI in the context of a changing global order, one needs to move beyond the realist debate and take ideas and interests into consideration. We challenge findings that applied realist frameworks to explain China's potential threat to the liberal order as they neglect perceptions of societal ideas. From a realist perspective, fast-rising states use military force to enhance their power (Waltz 1964). Realist approaches argue that states are driven by self-interest in their ambition to enhance their benefits while being subjected to constraints. The state is perceived as a unified actor. This means that preferences and societal ideas and interests are a given condition. States are purely motivated by their aim to enhance their benefits and power. Rather than focusing on the motivations and ideas of societal actors, the realist approach places emphasis on the constraints that the states faces (Goldstein and Keohane 1993). While realist approaches are important to explain power politics, this framework neglects forces within the nation state. As such, a realist explanation to our puzzle would be one-dimensional. The answer would be that the BRI is simply a vehicle to utilize China's benefits on its endeavour to become the next hegemon. Yet this answer does not take the underlying societal forces into account and fails to consider the political and economic agency of multiple stakeholders. In contrast to realist perspectives, our perspective implies that societal ideas, norms and values are crucial to determine the success of China's BRI as a vehicle to challenge the global system.

We argue that while one factor to launch the BRI was China's slowing economy in the context of the global financial crisis, ideas and interest on China's role in the global system played an additional role in the policy process. Evidently, China's leadership had to react to domestic challenges as a declining economy poses a threat to its authority. BRI serves as a vehicle to counterbalance overproduction and explore new markets. While the latter factors are certainly essential, this paper mainly explores determining factors such as societal ideas and interests to explain whether the BRI can serve as a vehicle to challenge the existing world order. As such, we take the importance of the societal perceptions based on ideas and interests into account. Applying China's perspective, one motivation behind the BRI is to support its political narrative of having the capability for world leadership.

The idea that China has been a great power for centuries and thus is reclaiming its leadership is one of the narratives of the BRI. Since the Xi presidency, China has been conveying the idea of its identity as a great power, one that is capable of shaping the international system (Harnisch, Bersick, and Gottwald 2016). Yet, policy is determined not only by China's leadership but by multiple actors as well (Weil 2017). As the BRI affects not only governments but also individuals, companies and societal actors such as think tanks or interest groups, the BRI is exposed to multiple national and international stakeholders. To the extent that different players' support BRI policies depends upon the interconnection between material interests and ideas of multiple societal actors. We will aim to shed light on these factors in regard of the BRI under the backdrop of the international system.

We argue that, perceived from a realist perspective, the BRI has the potential to challenge US hegemony. Moving beyond this state-centric approach, the BRI embodies ambiguous ideas and interests with 'Chinese characteristics', which not only stand in stark contrast to the West but are also perceived with scepticism. The current liberal world order consists of ideas, norms and values re-enforced and promoted by the West. Thus, albeit China's economic and material capabilities, which are reflected in the BRI, considering its communist political and cultural ideas and interests, it is not in the position to realistically challenge the international system. We will enfold our argument by asking the question: Can China use the BRI as a vehicle to challenge the current liberal international order?

To unravel the puzzle, we will first highlight and define the critical variables in the international system and elaborate on China's role in this system. Subsequently, we will introduce the analytical framework for understanding this further and elaborate on ideas and interests of the BRI narrative. In the last part, we will provide answers to our research question on whether China can use the BRI as a vehicle to challenge the current liberal international order.

CHINA'S LEADERSHIP IN THE LIBERAL INTERNATIONAL SYSTEM

When scholars propose that China will challenge the international order, the question arises as to what is meant by the international order. Multiple definitions of the international system are debated, even moving beyond the realist perspective. As argued before, realist approaches do not take societal and national agency into account. Therefore, in the framework of this research, we apply liberalist and global governance perspectives. We refer to global governance as rules, norms and values that define the agency of state and non-state actors in the international system. Accordingly, we embrace the argument, conveyed by global governance and liberalist views alike, that states as part of the international system are embedded and influenced by domestic and transnational societies, which eventually give momentum to transnational interactions (Hewson and Sinclair 1999; Kennedy 2017; Moravcsik 2008; Sinclair 2012).

Drawing from the global governance approach, multilateral institutions such as the World Trade Organization (WTO), the United Nations (UN) and the IMF share common values in their function to support political rule and capital investments in the absence of an overarching 'world government'. Most crucially, and in line with neoliberalism, national and transnational societies adjust themselves; they adopt ideas to the functional requirement of global capital. Multiple stakeholders convey their grievances based on their ideas and interests. These pressures are conveyed in commonplaces such as institutions, forums, interest groups and other transnational and national platforms (Van Apeldoorn 2002; Hewson and Sinclair 1999; Noelke 2012; Overbeek 2004; Sinclair 2012). In the creation of a liberal world order, multilateral institutions play a crucial role as vehicles for norm creation and the enhancement of information sharing, transparency, trust building and compliance (Sørensen 2011).

General ideas of liberalism, as well as ideas of a liberal world order, are those of welfare states, flexible labour markets, collective bargaining in form of interest groups, barrier-free international capital mobility and a free-market exchange rather than a state-led top-down economy (Smith 2003). These ideas are manifested in multilateral institutions such as the WTO or the IMF of the global system (Campbell and Pedersen 2001).

After 1945, the international liberal order evolved in the post-war period promoted by the USA in its necessity of free trade and global prosperity to gain global leadership. To stabilize the world economy, the USA established new multilateral institutions with the mission to not only steer economic but also political and security relationships (Ikenberry 2011).

The post-war liberal system was based on US values, interdependencies between the Western countries and multilateral decision-making in international institutions. China and the Soviet Union did not adopt US-led ideas of the international system. Milton's general assumption that only democratic societies can engage in liberal trade was a predominant idea of Western liberalism and certainly re-enforced by the isolation of the Soviet bloc and China (Friedman 1962).

Since the 1970s, and as a reaction to crisis of the system, public policy in the USA and other wealthy democracies have moved towards neoliberal direction (Campbell and Pedersen 2001). The 1970s are a good example of how the 'effective market hypothesis' is not as effective as once assumed. Crises of world affairs, such as falling oil prices and the decline of US ability to ensure a stable international financial system marked by the collapse of the Bretton Woods system, raised questions on the post-war order. Yet, US hegemony prevailed. The international economy remained to be driven and monitored by

US-dominated international institutions such as IMF, World Bank and GATT (WTO).

US hegemony proved to be resilient especially considering that the collapse of the Bretton Woods system was a major shock to the international system. After the Second World War, the USA and Britain led the negotiations to implement a stable monetary and trading system, which was manifested in the 1944 Bretton Woods agreement. It was named after the final conference in Bretton Woods, New Hampshire. In its attempt to learn from history, the Bretton Woods system aimed to implement consistent exchange rate policies. Great international payments imbalances in the years after the First World War were one crucial factor of the failure of the international gold standard and the international trading system. The Bretton Woods agreement offered a new innovative global monetary framework such as the establishment of international institutions and a pegged exchange rate system. The USA had the exchange rate obligation to pegging the dollar to gold. This decision was based on the assumption that great imbalances between deficit and surplus countries lead to instability within the international financial system. Payment deficits result in reserve (or gold) outflow, a decline in money supply, decreasing price, greater competitiveness, increasing exports and lesser imports. In turn, surplus countries receive reserves from deficit countries, with the result that deficit countries suffer weakening currencies. A payment deficit can be realized and lead to a loss of reserves (like gold) only if a country has a fixed exchange rate. With a flexible exchange rate, governments refuse to supply internationally acceptable assets to absorb an excess supply of the currency, so the consequence is a deprecation of the currency rather than a loss of reserves (Ugur 2002). In the 1920s, surplus countries such as the United States were in the position to avoid costly adjustments by counterbalancing the impact of gold inflows by central bank policies that eventually lead to a dissolution of the link between buying gold and domestic inflation. After the Bretton Woods system was long established, in the late 1960s, the USA asked surplus states like Germany to revalue the German Deutsch Mark against the dollar. As Germany and other surplus countries did not comply, the USA became increasingly dissatisfied with its obligation to peg the dollar against gold. Paired with a declining economy, increasing public spending on wars and the oil crisis, the USA took a bold decision. In August 1971, the Nixon administration officially de-pegged the dollar from gold and would therefore no longer trade gold to other governments in exchange for US dollars. In other words, the value of the dollar was no longer defined by gold reserves. As a result, in the course of the 1970s, other liberal markets moved away from the dollar–gold standard towards a flexible exchange rate system. The US decision was a shock to the international financial community (Foot and Walter 2011).

The failure of the Bretton Woods system was a low moment of the USA. The end of the Cold War, however, marked the rise of American unipolarity (Ikenberry 2011). It was the most powerful moment of the USA, a 'Western' triumphalist view of globalization. The notion that President Reagan 'won' the Cold War attested US hegemony. The end of the Cold War re-enforced again the idea of democratic and liberal values. China's continuous rise since 1978 posed questions as to whether China would eventually democratize. With its growing influence and an invigorated Communist Party, these voices silenced over time.

The Asian financial crisis further sparked the debate on China's capability to introduce new ideas to the international system. By keeping its currency stable during the Asian financial crisis, it was in the position to offer aid packages to struggling Southeast Asian countries. By providing loans, it set a new tone in the international financial system. In stark contrast to the dictatorial posture of the IMF, Chinese loans were not tied to strict monetary policies for the credit receivers (Shambaugh 2013). Clearly, China's economic actions had long-term political changes not only in the region but also worldwide. The emergence of the G20 as the principle body for the global economic management was one such example. China has used its increasing global financial power to become an active member not only of the G20 but also in the World Bank and the IMF. Yet, until 2008, China had been more of rule-taker than a rule-maker in the international system.

The 2008 global financial crisis again posed new questions to US hegemony (Kirshner 2014). In the wake of the crisis, new actors emerged and the question of China as a responsible caretaker or as the saviour in international economic affairs re-entered the scholarly debate (Gottwald and Duggan 2011). Once again, the US-led Washington consensus was under fire and voices became louder arguing for a China-modelled international order—'the Beijing Consensus' (Ramo 2004).

Returning to the initial puzzle of China's aim to challenge the US-led order, we argue that BRI policies might challenge the US-led liberal order which is defined along the ideas of (a) free trade with little market interference including flexible labour markets and barrier free capital move; (b) liberal economic policies that also serve as a role-model for other nation states; (c) the promotion and spread of liberal democracy; US hegemony of introducing mechanisms on how to organize global politics; (d) the existence of international institutions based on US norms and values such as conditionality; (e) democracy as a necessity for liberal trade.

IDEAS AND INTERESTS OF THE BRI NARRATIVE

In this section, we will define and apply our analytical framework and explain why ideas and interest matter when unravelling the puzzle. We draw on complementary analytical frameworks and combine approaches on ideas and interests (Campbell 2002, 2008; Goldstein and Keohane 1993; Hall 1993a, 1993b; Halpern 1993; Keck and Sikkink 1998; Keohane and Nye 2000; Schirm 2009, 2011, 2013, 2016, 2017) with interest group scholarship (Baumgartner and Leech 2001; Beyers, Eising, and Maloney 2010; Hanegraaff et al. 2015; Mahoney 2007). The way policy, including China's foreign policy on BRI, is made cannot be fully understood without taking ideas and interests into consideration (Hall 1993b). Ideas and interests affect governmental policies because multiple stakeholders aim to influence them by conveying their long-term ideas and short-term material interests into the policymaking process. As such, society lobbies the government on their preferences, which evolve from their ideas and interests (Schirm 2017). Ideas are defined as shared societal beliefs about how the government should act (Goldstein and Keohane 1993; Schirm 2017). They are reflected in societal attitudes as well as the variety of capitalism (Noelke 2012). Ideas relevant to the political content reflect what a society defines as a main task of the state in a given policy area (Halpern 1993; Schirm 2009). Interests and ideas are interconnected, yet interests are mainly motivated by economic reasons. As economic factors are more dynamic than deeply rooted societal ideas, stakeholders' interests in a policy issue are more short term.

The interest group approach depicts stakeholder influence on the policymaking process well, yet it has not been able to fully reflect on the consequences of ideas and interests on policymaking. Thus, we argue that material interests as well as societal ideas are fed back into the policymaking process by interest groups. Ideas and interests are reciprocal; they influence each other and can evolve over time (Blyth 2002). Interest groups are influenced by long-standing ideas as well as material interests. In line with interest group scholarship, we hinge on the argument that material interests of interest groups give momentum to their attempt to influence policies. However, a shared cultural perception on how policy is perceived and how appropriate a policy idea is are additional factors that are fed back into the policymaking process (Dobbin 1993). This is to say that Western interest groups in China determine whether a policy is appropriate according to their cultural background (Campbell 2002). As Western interest groups are shaped and established along democratic pluralist lines, which is in contrast to their Chinese counterparts, we argue that their general stance towards policies is based on liberal democratic ideas. However, Chinese groups are an integral part of the state corporatist system and thus are shaped along the lines of China's leadership.

We argue that foreign interest groups in China shape policies on their behalf to ensure their material benefits. Research showed that China's leadership is using Chinese interest groups as a tool to promote the BRI (National Development and Reform Commission 2015). As they are closely intertwined with China's state apparatus, they are easily used as a vehicle to support its policies. In contrast, Western interest groups are not part of China's state corporatist system, with their tools and organizational structure reflecting European and American values. This is to say that European interest groups in China aim to shape policies on the behalf of European business, according to European interests and values and US interest groups accordingly for the USA (Weil 2017, 2018).

To be clearer on the position of Western interest groups to convey their interests into BRI policies, we need to draw attention to China's way of interacting with its domestic groups. China's approach to civil society is state corporatist, which means that (a) interest groups are not membership driven but governmental influenced, (b) interest groups are established top-down by the government, (c) the main mission of corporatist groups is to support governmental policy implementation, (d) governmental officials work for the group and (e) grievances are not to be conveyed openly (Schmitter 1974).

Although foreign groups need to officially register with a governmental organization, the power of the Chinese state to directly influence the organizational structure and operations is limited. This means that state corporatist control mechanisms do not seize influence over such groups. EU and US groups operating in China are (a) membership driven and (b) established bottom-up by their members. In addition, (a) the mission of the groups is to influence governmental policies on behalf of its members rather than supporting Chinese governmental policy implementation; (b) China's state corporatist framework is not able to place Chinese governmental officials within the internal organization of the groups; and (c) in contrast to Chinese interest groups, Western groups in China are able to convey grievances more openly. As a result, while Western business is constrained, and think that they do not benefit reciprocally from BRI policies, it will be in the position to actively convey its material interests into the BRI policies. This stands in contrast to China's interest groups that are (a) not only in a weak position to convey their interests but also (b) are used as a vehicle to promote BRI policies. Albeit its liberal narrative, the BRI remains a campaign that is driven by China's communist leadership, which promotes its ideas domestically and internationally.

Ideas are defined as theories, conceptual models, norms, views, frames and beliefs (Campbell 2002). They can change if policymakers are facing political economic problems.

Existing literature differentiates between cognitive and normative ideas (Campbell 1998):

1. Cognitive ideas such as policy programmes on certain topics such as tax policies
2. Cognitive ideas such as neoclassical or supply side economics

3. Normative ideas such as public attitudes, for example general sentiments to budget deficits
4. Normative ideas such as frames, which include metaphorical pronouncements of political spin doctors and lobby groups on how high taxes are harmful to American values

Broadly, ideas can be differentiated between cognitive ideas based on causal relationships and explanations, and normative ideas that prescribe how things should be. Cognitive ideas provide an overall understanding between multiple layers of society of how the world works (Campbell 2002). Normative ideas consist of presumed assumptions on values, identities and expectations (Katzenstein 1996). While normative ideas serve as symbols and concepts that support the legitimation of policies, cognitive ideas are conveyed as policy explanations to support policymakers to draw clear and specific policies (Campbell 1998). The more straightforward the policy programme, the better policymakers are in the position to sell their ideas (Campbell 1998).

Ideas are rooted within society, based on norms and values, and are part of a certain shared societal perspective. Ideas can evolve over time; yet, in contrast to short-term interests, they are more deeply rooted within the system. They give momentum to interest-based action, influence political events and have a profound effect on national policies (Weber 1946). Policies are made within a system of ideas and standards which are embedded in the rationale and system of the actors involved (Hall 1993b).

Ideas can be influenced through the media (Hall 1993b). Policymakers strategically craft narratives to legitimize policies to the public and to each other (Campbell 2002; Fligstein and Mara-Drita 1996). As China's media is not entirely free, its leadership can influence ideas through the media more effectively than in democratic systems. For example, China's largest national news service has increased its news reports on the BRI to provide 'intellectual support with 'Xinhua Silk Road' information (Xinhuanet 2015).

However, China's leadership is not the only actor who can influence ideas on the BRI. International actors and governments also play a crucial role. China's BRI investments are not always welcome, as shown by how China had to defend its ambitions towards other governments such as India and Pakistan. This means that China's leadership can influence the idea of the BRI only to a certain extent, given that other actors interpret ideas in a different manner. Ideas significantly vary across countries and change over time. It is crucial to note that ideas are not always embedded in reality and actually have a more autonomous character based on the actor's interpretation (Hall 1993a). In the international sphere, networks of professionals and experts, who share a set of normative (capitalist) beliefs, are responsible for new ideas (Van Apeldoorn 2002; Van Apeldoorn and De Graaff 2016). These transnational capitalist actors aim to set the agenda and shape international politics. These networks are composed of multiple groups constituted based on a shared identity. A common identity evolves based on relations to production, reproduction and distribution of wealth. Naturally, each group further develops ideas based on their common belief or needs. These beliefs and collective identities are constructed through formal and informal organizations such as interest groups (Van Apeldoorn 2002). Depending on the group and the political environment, these actors seek to set the agenda and shape transnational politics. In their attempt to set the agenda on their behalf, ideas compete with each other. Multiple factors such as type of interest group, organizational structure, financial power and political system determine inasmuch each group is able to implement a generally accepted idea (Mahoney 2008).

As China's capitalists are not embedded in these networks, there is little chance that they can influence manifested ideas. This is not to say that Chinese actors are not embedded in international institutions such as the WTO, United Nations and the World Bank. However, in contrast to international institutions, Chinese capitalists are less visible in influential international groups. This is a result of distinctive concepts of Chinese and Western think tanks and interest groups. The distinct approach on Chinese interest groups, constrains Chinese capitalists to fully unfold their ability to make use of transnational influential think tanks to influence ideas. In the West, interest groups are part of civil society, established bottom up by their members based on their ideas and beliefs with the mission to actively shape the agenda on their behalf. In contrast, Chinese think tanks and interest groups are embedded in state corporatist structures. This means that the state uses think tanks to convey its ideas and messages from the top-down. As a result, Chinese actors are not experienced in influencing manifested ideas on transnational level through organizations.

Material interest of stakeholders is one of the determining factors whether BRI policies are perceived positively or negatively. To make a clear analytical distinction between long-term ideas and interests is not a straightforward practice, as they can be overlapping and may influence each other. Interests are another type of idea, with the crucial difference being that interests are rooted in people's perception of their material situation (Campbell 2008). Interests and ideas are interconnected, or, to apply Karl Marx's perspective, ideas become material forces as soon as they take hold of the masses (Hall and Gingerich 2009). As argued above, one of the motivations of the BRI is to discover new markets as a reaction to a slowing economy and the global financial crisis. This certainly serves material interests of some domestic sectors that benefit from the BRI. However, the lion's share of the projects of the BRI is executed by state-owned companies with little room for domestic nor foreign-owned companies doing business in China. This is most crucial because different identities of actors shape how they perceive their interests and therefore which policies and institutions they favour (Campbell 2002).

IDEAS OF THE BRI FROM A CHINESE PERSPECTIVE

We analysed statements of Chinese and Western interest groups and triangulated them with additional sources such as scholar articles, governmental statements and qualitative interviews. We do not claim that our results are exhaustive, yet analysis showed repeating pattern on the ideas of the BRI.

Ideas on the BRI are highly promoted by the Chinese government, supported by think tanks, banks and other government-supported organizations. The BRI has a clear signature of the President, with Xi promoting the concept personally on numerous occasions (Brown 2017b). He is the face of the BRI, a strong leader who stands personally behind the idea of 'China's grand strategy'. The narrative behind the BRI has been carefully drafted by China's leadership, portraying a discourse on 'mutual respect and trust, mutual benefit and win–win cooperation, and mutual learning between civilizations' (National Development and Reform Commission 2015).

The main ideas are (a) China's push to reclaim its leadership is based on a shared memory of its historical greatness. Rather than claiming global leadership, it is naturally re-establishing its global power. Based on historical memory, ancient Silk Roads flourished during the strong and outward-looking Han and Tang dynasties. BRI aims to resemble the ancient routes from the past to the modern era (Economy 2018; Rolland 2017). China's global power declined because of the Western invasion. After a period of 'keeping a low profile', China is now re-emerging to its initial strength and the BRI is promoted as a vehicle to retrieve its power. The Chinese leadership promotes the ancient Silk Road as a period of Chinese strength; (b) the BRI is a reaction to the global financial crisis, drawing on the experience of China's strong role during the 1997 Asian financial crisis. During those periods, China's leadership promoted the perception of a financial backbone during the global financial crisis within the international system. The idea that long-established rules for international trade need to be adjusted and that China has the capacity to invest during a period of uncertainty to stabilize the system is highly promoted by multiple Chinese stakeholders (National Development and Reform Commission 2015). By taking up financial responsibility, China is conveying the narrative of its ability to stabilize the international system; (c) China stands for a liberal world order and is thus against protectionism. In times of Brexit and the Trump administration, China is conveying the idea that it stands for economic globalization, global free trade and an open world economy (National Development and Reform Commission 2015; Xi 2017a). It aims to 'create new models of investment and financing' (Xi 2017b). In contrast, to establish international organizations, China is providing a model that provides loans without interference in political issues. This is based on the ideas of the 'Five Principles of Peaceful Coexistence: mutual respect for each other's sovereignty and territorial integrity, mutual non-aggression, mutual non-interference in each other's internal affairs, equality and mutual benefit, and peaceful coexistence' (National Development and Reform Commission 2015). This means that China's investment decisions are not based on the established conditionality approach of the IMF, World Bank or

Developing Banks. Rather than taking the political and economic situation into consideration, BRI investments are based on Chinese ideas. As such (d) the BRI is a vehicle to promote the idea of a community of common destiny, which is a new type of international relations featuring win-win cooperation based on the principles of amity, sincerity, mutual benefit and inclusiveness (enhance people-to-people and cultural ties). The BRI is portrayed as a peaceful alternative to the US-led system, in which plurality is fostered based on a world of harmony with differences (Xi 2014; Rolland 2017). The idea of a 'community of common destiny' (National Development and Reform Commission 2015) is promoted. In the 'Silk Road Spirit', China is promoting the idea of 'peace and cooperation, openness and inclusiveness, mutual learning and mutual benefit' (National Development and Reform Commission 2015). Furthermore, the main pillar of China's success story is economic development while maintaining its political system. It hopes to stabilize its weaker economic neighbours, the region and eventually the rest of the world. The BRI will mitigate frictions between China and its neighbours and thus legitimize undemocratic political rule (Rolland 2017). This is rooted in the idea that as countries rise with the help of China, a new Chinese way could be accepted within the international sphere.

When analysing the ideas promoted around the BRI, it became clear that concepts are ambiguous and not clearly defined and are conveyed with traditional tools of governmental and party communication. The BRI promotes multilateralism, global governance, free trade and a liberal order without actually defining it. Analysis showed that these concepts are perceived and interpreted very differently; even among Chinese scholars, there is little consensus on how to interpret these ideas.[1] Some of the ideas such as rising in harmony, peaceful co-existence and moving

---

[1] Interview 4 and Interview 5 on BRI, 2018 ('BRI and Multilateralism'). We conducted 15 qualitative interviews with Chinese, European and US government officials, interest group members and experts between March and October 2018. The interviews were held either face-to-face or via Skype and lasted between 1.5 hours and 3 hours. The face-to-face interviews were conducted in Germany, Belgium and China. Interviews were transcribed and analysed with conventional qualitative methods. The newly collected material allowed us to update data from previous research projects in the years between 2015–2018 on the BRI and research on interest groups in China and in the West.

away from Deng's 'keeping a low profile' are not new. There was a first attempt to construct the idea of peaceful rise in 2005. The idea that China's rise needs to be recognized inside and outside China was promoted by influential Chinese scholars. Xi's idea of the 'Chinese dream' that was launched in 2013 promoted that China has an alternative concept of development the USA, acknowledging the importance of China's society and the necessity to engage with the outside world. The idea that China would cooperate with other countries can be traced back to the 1950s. The 'Five Principles of Peaceful Coexistence' are reflected in the idea since the very beginning of the Republic that China is appreciating 'rule-based and secure trade' based on the principle of non-interference and respect of one another's sovereignty (Brown 2017b).

The Chinese perspective puts great emphasis on 'mutual understanding, consensus and deepening cooperation'. In this vein, goals and benefits for both parties are coordinated through a 'pluralist and open process'. The general idea is that China aims to consult and educate all countries along the BRI aiming to consider interests and benefits of all stakeholders (National Development and Reform Commission 2015). These ideas are perceived as Chinese propaganda from the Western stakeholders (Rolland 2017).

Chinese Ideas: Are They Liberal? A Perspective from the West

As part of our analysis, in this section, we focus on a Western perspective and argue that there are discrepancies between the Western and Chinese narratives (Breslin 2011, 2013; Pan Zhongqi 2012; Weil and Yijia 2012). When arguing from a Western perspective, the question of how to define the West in BRI discourse arises. Certainly, there is no one Western perspective, yet our analysis showed that there are prevailing general ideas among the Western actors such as interest groups, experts, academics, official governmental statements and other non-state actors. In China's attempt to stabilize the region, it is focusing on its neighbouring authoritarian countries. It speaks for itself that we certainly do not count these countries to the West. Thus, we have not included them in our analysis. Furthermore, BRI investments in Europe are more focused on the East, receiving governments like those of Hungary that regularly infringe norms and values of the liberal system.

One of the most salient findings is that Chinese ideas on the BRI are perceived as top-down Chinese concepts. This is to say that Western stakeholders do not use terms such as 'community of common destiny, Silk Road Spirit, peace and cooperation, openness and inclusiveness, mutual learning and mutual benefit'. In contrast to the specific Chinese wording on the BRI and the related policies, when describing the international system or international politics, China's leadership is using mainstream Western concepts such as multilateralism, global governance, democracy, etc. However, as argued in the previous section, these concepts are applied and described with 'Chinese characteristics', with little consensus between the West and the Chinese perspectives (Freeman and Geeraerts 2012; Pan Zhongqi 2012; Weil and Jing 2012).

Interest in the BRI among European scholars is high, yet explorative research showed that the interest of European interest groups that are located in China remains low. Other topics such as market access, intellectual property rights and government procurement remain to dominate the debate. However, topics such as government procurement are certainly related to the BRI. While seminars, roundtables or events are taking place, there is a lower number of special issues or reports on the BRI. One reason for this low attention could be that the lion's share of the current investments are taking place outside of Western Europe or the USA.[2] Our research showed that the general stance towards the BRI is critical, with Europe in particular having reservations against the BRI (Le Corre 2017).

Western governments that benefit from the BRI pose little questions on the economic rationale whereas others emphasize the risks of foreign investments in countries with unstable political institutions and regimes. This criticism is based on China's approach of unconditionality and its history of providing foreign aid in Africa. Chinese investments in the African continent raised critical questions on its motivation. Repeating

---

[2] Interview 1 on BRI, 2018 ('Western Business and the Belt Road Initiative').

a certain rationale of a Chinese neocolonial approach, scepticism towards Chinese investments and its support for non-democratic regimes remains embedded in Western ideas.[3]

Another idea of the West is that China is collecting and branding old projects under one single label. Thus, the BRI is simply a repetition of traditional diplomacy policies with Chinese characteristics. This view suggests that the BRI is an attempt to counterbalance Chinese overcapacity in sectors like steel; furthermore, to increase its exports and support its state-owned businesses, it is applying mercantilism tools. As such, the BRI is nothing more than an extended version of old ideas such as its 'Going Out' policy (Rolland 2017). The Western discourse associates ideas such as the 'Chinese dream' with the BRI. Analysis showed that these concepts are ambiguous and hardly understood by the West. As one Chinese scholar argues, 'The Belt and Road initiative is easily misinterpreted as China's grand strategy of geopolitics, which is sometimes worsened by the social and cultural differences between China and partners' (Yong 2016). The Chinese government aims to counterbalance this image with 'high-level guidance and facilitation' executed personally by President Xi and Premier Li 'to explain the rich contents and positive implications of the Belt and Road Initiative'. But the leadership wrongly assumes that 'their efforts have helped bring about a broad consensus on the Belt and Road Initiative' (National Development and Reform Commission 2015). There is actually a misperception between China and the West as these kinds of educational tours are perceived as propaganda[4] (Rolland 2017).

Another predominant idea is that of the 'China threat'. From this perspective, the BRI is seen as a tool to expand regional and global hegemony with little benefit for other stakeholders. Statements towards China are normative. As stated by the French President Macron during his visit to China in 2018, 'China's New Silk Road cannot be a one way' (Rose 2018), which may have implied that the French administration suggests that the Europeans will not participate unless European

---

[3] Interview 2 on BRI, 2018 ('Chinese Investments')
[4] Interview 1 on BRI 2018 (Western Business and the Belt Road Initiative).

and Chinese actors are mutually benefitting from the BRI. The German newspaper *Handelsblatt* reported (Heide et al. 2018) in August 2018 on an unpublished report signed by 27 out of 28 EU ambassadors located in China. This report is highly critical of China's BRI policy. The only ambassador that refrained from signing was of Hungary, given that it benefits directly from the BRI policy. In the same manner, the Western interest groups in China organize seminars for their members on 'dispute resolution mechanisms along the BRI' rather than on opportunities of engagement.

Furthermore, in a report published by the German Chambers of Commerce Worldwide Network and the state-funded agency Germany Trade and Invest (GTAI), it is argued that Chinese ideas such as 'peace and security, prosperity through exchange and mutual benefit' have little to do with reality. Rather, the Chinese government aims to benefit most from the BRI, which leaves little room for foreign business (German Chambers of Commerce Worldwide Network and GTAI 2018). The idea that Chinese, rather than foreign stakeholders, benefit is also a prevailing theory among US stakeholders. It is argued that 'as part of its One Belt, One Road project, China is pressing participating countries to buy Chinese high-speed trains, solar panels, and telecommunications equipment, which could reduce opportunities for American businesses beyond China' (Kennedy 2018).

China's establishment of the AIIB in 2016, a Chinese-led developing bank headquartered in Beijing has also been perceived with scepticism and at times even as a major threat to the liberal order. In this context, the AIIB is perceived as a vehicle to exert China's influence on the system; the idea that China could use the AIIB as a vehicle to influence liberal norms and values of the international system is spread widely. One of the concerns is that the AIIB is providing loans for projects that are executed in states with no rule of law, political instability and a high risk that the loan cannot be paid back. This concept of unconditionality stands in stark contrast to practices of those of the US-led multilateral institutions. Given the power of institutions as a multiplicator of norms and values (Campbell 2008), the absence of trust and non-acceptance of its practices is of particular importance.

Western and Chinese Interests

It is not straightforward to analyse Chinese interests in the BRI policies as the policies are implemented, promoted and driven as a top-down approach. Analysis showed that, in the framework of the BRI, China's leadership made a particular effort to embrace multiple societal stakeholders to promote its ideas. This is particularly crucial, as interest groups in democratic systems are the main players in articulating interests of society. In contrast, the Chinese Communist Party and the government are guiding Chinese interest groups and think tanks, diplomats and other leaders to convey a certain narrative to foreign stakeholders. Banks, state-owned enterprises, think tanks and media are in close interaction with the government. This resulted in mostly aligned ideas and interests (Rolland 2017). There are some critical voices on the economic rationale from Chinese scholars and think tanks, which is an indicator for material interests in the BRI. Concerns over stable investment environments have been addressed (Economy 2018).

Another challenge in the articulation of Chinese interests is that its business actors, the ones with material interests, are co-opted by the party (Dickson 2008) and not embedded in transnational networks. The party is co-opting business actors to align business with party ideas. Business actors are powerful members of China's society. Therefore, the party wants to ensure that Chinese capitalists act as a vehicle to spread party ideas and policies rather than contradicting state-driven ideas and policies. As argued before, being embedded in China's state corporatist system and aligned with the party constrains, these international actors integrate and participate with transnational think tanks and groups. This means that it is very likely that their interests deviate from those in the West.

However, our research showed that both Chinese and Western stakeholders' interests are not clearly conveyed and depend on their engagement and role in the BRI. This is not only valid for interest groups but also for government agencies, politicians and institutions. As one interviewee argued on the stance of the German government towards the BRI: 'The German Government doesn't have an opinion, there is no strategy on how to deal with the BRI. The government cannot reject it because it is too important and it cannot agree because of the political dangers the BRI bears for the German government'.[5] Thus, a salient result is that there is a correlation between material interests in the BRI and the manner of interest articulation. If stakeholders are involved and have a high material interest, the tone of the criticism remains positive.

As a result of a missing civil society, we found that Chinese interests are often interpreted by the West. Summing the material interests up: (a) BRI is a reaction of the global financial crisis and China has the interest to expand its role in the international system; (b) China is in the need to counterbalance its economic slowdown and thus is extending to other markets; (c) China wants to counterbalance its overcapacity and has an interest to stabilize the economies of its neighbouring countries; (d) Chinese companies can satisfy their material interests but foreigners are unlikely to benefit.

CONCLUSION

In this chapter, we addressed the question whether China's can use the BRI as a vehicle to challenge the US-led international system. By applying ideas and interest as an analytical framework, we can conclude that the BRI does not support China's attempt to challenge the current international order.

Our analysis confirmed the initial hypothesis and starting point of this research on the correlation between how actors interpret ideas, interests and successful policy implementation. To be more precise, ideas behind the BRI are ambiguous and perceived with scepticism from the West. Yet, how the West perceives and interprets Chinese ideas is decisive for China's attempt to challenge the US-led system. We showed that the power of ideas and interests give momentum to political agency. As Chinese ideas are not sellable, neither accepted by nor understood among the Western community, the possibility of

---

[5] Interview 3 on BRI, 2018 ('The German Government and the BRI').

political agency, as defined as the Western support to build a Chinese-led international order, is low. As shown in our analysis, one variable of international leadership is that ideas and interests are widely accepted and conveyed in international institutions and as a second step transferred to nation state level in form of accepted norms, values and policies. This means that if China would lead the international system, Chinese ideas and interests would be translated and conveyed to practices in the Western nation states. As the West doesn't accept or understand Chinese concepts, this scenario seems unlikely in the near future.

The current order consists of ideas and interests promoted and defined by the West such as (a) free trade; (b) liberal economic policies that also serve as a role model for other nation states; (c) the promotion and spread of liberal democracy; US hegemony of introducing mechanisms on how to organize global politics; (d) the existence of international institutions based on US norms and values such as conditionality; (e) democracy as a necessity for liberal trade.

The BRI is not perceived as a vehicle that promotes free trade. In contrast, our analysis showed that China is perceived as a threat to free trade, forcing Western businesses into contracts and business deals that are not of reciprocal benefit. In this sense, not much has changed since Chinese aid programmes in Africa, the BRI is perceived as another tool with 'Chinese characteristics' that utilizes Chinese benefits rather than serving a 'community of shared destiny'.

Instead of promoting liberal economic policies that might serve as a role model for the West, the West perceives ideas behind the BRI as 'old wine in new glasses' or communist ideas promoted in its traditional top-down manner. During the Asian financial crisis and the global financial crisis, Chinese ideas on how to tame the crisis were discussed as an alternative model. However, the BRI does not further support this image; on the contrary, it impairs China's capability to introduce alternative, peaceful-models to the US-led system. Yet China's strong role during the crisis enabled the participation in the G20. In such, China showed behaviour of compliance rather than a challenger. In the event of the BRI, China established the AIIB. It took the lead in the establishment of a multilateral institution and was in the position to introduce new rules such as un-conditionality. Whether this will support China's aim to gain leadership depends upon the long-term success of lending practices for BRI projects. China is helping its neighbours as a long-term political strategy, but this strategy has not proven effective yet. Drawing from experience in the Africa continent, it seems unlikely that Chinese unconditional investments results in loyal supporters, which would be essential as it aims for global leadership. Furthermore, China's neighbouring countries are currently not significant players in the international system. Thus, even if these states would follow China and support its attempt for leadership, their structural power remains limited.

In line with its top-down approach of international projects, the role of interest groups to promote the BRI is far from pluralist interest articulation. China's leadership is using its media and other long-established tools to promote ideas on the BRI among various stakeholders. Aligned interests of Chinese stakeholders constrain not only the bargaining process but also China's conveyed idea of 'pluralist and open process of cooperation'. As China is not acting along Western ideas of pluralism, Western ideas of mercantilist and state corporatist (as concept contrary to pluralism) practises are associated with China's pluralism, a very distinctive interpretation of the Western ideas. This is to say that the BRI undermines instead of supporting China's attempt to promote liberal ideas.

However, besides aligned Chinese stakeholders, material interests of the West play a role in the way they challenge or interpret Chinese ideas. Western stakeholders comment on and aim to influence BRI policies with caution, depending on whether they benefit or not from BRI projects. This was shown from the behaviour of the Hungarian government, which refrained from critical arguments. Another interesting result is the reserved stance of the German government towards the BRI. This could be the first sign that China is gaining power within the international system. However, it remains unlikely that China can challenge the liberal system with repressive tools.

The Chinese idea of a historical strong power that is simply reclaiming leadership is certainly part of Chinese collective memory, but is less so in the West. If discussed in the Western discourse, China's history is one reason that it is threatening the Western liberal values.

China is promoting the idea that it stands for a liberal world order, yet BRI practises are perceived very differently from the West. Concepts such as 'a community of common destiny' and 'a new type of international relations' are perceived with great scepticism. Furthermore, Western ideas on liberalism are aligned with democracy. In the context of the BRI, China's political system constrains the Western acceptance and challenges China as a trustworthy negotiation partner. In other words, Chinese investments are not always welcome because they are not associated with liberal practises and democratic values.

We showed the importance of cognitive ideas to support policy programmes: the clearer the policy programme, the better policymakers are in the position to sell their ideas. China has not effectively communicated about the BRI, not to the Western stakeholders nor to Chinese actors at least. Taking the importance of clarity into consideration, the BRI is unlikely to challenge current liberal practises. It is difficult to challenge a system if the ideas are not shared and practises are not imitated. Material interests won't change the fact that China's ideas are not fully understood or accepted. Our analysis showed that material interests are interpreted and perceived by the West as negative, as the BRI is portrayed as a vehicle to utilize Chinese benefits, to tackle its internal problems of overcapacity and a slowing economy. This analysis showed the relevance of ideas and interests and clearly indicated that the BRI does not have the potential to challenge liberal practices.

REFERENCES

Baumgartner, F., and B. L. Leech. 2001. 'Interest Niches and Policy Bandwagons: Patterns of Interest Group Involvement in National Politics'. *The Journal of Politics* 63 (4): 1191–1213.

Beyers, J., R. Eising, and W. Maloney., eds. 2010. *Interest Group Politics in Europe*. Oxon and New York: Routledge.

Blyth, M. 2002. *Great Transformations: The Rise and Decline of Embedded Liberalism*. Cambridge and New York: Cambridge University Press.

Braumoeller, B. F. 2012. *The Great Powers and the International System: Systemic Theory in Empirical Perspective*. Cambridge and New York: Cambridge University Press.

Breslin, S. 2011. 'The "China model" and the Global Crisis: From Friedrich List to a Chinese Mode of Governance?' *International Affairs* 87 (6): 1323–1343.
———. 2013. 'China and the Global Order: Signalling Threat or Friendship?' *International Affairs* 89 (3): 615–634.
Brown, K. 2017a. 'Restoring Faith in Globalization: Can China Push Against the Tide of Anti-Globalization?' *Beijing Review* (2). http://www.bjreview.com/Columnists/Kerry_Brown/201710/t20171011_800106601.html
———. 2017b. 'China's Foreign Policy Since 2012: A Question of Communication and Clarity'. *China Quarterly of International Strategic Studies* 3 (3): 325–339.
Campbell, J. 1998. 'Institutional Analysis and the Role of Ideas in Political Economy'. *Theory and Society* 27 (3): 377–409.
———. 2002. 'Ideas, Politics, and Public Policy'. *Annual Review of Sociology* 28: 21–38.
———. 2008. 'What Do We Know—or Not—About Ideas and Politics?' In *Institutions and Politics*, edited by P. Nedergaard and J. Campbell, 157–176. Copenhagen: DJOF Publishing.
Campbell, J., and O. K. Pedersen, eds. 2001. *The Rise of Neoliberalism and Institutional Analysis*. Princeton and Oxford: Princeton University Press.
De Graaff, N., and B. Van Apeldoorn. 2018. US–China Relations and the Liberal World Order: Contending Elites, Colliding Visions? *International Affairs* 94 (1): 113–131.
Dickson, B. J. 2008. *Wealth into Power: The Communist Party's Embrace of China's Private Sector*. Cambridge, New York: Cambridge University Press.
Dobbin, F. R. 1993. The Social Construction of the Great Depression: Industrial Policy During the 1930s in the United States, Britain, and France. *Theory Society* 22 (1): 1–56.
Duggan, N. 2014. 'The Rise of China within Global Governance'. In *Interpreting China as a Regional and Global Power*, edited by B. Dessein. Houndmills: Palgrave Macmillan.
Economy, E. C. 2018. *The Third Revolution: Xi Jinping and the New Chinese State*. New York: Oxford University Press.
Fligstein, N., and I. Mara-Drita. 1996. 'How to Make a Market: Reflections on the Attempt to Create a Single Market in the European Union'. *American Journal of Sociology* 102 (1): 1–33.
Foot, R., and A. Walter. 2011. *China, the United States and Global Order*. Cambridge and New York: Cambridge University Press.
Freeman, D., and G. Geeraerts. 2012. 'Europe, China and Expectations for Human Rights'. In *Conceptual Gaps in China–EU Relations*, edited by Z. Pan. Houndmills, Basingstoke, Hampshire: Palgrave Macmillan.
Friedberg, A. L. 2011. *A Contest for Supremacy: China, America, and the Struggle for Mastery in Asia*. New York: W. W. Norton & Company, Inc.
Friedman, M. 1962. *Capitalism and Freedom*. Chicago: University of Chicago Press.
Fukuyama, F. 2006. *The End of History and the Last Man*. New York: Free Press.

German Chambers of Commerce Worldwide Network, and GTAI. 2018. *Neue Seidenstraße: Chinas massives Investitionsprogramm [New Silk Road: China's Massive Investment Program]*. Bonn & Berlin: Author.

Gilpin, R. 1981. *War and Change in World Politics*. Cambridge: Cambridge University Press.

Goldstein, J., and R. O. Keohane. 1993. 'Ideas and Foreign Policy: An Analytical Framework'. In *Ideas and Foreign Policy: Beliefs, Institutions and Political Change*, edited by J. Goldstein and R. O. Keohane, 3–30. Ithaca and London: Cornell University Press.

Gottwald, J., and N. Duggan. 2011. 'Expectations and Adaptation: China's Foreign Policies in a Changing Global Environment'. *International Journal of China Studies* 2 (1): 1–26.

Hall, P. A. 1993a. 'Ideas and the Social Sciences'. In *Ideas and Foreign Policy: Beliefs, Institutions and Political Change*, edited by J. Goldstein and R. O. Keohane. New York: Cornell University.

———. 1993b. 'Policy Paradigms, Social Learning, and the State: The Case of Economic Policymaking in Britain'. *Comparative Politics* 25 (3): 275–296.

Hall, P. A., and D. W. Gingerich. 2009. 'Varieties of Capitalism and Institutional Complementarities in the Political Economy: An Empirical Analysis'. *British Journal of Political Science* 39 (3): 449–482.

Halpern, N. 1993. 'Creating Socialist Economies: Stalinist Political Economy and the Impact of Ideas'. In *Ideas and Foreign Policy: Beliefs, Institutions and Political Change*, edited by J. Goldstein and R. O. Keohane, 87–110. Ithaca and London: Cornell University Press.

Hanegraaff, M., C. Braun, D. De Bievre, and J. Beyers. 2015. 'The Domestic and Global Origins of Transnational Advocacy: Explaining Lobbying Presence During WTO Ministerial Conferences'. *Comparative Political Studies* 48 (12): 1591–1621.

Harnisch, S., S. Bersick, and J.-C. Gottwald, eds. 2016. *China's International Roles*. New York: Routledge.

Heide, D., T. Hoppe, S. Scheuer, and K. Stratmann. 2018. 'EU Ambassadors Band Together Against Silk Road'. *Hnadelsblatt*, April 17. https://www.handelsblatt.com/today/politics/china-first-eu-ambassadors-band-together-against-silk-road/23581860.html?ticket=ST-4861345-27BrvvuqBUBHDHhjgs9A-ap3

Hewson, M., and T. J. Sinclair, eds. 1999. *Approaches to Global Governance Theory*. Albany, NY: State University of New York Press.

Ikenberry, J. G. 2009. 'Liberalism in a Realist World: International Relations as an American Scholarly Tradition'. *International Studies* 46 (1–2): 203–219.

———. 2011. *Liberal Leviathan*. Princeton and Oxford: Princeton University Press.

Junxian Gan, and Yan Mao. 2016. 'China's New Silk Road: Where Does It Lead?' *Asian Perspective* 40: 105–130.

Katzenstein, P. J., ed. 1996. *The Culture of National Security, Norms and Identity in World Politics*. New York: Columbia University Press.

Keck, M., and K. Sikkink. 1998. *Activists beyond Borders: Advocacy Networks in International Politics*. Ithaca, NY: Cornell University Press.

Kennedy, S. 2018. 'Protecting America's Technology Industry from China'. *Foreign Affairs*, August 1.

———. ed. 2017. *Global Governance and China: The Dragon's Learning Curve*. London and New York: Routledge.

Keohane, R. O., and J. S. Nye Jr. 2000. Globalization: What's New? What's Not? (And so What?). *Foreign Policy* (118): 104–119.

Keohane, R. O., and J. S. Nye. 1974. 'Transgovernmental Relations and International Organizations'. *World Politics* 27 (1): 39–62.

———. 1989. *Power and Interdependence*. Glenview, Illinois and Boston: Scott, Foresman and Company.

Kirshner, J. 2014. *American Power after the Financial Crisis*. Ithaca and London: Cornell University Press.

Le Corre, P. 2017. Europe's Mixed Views on China's One Belt, One Road Initiative. *Brookings International Affairs*, July 15.

Mahoney, C. 2007. 'The Role of Interest Groups in Fostering Citizen Engagement: The Determinants of Outside Lobbying'. In *Politics Beyond the State*, edited by K. Deschower and T. M. Jans. Brussels: VUBPRESS Brussels University Press.

———. 2008. *Brussels Versus the Beltway: Advocacy in the United States and the European Union (American Governance and Public Policy)*. Washington, DC: Georgetown University Press.

McNally, C. A., and J. Gruin. 2017. 'A Novel Pathway to Power? Contestation and Adaptation in China's Internationalization of the RMB'. *Review of International Political Economy* 24 (4): 599–628.

Mearsheimer, J. J. 2010. 'The Gathering Storm: China's Challenge to US Power in Asia'. *The Chinese Journal of International Politics* 3 (4): 381–396.

Moravcsik, A. 1997. 'Taking Preferences Seriously: A Liberal Theory of International Politics'. *International Organization* 51 (4): 513–553.

———. 2008. 'The New Liberalism'. In *The Oxford Handbook of International Relations*, edited by Reus-Smith and D. Snidal. Oxford: Oxford University Press

Morgenthau, H. J. 1978. *Politics among Nations: The Struggle for Power and Peace*. New York: Alfred A. Knopf.

National Development and Reform Commission and Ministry of Commerce. 2015. *Vision and Actions on Jointly Building Silk Road Economic Belt and 21st-Century Maritime Silk Road*. Beijing: People's Republic of China.

Noelke, A. 2012. 'The Rise of the B(R)IC Variety of Capitalism: Towards a New Phase of Organized Capitalism'. In *Neoliberalism in Crisis*, edited by H. Overbeek and B. Van Apeldoorn. Houndmills: Palgrave Macmillan.

Nordin, A., and M. Weissmann. 2018. 'Will Trump Make China Great Again? The Belt and Road Initiative and International Order'. *International Affairs* 94 (2): 231–249.

Nye, J. S. 2016. 'Limits of American Power'. *Political Science Quarterly* 131 (2): 267–283.
Nye, J. S. Jr., and R. O. Keohane. 1971. 'Transnational Relations and World Politics: A Conclusion'. *International Organization* 25 (3): 721–748.
Overbeek, H. 2004. 'Transnational Class Formation and Concepts of Control: Towards a Genealogy of the Amsterdam Project in International Political Economy'. *Journal of International Relations and Development* 7 (4): 113–141.
Pan Zhongqi. 2012. *Conceptual Gaps in China–EU Relations: Global Governance, Human Rights and Strategic Partnerships*. Houndmills: Palgrave Macmillan.
Ramo, J. C. 2004. *The Beijing Consensus*. London: The Foreign Policy Centre.
Rolland, N. 2017. 'China's "Belt and Road Initiative": Underwhelming or Game-Changer?' *The Washington Quarterly* 40 (1): 127–142.
Rose, M. 2018. 'China's New "Silk Road" Cannot be One-Way, France's Macron says'. *Reuters*, January 8. https://www.reuters.com/article/us-china-france/chinas-new-silk-road-cannot-be-one-way-frances-macron-says-id USKBN1EX0FU
Schirm, S. A. 2009. 'Ideas and Interests in Global Financial Governance: Comparing German and US Preference Formation'. *Cambridge Review of International Affairs* 22 (3): 501–521.
———. 2011. 'The G20, Emerging Powers, and Transatlantic Relations'. *Transatlantic Academy Paper Series*, 1–16.
———. 2013. 'Global Politics are Domestic Politics: A Societal Approach to Divergence in the G20'. *Review of International Studies* 39 (3): 685–706.
———. 2016. 'Domestic Ideas, Institutions or Interests? Explaining Governmental Preferences towards Global Economic Governance'. *International Political Science Review* 37 (1): 66–80.
———. 2017. 'Societal Foundations of Governmental Preference Formation in the Eurozone Crisis'. *European Politics and Society* 19 (1): 63–78.
Schmitter, P. C. 1974. 'Still the Century of Corporatism?' *The Review of Politics* 3 (6): 85–131.
Shambaugh, D. 2013. *China Goes Global*. Oxford and New York: Oxford University Press.
Sinclair, T. J. 2012. *Global Governance*. Cambridge and Malden: Polity Press.
Smith, A. 2003. *The Wealth of Nations*. New York: Bantam Books.
Sørensen, G. 2011. *A Liberal World Order in Crisis: Choosing Between Imposition and Restraint*. Ithaca, NY: Cornell University Press.
Ugur, M., ed. 2002. *An Open Macroeconomics Reader*. London and New York: Routledge.
Van Apeldoorn, B. 2002. *Transnational Capitalism and the Struggle over European Integration*. London and New York: Routledge.
Van Apeldoorn, B., and N. De Graaff. 2016. *American Grand Strategy and Corporate Elite Networks: The Open Door since the End of the Cold War*. London and New York: Routledge.

Waltz, K. 2001. *Man, the State, and War: A Theoretical Analysis, Revised Edition.* New York: Columbia University Press.
Waltz, K. N. 1964. 'The Stability of a Bipolar World'. *Daedalus* 93 (3): 881–909.
Wang, J., and W. Song, eds. 2016. *China, the European Union, and the International Politics of Global Governance.* Houndmills and New York: Palgrave Macmillan.
Weber, M. 1946. 'The Social Psychology of the World Religions'. In *From Max Weber: Essays in Sociology*, edited by H. H. Gerth and C. W. Mills. New York: Oxford University Press.
Weil, S. 2017. *Lobbying and Foreign Interests in Chinese Politics.* Houndmills and New York: Palgrave Macmillan.
———. 2018. 'The Strange Case of Pluralist Lobbying in a Corporatist Setting: Defending Western Business Interests in China'. *Business and Politics* 20 (1): 70–97.
Weil, S., and J. Yijia. 2012. 'The EU and China's Perceptions of Democracy and Their Impacts on China–EU Relations'. In *Conceptual Gaps in China–EU Relations: Global Governance, Human Rights and Strategic Partnerships*, edited by Z. Pan. Houndmills: Palgrave Macmillan.
Weil, S., and Y. Jing. 2012. 'The EU and China's Perceptions of Democracy and Their Impacts on China–EU Relations'. In *Conceptual Gaps in China–EU Relations*, edited by Z. Pan. Houndmills, Basingstoke, Hampshire: Palgrave Macmillan.
Xi, J. 2017a. 'Keynote Speech by H. E. Xi Jinping, President of the People's Republic of China'. *Opening Session of the World Economic Forum Annual Meeting 2017.* http://www.china.org.cn/node_7247529/content_40569136.htm
———. 2017b. 'Work Together to Build the Silk Road Economic Belt and The 21st Century Maritime Silk Road'. *Keynote speech at the Belt and Road Forum for International Cooperation.* http://www.xinhuanet.com/english/2017-05/14/c_136282982.htm
———. 2014. *The Governance of China.* Beijing: Foreign Languages Press.
Xinhuanet. 2015. 'Xinhua Asia-Pacific Regional Bureau promotes "Xinhua Silk Road" Information Products at "One Belt, One Road" Forum'.
Yong, W. 2016. 'Offensive for Defensive: The Belt and Road Initiative and China's New Grand Strategy'. *The Pacific Review* 29 (3): 455–463.

Chapter 5

Soft Infrastructures and the Belt and Road Initiative

Bala Ramasamy, Matthew Yeung,
Yann Duval and Chorthip Utoktham

INTRODUCTION

The Belt and Road Initiative (BRI) is an ambitious vision that encourages a new level of cooperation among countries along the various corridors identified by the Chinese government. The Vision document (National Development and Reform Commission [NDRC] and Ministry of Commerce 2015) states a number of cooperative initiatives that will bring member countries closer together, politically, economically and culturally. These range from free trade areas along the corridors to an international summit forum on the BRI. However, two main initiatives that make up a significant portion of the Vision document are as follows:

1. To improve the region's infrastructure and put in place a secure and efficient network of land, sea and air passages, raising the connectivity to a higher level, and
2. To further enhance trade and investment facilitation, establish a network of free trade areas that meet high standards so that economic ties among member economies can be further deepened.

In other words, the BRI has a dual objective of improving both the hard and soft infrastructure of the economies aligned to the initiative. Portugal-Perez and Wilson (2010) explain that trade facilitation in a broad sense can be undertaken along these two broad dimensions. The hard dimension relates to tangible infrastructure such as roads, ports, highway and telecommunications whereas the soft dimension relates to transparency, customs management, the business environment and other institutional factors. The distinction between the two can assist in policy decisions. Portugal-Perez and Wilson (2010) also state that both dimensions are complementary in nature, as one dimension reinforces the other in lowering the cost of trade. They do however find that improvements in infrastructure quality have the greatest benefits for export growth, particularly for lower income countries. The marginal impact of ICT usage on export performance, on the other hand, is greater for richer countries.

The impact of infrastructure improvement (air, land and sea) is simulated by Herrero and Xu (2016) for the BRI countries. Using a gravity model and using distances as proxy for transportation costs, they find that a 10 per cent reduction in railway, air and maritime costs will increase export by 2, 5.5 and 1.1 per cent respectively. This implies that the marginal impact of a reduction in air and railway costs is greater than a reduction in ad valorem tariffs.

We conducted an in-depth analysis to compare the magnitude of impact of these hard and soft infrastructures along the six corridors of the BRI, namely the New Eurasian Land Bridge (NELB) economic corridor, the Central Asia–West Asia (CAWA) economic corridor, the Indo-China Peninsula (IP) economic corridor, the Bangladesh–China–India–Myanmar (BCIM) economic corridor, the China–Mongolia–Russia (CMR) economic corridor and the China–Pakistan (CP) economic corridor.[1] No doubt, both physical infrastructure and trade facilitation are important for trade to flourish. However, physical infrastructure has been found to be financially expensive and risky. ADB (2017) reported that developing Asian economies need to spend

---

[1] The countries along each corridor covered in our analysis are shown in Appendix 5.1.

$1.7 trillion annually from 2016 to 2030 if the region wants to maintain its economic momentum. Hurley, Morris, and Portelance (2018) considered the risk of debt distress among 68 BRI countries and find that countries such as Laos, Kyrgyzstan, Mongolia, Pakistan and Tajikistan will face debt sustainability problems. Hard infrastructure also requires strong political cooperation and will definitely be scrutinized by public opinion on its social and environmental impact. On the other hand, the soft infrastructure, more specifically trade facilitation is relatively cheaper and is less obvious to the public eye. Reducing trade barriers are policy driven initiatives. They are also within the jurisdiction of national governments. Although both hard and soft infrastructures are mutually supportive, our comparison between the two shows the importance of the latter.

DATA, MODELS AND METHODS

Rather than developing a unique data set for the issues of interest as done by Portugal-Perez and Wilson (2010), Otsuki (2011) and Herrero and Xu (2016), we use the pillar-level indicators calculated by the World Economic Forum's Enabling Trade Index (ETI). The ETI comprises of 7 pillars: (a) domestic markets access, (b) foreign market access, (c) efficiency and transparency of border administration, (d) availability and quality of transport infrastructure, (e) availability and quality of transport services, (f) availability and use of ICTs and (g) operating environment. We are particularly interested in the third, fourth and sixth pillars. Among the variables considered in the third pillar include customs services, customs transparency, number of documents, days and cost to import and export as well as irregular payments involved. The fourth pillar on the other hand includes the quality and availability of air, rail, road and port infrastructure. The sixth pillar includes the Internet penetration rate as well as the extent of ICT use in business transactions. The first and second pillars were not included as these are not our main focus in this chapter while the fifth and seventh pillars, although relevant, were excluded to avoid multicollinearity issues in modelling.

Each pillar in the ETI is normalized within a range of 1 (lowest quality) to 7 (highest quality). Our gravity model based on Portugal-Perez and Wilson (2010) and Otsuki (2011) uses mixed effects model of panel data estimation with more than 70,000 bilateral trade relationships among 139 countries worldwide for the period between 2008 and 2014 (years for which consistent ETI data is available). The gravity modelling method is proven to be remarkably successful in predicting bilateral trade flows based on the mass of the exporting and importing economy, the geographical distance between the two economies, and other attributes according to the researcher's interests.

As our main interest is the impact of improvements in trade facilitation and infrastructure along the various corridors of the BRI, we specify the following gravity model to which we append the selected enabling variables of the exporting country:

$$y_{ij} = \alpha_{j[i]} + b_1(\text{Border}_i) + b_2(\text{Infra}_i) + b_3(\text{ICT}_i) + \beta X + \delta T + \in_{ij} \quad 1$$

where y_{ij} is the value of exports from country i to country j; Border is the efficiency of border administration in the exporting country i; Infra is the quality and availability of transport infrastructure in the exporting country i; ICT is the availability and quality of ICT in the exporting country i; $\alpha_{j[i]}$ is fixed effects for importer j; T is fixed effects for each year t; and $\in_{ij}$ is the random error term. X consists of a basket of variables that are commonly included in a gravity model, which comprise of real GDP of both countries, the size of population of both countries, the physical distance between trading partners, dummy variables for sharing a common border, a shared language, colony–colonizer relationship, land-locked countries and if a regional trade agreement (RTA) exists with the trading partner.

All variables are log-transformed, except for dummy variables. Equation 1 is a varying intercept model and controls for the importing country j. Sources of data are reported in Table 5.1.

As mentioned earlier, the hard and soft infrastructures do not only impact trade individually. There is also synergy between the two. We extend our analysis by considering the possible interacting effects of various pillars on export performance. We added three interaction variables, namely [Border × Infra], [Border × ICT] and [Infra × ICT], to the original model as shown in Equation 2. To reduce multicollinearity, all the right hand side variables in Equation 2, except for the

Table 5.1 *Variables and Data Source*

Variable	Details	Source
Border	Efficiency and transparency of border administration	Various issues of the World Economic Forum's Global Enabling Trade Report 2008 – 2014
Infra	Availability and quality of transport infrastructure	
ICT	Availability and use of ICTs	
Exports	Amount of exports from country i to country j (in million $)	UNCTAD's Data Centre
GDP	Real GDP of country i and j (in million $, constant)	
Population	Size of population in country i and j (in 1,000)	
Distance	Geographic distance between country i and j	dist_cepii.xls from CEPII
Contig	Dummy variable set equal to 1 if country i and j share a common border	
Comlang	Dummy variable set equal to 1 if country i and j share a common language	
Col45	Dummy variable set equal to 1 if country i and j had a colonial relationship after 1945	
Comcol	Dummy variable set equal to 1 if country i and j had a common colonizer after 1945	
Landlocked	Dummy variable set equal to 1 for landlocked countries, 0 otherwise	geo_cepii.xls from CEPII
RTA	Dummy variable set equal to 1 if country i and j are members of an RTA, 0 otherwise	De Sousa (2012) http://jdesousa.univ.free.fr/data.htm

Source: The authors.

dummy variables, are centred. The model also takes into account the fixed effects of importer country j and time T.

$$y_{ij} = \alpha_{j[i]} + b_1(\text{Border}_i) + b_2(\text{Infra}_i) + b_3(\text{ICT}_i) + \\ b_4(\text{Border}_i \times \text{Infra}_i) + b_5(\text{Border}_i \times \text{ICT}_i) + b_6(\text{Infra}_i \times \\ \text{ICT}_i) + \beta X + \delta T + \in_{ij} \qquad 2$$

RESULTS OF ANALYSIS

The fitted model for Equations 1 and 2 is reported in panels A and B of Table 5.2, respectively. The fitted model yielded a goodness of fit (Snijders and Bosker) of $R2 > 0.8$. In the fitted equation (1), the usual

Table 5.2 Effects of Border Administration, Physical Infrastructure and ICT on Exports

Panel A: Equation 1 [Main Effect Model]; n = 73,868			
Variable	Coefficient	Std. Error	z
Landlocked	−0.765**	0.137	−5.58
Contig	1.368**	0.052	26.28
Comlang	0.684**	0.026	26.02
Col45	0.763**	0.083	9.18
Comcol	0.963**	0.033	28.81
Distance	−1.111**	0.013	−87.25
GDP(*i*)	0.724**	0.013	55.34
GDP(*j*)	0.935**	0.034	27.51
Population(*i*)	0.525**	0.013	40.04
Population(*j*)	0.088**	0.044	1.99
Border	1.532**	0.061	25.05
Infra	0.686**	0.054	12.81
ICT	1.400**	0.057	24.54
RTA	0.571**	0.025	23.16

(Table 5.2 continued)

(Table 5.2 continued)

Panel B: Equation 2 [Interaction Model with Centred Data]; n = 73,868			
Variable	Coefficient	Std. Error	z
Landlocked	−0.765**	0.137	−5.57
contig	1.369**	0.052	25.86
comlang	0.683**	0.026	25.46
col45	0.758**	0.083	9.70
comcol	0.960**	0.033	28.57
distance	−1.111**	0.013	−88.01
GDP(i)	0.724**	0.013	54.36
GDP(j)	0.934**	0.034	27.48
Population (i)	0.525**	0.013	39.40
Population(j)	0.089*	0.044	2.03
Border	1.701**	0.063	27.17
Infra	0.686**	0.054	12.67
ICT	1.264**	0.058	21.69
RTA	0.574**	0.025	23.28
Border × Infra	2.943**	0.236	12.47
Border × ICT	−0.510**	0.139	−3.66
Infra × ICT	−1.701**	0.153	−11.09

Note: * and ** refers to level of significance at 1 per cent and 5 per cent respectively.

variables used in gravity models have the right sign and are significant. A larger geographic distance between trading partners have a negative effect on exports. Similarly, when one partner is landlocked, the effect on export is also negative. Other variables that reduce the liability of foreignness (Zaheer 1995) like sharing a common border, language, etc., have significant positive impact on exports. A larger GDP and population of both trading partners also result in more exports. More importantly, the coefficients for Border, Infra and ICT are all positive and significant indicating that these are indeed enablers of export. Our analysis also finds significant positive results for RTA.

A 1 per cent increase in the efficiency of border administration and transport infrastructure will increase exports by 1.5 per cent and 0.7 per cent, respectively. A 1 per cent improvement in the quality of ICT on the other hand can increase exports by 1.4 per cent. Clearly, among the three enablers in the model, improvements in the efficiency of border administration have the largest impact on exports, ceteris paribus. In fact, the border administration co-efficient is the largest among all our variables.

Using the estimations from Equation 1, we can calculate the improvements in export performance that will accrue to countries if they reach higher standards of performance in border administration, infrastructure and ICT, presumably through the support provided by the BRI in these areas. Two scenarios are considered: (a) countries involved in BRI whose standards were lower than that of China improve their performance to the level of China and (b) countries involved in BRI improve their performance to that of the top performer.[2]

The results of selected countries are shown in Table 5.3. Our estimations suggest that Mongolia, Tajikistan and Uzbekistan could see their exports more than triple if they can align the efficiency of their border administration with that of China (Scenario 1). Mongolia is found to gain most from advances in trade facilitation under the China benchmarking scenario, as do most other countries. On the other hand, Myanmar gains relatively more from improvements in transport and ICT infrastructure and services.

Thailand and Turkey, whose performance on trade facilitation are higher than China, are two other countries who gain most from hard infrastructure improvements under Scenario 1. However, considering Scenario 2, where BRI economies all upgrade their performance to that of the best performer among them, improvements in trade facilitation and ICT are generally found to be most important in raising exports.

---

[2] Singapore is chosen as the reference for this second scenario since it ranked as number one for border administration (third pillar) and infrastructure (fourth pillar) and among the top 10 countries for ICT (sixth pillar) in the ETI 2014.

Table 5.3 Changes in Exports in Selected BRI Economies from Improvements in Hard and Soft Infrastructure (%)

Economy	% Change in Exports under Scenario 1: Improvement to China's Performance Level			Percentage Change in Exports under Scenario 2: Improvement to Top BRI Performer's Level		
	Border Admin	Infra-structure	ICT	Border Admin	Infra-structure	ICT
Myanmar	95.9	104.3	188.5	200.4	141.3	454.1
Bangladesh	106.4	72.7	72.8	216.5	103.9	231.9
Mongolia	236.7	72.7		416.3	103.9	85.7
Lao PDR	86.2	50.9	82.4	185.5	78.2	250.2
Cambodia	86.2	63.1	25.1	185.5	92.6	140.2
Tajikistan	234.4	26.3	107.1	395.1	35.8	188.7
Uzbekistan	232	19.2	119	409.1	40.7	320.6
Kyrgyz Republic	95.9	58.8	11.3	200.4	87.5	113.7
Iran, Islamic Rep.	95.9	29.5	36.1	200.4	52.9	161.3
Pakistan	24.9	32.1	64.1	91.5	56	215.2
Kazakhstan	130.4	27		253.3	50	34.6
India	30	12.4	36.1	99.3	32.8	161.3
Vietnam	41.2	34.8		116.6	59.2	68.7
Indonesia	20.1	27		84.1	50	92
Russian Federation	68.9	20.2		159.1	42	34.6
Thailand	7.3	10.7		64.6	30.7	79.7
Turkey		9		53.3	28.7	85.7
China				53.3	18.1	92
Malaysia				38.6	15	31.2

Looking at these numbers from a corridor perspective (see Table 5.4), results from the improvement of trade facilitation to China level suggests that exports would increase most for countries along the NELB as well as the CMR, essentially due to the fact that countries along these

Table 5.4 Changes in Exports along BRI Corridors from Improvements to China's Performance Level

Corridors	Border Admin (%)	Infrastructure (%)	ICT (%)
ICP	17.51	18.06	2.17
BCIM	39.43	20.63	43.00
CP	24.90	32.10	64.10
CMR	68.90	20.20	0.00
CAWA	60.17	19.11	3.95
NELB	76.12	21.00	–

Note: numbers shown reflect aggregate changes in exports to the world of all Asian economies in each corridor other than China.

corridors currently stand well below China's performance in this area. In contrast, the CP corridor stands out in terms of potential export increases if infrastructure and the use of ICT can be improved.

Turning now to interactions between hard and soft infrastructure as modelled in Equation 2, we find strong evidence to show that border administration and infrastructure complement each other. Figures 5.1 and 5.2 provide a visual of the interaction effects. Our results strongly suggest that improving hard infrastructure in a context of inefficient border crossings and trade procedures may not result in an increase in trade (the rather flat line in Figure 5.1). At the same time, however, countries with better quality infrastructure tend to gain more from a more efficient border administration (Figure 5.2). These results do confirm our earlier findings that trade facilitation is a critical driver of export performance.

Significant interactions are also found between ICT and infrastructure. In particular, while improving ICT has a positive effect on exports for countries with both high- and low-quality infrastructure, the effect is greater in countries with lower levels of infrastructure (Figure 5.3). As for ICT and trade facilitation, improvements in ICT have similar positive effects on exports, regardless of the level of trade facilitation (Figure 5.4).

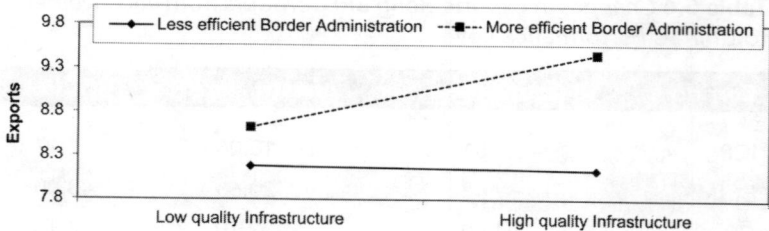

Figure 5.1 *Effect of Infrastructure Improvements on Exports in a Low/High Trade Facilitation Environment*

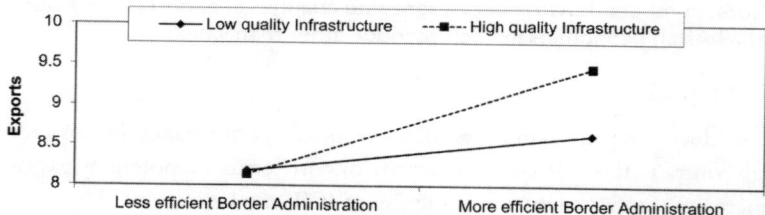

Figure 5.2 *Effect of Trade Facilitation Improvements on Exports in a Low/High Quality Infrastructure Environment*

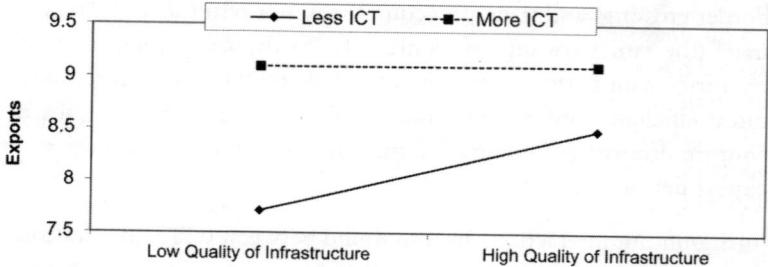

Figure 5.3 *Effect of Infrastructure Improvements on Exports in a More/Less ICT Input*

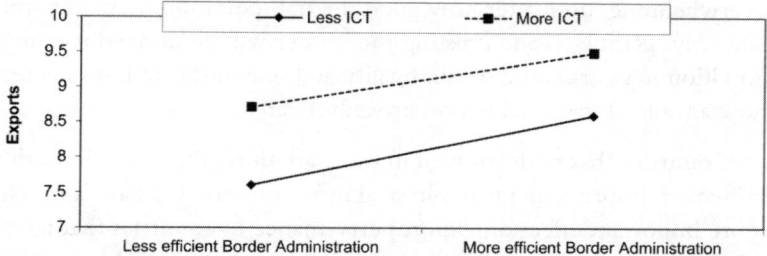

Figure 5.4 *Effect of Trade Facilitation Improvements on Exports with More/Less ICT Input*

DISCUSSION

Banomyong (2013) explained that a transport corridor is one where an area or region is connected physically by transportation networks. A logistics (or a trade facilitation) corridor takes the transport corridor to another level as the institutional framework is harmonized such that freight, people and information are able to move within the corridor much more efficiently. Finally, an economic corridor is one that is able to attract investments into the region, which will generate greater economic activities. Since the BRI is designed to develop economic corridors, efforts that focus on transport and trade facilitation corridors as a pre-requisite make strategic sense.

Our analysis of the trade and trade facilitation data of countries affected by the BRI clearly points to the fact that the improvement of both transportation networks and trade facilitation procedures as well as ICT capacities do indeed encourage and increase trade flows between countries. Our findings suggest that on average, a 1 per cent improvement in trade facilitation will increase exports by more than 1.5 per cent, while a 1 per cent improvement on the quality of transport infrastructure will increase exports by about 0.69 per cent. In fact, we find that both strategies complement each other and that an integrated cross-sectoral approach would be most effective. The movement of people and freight will be delayed at the border if procedural issues are overwhelming, no matter how good the transportation networks are. Similarly, getting to and crossing the border will be delayed if transportation networks are poor in quality and uncoordinated, no matter how advanced trade facilitation procedures are.

Countries that perform well in trade are those that excel in both. However, improvements in physical infrastructure will have a much more important effect on export performance in countries that have relatively more efficient border administration. This highlights the need for countries with weak trade facilitation to take stock of their weaknesses and work on improving their border administration if they wish to receive the full effect of better infrastructure. This also implies that the BRI has to dedicate enough importance on both strategies—border administration and physical connectivity—although not necessarily equal emphasis as the impact differs from one corridor to another.

A review of the literature on trade facilitation efforts of the Asian sub-regions covered by the six corridors in the BRI tends to point to a common set of problems in each of the corridor: customs and other authorities that require excessive documentation and/or do not apply modern ICT to trade procedures; a lack of harmonization of various standards and procedures within and between countries; and inadequate border infrastructure facilities at the border and between borders.[3]

However, there is still insufficient knowledge about the bottlenecks that hamper the seamless flow of freight along the corridors. While business process analyses (BPA) of trade procedures have been carried out for more than 50 goods involving 13 countries in the Asia Pacific region since 2010 (UNESCAP 2014), only a few of them have focused on cross-border trade and transport processes directly relevant to the BRI. Therefore, there is an urgent need to better understand the procedures involved in moving popular products along the various

---

[3] For example, refer to UNNExT Brief No. 11, Insights from ESCAP's Trade Process Analysis Database. http://www.unescap.org/resources/unnext-brief-no-11-insights-escap%E2%80%99s-trade-process-analysis-database

corridors in the BRI. In particular, BPA and BPA+ studies[4] of the top products crossing borders as well as along the corridors to identify the bottlenecks are necessary. Identifying and releasing the bottlenecks for these goods will be the low-hanging fruits that can be harvested and gain support from the various players, both public and private, in the trading activity. These studies should also identify which type of infrastructure—soft or hard—contributes more towards the bottlenecks so that policies and projects can be prioritized effectively.

In the case of building and utilizing fully ICT capabilities, first, a technological leapfrogging is required (Fong 2009). Without capacity building in ICT and its widespread use, paperless system will be a mirage. Investing in broadband and leapfrogging into future Internet systems and extending the use of mobile phone and its various applications in facilitating trade procedures are all strategies well worth considering. In fact, given that the BRI consists of China as a leading country in computer and mobile phone hardware and India as a leading software developer, eradicating digital poverty in the BRI is well within reach. This requires governments of individual countries to allocate a larger portion of their resources into building these digital capabilities. This could also be achieved by attracting more multinationals from China, India and other countries to invest in their countries. We have shown elsewhere five simple policies that attract Chinese companies (Ramasamy and Yeung 2016). These include minimizing institutional risks by reducing corruptive practices and establishing free trade agreements (FTAs) with China. Liberalizing the telecommunication industry and inviting foreign investors can achieve technological leapfrogging and building human resource capacity in ICT. Building ICT capacity would be an important step towards cross-border paperless trade facilitation in the BRI.

Second, an extensive usage of ICT in facilitating trade procedures is necessary. In other words, a paperless initiative at a national level should

---

[4] BPA+ extends the BPA to the time-cost-distance (TCD) and time-release studies (TRS) methodologies, providing reliable and detailed data so that bottlenecks can be identified and addressed. This information can provide the basis for establishment of integrated and sustainable Trade and Transport Facilitation Monitoring Mechanisms (TTFMM) at the national or regional levels (UNESCAP 2014).

be a policy priority (UNESCAP 2014). The paperless system should consider decreasing the need for repetitive information, and connect digitally the various national agencies involved in regulating the movement of goods and services. Further, allowing exporters and importers to make online submissions of relevant documents should be encouraged (Rastogi and Arvis 2014). The UN Global Survey on Trade Facilitation and Paperless Trade Implementation finds that even when Internet connection is available among customs and other regulatory bodies within a country, electronic application and the issuance of various certificates like the Certificate of Origin is yet to be implemented (UNESCAP 2015). Once a single window system can be implemented at a national level, harmonizing the necessary rules, regulations and requirements can be considered at a sub-regional, regional and corridor level. The adoption in May 2016 at UNESCAP of a Framework Agreement on Facilitation of Cross-border Paperless Trade in Asia and the Pacific is worth noting in this context, as it could provide the neutral and dedicated platform for countries to reduce non-tariff barriers and trade costs through digitalization of procedures.

Our econometric models also pointed to the significant positive effects that RTAs have on exports. RTAs among countries within specific corridors can act as a catalyst towards greater cooperation between countries. In most of the corridors of the BRI, there are often at least one or two FTAs that unite a majority of the corridor countries—ASEAN and ASEAN–China FTA for the IC, CP FTA for the CP corridor, South Asian FTA (SAFTA) and Bay of Bengal Initiative for Multi-Sectoral Technical and Economic Cooperation (BIMSTEC) for BCIM, and the Eurasian Economic Community (EAEC) for Central Asia. However, two points needs to be considered. First, China needs to step up its relationship with other regions. Currently, only its relationship with ASEAN seems to be at an advanced stage with the China–ASEAN FTA. There is no such agreement with the EAEC nor with the Russian Federation while, with South Asia, the only link that China has with India is the Asia Pacific Trade Agreement (APTA), which is relatively weak. No doubt, the proportion of China's exports in 2015 to the Commonwealth of Independent States (CIS) and the South Asian Association for Regional Cooperation (SAARC) were only 3 per cent and 4 per cent of total exports respectively; these are also regions with high potential. Second, a coordinating body needs to be established to facilitate greater trade relationships between regions as well as to share capacities and knowledge among regions. In this regard, existing institutions like the UNESCAP or the Asian Infrastructure and Investment Bank (AIIB) could act as initiators. A less formal organization (e.g., APEC) to forge closer political and economic ties among the countries of the BRI could also be considered.

CONCLUSION

The BRI is an ambitious initiative that aims at developing economic corridors connecting China to Europe by land and sea and enhancing the trading relationships between all economies involved. However, there is great diversity among the BRI economies and the various corridors in terms of level of trade development and integration. The IP corridor is ready to become a major economic corridor due to the China–ASEAN FTA legacy, while other corridors such as the CAWA or NELB corridors will likely take longer to develop.

In this chapter, we showed that trade facilitation and the development of soft infrastructure are keys to trade development along all the BRI corridors. Most countries along the corridors still have significant trade barriers and inefficient procedures in place. Our empirical analysis indicated that average export growth that could be expected from a 1 per cent improvement in trade facilitation performance in BRI countries was twice what could be expected from a similar change in terms of transport infrastructure. The quantitative analysis also highlighted that trade benefits from improvement in transport, and logistics infrastructure development could not be reaped in an environment where trade regulations are not harmonized and implemented in a transparent and efficient manner.

While the CP and the IP corridors are well covered by trade agreements, China appears to have limited formal trade arrangements with countries in the CAWA, NELB and CMR corridors. Accordingly, it may need to step up its efforts in concluding trade agreements with South and Central Asia to ensure that improved physical connectivity can effectively lead to more intra-regional trade. Given the relatively large number of existing and overlapping trade agreements in the region, this may best be done through expansion of existing agreements and initiatives, or through agreements between China and existing trade blocs.

While physical infrastructure may require investment from foreign firms and governments, trade facilitation is very much an internal effort that requires commitment and actions of national governments. The returns on investment in physical infrastructure along the BRI corridors is likely to be limited unless the political will for trade facilitation is secured. Thus, there is an urgent need for further studies to be conducted to identify the major bottlenecks that reduces smooth movement of goods across borders along the corridors. The potential use of ICT to release these bottlenecks should also be considered.

Our empirical analysis and the findings that follow assume that factors other than those that are controlled for (common language, common border, etc.) are held constant. In reality, other factors can also influence the trade that takes place between countries. Political stability and economic freedom influences trade, independent of how advanced the infrastructure and ICT of a country is or how efficient the border administration might be. These important factors also need to be when evaluating trade between countries.

Appendix 5.1. Economies along the BRI Economic Corridors

New Eurasia Land Bridge (NELB)	China, Kazakhstan, Russian Federation, Belarus, Poland (EU), Germany (EU)
China–Mongolia–Russia (CMR)	China, Mongolia and Russian Federation
China–Central Asia–West Asia (CAWA)	China, Kazakhstan, Kyrgyzstan, Tajikistan, Uzbekistan, Turkmenistan, Iran, Turkey, Greece (EU)
Indo-China Peninsula (ICP)	China, Thailand, Vietnam, Laos, Cambodia, Myanmar, Malaysia, Singapore, Indonesia
China–Pakistan (CP)	China, Pakistan
Bangladesh–China–India–Myanmar (BCIM)	China, Bangladesh, India, Myanmar

REFERENCES

ADB. 2017. *Meeting Asia's Infrastructure Needs*, Manila: Asian Development Bank. Mandaluyong City, Philippines: Author. https://www.adb.org/sites/default/files/publication/227496/special-report-infrastructure-highlights.pdf

Banomyong, Ruth. 2013. 'The Greater Mekong Sub-region of Southeast Asia: Improving Logistics Connectivity'. In *Handbook of Global Logistics: Transportation in International Supply Chains*, edited by J. H. Bookbinder, 69–96. International Series in Operations Research and Management Science. New York: Springer.

De Sousa, J. (2012), 'The Currency Union Effect on Trade is Decreasing over Time', *Economics Letters* 117(3): 917–920.

Fong, Michelle W. L. 2009. 'Technology Leapfrogging for Developing Countries'. IGI Global. http://journalistsresource.org/wp-content/uploads/2013/04/Technology-Leapfrogging-for-Developing-Countries.pdf

Herrero, Alicia Garcia, and Jianwei Xu. 2016. 'China's Belt and Road Initiative: Can Europe Expect Trade Gains?' Bruegel Working Paper Issue 5, Brussels, Bruegel.

Hurley, J., S. Morris, and G. Portelance. 2018. 'Examining the Debt Implications of the Belt and Road Initiative from a Policy Perspective'. Center for Global Development Policy Paper 121, March 2018. https://www.cgdev.org/sites/default/files/examining-debt-implications-belt-and-road-initiative-policy-perspective.pdf

NDRC and Ministry of Commerce. 2015. 'Vision and Actions on Jointly Building Silk Road Economic Belt and 21st-Century Maritime Silk Road'. http://en.ndrc.gov.cn/newsrelease/201503/t20150330_669367.html

Otsuki, Tsunehiro. 2011. 'Quantifying the Benefits of Trade Facilitation in ASEAN'. OSIPP Discussion Paper 11E006, Osaka School of International Public Policy, Osaka University.

Portugal-Perez, Alberto, and John S. Wilson. 2010. 'Export Performance and Trade Facilitation Reform: Hard and Soft Infrastructure'. Policy Research Working Paper 5261, World Bank.

Ramasamy, Bala, and Matthew C. H. Yeung. 2016. 'Wooing the New Chinese Businesses: Five Short-term Policies to Attract Direct Investment'. *Journal of Business Strategy* 37 (5): 3–11.

Rastogi, Cordula, and Jean-François Arvis. 2014. *The Eurasian Connection: Supply-Chain Efficiency along the Modern Silk Route through Central Asia*. Washington, DC: World Bank.

UNESCAP. 2014. *Towards a National Integrated and Sustainable Trade and Transport Facilitation Monitoring Mechanism: BPA +*. Bangkok: Author. http://www.unescap.org/resources/towards-national-integrated-and-sustainable-trade-and-transport-facilitation-monitoring

UNESCAP. 2015. 'Trade Facilitation and Paperless Trade: State of Play and the Way Forward for Asia and the Pacific'. Studies in Trade and Investment No. 85, ST/ESCAP/2742, Bangkok. www.unescap.org/resources/trade-facilitation-and-paperless-trade-state-play-and-way-forward-asia-and-pacific

Zaheer, Srilata. 1995. 'Overcoming the Liability of Foreignness'. *The Academy of Management Journal* 38 (2): 341–363.

Chapter 6

The Belt and Road Initiative and Sino-Russo-Japanese Relations

Nikolay Murashkin

INTRODUCTION

When Russian and Japanese foreign and defence ministers held their inaugural '2 + 2' talks in November 2013, dealing with China's rise appeared as a key undertone at that time, even though both sides expressly highlighted that the consultations were not directed against any third party. The Russo-Japanese meeting took place shortly after Chinese President Xi Jinping's announcement of the Silk Road Economic Belt (SREB) in September 2013 in Russia's key ally Kazakhstan, and the October 2013 announcement of the 21st Century Maritime Silk Road in Indonesia, a major ASEAN country. Five years later, however, the nature of relations within the Sino-Russo-Japanese triangle has changed for both internal and external reasons, as Russia and Japan, to a lesser extent and with lower speed, gradually warmed up to the Belt and Road Initiative (BRI).

One of the key challenges that China is facing with regards to implementing its BRI is the associated management of relationships with major powers that were potential or prospective stakeholders in the BRI as well as overcoming risk-averse perceptions of the initiative (for instance, debt-trap diplomacy). This chapter looks at respective

China's relations with Japan and Russia, its key counterparts in Northeast Asia and Eurasia. While media discourse and scholarship tend to emphasize Sino-Japanese rivalry and Sino-Russian rapprochement, both of those relationships of China's display cooperative and competitive patterns as well as a gradual evolution of policy responses to the BRI, from initial wariness to more accommodating, even if still cautious, postures. In the case of Russia, despite remaining Sino-Russian competition over Central Asia and differing interpretations of what the Shanghai Cooperation Organisation's (SCO) economic functions should be—the 'warming up' was significantly quicker than in the case of Japan. Japan sees its position of 'go-to' infrastructure finance provider in Asia challenged by China. Furthermore, Japan had also experienced in the past similarly risk-averse external perceptions of the historical growth of Japan's financial power and initiatives in Asia. These criticisms came from both Asian recipients of FDI and Japan's Western counterparts, ultimately forming a part of the 'Japan bashing' discourses. Still, although the initial reaction to the BRI in both Japanese and Russian cases was 'a cold shoulder', we are starting to observe, even in the case of Japan, a slow 'thaw' over the past years; so it is worth examining the reasons for these changes in attitudes. Furthermore, this paper explores how China's policy vis-à-vis Russia's involvement in the BRI and the Asian Infrastructure Investment Bank (AIIB) turned out to be relatively more inclusive than Japan's earlier policies vis-à-vis Russia's involvement in Asia, such as, for instance, its application for membership of the Asian Development Bank (ADB) in the mid-2000s. Although several years into the BRI's life the Chinese authorities started positioning the BRI and the AIIB increasingly separately, those two initiatives are treated in conjunction with each other—albeit not as a whole—for the purposes of this chapter. The reason for this treatment is that both the BRI and the AIIB, as well as the ADB, have major implications for Central Asia—a region that the Russian government views as vital and strategic for the Russian national interests. By encouraging rather than discouraging Russia to join the respective Asian multilateral development bank, China did the opposite of what Japan did, despite Japan's regular calls for open regionalism. This aspect fits within a broader inquiry whereby we explore a hypothesis according to which China has the potential to attain achievements in Asian connectivity infrastructure that Japan also could have attempted and, at times, had attempted to pursue but did not always succeed in accomplishing.

Let us start by contextualizing the two relationships within the background of Japan's financial and infrastructural diplomacy in Asia until Tokyo's engagement with the BRI. We will then proceed to Moscow's approaches to BRI. The purpose of this analysis is not to provide an all-around comprehensive review of China's, Japan's and Russia's bilateral ties with each other. These relationships per se have been extensively examined in numerous authoritative scholarly accounts (to name only a few, Chugrov and Streltsov 2017; Jerdén and Hagström 2012; Kireeva and Sushentsov 2017; Lukin and Denisov 2015; Pugliese and Insisa 2017; Voskressenski 2015). Rather, this paper focuses on the comparison of China's and Japan's infrastructure and development policies in Eurasia that have affected Russia and its bilateral relations with the two Asian economic powerhouses.

JAPAN AND ASIAN INFRASTRUCTURE: FIGHTING FOR THE 'KING OF THE HILL' POSITION?

In the media coverage and scholarship, the BRI's intended giant scale and associated publicity have seemingly overshadowed Japan's footprint and track record in Asia's connectivity-related infrastructure. On par with China's growing role in the World Trade Organization and other international institutions, the BRI became one of the symbols of China's rise and the much-forecast power shift in favour of Beijing on the world stage. Yet, over the past four decades, Japan has been attempting, with intermittent success, a number of diplomatic and economic initiatives in Asian infrastructure that can be viewed as predecessors, prototypes or sources of benchmarking for the BRI. This track record also created a solid foundation upon which Japanese policymakers (for instance, incumbent Prime Minister Abe Shinzō) could capitalize when designing foreign policies in the realm of Asian infrastructure and its financing. The next section provides a brief overview of these projects in order to understand the regional context and Japan's role in Asian infrastructure prior to the BRI's announcement.

When Japan played a key part in establishing the ADB in 1966, it highlighted, first, Japan's new stature among developed nations, as Japan was about to graduate from the World Bank's borrower status, and, second, Japan's central role in the Asian financial and economic system with regards to regional borrowing nations. However, as Japanese Prime Minister Tanaka Kakuei toured Southeast Asian states in 1974, he faced strong anti-Japanese protests from local residents over Japan's way of investment and industrial management in these countries (Halloran 1974). Consequently, Tanaka's successor Fukuda Takeo announced a pivotal policy for Tokyo's cooperation with Southeast Asian countries which included an increase in Japan's official development assistance (ODA), inter alia, involving infrastructure improvement (Fukuda 1977). A decade later, in 1987, Prime Minister Nakasone Yasuhiro announced the ASEAN–Japan Development Fund, while Minister of International Trade and Industry Tamura Hajime promoted the new Asian Industries Development Plan (new AID), aimed at supporting industrial development in Asian countries hosting Japanese supply chains by improving regional port infrastructure and associated international trade (Sudo 2015, 120). Despite Japan's improved relations with Southeast Asian states and solidified credentials among industrially developed nations, Japan's proposals did not eventuate due to hindrances both domestically in Japan and abroad, in East Asia as well as the USA, the World Bank and the IMF (Katzenstein and Rouse 2001; Shiraishi 1997; Terry 2002). Similar to present-day risk-averse perceptions of China's BRI in the media and scholarship, pundits and researchers outside Japan at the time had drawn historic parallels between new AID and the Greater East Asia Co-Prosperity Sphere by interpreting Japan's activities as a 'nicer' or a new and more prosperous version of it (Johnson 1992, Terry 2002). Another similarity between external perceptions of the economic statecraft of Japan in the 1980s and that of China in the 2010s can be found in the fact that the risk-averse discourse of Japan's initiatives was preceded and stimulated by Japan's major boost of its overseas investment: According to Calder (1991), it grew fivefold between 1985 and 1990, reaching over $67 billion, or approximately $130 billion in the 2018 prices (Murashkin 2018).

After the Cold War ended, the ADB, in which Japan historically had been playing a key role, established the Greater Mekong Subregion

(GMS) programme, seeking to improve connectivity between the six states of that Southeast Asian region. In 1997–1998, several years after the break-up of the Soviet Union, Japanese Prime Ministers Hashimoto Ryūtarō and Obuchi Keizō announced Japan's Eurasian Diplomacy and Silk Road Action Plan initiatives, targeted at Central Asia, China and Russia, and involving infrastructure development. Finally, in 1997–1998, the ADB launched its Central Asian Regional Economic Cooperation (CAREC) programme, an equivalent of the aforementioned GMS programme, but aimed at the heart of Eurasia. Initially focusing on transport connections between China's Xinjiang, Kazakhstan, Kyrgyz Republic and Uzbekistan, from 2001 onwards, CAREC has gradually developed into a six-corridor framework, involving $32.9 billion worth of projects, 10 countries of Central and South Asia and five other financial institutions: the European Bank for Reconstruction and Development (EBRD), the International Monetary Fund, the World Bank, the United Nations Development Programme, and the Islamic Development Bank. The community of Japanese Finance Ministry's and ADB's officials played an instrumental role in CAREC's implementation. These included the ADB's President Chino Tadao (1999–2005), whose role in Japan's and ADB's financial policies in Asia was crucial at the turn of the century for a number of reasons examined in the next section.

First, during Chino's tenure as Vice Minister of Finance for international affairs (*zaimukan*), a key policymaking position in Japan's Finance Ministry (1991–1993), he told the *New York Times* in 1991, 'Japan wanted to transform its substantial foreign aid into a magnet for private capital ... [and] will increasingly use its aid ... as seed money to attract Japanese manufacturers or other industrial concerns with an attractive investment environment' (Sterngold 1991). This approach reflected the traditional patterns of Japanese aid, as Japan was to maintain its focus on Asia, given the nature of its industrial strategy and the regional pre-eminence of Japanese companies. Chino's thinking demonstrated a degree of continuity with the 1987 New AID plan (Terry 2002), even though the plan itself was not implemented. Second, another notable stance that Chino expressed in 1991 was that Japan should refrain from providing any financial aid to the USSR until the latter clarified the relationship between the central government and the republics, reformed its economy, transferred the Southern Kurils to Japan, and reduced its military presence in Asia (Sterngold 1991).[1] After the USSR collapsed, Chino toured newly independent Central Asia and built good ties with some of their leaders, supporting their gradual economic reforms, as opposed to shock therapy. As Chino went on to become the ADB's president in 1999, this trust undoubtedly helped him in pursuing the development of the bank's major Central Asia infrastructure project CAREC. Third, Chino advocated Asia-specific approaches for regional development, explaining them by Asia's difference from Europe (Rafferty 2002). Finally, it was during Chino's ADB presidency that Chinese officials became the bank's vice presidents—starting in 2003 with Vice-President Jin Liqun (who later became President of the AIIB) and started covering West, Central and South Asia, including the CAREC programme.

In this context, when the Japanese government announced a $110 billion package of infrastructure financing for Asia in 2015 (both bilaterally and via an increased commitment to the ADB) and subsequently expanded to $200 billion in 2016, it was logically interpreted as a competitive offer-matching to the BRI. Japan's financial footprint is particularly extensive in Southeast Asian infrastructure but also tangible in Central Asia. Recent media reports estimated Japan's completed and on-going infrastructure investment in Southeast Asia at $230 billion as opposed to China's $155 billion (Alegado 2018). Figures for Japan's FDI stock in Central Asia exhibit discrepancies between different sources, varying from $5 billion to $9 billion, while Japan's ODA in Central Asia is about $5 billion. Furthermore, the ADB's multi-billion financial footprint in Central Asia also became possible largely due to Japanese policymakers.

While the strong presence of the Japanese private sector in various Asian subregions is well-known, many of the aforementioned Japan-driven regional master plans, with the notable exception of the ADB's programmes such as CAREC, GMS and SASEC, turned out to be

---

[1] As Miyashita (2003) suggested, Japan subsequently changed its reluctance to provide aid to Russia in the early 1990s in favour of a positive stance following pressure from the United States of America.

either short-lived or understated in Japan's public diplomacy as compared to the BRI—even if the BRI's fate is still unclear. Furthermore, Japan's and the ADB's pre-BRI regional programmes (CAREC, GMS) were inclusive of China and, given the fact that Abe showed both cooperative as well as competitive postures to Beijing during his second premiership, it would be inaccurate to downplay Japan's interest in cooperative Sino-Japanese relations.

At the same time, while Abe's second premiership (2012 to the present) was marked by a proactive and consistent policy of normalizing ties with Russia, the governments of Abe's predecessors and that of Abe himself during his first premiership (2006–2007) demonstrated a more antagonizing position towards Russia by withholding their approvals of Russia's application for a membership in the ADB. The next section provides a detailed account of these disagreements that partially shaped Russia's current position in multilateral development banks.

JAPAN AND NOT-SO-OPEN REGIONALISM: REJECTIONS OF RUSSIA'S ADB MEMBERSHIP BID

Among one of the drivers behind China's decision to establish the AIIB was Beijing's dissatisfaction with its limited influence and limited prospects to increase clout at the ADB, where Japan has a dominant administrative presence and a voting share more than twice the size of China's (Wang 2015). As for Russia, it has never succeeded to join the ADB even as a member, despite having made at least two attempts and being an obvious stakeholder with three quarters of its territory in Asia and growing economic ties to various Asian subregions. As this section shows, Russia's inability to join the ADB was partially caused by opposition from Japan and, to a lesser extent, the United States of America.

According to the Ministry of Foreign Affairs of the Russian Federation (MoFA 2007a), although the Soviet government was involved in the ADB's establishment in 1966, for political reasons, it had nonetheless refrained from joining as member. Nevertheless, the Russian government has been sending delegations as observers to the bank's annual meetings. The first time Moscow filed a full membership application to the ADB was in 1997. This bid was rejected by several shareholders of the bank for economic considerations (Finmarket 2007). While outlining specific reasons for that rejection is outside the scope of this chapter, the plausible causes are self-evident: Russia's economic weakness at the time, which was confirmed by its financial crisis a year later, and the 1997 Asian financial crisis. Besides, in this bid, the Russian government did not indicate an intention to become a regional donor (MoFA 2007a). Furthermore, it is important to note that the ADB's initiatives regarding Central Asia's infrastructure and cooperation sought to reduce the region's dependence on Russia-bound pipeline, railway and road routes (ADB 1998). It is therefore possible that the ADB's 1997 rejection of Russia's bid was motivated by the bank's fears of Russia's potential interference in relations between the bank and Central Asia. However, the bid's rejection contradicted the Japanese government's Russian policy at the time. Prime Minister Hashimoto and his Foreign Minister Obuchi announced the aforementioned Eurasian Diplomacy, which implied Japan's engagement with Russia, China and the Silk Road region. Furthermore, Hashimoto and Obuchi supported Russia's accession to the Group of Seven (making it the Group of Eight) in 1997, as part of normalizing bilateral ties and intending to solve the territorial dispute and sign the peace treaty. Furthermore, according to the Russian MoFA, Japan never linked the question of Russia's accession to the bank to any conditionality involving political concessions, including the territorial dispute (MoFA 2007a). Some ADB's former officials (Tsuruoka 2017), however, suggested that the dispute did sour Tokyo on Russia's ADB accession prospects.

In the mid-2000s, however, Japan rejected Moscow's second bid to join the ADB, this time despite Russia's markedly improved economic standing, plans to contribute as donor and support for that bid from the ADB's other member states.[2] According to the Russian MoFA (2007b), the second application was initially filed around 2005, a year when Chino Tadao was succeeded at the ADB's helm by Kuroda Haruhiko. In the following two years, during several rounds of consultations with

---

[2] See, for instance, Malaysia's position on Russia's accession indicated during the 40th Annual Meeting of the Board of Governors of the ADB.

Russia, the Japanese government initially expressed a number of concerns regarding Russia's ADB bid and then delayed making that decision, ultimately stating in 2007 that Japan would formulate its own position only after all the Bank's other shareholders decided on theirs. Japan's initial concerns were related to Russia's potential impact on the ADB's balance of power and to Moscow's desire to join the ADB as a regional member, which would enable it to bid for the bank's presidency and request financial support as borrower in the event of adverse market conditions. At the time, experts said that Russia's accession to the ADB was welcomed by the locomotives of Asian growth, such as China and India, as it would have helped dilute the US influence in the bank, making the organization more Asian and increasing its contribution to Asian development (Finmarket 2007).

The Russian MoFA suggested that Japan's fears were unfounded because Russia's initial share capital would have been limited to about 2 per cent, thus ruling out any presidency ambitions, whereas its creditworthiness had been drastically improving since 1999 on the back of commodity boom and government policies, leading Russia to propose participation not only in the ADB but also in its Asian Development Fund. Russia's ADB bid had the backing of then Finance Minister Alexey Kudrin (St. Petersburg International Economic Forum [SPIEF] 2012), who had earned a solid international recognition for his fiscal prudency, successful reforms and early repayment of Russia's sovereign debt to the Paris Club of Creditors in 2006. Russia's robust prospects as donor were also demonstrated by the 2006 establishment of the Eurasian Development Bank (EDB) by the Russian and Kazakh governments with $7 billion capital, aimed at financing the development needs of Armenia, Belarus, Kyrgyzstan, Tajikistan and the two founders. Furthermore, the ADB's CAREC programme was designed to improve Central Asia's connectivity and trade across corridors, some of which involved Russia (CAREC 2007). Academic accounts of Russia's involvement in Asian integration processes of the time showed that Russian scholars perceived the country's chances to join the ADB as certain (Abalkina 2007, 172).

Nonetheless, Japan's position at the time did not warm up, becoming a permanent delay without expressing clear preferences. The US

Secretary of the Treasury Henry Paulson, for instance, was initially expressing a positive attitude towards Russia's ADB bid. However, during the 40th Annual Meeting of the ADB Board of Governors in 2007, where Russia dispatched the second largest observer delegation next to the World Bank's (ADB 2007, 270–272), the US revised its stance and made its approval of Russia's bid conditional upon the Russian government's writing off sovereign debts of Iraq and Afghanistan. According to a former official of the Japanese Ministry of Finance (MoF), the Japanese government was also wary of the implications of Russia's position regarding Afghanistan and wider Central Asia for the ADB.[3] For instance, at that time, Moscow was critical of the ADB-backed Turkmenistan–Afghanistan–Pakistan–India gas pipeline project, viewing it as a threat to its gas cooperation with Turkmenistan (Jamestown Foundation 2011).[4] In turn, denying Russia membership in 2007 prevented the ADB from accepting other new members since that year, despite the expressions of interest made by Hungary and Brazil (Tsuruoka 2017).

On the other side of the finance–geopolitics nexus, Japan's opposition to Russia's ADB bid struck a contrast with Japan's calls for open regionalism in Eurasia, recurrent in Japanese diplomatic rhetoric of the second half of the 2000s and repeated in the mid-2010s with regards to the BRI. As the SCO, propelled by increasing cooperation between China, Russia and Central Asian states, raised its profile in Eurasia, Japan responded with boosting its Central Asia plus Japan dialogue and advancing the diplomatic concept of 'Arc of Freedom and Prosperity' (AFP). AFP was launched by Foreign Minister Tarō Asō and formulated by officials who ultimately became key members of Prime Minister Abe's foreign policy team, in particular, Yachi Shōtarō, Kanehara Nobukatsu and Taniguchi Tomohiko. The AFP stressed the importance of supporting democratization and development in emerging unstable economies across various subregions of Eurasia, including Central Asia, and sought to reinforce Japan's value-oriented diplomacy in that regard with the EU, NATO and the USA. Japanese rhetoric interpreted the brand of Eurasian regionalism promoted by China and Russia via the SCO as closed to others and advocated the need for an open approach, similarly

---

[3] Interview with a former official of Japan's MoF, 2012.
[4] Moscow revised its position on TAPI in the 2010s.

to its criticism of the BRI a decade later. The AFP concept generated suspicion from Moscow and Beijing who viewed it as an attempt to contain their power or encircle them in Eurasia.

The US diplomatic cables showed that Washington did not share Tokyo's zero-sum-game perception of China's and Russia's rise in Eurasia at the time:

> The opportunity to discuss development assistance programs in Central Asia with representatives of [Japanese government] was extremely beneficial. All participants agreed there is much to be gained by further such engagements and that efforts should be made to enhance cooperation among donors. DAS Feigenbaum stressed throughout that, while there inevitably will be some competition among outside powers, the primary strategic purpose of U.S.-Japan cooperation is not to 'compete' with Russia or China for its own sake.... It is unclear whether the Japanese, who still tend to view the region through a traditional 'Great Game' prism, focused on both Russia and China, fully agree. (WikiLeaks 2006)

Later, Taniguchi (2010, 2) contended that AFP was not construed as antithetical to the emerging Sino-Russian axis. Rather, it was 'Japan's first ever branding exercise to "sell" its commitment to values' and an attempt to 'bring the Russians to the negotiating table' regarding the territorial dispute 'while enriching the diplomatic capital of Japan's ally the United States in areas, such as Eastern Europe, that were critical to the its global strategy'.

Yachi[5] also argued that Japan's intention behind the AFP was misconstrued by China and Russia, and there was no intention of encircling the two. Nevertheless, looking at the situation from a broader perspective, the calls for open regionalism made by Japanese diplomats in 2005–2007 regarding closer Sino-Russian cooperation in Eurasia were contradicted by the Japanese financial officials' opposition to Russia's application for ADB membership.

The 2008 global financial crisis shifted the agendas of many governments, including the Russian and Japanese ones, sidelining the issue of

---

[5] Interview with Yachi Shōtarō, 2012.

Russia's ADB accession, as well as the AFP concept, even when one of its architects Asō served as prime minister in 2008–2009. The 2009 change of power from the Liberal Democratic Party (LDP) of Japan to the Democratic Party of Japan (DPJ) did not seem to have an impact on the state of Russia's ADB bid, although the DPJ's China-friendly position led it to scrap the AFP. According to the Russian government (SPIEF 2012), Russia's application was still under consideration as of June 2012. The ADB Institute's Dean Kawai Masahiro (2013) made the case for establishing a Northeast Asian Infrastructure Investment Fund involving both ADB and Russia among other parties but via the EBRD rather than through an eventual accession of Russia to the ADB. Russia's accession to the AIIB in 2015 further contributed to the caution exercised by the ADB vis-à-vis the China-led bank, this time striking a contrast with the US-led World Bank, which cooperated with the AIIB, as Russia was a member in both (Tsuruoka 2017). Subsequently, Russia and the ADB increased indirect cooperation via the EDB. The EDB's and ADB's co-financing partnership started in 2013 with the signing of a framework agreement, and initial volumes of co-financing totalled around $310 million (ADB 2016). In 2016, however, the ADB and the EDB signed their first framework co-financing agreement aimed at projects in Central Asia and Caucasus, committing $2 billion and $1 billion, respectively, until 2021 (EDB 2016). This cooperation was accompanied by improving Russo-Japanese ties during the second Abe premiership (2012–present) and occurred after the EDB had obtained wider international peer recognition, becoming a multilateral financial institution recognized by the Organisation for Economic Cooperation and Development (in 2013), and an institutional member of the World Economic Forum (in 2014). The dramatic worsening of US–Russia relations in the 2010s is likely to further hinder Russia's potential accession to the ADB, unless Moscow abandons that plan.

In retrospect, considering the contemporary position of Russia as an AIIB member with the third-largest voting share, a co-founder of the New Development Bank of BRICS and the founder of the EDB, one may argue that by obstructing Russia's accession to the ADB in the mid-2000s, Japan acted short-sightedly and reduced its bargaining power vis-à-vis Russia. By keeping the ADB's door, and Asian regionalism, closed for Russia, Japan obtained little tangible benefits but reinforced Russia's inclination to cooperate with China. In the mid-2010s, a decade after the AFP's announcement, Abe's foreign policy team, involving several AFP authors, again promoted diplomatic rhetoric emphasizing the importance of open regionalism, albeit without referring to Russia—this time as part of Japan's response to the BRI, which the next section will examine.

JAPAN AND THE BRI: HEDGING BY COMBINING ENGAGEMENT AND BALANCING?

Japan's approach towards the BRI appears filled with mixed feelings. Prima facie, one may find this attitude self-evident, attributing it to Japan's desire to defend its long-standing centrality in Asian infrastructure and Abe's reputation as a politician with a tough position vis-à-vis China. However, a closer look reveals a greater degree of hesitation and cooperative postures, especially looking at Sino-Japanese diplomatic exchanges in 2017 and 2018, many of which showed positive dynamics rather than antagonism.

Between Xi Jinping's announcement of BRI in 2013 and Abe's promotion of the Indo-Pacific Strategy/Indo-Pacific Vision in 2017–2018,[6] Tokyo's bilateral response to China's infrastructure initiatives

---

[6] Prime Minister Abe has been continuously promoting the idea of Japan's cooperation with Australia, India and the United States of America since as early as 2006. In his 2006 manifesto book, *Towards a Beautiful Country*, Abe calls this framework Asian Democratic G3 plus America. His 2007 speech 'Confluence of the Two Seas' at the Indian Parliament is often considered the earliest incarnation of the concept in practical diplomacy. While support for the concept of Indo-Pacific has been voiced in Indian and Australian policy communities at the time, change of governments in Japan and Australia impeded further materialization of this cooperation. In 2012, upon returning to power, Abe again sounded out the idea of this quadrilateral cooperation in his *Project Syndicate* article as Asia's Democratic Security Diamond. Since mid-2010s, and especially starting from 2016, the Japanese government has been increasingly pursuing the policy dubbed Free and Open Indo-Pacific (FOIP) Strategy, subsequently replacing 'Strategy' with 'Vision'. The quadrilateral security dialogue of Australia, India, Japan, and the United States was resuscitated in 2017. https://www.mofa.go.jp/files/000259285.pdf

gradually shifted from balancing to a mixture of engagement and balancing (Michishita 2018). Japan's initial rhetoric on the BRI and FOIP stressed economic feasibility, creditworthiness and quality, thereby emphasizing Japan's competitive edge in this sector. This language can be seen in Tokyo's corresponding initiative, Partnership for Quality Infrastructure, which includes three key Japanese ministries: the MoF, Ministry of Economy, Trade and Industry (METI) and the MoFA. The partnership was announced simultaneously with the 2015 pledge by Abe to commit $110 billion to infrastructure finance in Asia in 2015–2020. In 2016, this commitment was increased to $220 billion, and in June 2018, Abe announced plans to establish a $50 billion fund to boost infrastructure investment in Indo-Pacific. In November 2018, the USA, Australia and Japan announced a separate partnership for jointly financing infrastructure in the region, especially in the South Pacific. Emphasis on the quality of infrastructure and debt sustainability has become the leitmotiv of Japan's policies in this field.

At the same time, the promotion of infrastructural exports by the Japanese government in the recent years should not be reduced to simply competing with the BRI, as Japan's contribution to Asian infrastructure pre-dated the BRI and initially followed a predominantly mercantilist logic, while its strategic dimension was subsequently stimulated by the BRI (Murashkin 2018). Prior to Abe's second premiership, the DPJ's governments stressed the importance of promoting Japanese infrastructure exports as early as 2009 under Prime Minister Hatoyama Yukio, as they saw Japanese companies lose bids to competitors from other countries (Nikkei 2016).

Year 2017 was particularly intensive in terms of the Japanese government's statements on the BRI, which contained numerous mixed signals, alternating direct calls for cooperation in May and June, with calls for competition in October–November, and again cooperation with elements of competition in December and early 2018. This alternation and its frequent channelling via outlets considered close to the LDP, such as Yomiuri and Nikkei, produced an impression that infrastructure announcements were being used as signalling and strategic communications to influence China's foreign policy. At one stage, Yomiuri directly acknowledged that the Japanese government's proposals to partner with China in Africa were aimed at getting Beijing to be more cooperative on the North Korean issue (Yomiuri 2017).

In May 2017, two of Japan's 'China hands', the ruling LDP's Secretary General Nikai Toshihiro and Abe's political secretary Imai Takaya, participated in the inaugural BRI Forum and hinted at prospects of Sino-Japanese cooperation over the BRI. In June 2017, Abe highlighted the basis upon which Japan would cooperate with the BRI and AIIB. He expressed hope that the BRI would fully incorporate a common frame of thinking and come into harmony with the free and fair transpacific economic zone, and contribute to peace and prosperity. However, Abe urged that infrastructure should be open to use by all, procurement ought to be transparent and fair, while projects needed to be economically viable, financed by debt that can be repaid and not harm the soundness of the debtor nation's finances. This rhetoric, apart from stress on creditworthiness and responsibility, also exhibited continuity with Japan's above-described demands for open regionalism in Central Asia in response to the SCO's rise in the mid-2000s.

As of early 2018, salient points of Sino-Japanese bilateral rivalry over strategic (rather than purely commercial) infrastructure included several Indian Ocean countries, such as Myanmar, Iran, Sri Lanka, Maldives and even Pakistan, rather than Central Asia. For instance, during a 2017 meeting with the Myanmar's leader Aung San Suu Kyi, Abe promised to provide $1.1 billion in assistance for infrastructural and agricultural development (in particular, the Yangon–Mandalay railway). This decision was in line with Japan's long-established policy of reducing Myanmar's dependence on China, including through financial assistance. Another vivid example is Japan's assistance to the Iranian port project of Chabahar, a competitor of the Pakistani port of Gwadar that, in turn, is part of the China–Pakistan Economic Corridor and part of the BRI. India is interested in Chabahar as a hub for developing communications with Central Asia bypassing Pakistan, whereas Japan is 'killing two birds with one stone': continuing to develop its relations with Iran outside the oil sector and helping India as its Indo-Pacific partner to balance China and its ally Pakistan. In early 2018, Foreign Minister Kōno went on a diplomatic tour of Sri Lanka, Maldives and Pakistan, seeking to promote Japan's infrastructure offer as a means of helping these countries avoid what the BRI critics called China's 'debt-trap' diplomacy (Laruelle 2018; MoFA 2018).

The most intensive and perhaps the most seemingly confusing period (whether by miscalculation or by design) of Japan's strategic communications on the BRI occurred in the fourth quarter of 2017. Shortly after Abe's announcement of the Indo-Pacific Strategy together with US President Donald Trump, and a new attempt at furthering the quadrilateral partnership between Australia, Japan, India and the USA (the 'Quad'), Kōno openly called the Quad antithetical to China's BRI-related expansion. In this respect, Tokyo invited its 'Quad' partners to expand the dialogue's agenda by including infrastructure development in Asia and Africa, in particular, East Africa, where India has historical ties that Japanese companies were also trying to use. Thus, the geography of possible infrastructural cooperation between Japan, the USA, Australia and India may affect the countries of the BRI's maritime segment, the Maritime Silk Road. The continental SREB was not mentioned, possibly in line with Abe's avoidance of antagonizing Russia. At the time of writing this chapter, Quad-related infrastructure cooperation is yet to materialize, making the matter speculative.

More importantly, the reason why Kōno's anti-BRI rhetoric may appear inconsistent or deliberately aimed at hedging was that it struck a contrast with both preceding and subsequent pro-cooperation speeches of Abe and Nikai, made in May, June and November. In November, shortly after calls for quadrilateral cooperation, Abe called on the PRC to boost Sino-Japanese cooperation and agree to a trilateral summit between Japan, China and South Korea. Commenting on Abe's Manila meeting with the Chinese Prime Minister Li Keqiang, the Yomiuri daily noted that Abe wanted to develop economic diplomacy with China, since he had little progress on the peace treaty with Russia.

Upon return from the 2017 East Asian Summit and APEC, Abe was tacit on both the Indo-Pacific and the Quad in his speech before the National Diet. The rationale for this is likely to stem from auspicious opportunities to mend ties with China, as 2018 marked the 40th anniversary of the conclusion of the Sino-Japanese Peace and Friendship Treaty. Furthermore, in 2019, Japan is to host the G20 Summit for the first time, and Xi Jinping's attendance creates the rationale for emphasizing positive aspects of the bilateral relationship. A week after meeting with Abe in November 2017, Li Keqiang received a 250-strong delegation of Japanese businessmen from the Japan–China Economic Association, the largest since 1975. The delegates called for the early conclusion of the Sino-Japanese–South Korean FTA and expressed interest in the BRI's infrastructure projects. During the visit of China's State Councillor and Foreign Minister Wang Yi to Japan in April 2018, Japanese officials again expressed intention to cooperate with the BRI. As Abe attempted to improve Sino-Japanese relations by paying a state visit to China in October 2018, the two countries signed a memorandum of understanding seeking to promote cooperation over approximately 50 infrastructure investment projects in third countries totalling about $892 million (Cho and Suga 2018).

Japanese companies are already cooperating with the BRI, while the government and scholars have made a point of mentioning that Japan was part of the historical Silk Road via Osaka, its medieval merchant capital. One notable example of Japanese BRI-savvy companies is Nippon Express, one of the largest 10 global logistic operators, which is involved in BRI, thanks to an agreement with the Kazakhstan Railways for port-to-rail container service between Lianyungang–Kazakhstan–Europe (Nikkei 2017a). The lucrative prospects of such cooperation are tangible: Kazakhstan Railways reported that the transit volume of China–Europe cargoes has grown 200 times between 2011 and 2017, from 1,000 to 200,000 containers a year. Future areas of cooperation, according to Japanese media reports (especially Yomiuri 2017), may include joint Sino-Japanese projects in Thailand and Africa. Then again, Yomiuri's reports about Japan's plans for Africa mentioned the government's plans for both cooperation with China and cooperation with India and France against China, while also revealing that Abe and Xi reached agreements over loans to joint projects in July 2017, before Kōno's and Abe's autumnal statements on the Indo-Pacific and the Quad.

Does the Japan's back-and-forth rhetoric on the Quad the Indo-Pacific and the BRI suggest reactivity and inconsistency? Not necessarily. Similar to the AFP's usage in Russo-Japanese relations a decade earlier, various incarnations of Abe diplomacy's coalition manoeuvres around China may have been aimed not at balancing or competition per se, but rather at stimulating Beijing by 'carrots' and 'sticks' towards greater cooperation over various issues, such as security on the Korean peninsula, the East China and South China seas (Yomiuri 2017). Furthermore, although Japan exhibits a competitive posture vis-à-vis Chinese infrastructural initiatives partially as part of promoting its own infrastructural exports, its calls for financial prudence and debt sustainability in providing concessional lending are based on its own past experiences in Asia, learning from which is likely to benefit China's interests. Financially, Japan and China as concessional lenders are both likely to pursue the diversification of risks and to avoid overexposure to uncreditworthy borrowers.

RUSSIA AND THE BRI: WARINESS, ENTHUSIASM AND REALISM

Russia's engagement with the BRI is a complex and multifaceted one. It has received extensive analytical coverage in the expert community (Gabuev 2016; Karaganov et al. 2015) without, however, being examined in the context of other New Silk Road initiatives, including Japanese ones. While Sino-Russian relations per se have been steadily improving during Xi Jinping's rule (2012 to the present), Russia's position towards the BRI has evolved from cautious observation to an embrace, with subsequent adjustments. From a comparative perspective, however, China's megaproject has been the most Russia-inclusive of various New Silk Road initiatives advanced in Eurasia by major powers in the post-Cold War era. The US initiatives concerning the New Silk Road in 1999 and especially 2011 were primarily aimed at helping Central Asia countries develop their connectivity through routes alternative to Russia, such as South Asia. Neither was Russia involved in the European Union's Transport Corridor Europe-Caucasus-Asia (TRACECA) programme—a multilateral programme on transport cooperation between European countries and the Caucasus and Central Asia. Japan's initiatives in Central Asia (1997–1998, 2006) were less antagonizing vis-à-vis Russia or at least declaratively so, as is shown in the previous sections, but Japan's risk-aversion also saw Russia's influence in Central Asia more as a problem than as an opportunity. By contrast, the BRI, or, more specifically, its continental segment known as the SREB, has not sought to exclude Russia from the region, although some of its corridors can be seen as competing with the Trans-Siberian. On one hand this observation can be qualified by the fact that Xi Jinping's inaugural SREB speech in Astana (Xi 2013) did not mention Russia. And Beijing's expanding economic clout in Central Asia has been a recurrent source of concern for Moscow, probably not dispelled by China's intent to promote southern corridors via the SREB. On the other hand, the actual development of the BRI in the last four years was rather marked by China's and Russia's willingness to cooperate, even if to a limited extent, rather than being fraught with tensions.

Russia's geographic location between such global economic growth centres as Europe and the Asia Pacific and unique transport networks, such as the Trans-Siberian railway, have encouraged the country's attempts to promote international transit, especially after the end of the Cold War. The development of the Eurasian Land Bridge, via Russia, and of the Northern Sea Route were recurrent on the agenda of successive Russian governments and during exchanges between Russian experts and their foreign colleagues (Baydakov et al. 2012, 132–133). In 2012, a little over a year before SREB's announcement, a group of Russian, Italian and German experts, previously involved in Eurasian Land Bridge discussions, including some affiliated with Russian Railways, came up with the concept of a so-called Trans-Eurasian Belt Razvitie (TEBR) [Development]. The TEBR concept was rather a grand design regarding international transport corridors and a broad worldview than a specific policy with recommendations. Nevertheless, it had some foresight, as it showed a degree of similarity with the subsequently announced SREB, and the then President of Russian Railways Vladimir Yakunin, who made several attempts to promote TEBR, even proposed to integrate the two concepts in 2015 (Gudok 2015). Although neither this integration proposal nor TEBR itself ever gained traction in China or Russia, they indicated the interest in Russia towards large-scale projects of that kind shortly before the BRI's launch.

While 2014 was pivotal for Russia's foreign policy due to the Ukrainian crisis, related Western sanctions and the tumble of oil prices, it was also beneficial for Sino-Russian relations. Bilateral ties grew in the aforementioned international context and on the back of the Gazprom–CNPC jumbo gas deal and other agreements signed during President Putin's 2014 visit to China. However, it was not until early 2015 that Russia openly formulated an official policy regarding the BRI. This delay was likely caused by a protracted absence of Chinese official documents detailing the BRI, which appeared in March 2015, and by Russia's efforts to establish the Eurasian Economic Union (EEU), the foundation treaty of which came into force on 1 January 2015. On 28 March 2015, during the Boao Forum for Asia, the Chinese government published its action plan on jointly building the SREB and 21st Century Maritime Silk Road (NDRC, MoFA, and Ministry of Commerce 2015). At the same forum, Russia's First Deputy Prime Minister Igor Shuvalov announced Russia's intention to join the AIIB and to cooperate with China on jointly developing the SREB with the EEU. Russia's policy on the EEU's linkage (*sopryazhenie*, a term informally attributed to the officials of the Russian Economy Ministry) with SREB was formulated on 8 May 2015, shortly after the Boao Forum, in a joint Russo-Chinese declaration (President of Russia 2015). In May 2017, President Putin became the main guest of honour at the Belt and Road Forum.

To some extent, Russia's participation with the BRI increased its multilateral exposure to Asian countries and access to Chinese capital. However, to date, the Silk Road Fund's exposure to Russia is mostly represented by its purchases of a 9.9 per cent $1.2 billion stake in Russia's Yamal LNG plant and a 10 per cent circa $1.2 billion stake in Russia's largest petrochemical company Sibur, both in 2016. The scope of BRI-related Sino-Russian cooperation remains nebulous, sometimes mistakenly including unrelated Sino-Russian projects (Kommersant 2018). Some Russian experts estimated that only 1 per cent of circa $100 billion of Chinese infrastructural investment worldwide went to Russia, not least because of Russia's wariness of Chinese investments (Polubota 2017).

Furthermore, inside the AIIB, Russia has presented at least 10 projects for financing in 2016, but none of them had been approved to date, despite President Putin's personal involvement at the proposal pitch stage and meetings with AIIB President Jin Liqun (Interfax 2017).

According to Russia's and EDB's officials, the main stumbling block here is the policy of state guarantees: While AIIB demands them, the Russian MoF seeks to minimize guarantees issued to international financial institutions for investment projects (RIA Novosti 2016). As of October 2018, the MoF was awaiting from the AIIB to prepare norms for financing projects in Russia (Vesti.Ekonomika 2018). At the same time, the EDB and the AIIB signed a memorandum of cooperation hinting at possible progress (AIIB 2018). Other explanations of AIIB's low-profile in Russia may be both financial and political. The bank has only disbursed $4.4 billion during its two years of existence, despite initial expectations of $10–15 billion a year (Babones 2018). On one hand, this policy is likely to reflect limited personnel resources but also prudency and desire to maintain the AIIB's investment rating, especially at this early stage of its existence. On the other hand, the AIIB visibly sought to dispel perceptions of risk regarding its ambitions and opted for co-financing with established Western institutions, including the ADB, in its first batch of approved projects. Still, approximately one quarter of the disbursed $4.4 billion went to India—second-largest shareholder of the AIIB but also the key participant of the Quad, often viewed as antithetical to the BRI.

While Russia has rapidly warmed up its position towards the BRI and the AIIB, despite an initially cautious start, and China has accommodated Russia's involvement, the record of Sino-Russian bilateral cooperation in this specific field so far remains below expectations as compared to non-BRI/non-AIIB Sino-Russian projects. Curiously, although Russia's ADB bid has been opposed by Japan and the USA, the current volume of ADB–EDB co-financing exceeds that of EDB and AIIB. As of end 2016, Japan still ranked the first among Asian countries in terms of FDI stock in Russia with $15.1 billion as opposed to China's $8 billion (EDB 2017).

CONCLUSION

Although China has a dominant position in the AIIB with 28.7 per cent voting power, Russia ranks third in that regard (6.6%) after India (8.3%). Russia's speedy accession to the upstart AIIB as a key member was the opposite of its earlier multiple unsuccessful attempts to join the more long-established ADB, opposed by the Japanese and US governments. Similarly, while the ADB's CAREC envisaged little, if any, role for Russia, the BRI made Russia one of many stakeholders and, arguably, a major one, given its transit position, even though Russia and China still have differences and rivalries regarding Central Asia, including China's ever-growing economic clout in the region. While Japan in the mid-2000s saw Russia's (and China's) emergence as risks to the international status quo and attempted to reinsure itself against that emergence, China in the mid-2010s ventured, even if cautiously, into laying groundwork for a change in that status quo and included Russia.

However, the benefits of Russia's involvement in the BRI and AIIB so far remain limited and dependent on direct support from the leaders. Western sanctions on Russia significantly reduced the risk appetite of Chinese banks and Chinese investors, making it harder than expected for Russian borrowers to raise funds in China.

Therefore, the BRI's 'Russian challenge' will be to institutionalize genuine win-win cooperation beyond top-down push from leaders and avoid becoming confined to existence purely in the rhetoric. The AIIB's 'Russian challenge' will be to avoid becoming another version of the ADB with regards to Russian initiatives and, instead, treat its third-largest regional member in accordance with its contribution. As for both the BRI's and the AIIB's 'Japanese challenge', it is fairly straightforward: getting Japan on board, which is not only in the long-term interest of both China and Japan but also feasible, as evidenced by the instances of Sino-Japanese economic cooperation and interdependence.

REFERENCES

Abalkina, Anna A. 2007. 'Rossiya i integratsionnye protsessy v Vostochnoy Azii' [Russia and integration processes in East Asia]. In *Rossiya i mir v XXI veke* [*Russia and the World in the 21st Century*], 161–172. Moscow.

ADB. 1998. *Regional Economic Cooperation in Central Asia*. Mandaluyong, Philippines: Author.

ADB. 2007. *Summary of Proceedings of the 40th Annual Meeting of the Board of Governors*. Kyoto International Convention Center, Japan, May 5–7.

ADB. 2016. 'ADB Signs $1 Billion Cofinancing Agreement with Eurasian Development Bank'. March 4. https://www.adb.org/news/adb-signs-1-billion-cofinancing-agreement-eurasian-development-bank

AIIB. 2018. 'AIIB, EDB Strengthen Cooperation to Increase Development across Eurasia'. October 31. https://www.aiib.org/en/news-events/news/2018/20181031_001.html

Alegado, Siegfrid. 2018. 'Japan Still Beating China in Southeast Asia Infrastructure Race'. *Bloomberg*, February 8. https://www.bloomberg.com/news/articles/2018-02-08/japan-still-beating-china-in-southeast-asia-infrastructure-race

Alexei D. Voskressenski. 2015. Russia and China: A Theory of Inter-State Relations, Routledge.

Babones, Salvatore. 2018. 'China's AIIB Expected to Lend $10–15B a Year, but Has Only Managed $4.4B in 2 Years'. *Forbes*, January 16. https://www.forbes.com/sites/salvatorebabones/2018/01/16/chinas-aiib-expected-to-lend-10–15b-a-year-but-has-only-managed-4–4b-in-2-years/#7721f16d37f1

Baydakov, Mikhail, Bassanini Franco, Yuriy Gromyko, Viktor Zyukov, Paolo Raymondi, Edoardo Reviglio, and Jonathan Tennenbaum. 2012. *Transevraziyskiy poyas Razvitie [Trans-Eurasian Belt Development]*. Moscow: Praxis.

Calder, Kent E. 1991. *Japan's Changing Role in Asia: Emerging Co-prosperity*. New York: Japan Society.

Central Asia Regional Economic Program (CAREC) Cooperation. Inaugural Meeting of CAREC Research Institutes Astana, Kazakhstan, 12 March 2009 https://www.carecinstitute.org/wp-content/uploads/2009/03/01-Introduction-to-the-Central-Asia-Regional-Economic-Cooperation-Program.pdf

China's Belt and Road Initiative and Its Impact in Central Asia, Marlene Laruelle, ed. Washington, D.C.: The George Washington University, Central Asia Program.

Cho, Yusho, and Kyohei Suga. 2018. 'Xi-Abe Summit to Trigger Dozens of Cross-Border Deals'. *Nikkei Asian Review*, October 24.

Chugrov, Sergey V., and Dmitry V. Streltsov. 2017. 'Interdependence of Russo-Japanese Relations and Mutual Images of Japan and Russia'. *Japanese Journal of Political Science* 18 (1): 22–40.

EDB. 2017. *EAES i strany evraziyskogo kontinenta: monitoring i analiz pryamykh investitsii 2017* [The EAEU and the Countries of the Eurasian Continent: Monitoring and Analysis of Direct Investment 2017]. https://eabr.org/analytics/integration-research/cii-reports/eaes-i-strany-evraziyskogo-kontinenta-monitoring-i-analiz-pryamykh-investitsiy-2017-/

Finmarket. 2007. 'SShA blokirovali vstupleniye Rossii v Aziatskiy bank razvitiya' [The USA blocked Russia's accession to the Asian Development Bank]. *Finmarket.ru*, May 11. http://www.finmarket.ru/news/597914

Foreign Minister Kono Visits Pakistan, Sri Lanka and Maldives (January 3-7, 2018) https://www.mofa.go.jp/s_sa/sw/page3e_000799.html

Fukuda Takeo. 1977. 'Speech by Prime Minister Takeo Fukuda (Fukuda Doctrine Speech)'. Manila, August 18. http://worldjpn.grips.ac.jp/documents/texts/docs/19770818.S1E.html

Gabuev, Alexander. 2016. 'China's One Belt, One Road Initiative and the Sino-Russian Entente'. Carnegie Moscow Centre, August 9. http://carnegie.ru/2016/08/09/china-s-one-belt-one-road-initiative-and-sino-russian-ententepub-64297

Gudok. 2015. 'Trans-Evraziyskiy Poyas Razvitiye na Shelkovom Puti' [Trans-Eurasian Belt Development on the Silk Road]. Gudok.ru, May 25. http://www.gudok.ru/transport/zd/?ID=1274472

Halloran, Richard. 1974. 'Violent Crowds in Jakarta Protest the Visit by Tanaka'. *The New York Times*, January 16.

Interfax. 2017. 'Russia Presents 10 Projects to AIIB for Financing, None Yet Approved'. *Interfax*, March 1. http://www.interfax.com/newsinf.asp?id=737921

Jamestown Foundation. 2011. *Central Asia, Afghanistan and the New Silk Road: Political, Economic and Security Challenges* (Conference Report). Washington, DC: The Jamestown Foundation. https://jamestown.org/wp-content/uploads/2011/11/Afghan_Silk_Road_conf_report_-_FULL.pdf?x87069

Jerdén, Björn, and Hagström, Linus. 2012. "Rethinking Japan's China Policy: Japan as an Accommodator in the Rise of China, 1978–2011," *Journal of East Asian Studies* 12: 215–250.

Johnson, Chalmers. 1992. *History Restarted: Japanese-American Relations at the End of the Century*. Canberra: Australian National University Peace Research Centre.

Karaganov, Sergey A., Oleg Barabanov, Alexey Bezborodov, Timofei Bordachev, Alexander Gabuev, Konstantin Kuzovkov, and I. Timofeev. 2015. *Towards the Great Ocean – 3: Creating Central Eurasia—The Silk Road Economic Belt and the Priorities of the Eurasian States' Joint Development*. Valdai Discussion Club, Analytical Report, June. Moscow. http://karaganov.ru/content/images/uploaded/a7a117d7310c6e15bf14bf0f6d2f56ae.pdf

Katzenstein, Peter, and Martin Rouse. 2001. 'Japan as a Regional Power in Asia'. In *Japan and South East Asia*, edited by Wolf Mendl, 193–224. London: Routledge.

Kawai, M. 2013. 'Financing Development Cooperation in Northeast Asia'. *The Northeast Asian Economic Review* 1 (1): 1–40.

Kireeva, Anna, and Andrey Sushentsov. 2017. *The Russian-Japanese Rapprochement: Opportunities and Limitations*. Valdai Discussion Club Report, August.

Kommersant. 2018. 'ShOS splotili SShA i terroristy' [The USA and Terrorists Consolidated the SCO]. *Kommersant*, April 25. https://www.kommersant.ru/doc/3613413

Lukin, Alexander, and Igor Denisov. 2015. 'Russia and the Conception of "pivot to Asia"'. In *Yearbook of the International Studies Institute*, 194–203. Moscow, Russia: MGIMO University.

Michishita, Narushige. 2018. 'Cooperate and Compete: Abe's New Approach to China'. *The Straits Times*, November 13.

Miyashita, Akitoshi. 2003. *Limits to Power: Asymmetric Dependence and Japanese Foreign Aid Policy*. Langham, MD: Lexington Books.

MoFA. 2007a. 'Interview of the Director of the Ministry's Economic Cooperation Department A.L. Kondakov on the Problems of Regional Financial

Institutions'. *Vremya Novostei*, April 24. http://www.mid.ru/aziatskij-bank-razvitia-azbr-/-/asset_publisher/KrRBY5EMiHC1/content/id/375488

MoFA. 2007b. 'Comment by the Ministry's Official Representative M.L. Kamynin in Connection with a Question from the Media Regarding Main Results of the Participation of the Russian Delegation in the Annual Session of the Asian Development Bank's Governors'. May 1. http://www.mid.ru/aziatskij-bank-razvitia-azbr-/-/asset_publisher/KrRBY5EMiHC1/content/id/373900

Murashkin, Nikolay. 2018. 'Not-So-New Silk Roads: Japan's Foreign Policies on Asian Connectivity Infrastructure under the Radar'. *Australian Journal of International Affairs* 72 (5): 455–472.

NDRC, MoFA, and Ministry of Commerce. 2015. *Tuīdòng gòng jiàn sīchóu zhī lù jīngjì dài hé 21 shìjì hǎishàng sīchóu zhī lù de yuànjǐng yǔ xíngdòng* [*Vision and Action to Promote the Construction of the Silk Road Economic Belt and the 21st Century Maritime Silk Road*]. March 28. http://www.chinagoabroad.com/zh/article/action-plan-on-the-china-proposed-belt-and-road-initiative

Nikkei. 2016. 'Abe's "New Mercantilism" Bears Fruit for Japan'. *Nikkei Asian Review*, January 4. http://asia.nikkei.com/Politics-Economy/Policy-Politics/Abe-s-new-mercantilism-bears-fruit-for-Japan

Nikkei. 2017a. 'Nippon Express Climbs Aboard China's Belt and Road Initiative'. *Nikkei Asian Review*, September 30. https://asia.nikkei.com/Business/Companies/Nippon-Express-climbs-aboard-China-s-Belt-and-Road-Initiative

Polubota, Aleksei. 2017. 'Rossiya okazalas' na obochine Novogo shelkovogo puti' [Russia Ended Up on the Sidelines of the New Silk Road]. *Svobodnaya Pressa*, May 15. http://svpressa.ru/economy/article/172322/

President of Russia. 2015. 'Sovmestnoe zaiavlenie Rossiiskoi Federatsii i Kitaiskoi Narodnoi Respubliki o sotrudnichestve po sopriazheniiu stroitel'stva Evraziiskogo ekonomicheskogo soiuza i Ekonomicheskogo poiasa Shelkovogo puti' [Joint Declaration of the Russian Federation and the People's Republic of China on Cooperation in Linking the Eurasian Economic Union and Silk Road Economic Belt]. The President of Russia, May 8. www.kremlin.ru/supplement/4971

Pugliese, Giulio, and Insisa, Aurelio. 2017. *Sino-Japanese Power Politics: Might, Money and Minds*. Basingstoke: Palgrave Macmillan.

Rafferty, Kevin. 2002. 'Chino Cements Image as ADB's Best Chief Ever'. *Japan Times*, February 21.

RIA Novosti. 2016. 'EABR: pravila vydachi gosgarantii RF ne pozvolyayut ABII investirovat' v nee' [EDB: The Rules of Issuing State Guarantees of the Russian Federation Don't Allow the AIIB to Invest in It]. *RIA Novosti*, June 17. https://ria.ru/economy/20160617/1449045201.html

Shiraishi, Takashi. 1996. 'Japan and Southeast Asia'. In *Network Power. Japan and Asia*, edited by Peter J. Katzenstein and Takashi Shiraishi, 169–196. Ithaca: Cornell University Press.

St. Petersburg International Economic Forum [SPIEF]. 2012. *Minutes of the Panel Creating a Reliable Future. The Asia-Pacific Region's Economy. Challenges and*

Opportunities. https://forumspb.rcfiles.rcmedia.ru/upload/iblock/d59/d5924280e790fd4db497fa2e3ff751db.pdf

Sterngold, James. 1991. 'Japan's New Finance Official Plots an Independent Course'. *New York Times*, August 5.

Sudo, Sueo. 2015. *Japan's ASEAN Policy: In Search of Proactive Multilateralism.* Singapore: Institute of Southeast Asian Studies.

Taniguchi Tomohiko. 2010. 'Beyond "The Arc of Freedom and Prosperity": Debating Universal Values in Japanese Grand Strategy'. Asia Paper Series, the German Marshall Fund of the United States.

Terry, Edith. 2002. *How Asia Got Rich: Japan, China and the Asian Miracle.* Armonk, NY: M.E. Sharpe.

Tsuruoka, Doug. 2017. 'Asian Development Bank Wary of Russia's AIIB Membership'. *Asia Times*, July 18. http://www.atimes.com/article/asian-development-bank-wary-russias-aiib-membership/

Vesti.Ekonomika. 2018. 'Aziatskii bank infrastrukturnykh investitsii nameren finansirovat' proyekty v Rossii' [The Asian Infrastructure Investment Bank Intends to Finance Projects in Russia]. *Vesti*, October 15. https://www.vestifinance.ru/articles/108510

Wang, Zheng. 2015. 'China's Alternative Diplomacy'. *The Diplomat*, January 30.

WikiLeaks. 2006. 06TOKYO7164. 'U.S.-Japan Central Asia Dialogue: Part Two, Foreign Assistance and Project Finance'. US Embassy in Tokyo, ID 06TOKYO7164_a. https://wikileaks.org/plusd/cables/06TOKYO7164_a.html

Xi Jinping. 2013. 'President Xi Jinping Delivers Important Speech and Proposes to Build a Silk Road Economic Belt with Central Asian Countries'. Embassy of the People's Republic of China in the Cooperative Republic of Guyana. http://gy.china-embassy.org/eng/zgyw/t1076334.htm

Yomiuri. 2017. 'Afurika shien, chūgokukōsō ni kyōchō. Nicchū kyōryoku teian he' [Aid to Africa to Stress China Vision. Toward a Sino-Japanese Cooperation Plan]. *Yomiuri*, December 31. http://www.yomiuri.co.jp/feature/TO000301/20171230-OYT1T50087.html

Chapter 7

China's Infrastructure Investment in Africa

Saite Lu

INTRODUCTION

The pace of economic development in China over the past few decades has been astounding. Less than half a century ago, China was one of the world's poorest nations. Transformational socio-economic change has been achieved, with hundreds of millions of people no longer facing poverty in what has now become the second largest national economy on Earth. Gazing at the skylines of Beijing, Shanghai, and many other Chinese cities today, one may justifiably be amazed that only 25 years ago, the GDP per capita of China was below the level of Sub-Saharan Africa (SSA). Today, China is Africa's most important contributor of foreign direct investment (FDI), and, after the European Union, its second largest trading partner. China is currently also a significant financier of African infrastructure development.

Like the arteries of the human body, infrastructure is fundamental to the functioning of any economy, providing the vital material foundation and connectivity for economic activities. Despite being one of the fastest growing regions in the world,[1] SSA lacks infrastructure. Until today,

---

[1] The region achieved an average GDP growth of 5.09 per cent between 2000 and 2017.

442 million people still have no access to electricity in SSA. It is also the only region witnessed a decline in road density over the past two decades (Calderon et al. 2017). Woetzel et al. (2017) estimate that, between 2017 and 2035, the average financing need for infrastructure investment in the world is $3.7 trillion per annum. To achieve UN's Sustainable Development Goals (SDGs) by 2030, the annual financing need could increase further by up to $1 trillion. Africa only accounts for 2 per cent of the estimated global investment, which is the smallest among all regions. As noted by Goldin (2016), with limited domestic resources in developing countries, around half of infrastructure financing rely on external sources such as the World Bank, African Development Bank, and China EXIM Bank. The implementation of China's Belt and Road Initiative (BRI) may offer further realization of African infrastructural and economic development.

This chapter seeks an understanding of China's current infrastructure investment projects in Africa and explores implications for future BRI projects. The first section discusses how China finances its infrastructure projects in Africa. The second and third sections, through two different case studies, take a closer, critical look at Chinese official investments in Africa. While the South Sudan case provides evidence which refutes stereotypical critiques that China is mainly interested in resource grabbing from Africa, the Sierra Leone case highlights significant limitation to China's bilateral financing arrangements in Africa. Based on these observations, the final section further explores the potential impacts of the BRI on China's infrastructure investment in Africa.

HOW CHINA FINANCES INFRASTRUCTURE INVESTMENT

'To achieve prosperity, one must build roads first'. A well-known slogan that was widely adopted by local governments in China in the early 1980s, it has become accepted wisdom and remains relevant today. The positive economic impacts of infrastructure development are not unique to China. Similar outcomes have been seen in SSA (Kodongo and Ojah 2016), South Asia (Sahoo and Dash, 2012), and even in the early periods of industrialization in Britain and the USA (Allen 2011).

Although the benefits are widely recognized, financing infrastructure projects across the globe have proved challenging. First, the high fixed costs (e.g., capital expenditure) in the initial construction phase are formidable. Second, various sources of uncertainty associated with infrastructure projects in developing countries may prevail, such as external macroeconomic shocks (the fourth section), political instability (the third section), and potentially low returns. These factors deter entry of the private sector and together create a market failure. Hence most infrastructure investments are financed by public money from either the domestic authority or international community.[2]

No exception to this pattern, the majority of China's infrastructure investment in Africa is funded by state finance, which can be classified into two broad categories:

- Official development assistance (ODA)
- Other official finance (OOF)

ODA includes grants, interest-free loans and concessional loans, while OOF comprises those financing sources that are not qualified for ODA. Unlike members of the Development Assistance Committee (DAC), who typically make regular updates of their official finance data available to the public; official finance data from the Chinese government relatively lacks transparency.

Many analyses on China's ODA still rely on the data provided in two publications of the *White Paper of China's Foreign Aid* (2011, 2014) prepared by the Chinese State Council. According to official claims, until 2012, the accumulated amount of foreign aid had reached $53.2 billion.[3] Of this amount (see Figure 7.1), $21.3 billion were grants for technical assistance, humanitarian responses and social welfare projects; interest-free loans amounted to $12.9 billion, mainly used for the construction of public facilities and projects that may improve people's livelihoods; there were $19 billion in concessional loans, supporting economically and socially productive projects, medium to large-scale infrastructure development and equipment procurements.

The budget for foreign aid expenditure is set by the Ministry of Finance, while its management is mainly under the Ministry of

---

[2] The public–private partnership (PPP) has become increasingly popular, as it creates additional space for financing when the public sector is heavily in debt.

[3] Using an exchange rate of $1 = 6.5RMB.

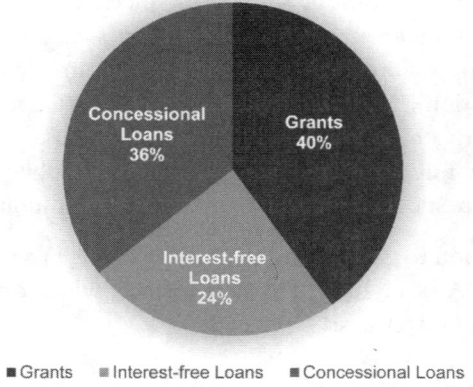

Figure 7.1 *Chinese ODA by Categories*
Source: *White Paper of China's Foreign Aid* (2011, 2014)

Commerce and various other MDAs[4] based on their respective jurisdictions. For example, the Ministry of Health is responsible for dispatching Chinese medical teams to 42 countries in Africa. The concessional loans are managed directly by the Export–Import (EXIM) Bank of China.

However, the AidData[5] database indicates that the size of Chinese ODA is considerably more than that stated by the government. Between 2000 and 2014, the Chinese ODA reached $81.1 billion. An ODA flow of $27.9 billion in 2013 and 2014 alone may seem unlikely. The White Papers do not offer data at the project level or data by the recipient country. Therefore, it is not possible to crosscheck the differences between the two sources.

---

[4] Ministries, departments and agencies.

[5] AidData is managed by the College of William and Mary. It provides comprehensive Chinese official finance data at project level. These information are collected from the actual media reports, government contracts, field research, etc. The database should be used with caution especially when verifying projects (Brautigam and Hwang 2016). As many China-funded projects reported by local media never materialized in the end, AidData tends to exaggerate the scale of official finance from China. See the case of Mamamah Airport for an example.

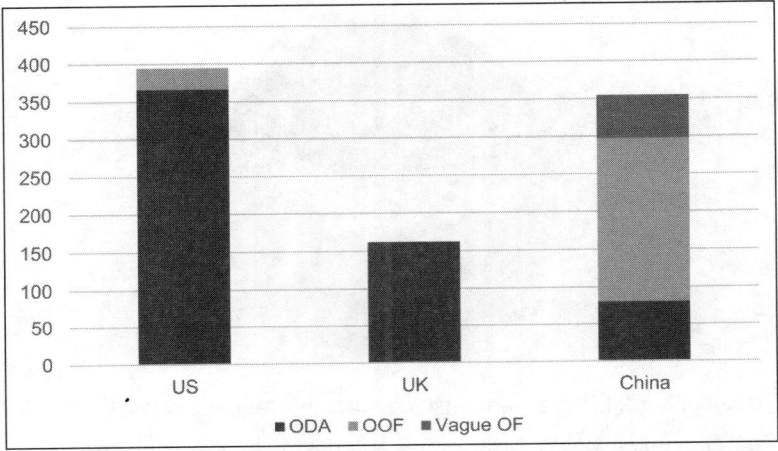

Figure 7.2 *Comparing Official Finance (2000–2014): USA, UK and China*

Source: AidData and OECD
Note: OOF data for the UK is not readily available.

During the same period, AidData also records $216.3 billion of OOF, and a further $57 billion of official finance sources, that do not have enough information for classification. The total official finance from China stood at $354.3 billion, second only to the USA, with total official finance of $394.6 billion (see Figure 7.2).

The lack of transparency in official statistics can arouse concern and some suspicion in the international community about the motivation behind such financing, allowing a misreading of the potential impacts from Chinese lending.

The following sections narrow down the focus on two specific cases. Each case highlights particular features of Chinese infrastructure investment in Africa in the hope of shedding some light on the future of BRI.

IS CHINA ALL ABOUT NATURAL RESOURCES IN AFRICA?

A common belief maintains that Chinese investment and aid are heavily biased towards mining and natural resources in Africa. However,

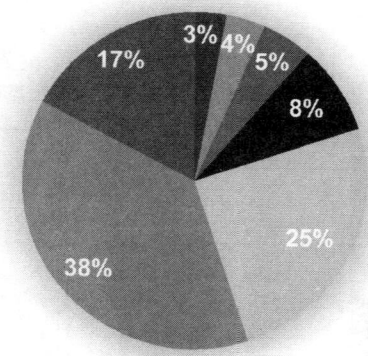

- Agriculture, Forestry and Fishing
- Communications
- Transport and Storage
- Others
- Action Relating to Debt
- Industry, Mining, Construction
- Energy Generation and Supply

Figure 7.3 *Chinese Official Finance by Sector*
Source: AidData

according to the AidData database, official finance from China covers more than 140 countries and a wide range of sectors.[6] In 2014, the total official commitments from China amounted to $354.4 billion. Projects related to industry, mining and construction together only account for 8.5 per cent of the total. Much of the financing end up in infrastructure projects such as energy ($134.1 billion), transport ($88.8 billion) and communication ($16.9 billion). The rest went to agriculture, debt relief and everything else (Figure 7.3). Brautigam (2009) also described the diverse nature of the Chinese presence in detail, citing numerous case studies across Africa.

---

[6] According to Chen, Dollar, and Tang (2016), both Chinese investments and Western investments are positively correlated to natural resource wealth in African nations. Comparing with the latter, Chinese investments are relatively equally distributed between good and bad governance environments.

THE SOUTH SUDAN CASE

The world's youngest nation, oil-rich South Sudan, is a textbook example of a small isolated economy. The GDP of South Sudan contributed less than 0.01 per cent of global GDP in 2016. It is landlocked, with limited infrastructure connecting to the rest of the world. Production and exports other than oil are minimal. As a result, South Sudan must rely on imports to meet its daily consumption demands.

Living in a country geographically larger than France, South Sudan's population is only one-fifth the size of France's. About 80 per cent of the South Sudanese live in rural areas. The highly dispersed population means it is difficult to harness economies of scale and specialization. There are significant barriers to rapid industrialization, rising productivity and ascent from poverty. Poverty and economic stagnation often go hand in hand with conflict and war (Collier 2007). The top priority for South Sudan has been to end the vicious cycle of violence and poverty. China's involvement could be a game changer by boosting the economy which may contribute to ending the conflict in the country.

China has been the biggest trading partner of South Sudan since its independence. About 80 per cent of its exports are shipped to China. At the same time, according to the UN Comtrade Database, China is the supplier of more than a quarter of South Sudanese imports. The oil industry has always been under the spotlight. The sector contributes over one-third of GDP, more than 80 per cent of total exports, and over 90 per cent of fiscal revenues. However, the pursuit of vast oil reserves in South Sudan has been far from a smooth operation.

The China National Petroleum Corp (CNPC) first opened its subsidiary in the newly constituted South Sudan in 2011. Before independence, CNPC enjoyed a rate of return of roughly 15 per cent on investment in Sudanese oil fields. This has since been impacted by the unrest in South Sudan. In 2012, due to severe disputes between South Sudan and the North, the operation was stopped by the Government of South Sudan (GoSS). Subsequently, the conflict escalated into fighting, leading to the Heglig Crisis.[7] CNPC's operation in South Sudan did not resume until May 2013, but did not last very long too. In December 2013, the country fell into civil war again, and oil fields were at the epicentre of the conflict. All the foreign workers from other stakeholders were evacuated, but not the Chinese. CNPC kept a small team on the ground to operate at a minimal level, which won over appreciation, support and trust from the GoSS.

The complex nature of oil exploitation means CNPC is only one of the major players in the sector. There are various other foreign and local state companies, such as Petronas (Malaysia), ONGC Videsh Ltd (India) and Nilepet (South Sudan), that own significant shares in various oil blocks. Given the lack of refinery facilities in South Sudan, crude oil must be first transferred to Khartoum for processing, and then to Port Sudan for shipping. For every barrel of crude oil produced in South Sudan, CNPC must pay an overall $24 in transit fees charges to Sudan as well as costs for processing. Thus, combined with low international oil prices, the company is making a loss on every barrel it sells (Yan 2016). CNPC could have shut down the operation temporarily to reduce its financial burden, but has instead kept production running, howsoever small. Irrespective of underlying intentions, this continuing production acts as an essential stabilizer for the South Sudanese economy.

Finally, apart from the oil sector, Chinese state-owned and private companies invest in various industries such as construction, telecommunications, hotels and services. Up to May 2015, there were over 140 Chinese companies and institutions registered. However, without the military protection that exists in the oil fields, their operations have faced immense difficulties. The Juba Airport Renovation Project is a good example. The China Harbour Engineering Company is contracted for this $160 million project, but it ground to a halt due to the ongoing conflict. The Chinese government is also actively involved in financing the construction of hospitals, schools, providing medical aid and inviting officials from various MDAs to China for training.

---

[7] The disagreements between South Sudan and Sudan over the ownership of the oil-rich regions elevated into armed conflicts on 26 March 2012.

Many China–South Sudan analyses take a primary focus on questioning China's fundamental interests and motivations in South Sudan. The dire needs of South Sudan at its current development stage are forgotten. The domestic conflict and low oil prices have very severely damaged the South Sudan economy. Consumer Price Index (CPI) skyrocketed from 161.5 in 2014 to 1184.2 in 2016, and exchange rates in the parallel market depreciated dramatically from 5.8 SSP/USD in December 2014 to 90.9 SSP/USD. After November 2015, the official rate was also forced to adjust downward from 2.9 SSP/USD to 78.4SSP/USD. No country can prosper under such conditions. China has continued to work with South Sudan throughout this political and economic crisis (Lu 2017).

Although it is still unknown precisely which African countries will be involved in the BRI,[8] geographically speaking, North and East Africa fit perfectly into the concept of a Maritime Silk Road. However, the participation of Senegal seems to suggest that the coverage of the BRI in Africa could well extend to other regions in Africa.

The BRI may bring new opportunities in improving transport corridors which boost trade and economic development, but its success relies heavily on political and economic stability in member countries and their neighbours. For instance, the continuing civil conflict in South Sudan has led to one of the greatest humanitarian crises in the modern world. Three out of the world's largest five refugee camps are in its neighbouring countries,[9] which severely destabilize the regional economy (Ajak 2017). While the refugee crisis in Europe dominated much debate in the media, the majority of the refugees reside in developing countries. According to Collier (2007), international peacekeeping forces have a vital role to play in ending the violent conflict and preventing the risk of the recurrent cycle of violence. Among the 1,700 UN peacekeeping troops that China deployed in Africa, South Sudan and Sudan host 1,300 Chinese peacekeepers. Due to the increasing

---

[8] The official BRI website has included the following African nations: Morocco, Madagascar, Ethiopia, Egypt, Libya, Senegal, Tunisia and South Africa. See https://eng.yidaiyilu.gov.cn/info/iList.jsp?cat_id=10076

[9] Bidibidi, Uganda (285,000); Dadaab, Kenya (239,500); Kakuma, Kenya (185,000).

economic presence in the region, the Chinese government is quietly deviating from its long-standing policy of non-interference in other nation's internal affairs policies. Therefore, it can be seen that the issue of what policy framework to adapt to safeguard the implementation of BRI posts a series of new challenges for China.

ARE LOANS FROM CHINA TOO COMMERCIAL?

Since the mid-1990s, the public debt level as a percentage of the gross national income (GNI) in SSA continued to increase and reached nearly 70 per cent in the early 2000 (Figure 7.4). In 2005, the World Bank and (International Monetary Fund) IMF, along with other bilateral and commercial creditors, decided to offer debt relief for Heavily Indebted Poor Countries (HIPC) through the Multilateral Debt Relief Initiative (MDRI). A total of 30 SSA countries received the full amount of debt relief, which drastically improved the debt positions in these states. However, Figure 7.4 shows that the gross debt to GDP ratio in SSA started to pile up again after the global financial crisis. The ratio is still relatively low by international standards, but interest rates are also higher in these countries (*The Economist* 2018).

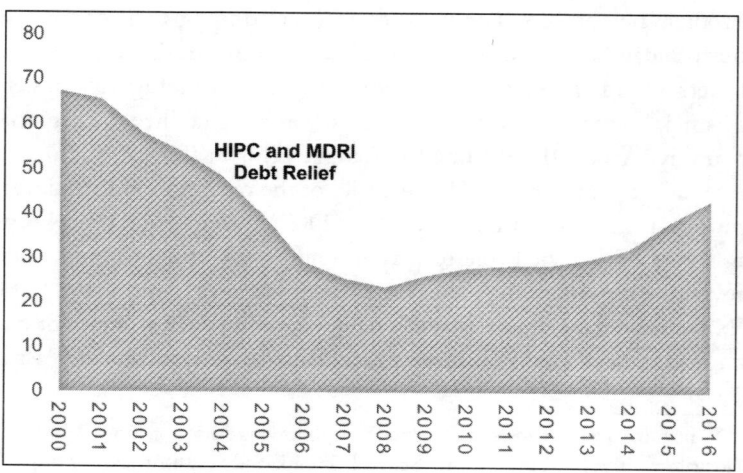

Figure 7.4 *Gross Debt in Sub-Sahara Africa (% of GDP), 2000–2016*
Source: IMF

Some perceive that Chinese investments and aid projects are too commercially driven, and hence the BRI will leave some governments under increasingly alarming debt distress (Hurley, Morris, and Portelance 2018). Figure 7.2 shows that the scale of official finance from China is already on par with the USA, but compared with traditional donor countries, the percentage of ODA is indeed much lower. Studying the Mamamah Airport case provides some insight at the project level, and demonstrates some of the limitations of the current bilateral approach that China practises, and illuminates some of the misunderstandings from the international community.

THE MAMAMAH AIRPORT CASE

Despite being regarded as a successful example of a post-conflict state, Sierra Leone remains one of most impoverished countries in the world. The civil war between 1991 and 2001 not only disabled 490,000 people[10] but also severely damaged domestic infrastructure stock. The Government of Sierra Leone (GoSL) launched a 5-year national development strategy—*Agenda for Prosperity in 2013*. The goal was to set out the eight pillars that would enable Sierra Leone to become an inclusive, green and middle-income country by 2035.[11] The Mamamah Airport is one of the most critical infrastructure projects that is believed to massively improve the international competitiveness of Sierra Leone.

The journey between the Lungi International Airport and the capital city Freetown is memorable. Upon arrival, passengers face a choice between a costly 6-hour road trip or an hour speedboat ride ($40 for a one-way ticket) to cross the sea estuary that separates Lungi and Freetown. The latter choice is eminently preferable. The service was under the monopoly of Sea Coach Express for many years until a new

---

[10] This is the UN estimation. The population is estimated to be 7.39 million in 2016.

[11] Pillar 1: Economic Diversification; Pillar 2: Managing Natural Resources; Pillar 3: Promoting Human Development; Pillar 4: International Competitiveness; Pillar 5: Labour and Employment; Pillar 6: Social Protection; Pillar 7: Governance Public Sector and Statistics Reform; Pillar 8: Gender Equality and Women's empowerment. For more details, see GoSL (2013).

rival, Sea Bird Express, appeared in 2014. This duopoly of competition has helped bring about bigger boats and better and more reliable services. However, delays are not unfamiliar for frequent travellers. Sometimes, one must wait for hours at the port before boarding the boat for a range of reasons (weather being a common one during rainy season).

It was against this background, in 2011, that the Chinese government agreed to finance a new airport with easier land access to the city. The project was to be financed by a flagship concessional loan from the EXIM Bank of China. The contract was awarded to the China Railway International Group Ltd., a subsidiary of the engineering and construction giant China Railway Group Ltd. The Mamamah site is located at the outskirts of Freetown, about 38 miles away.

The project received intense criticism from the World Bank and IMF, institutions which serve as the anchor for almost all the traditional donor agencies. IMF officials reiterated that the financing from China is non-concessional, and current international arrival statistics cannot justify the economic viability of the project. IMF (2014) believes it will impose substantial macroeconomic risks and make the local authority vulnerable to debt distress.

To investigate the IMF claims, it is useful to understand the concept of grant element (GE),[12] which is used to define concessionality. According to the OECD, using the cash flow system, if the GE of a loan is above 25 per cent of total face value, then the loan should be concessional enough to be classified as ODA. As revealed by the IMF, the financing terms for Mamamah project are as follows:

- Estimated costs: $198 million
- Annual interest rate: 2 per cent
- Maturity period: 20 years
- Grace period: 5 years
- Assume equal principal payments

---

[12] The definition of the GE is updated after 2015. However, given the project is evaluated before the change of concept, so an old version of GE concept is used here for discussion.

Under the OECD standard discount rate of 10 per cent per annum, the GE of the loan is 52 per cent. That is way above the cut-off level for a concessional loan. What the IMF used was a unified discount rate of 5 per cent per annum (IMF 2013), which is very low for a low-income country.[13] Those same financing terms now only generate a GE of 27.2 per cent. At the same time, the IMF also sets a minimum level of 35 per cent for concessionality, hence claims that the loan is non-concessional.

If the loan is regarded as non-concessional, it will exceed the ceiling of $30 million per annum for non-concessional debt set by the IMF under the performance criterion. In fact, these financing terms are the most concessional that China currently offers. Agreement with the IMF could imply that the GoSL should no longer be able to access any interest-bearing financing from China, even though it meets OECD–ODA standards.

Following the IMF request, the project came to a halt in 2014, and new feasibility analysis was contracted to Ernst & Young. In the following year, the country was hit badly by two external shocks—the Ebola crisis and falling iron ore prices—that further dimmed economic prospects. The IMF continued to advise pursuit of prudent borrowing policies and not signing the loan contract with China (IMF 2016).

In February 2018, only a month before the general election, President Koroma signed the contract with EXIM Bank of China and inaugurated the construction of the airport in March. The Chinese Ambassador to Sierra Leone, Peng Wu, expressed a different opinion from the IMF. He stated his belief that the project is more than an airport. It will bring economic transformation by attracting more investments and tourists. There will also be a new economic zone and airport city. He has added that a grant of $30 million will be delivered to cushion the possible risks related to interest payments (Cham 2018). In October 2018, seven years since the initial proposal, the newly elected government has cancelled the project. The current aviation minister told the BBC that instead of building a new airport, the

---

[13] The annual interest rates for private lending offered by the commercial banks in Sierra Leone can be way above 20 per cent.

government was considering to build a bridge that connects Freetown and Lungi Airport directly (BBC 2018).[14]

The project is a 'miniature' of many of China's infrastructure investments in Africa. Little evidence suggests that there will be major changes in China's development financing strategies. Hence, the BRI is likely to be an expansion of its current financing model. If the IMF's concerns are valid, then China may again face similar issues for other BRI projects. Experience, in this case, urges the Chinese authorities to coordinate and communicate closely with other donor agencies in the future and create a more credible internal evaluation process for proposed projects.

Dollar (2017) maps the top recipient countries of China's official finance between 2012 and 2014. Many of them are countries coincident with the BRI. Over half of the top recipients rank poorly in the Worldwide Governance Indicators for the rule of law. If the GE of the financing is too low to be ODA, then it is likely to burden these countries with increasingly high levels of debt and create default risks. Many of the project financing under the OOF requires the recipient countries to provide sovereign guarantees. However, if default happens, it is unlikely that China would apply punitive actions, so debt reliefs seem to be the only way out (Hurley et al. 2018). Such an awkward situation is unfavourable for both parties.

If the IMF is wrong, which is not unheard of—it utterly failed to foresee the global financial crisis in 2008, for example—then it may need to revise its policy programme in developing countries like Sierra Leone. Lacking flexibility and failing to recognize heterogeneity among developing countries can hinder economic development. The unified discount rate may need to be revised. The OECD grant equivalent system offers a way forward. From 2018, different discount rates will be applied to countries under different income groups by adding a premium rate to the IMF unified discount rate.[15]

---

[14] The 'battle' between the IMF and the GoSL over its external borrowing is likely to continue, as building a bridge crossing the sea channel seems to be another expensive project.

[15] 1 per cent premium for upper-middle income countries (UMICs); 2 per cent for lower-middle income countries (LMICs); 4 per cent for low-income countries (LICs). In addition, a new 45 per cent GE floor is set for loans to LICs; 15 per cent for LMICs and 10 per cent for UMICs (OECD 2019).

LOOKING AHEAD: THE BRI

Development finance is not a one-way street. A win-win situation for both donor and recipient countries can be achieved. In the era of globalization, the political and economic instability of any nation can have significant ramifications for its neighbouring region and even the world (e.g., refugee crises in Europe, nuclear tests in North Korea). The success of BRI rests on the premise that the shared prosperity of all member countries is ultimately guaranteed. Therefore, it is in China's interests to come up with a new model of foreign assistance to develop more innovative development financing products and to seek more international collaboration.

The Sierra Leone case reveals that significant limitations exist in bilateral financial arrangements. The lack of representation of interests from developing countries in the existing multilateral institutions has led to the establishment of new multilateral development agencies such as the Asian Infrastructure Investment Bank (AIIB) and the New Development Bank (NDB). The fundamental idea is to have developing nations become the majority shareholders so that the development agenda can be aligned to their development needs. Both institutions may offer alternative solutions and additional financing for future BRI projects.[16]

It is also essential to draw a clear distinction between ODA and OOF. Dreher et al. (2017) point out that the positive impact from the Chinese ODA on the economic growth of recipient countries (an average of 0.7% increase in GDP growth is identified) is no less than any other donor agencies; but no such impacts are observed using OOF data. This finding has important implications for BRI projects. Increasing the share of ODA in prudently selected infrastructure investments not only reduces the risk of debt distress but also enables economic growth, both of which are fundamental to the success of the BRI. Considering the heterogeneous nature of the BRI countries, OOF can be used to finance projects in countries with relatively low risks of debt distress.

---

[16] However, both institutions have limited role to play in Africa, at least for now. The AIIB still heavily focuses on the infrastructure projects in Asia, and the NDB is now solely financing projects in five BRICS countries.

Currently, ODA statistics from the Chinese government are likely to include the two flagship credit programmes from EXIM Bank: concessional loan and preferential buyer's credit. The former does satisfy the GE condition for ODA, but the latter, as a type of export credit,[17] according to the OECD definition, does not. The risks associated with both the programmes are low because of the favourable financing terms they offer. The loans from EXIM bank typically have an interest rate lower than 3 per cent per annum, and maturity ranges between 15 and 20 years. Confusion could arise when dealing with commercial financing from state-owned banks in China. The OOF statistics in AidData include several commercial loans from the Bank of China and the Industrial and Commercial Bank of China. Such loans are more likely to reflect private lending than official financing, as non-concessional loans tend to have higher interest rates than official financing.[18]

Also, there is an urgent need to improve data transparency. More engagement in multilateral agencies (e.g., AIIB and NDB) is one solution. China's newly established development agency may also play an important role. The agency is now directly under the State Council of PRC, which has taken over management and coordination functions from the Ministry of Commerce and the Ministry of Foreign Affairs. Having aid policy separated from the nomenclature of 'commerce' is a good start (Lu 2018). Having international standard guidelines in respect of data transparency and operational transparency should greatly reduce misunderstandings from the international community.[19] Domestically speaking, official finance is part of fiscal expenditure. More transparency and more effective internal evaluation processes are critical to ensure taxpayers' money is well spent and accounted for.

According to the UN Resolution of 1970, DAC member countries should aim to raise ODA to 0.7 per cent of their GNI.[20] However, the

---

[17] Other DAC members, such as the USA and Germany, also provide such credits.

[18] The annual interest rate of an OOF loan can reach well above 6 per cent, which is much higher than the interest rates offered by the China EXIM bank.

[19] The lack of systemic guideline in the public sphere has led to various speculations about China's intentions behind its lending to African nations. For a debt-trap diplomacy story, see Love (2018).

[20] GNI = GDP + net income from overseas investments and remittances.

target is often put aside when these countries face domestic political and economic pressures. In 2016, only the UK, Denmark, Norway, Luxembourg and Sweden met the target. The USA is leading the table regarding the absolute amount, but its ODA to GNI ratio was only 0.18 per cent in 2016.

As the second largest economy in the world, the average ODA to GNI ratio for China averaged at 0.1 per cent between 2000 and 2014. Through the lens of GDP per capita, China is still a middle-income country, and hence the 0.7 per cent target may seem a bit harsh considering China's current development stage. However, if taking OOF into account, the OOF to GNI ratio is up to 0.5 per cent. With the BRI, official finance from China and outward FDI are expected to expand much further. In the meanwhile, China may need to focus on how to increase the GE of much OOF to make it ODA so that the potential debt distress in some countries could be alleviated.

Finally, BRI will require an 'army' of development professionals from China. Developing its soft power is by far its weakest link, at least in comparison with traditional donors like the USA and the UK. Having established Confucius Institutes overseas and inviting middle-level government officials from developing countries to attend training will promote mutual understanding and cultural exchange in the long run. In the short-term, however, China's new development agency could learn from its international counterparts (e.g., DFID and USAID), collaborating closely with universities, NGOs and think tanks to have more Chinese development professionals engaged in technical assistance and development research.

CONCLUSION

Investment in infrastructure is a crucial driver in economic development. It reflects much of China's own development experience. China's heavy focus on infrastructure investment in Africa has offered the continent an alternative development model. Given the financing gap that is faced by most African states and many other developing countries, the BRI deserves to be welcomed with open arms by host countries and the international community. Although the scale of the

BRI is still unknown, the inclusion of East Africa and North Africa seems logical regarding sea routes, and the initiative may well extend to other regions in Africa. This chapter has taken a closer look at Chinese infrastructure investment in South Sudan and Sierra Leone, with insights for future BRI projects.

Unlike the common claim that Chinese investment is biased towards natural resources, the data and various case studies suggest otherwise. China's involvement is more diverse than imagined. In South Sudan, China has demonstrated itself to be a trading partner, a pillar in the extractive industry even in times of crisis, and a supporter of South Sudanese infrastructure. The strong correlation between poverty, economic stagnation and war create a vicious endogenous cycle in countries like South Sudan. China and the BRI could well be a positive external force that breaks that cycle, but this implies the need for the Chinese government to deviate from its non-interference policy model and create a new one.

The Mamamah Airport project is a compelling case to examine the limitations of bilateral cooperation, in this case, favouring China but facing heavy criticism. On the one hand, there is a lack of communication and collaboration between the Chinese authority and multilateral institutions (such as the IMF). On the other side, there is also a lack of flexibility from the IMF; it fails to recognize the heterogeneities among developing countries and its tight rules on concessionality could severely restrict the development process. However, the prudent borrowing policies advocated by the IMF in recipient countries may also benefit China in two ways. First, they urge China to be prudent regarding its lending. Non-concessional finance in countries with weak governance is likely to result in an awkward situation for both parties in the case of defaults. Second, they also inspire China to come up with more innovative ways of development financing.

The success of the BRI rests on mutual benefits for both donor countries and recipient countries. To achieve this purpose, it is essential that multilateral agencies (e.g., the IMF) align their broader policies with the development agenda of the recipient countries. Having the developing countries as the majority shareholders in the AIIB and NDB provides a practical way forward. China's new development agency also has an important role to play in the BRI. The first and foremost mission is to improve the transparency of official finance data and draw a clear distinction between ODA and commercial loans. Such data transparency will not only help reduce misunderstandings in the international community but also improve the accountability of public expenditure. Then, to avoid potential default risks and a consequent failure of China's development financing model, China must dedicate itself to increasing the share of ODA in overall official finance.

REFERENCES

Ajak, P. 2017. 'China's Success in Africa Depends on Peace in South Sudan'. *Mail & Guardian*. Retrieved from https://mg.co.za/article/2017-05-10-chinas-success-in-africa-depends-on-peace-in-south-sudan

Allen, R. C. 2011. *Global Economic History: A Very Short Introduction* (Vol. 282). Oxford University Press.

BBC News. 2018. 'Mamamah Airport: Sierra Leone Cancels China-Funded Airport'. BBC UK. https://www.bbc.co.uk/news/world-africa-45809810

Brautigam, D. 2009. *The Dragon's Gift: The Real Story of China in Africa*. Oxford University Press.

Brautigam, D., and J. Hwang. 2016. *China–Africa Loan Database Research Guide Book*. Washington, DC: Johns Hopkins University School of Advanced International Studies.

Calderon, Cesar, Gerard Kambou, Vijdan Korman, Megumi Kubota, and Catalina Cantu Canales. 2017. *Africa's Pulse: An Analysis of Issues Shaping Africa's Economic Future, vol. 19*. Washington, DC: World Bank.

Cham, K. 2018. 'Sierra Leone Launches U.S.$318 Million Chinese-Funded Airport'. *The East African* (Nairobi), March 9.

Chen, W., D. Dollar, and H. Tang. 2016. 'Why is China Investing in Africa? Evidence from the Firm Level'. *The World Bank Economic Review* 32 (3): 610–632.

Collier, P. 2007. *The Bottom Billion: Why the Poorest Countries are Failing and What Can Be Done About It*. New York: Oxford University Press.

Dollar, D. 2017. 'Where is China's Development Finance Really Going?' Brookings.edu https://www.brookings.edu/blog/order-from-chaos/2017/10/12/where-is-chinas-development-finance-really-going/

Dreher, A., A. Fuchs, B. Parks, A. M. Strange, and M. J. Tierney. 2017. 'Aid, China, and Growth: Evidence from a New Global Development Finance Dataset'. *AidData Working Paper No. 46*. https://doi.org/10.2139/ssrn.3051044

Goldin, I. 2016. *The Pursuit of Development: Economic Growth, Social Change, and Ideas*. New York: Oxford University Press.

GoSL, 2013. The Agenda for Prosperity - Road to Middle Income Status, Sierra Leone's Third Generation Poverty Reduction Strategy Paper 2013-2018.

Graves, C. 2015. 'Why Modernise Official Development Assistance?' *The OECD Observer* (303): 18. http://oecdobserver.org/news/fullstory.php/aid/4956/Why_modernise_official_development_assistance_.html

Hurley, J., S. Morris, and G. Portelance. 2018. 'Examining the Debt Implications of the Belt and Road Initiative from a Policy Perspective. *CGD Policy Paper, 121.*

IMF, 2013. Unification of Discount Rates Used in External Debt Analysis for Low-Income Countries, Policy Papers.

IMF African Dept, 2014. Sierra Leone : First Review Under the Extended Credit Facility Arrangement, Request for Modification of Performance Criteria, and Financing Assurances Review-Staff Report; and Press Release, Country Report No. 14/171.

IMF African Dept, 2016. Sierra Leone: 2016 Article IV Consultation and Fifth Review Under the Extended Credit Facility and Financing Assurances Review and Request for an Extension of the Extended Credit Facility-Press Release; Staff Report; and Statement by the Executive Director for Sierra Leone, Country Report No. 16/236.

Kodongo, O., and K. Ojah. 2016. 'Does Infrastructure Really Explain Economic Growth in Sub-Saharan Africa?' *Review of Development Finance* 6 (2): 105–125.

Love, D. 2018. 'China Threatens Sovereignty of Several African Nations as It Takes Over their Resources to Cover Debt'. *Atlanta Black Star*, September 16. https://atlantablackstar.com/2018/09/16/china-has-tightened-its-grip-on-africas-resources/

Lu, S. 2017. 'China's Role in South Sudan's Economic Development'. A-id: Agenda for International Development. http://www.a-id.org/2017/10/12/chinas-role-south-sudans-economic-development/

Lu, S. 2018. 'An Overview of China's International Development Finance: Issues and the Way Forward'. A-id: Agenda for International Development. http://www.a-id.org/wp-content/uploads/2018/10/aid-commentary-051018.pdf

Sahoo, P., and R. K. Dash. 2012. 'Economic Growth in South Asia: Role of Infrastructure. *The Journal of International Trade & Economic Development* 21 (2): 217–252.

The Economist. 2018. 'Increasing Debt in Many African Countries is a Cause for Worry. *The Economist*, March 8. https://www.economist.com/middle-east-and-africa/2018/03/08/increasing-debt-in-many-african-countries-is-a-cause-for-worry

Woetzel, J., N. Garemo, J. Mischke, P. Kamra, and R. Palter. 2017. 'Bridging Infrastructure Gaps. Has the World Made Progress?' *McKinsey & Company, 8.*

Yan, K. 2016. 'CNPC's South Suddan Dilemma'. *China Entrepreneur* (10): 57–61. http://www.cqvip.com/qk/94251x/201610/668865112.html

Chapter 8

Urban Development along the Belt and Road
A Case Study of North Africa

Chuchu Zhang and Chaowei Xiao

BACKGROUND

In recent years, driven by the Belt and Road Initiative (BRI), China has unprecedentedly engaged in global economic cooperation. In this process, many regions in Central Asia, West Asia and North Africa have become China's important economic partners. It should be noted that the historical development of these places has undergone several periods of serious disruption, and the urban development in these regions often shows a distinct feature of fragmentation, of which North Africa is the most typical case. An analysis of the background, process and features of urban development in North Africa provides new perspectives and important implications for China's current Belt and Road urban planning and infrastructure construction in the region.

EVOLUTION OF CITIES IN NORTH AFRICA

The evolution of cities in North Africa could be divided into five stages according to different historical periods: ancient Egypt and Carthage period (32nd century BC–2nd century BC), Roman and Byzantine period (2nd century BC–6th century AD), Arabian Empire and Ottoman period (7th century–18th century), European colonial period (19th century–mid-20th century) and the independence period (mid-20th century–21st century). In different historical stages, the impact of the collision between different cultures has affected the process of urban development in North Africa for thousands of years, thus leading the urban spatial structure and functional changes in the region to demonstrate different characteristics in the five historical stages.

Ancient Egypt and Carthage Period (32nd Century BC–2nd Century BC)

The Nile Valley, located in the east of North Africa, is one of the important birthplaces of human civilization. As early as in 3,000 BC, the urban civilization rose in the Old Kingdom of Egypt (Ha 2010). Early Egyptian cities were built along the Nile, including Memphis, Thebes and Calhoun. Take Lahan as example, where the major cities of ancient Egypt were flat squares with complete brick walls. In ancient Egypt, totemism and nature worship were prevalent, so the temple became the centre of the early Egyptian city. At the east side of the city was a bazaar, while the southeast corner was a large cemetery. Residential areas were located in the central and western parts of the city. Due to the distinct hierarchy of ancient Egypt, royal aristocrats and monks lived in deep-occupied courtyards facing south to the north, while the humble slaves lived in a narrow space facing the desert, and the space between the aristocrats and the slaves was the freeman's zone.

Around the 12th century BC, Tyre, the most powerful Phoenician city-state in the eastern Mediterranean, was colonizing along the Mediterranean Sea to the west. They set up temporary moorings in promontories and islands on the western coasts of North Africa, which gradually developed into settlements. The oldest city established by Punics (an ethnic group emerged from intermarriage between the Phoenicians and Berbers) in North Africa was Utica (Fage 1978), and the largest city was the well-known Carthage. As shown in Figure 8.1, Carthage was built between the salt marsh and the isthmus of Tunis,

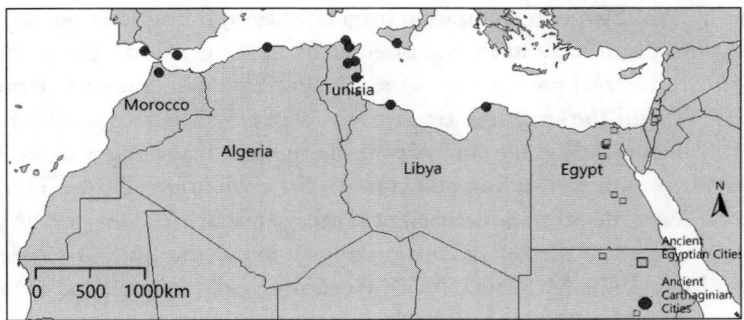

Figure 8.1 *City Layout in North Africa in the Ancient Egypt and Carthage Periods*
Source: The authors; data taken from Parragon (2010).

making it easy to hold but hard to attack. In the west end of the isthmus, the Punics built a three-story wall, which was connected by a vault, forming a huge fortress. Meanwhile, the Punics built artificial canals in the shoals along the northern coast as a fortification as well as lakes for the sake of merchant shipping and war shipping. The low hills at the south of the city was where the city centre was situated, known as Byrsa. The most important building in the city centre was the temple. North of the city centre was the outer city, which was mainly composed of residential areas. The residential buildings in Carthage were high, and the roads were narrow so that residents could lure the enemy into street fighting during the war. The city centre was surrounded by high walls, becoming 'the city in the city'. Such a layout was designed to enable residents in the outer city to move into the city centre to avoid wars.[1]

As shown in Figure 8.1, the cities in the Ancient Egypt and Carthage period followed certain principles in location selection. For instance, whereas most Ancient Egyptian cities were located along the Nile, cities in Carthage were mostly distributed along the coast of Tunis. As

---

[1] This information is taken from 'Encyclopedia of History' (online), s.v. 'Carthage', accessed August 23, 2017. http://www.daviddarling.info/encyclopedia_of_history/C/Carthage.html

the ancient Egyptian civilization originated from the agricultural civilization, the urbanization rate of Ancient Egypt is relatively low. By 350 BC, the total population of the Ancient Egyptian cities was about 200,000 and the urbanization rate was about 5.55 per cent (Depew 2000; Dunn 2011). By comparison, there were many more cities in Carthage with well-developed commercial civilization. By the Third Punic War, the urban population of Carthage reached 700,000, exceeding one-fifth of the total Carthage population at the time (McEvery and Jones 1978; McKenna 2011). Regarding city planning and management, although the Ancient Egyptian and Carthage cities showed the early traces of city planning such as functional zoning of the city, a complete planning system was hardly formed, and there were no consistent principles to unify the urban planning of different cities.

Roman and Byzantine Periods (2nd Century BC–6th Century AD)

From 264 BC to 146 BC, the Punics and Romans in the northern shore of the Mediterranean launched wars that lasted for centuries, which ended with the victory of the latter. The Maghreb region was subsequently included in the territory of the Roman Republic. Around the same time, General Ptolemy I of Alexander the Great of Macedonia established the Ptolemy Dynasty in Egypt. Until 30 BC, Octavian repealed the Egyptian Queen of Cleopatra VII and annexed Egypt as a Roman province.

The Roman invasion greatly changed the population composition and spatial structure of North African cities. First, Rome's policy of immigration to North Africa changed the composition of the urban population in the region. To ease the conflict between the large population and insufficient land in Italy, especially in Rome, and to ease the placement of veterans, Caesar and Augustus both pursued policies of large-scale immigration to North Africa. Around 80,000 immigrants moved to North Africa from Italy during this period (McKenna 2011). Meanwhile, as shown in Figure 8.2, the number of cities in North Africa greatly increased during the Roman Empire period. In addition to the previous cities at the Nile River basin and the coast of Tunisia, many new cities were built along the coastal areas of Algeria, Morocco and Libya,

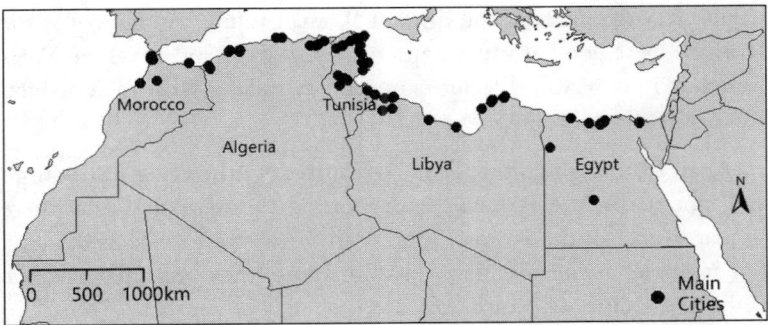

Figure 8.2 *Distribution of Cities in North Africa under the Roman Reign*
Source: The authors; data is taken from Parragon (2010).

and a small number of inland cities were built in Tunisia and Egypt. Meanwhile, the functions of the city were greatly expanded, and most cities had multiple functions including military, political, economic and cultural functions. In terms of urban form and spatial structure, it is worth noting that the cities designed by Romans were characterized by luxury and majesty. The ancient Romans changed the characteristics of the narrow open space of Carthage in the past. The city's new layout was more open and the architecture was grander. The city built by Romans usually used two crossroads as urban arterial roads. The auxiliary roads that extended around were straight and tidy (Graham 1902). An important landmark of the city was the rectangular square in the city centre, and the square and the monument formed an orientation axis (Kostof 1999). The square was embraced by tall colonnades, forming a three-dimensional open space, and was surrounded by large public buildings such as Roman temples, city halls, theatres, amphitheatres, libraries and public baths. The outskirts of the city were shops, workshops and private houses. When the Romans ruled North Africa, they brought their beliefs into the region. After the birth of Christianity, the temples were gradually replaced by churches. It is worth noting that as the Romans considered politics, culture and military as the main functions of the city, they did not set up temples and churches in the centre, but on the edge of the city (Guidobaldi 2000), which also reflected secular characteristics at the time of Roman ruling. Additionally, the Romans were good at water conservancy projects and developed brilliant water conservancy facilities in the city such as Roman aqueducts and sewers (Naylor 2015).

Apart from highlighting Roman features in urban spatial structures and landmarks, the Romans endeavoured to create an atmosphere similar to that of the Roman Empire in the abstract space of the city. For instance, ancient Romans loved bathing, they built many public baths in the cities of North Africa.

During Roman ruling, the Romans transplanted the planning system of Rome to North Africa. Not only were the spatial structure and public service facilities of major cities in Roman-ruled areas highly consistent, but the government also had strict requirements for road width and block size. For example, the width of roads in major cities must be greater than 2.9 meters (Tan 2005) and the single block size was approximately 120 × 240 Roman feet (LeGates and Stout 1998). In terms of city management, cities had much autonomy.

Compared with the Carthage period, the urban population of the North African region during the Roman reign slightly increased, but urbanization rate did not grow significantly. According to data, in 100 AD, the urban population in North Africa was about 1.02 million, and the urbanization rate was 18.9 per cent (Scheidel 2007).

Arabian Empire and Ottoman Empire (7th Century-18th Century)

In 639 AD, the general of the Arab empire, Amr ibn al-'As led troops to Egypt. From then on, large numbers of Arabs moved westward, which changed the population composition of North African cities. The Arab population exceeded the Berbers and Romans in North Africa and became the dominant ethnic group. In this period, the North African region underwent the Arabization and Islamization process.

Influenced by the integration of politics and religion in the Arab Empire, religion became an important function of North African cities.

Although the Arabs inherited the walls and moats that played a defensive role in the cities of North Africa during Roman reign, they greatly changed the original urban spatial structure. First, the orientation of the city's buildings were changed, and most buildings were oriented towards Mecca. Second, all cities have a mosque at their centre, surrounded by bazaars, religious schools, public baths and other public buildings. The Arabs attached importance to privacy, so there was a clear demarcation between the public space and the private realm. The private realm was generally located on the edge of the city, where the streets were narrowly stretched, and there were more end-of-roads to protect the privacy of residential areas. The houses of Arabs were mostly deep dwellings surrounded by high walls. The central courtyard usually had a pool which allowed Muslims to perform ritual purification before worship.

As shown in Figure 8.3, major cities in North Africa were mainly distributed along the Mediterranean in this period. Meanwhile, the urban population in the region also increased significantly. At the beginning of the 19th century, on the eve of the fall of North Africa into a European colony and protectorate, the urban population of the region reached 1.95 million, which was twice of what it was in the 1st century AD. However, during the Arab and Ottoman periods, four-fifths of the

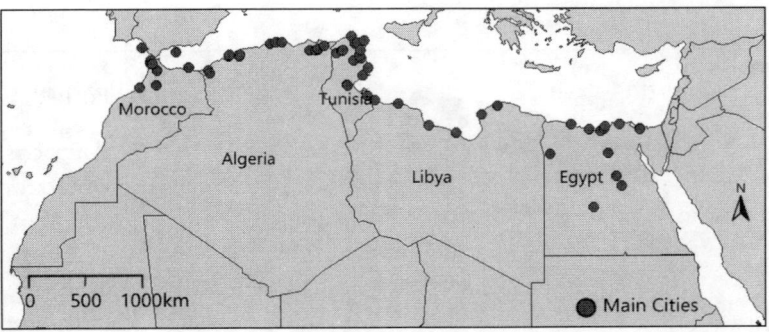

Figure 8.3 *City Distribution in North Africa during Arabian and Ottoman Ruling*

Source: The authors; data is taken from Parragon (2010).

North African population still lived in rural areas (McEvery and Jones 1978; Saoud 2004).

European Colonial Period (19th Century–mid-20th Century)

As North Africa is located at the border of Asia and Africa, and connects the Mediterranean and southern Africa, it became an important hub for western European colonists to expand in Asia and Africa due to the opening of a new sea route. In 1830, Algeria became a French colony. Tunisia and Egypt later became the protectorates of France and Britain; Libya became an Italian colony; and coastal areas in northern Morocco were controlled by Spain while the remaining regions were seized by France.

Europeans' infiltration of North Africa was accompanied by significant population movements. By mid-20th century, French colonists accounted for about 6–10 per cent of the population of Tunisia, Algeria and Morocco. Italian colonists once occupied 16 per cent of the population of Libya (Brown 1973), and most settlers settled in cities in North Africa. Consequently, the number of cities in North Africa increased (Figure 8.4), and the size of cities was enlarged significantly. Since European immigrants were unwilling and unable to be integrated into the original Arab urban society, European colonial authorities established

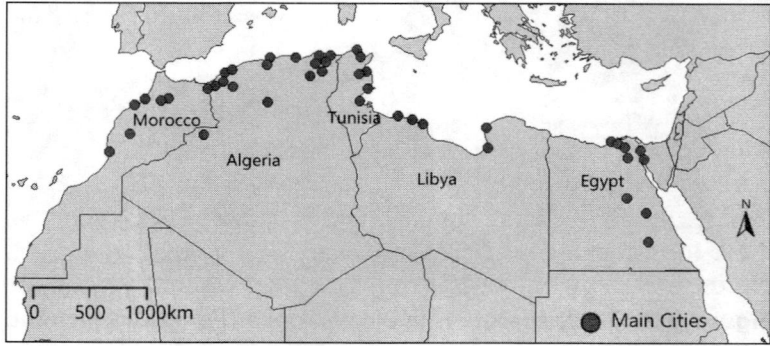

Figure 8.4 *City Distribution in North Africa during the Colonial Era*
Source: The authors; data is taken from Parragon (2010).

a new town next to the Arab old city as a colonists' place of residence and the city's trade and service centre (Findlay and Paddison 1986). Therefore, modern cities such as Casablanca, Tunisia, Algiers, Tripoli and Cairo in North Africa all have the old city (*medina*) and the new city (*ville nouvelle*). The Europeans demolished the original walls of the old city of North Africa and built roads between the new city and the old city for easy access. French and Italians set up circular, radial or grid-shaped streets in the new city and transplanted the European street layout and architectural styles to North Africa. For example, at the beginning of the 20th century, the layout of the main street in the new city of Tunis, Jules Ferry Street, imitated that of Parisian Champs-Elysées, and both sides of the street were filled with western-style cafes, western restaurants, clothing stores and perfume stores. This east–west main road ran through the centre of the capital. Like the Champs-Elysées Street which had the Place de la Concorde at its east end and Charles de Gaulle Square and the Arc de Triomphe at the western end, Jules Ferry Street had an independent square located at its western end and Victory Square and arched French gates at the eastern end.

To create a Western-style cultural atmosphere and create a European city image, European colonists established theatres, public gardens, indoor food markets and churches in North African cities, and Western architectural style such as the Baroque revival style.

Compared to the urban planning and management of the former Romans, Arabs and Ottomans, the European colonists introduced the institutional framework of modern Western urban planning to North Africa, but its negative impact was that planning was often used as a tool by European decision-makers to safeguard the assets and interests of the colonists. This system not only excluded local stakeholders from participating in urban planning and management but also prevented local residents from living in neat and orderly new cities, resulting in the residential separation between Arabs and Europeans (Loyal 2009). On the other hand, Europeans paid attention to the planning of the urban system. For example, French colonists built a national highway (No. 5) across the northern and eastern coasts in Algeria to facilitate transportation between Algiers, Setif, and Constantine. Meanwhile, the French built small and medium-sized towns along the national highways as regional hubs between rural dwellings and large cities (Silva 2016).

The urbanization in North Africa during the colonial period was accelerated, which was on one hand attributed to the colonists' policy of vigorously developing towns and cities, and on the other hand to the fact that large amount of the farmers and pastoralists' land in the colonial time was plundered by colonialists. During the later period of the colonial era, a forced zoning plan was adopted. Some of the inhabitants living in remote areas such as the Oran Mountainous Region were relocated to new towns, forcing farmers and herdsmen in the mountains to abandon their traditional production methods and lifestyle but to get adapted to new economic activities and urban lifestyle. By the end of the colonial rule in the mid-20th century, the population of North African cities had reached 12.806 million, an increase of 556.7 per cent compared to the 19th century (Silva 2016). However, as feudal relations still dominated the broad rural areas and the liberation of rural labour was limited, the progress of urbanization in Algeria was slow. In 1950, the urbanization rate in North Africa was 26 per cent, an increase of 6 percentage points compared with 1800 (Silva 2016).

Independence Period (Mid-20th Century to the Present)

After the Second World War, the North African nationalist movement reached its climax and many Europeans withdrew from North Africa. After independence, North African countries including Egypt, Libya, Algeria, Tunisia and Morocco implemented decolonization policies. In the process of reshaping urban representational and abstract space, monument statues of martyrs (such as Maqam Echahid in Algiers) and the presidents (such as Bourguiba statue in Tunis and Nasser Half statue in Cairo) were built and the National Day was set up to commemorate the war of independence and national liberation. On the other hand, in many areas of the city, especially the new city area, the European urban architecture and layout features of the colonial period were preserved, which meant that both Arab elements and European elements could be found in today's North African cities.

In the Early days after independence, North African countries launched economic reforms. The implementation of nationalization, industrialization and land reform policy profoundly changed the social order, which accelerated the urbanization process of North Africa. Oil-rich countries such as Algeria and Libya used oil revenues to expand the scale of the city, improve public service facilities and encourage the immigration of the rural population to the city to provide labour forces to the growth of urban industry. The North African governments expanded the colonial towns into medium-sized cities. Meanwhile, North African countries after independence attempted to develop capitals like Algiers, Tunis and Tripoli into international metropolis, so they expanded the scale of these cities and improved their infrastructure. As parliament, the presidential palace, mosques, commercial streets, sports venues and universities were widely set up in different areas of the capital, the capital cities demonstrated the trend of integrating multiple functions such as economic, political, religious, and cultural together. Additionally, after independence, North African governments retained the original functions of the city centre and broke the previous racial segregation, embedding the old city into the new urban profile. Many Arab political elites moved to the city centre previously occupied by Europeans. Typical urban spatial structures in this region also changed from a dual centre structure of new town and old town before independence to multiple centre structure with new political, religious and cultural centres, colonial new towns and old towns coexisting with each other. Furthermore, to adapt to the needs of population growth and economic development, governments included the original city suburbs into the range of the city and established many satellite towns around big cities (Silva 2016). Hence, North African countries now have a cluster of cities centred on the capital and large cities (Figure 8.5). Three satellite cities have been formed over the past five decades around Cairo including 6 October City, 15 May City, and El Obour. In 2010, the urban population of North Africa reached 100.776 million, and the urbanization rate of the North African countries rose to 50.5 per cent from 26 per cent in 1950 (Silva 2016).

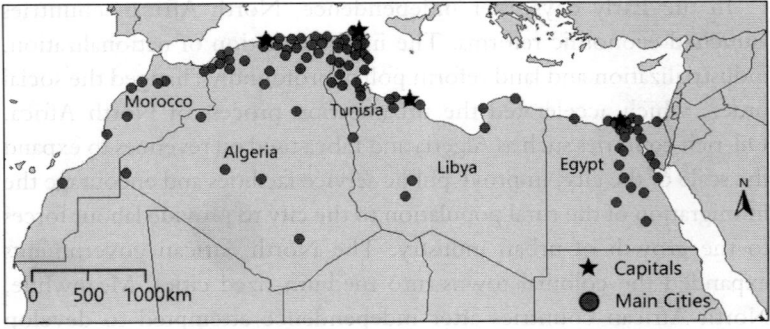

Figure 8.5 City Distribution in North Africa after Independence
Source: The authors; data is taken from Parragon (2010).

EVOLVEMENT OF URBAN SPATIAL STRUCTURE AND FUNCTION IN NORTH AFRICA UNDER THE BACKGROUND OF CULTURAL COLLISION

In sum, as shown in Table 8.1, the evolution of North African cities has encapsulated the periods of ancient Egypt and Carthage, Roman and Byzantine rule, Arabian Empire and Ottoman Empire, European colonization and independence. At different stages, cities in the region were featured by different characteristics in terms of urban population composition, urban functions, urban spatial structure, urban abstract space, urban development planning and management system.

Nietzsche (1998) stated, 'Architecture is a kind of power-eloquence in forms'. The history of multiple invasions by different ethnic groups and the collisions of multi-civilizations had an important impact on the current urban spatial structure and function in North Africa. First, at the physical space level of the city, the spatial structure of North African cities embodies multiple civilized characteristics, as the historical conquerors transformed the conquered cities according to their own urban layout and architectural style. Hence, the contemporary urban spatial structure of the region is characterized by a multi-centre structure in which new cities built in the colonial time and after the independence and old cities created in the Arab and Ottoman periods co-existed. Also, the characteristics in different stages of urban layouts intertwined with each other.

Table 8.1 Historical Evolvement of Cities in North Africa

Period	Time	Population Structure	Major City Functions	Urban Spatial Structure	Major Landmarks	System Evolvement of Urban Planning & Management	Urban Population	Urbanization Rate (%)
Ancient Egypt and Carthage Periods	Ancient Egyptian: 32nd century BC to 4th century BC; Carthage: 5th century BC to 2nd century BC	Ancient Egypt: Ancient Egyptians; Carthage: The Punics	Economic and religious functions	Religious temples located in the centre of the city; Cities were small in scale and had high density; Streets were narrow	Square, temple, trading market	Urban functional zoning appeared; Planning management system was hardly formed	Ancient Egypt: 200,000 (about 350 BC); Carthage: 700,000 (about 140 BC)	Ancient Egypt: 5.55; Carthage: 21.2

(Table 8.1 continued)

(Table 8.1 continued)

Period	Time	Population Structure	Major City Functions	Urban Spatial Structure	Major Landmarks	System Evolvement of Urban Planning & Management	Urban Population	Urbanization Rate (%)
Roman and Byzantine Periods	2nd century BC–6th century AD	Large numbers of Romans migrated to North Africa	Political, military and cultural functions	The city had squared walls and broad and crisscrossed main roads; The city centred around the square, which was surrounded by shops and manual workshops; Temples (early) and churches (late) are located on the edge of the city.	Squares, temples, arenas, public baths, theatres, aqueducts	The Romans transplanted the planning system and model of Rome to North Africa. There were strict rules for road width and block size.	1.02 million (about 100 AD)	18.9

| Arab Empire and Ottoman Empire Periods | 7th century–18th century | Westward Arab immigrants became the majority ethnic group | Religious and political functions | The building was facing Mecca; The city centred around a mosque; There was a clear demarcation between public and private areas; Streets were narrow | Mosques, religious schools, public baths, bazaars | Arab and Ottoman City Management Acts and Judicial Systems were implemented; The central government negotiates with local aristocrats to decide on the planning of large-scale projects, urban land use, urban public service facilities and public space planning | 1.95 million (1800) | 20 |

(Table 8.1 continued)

(Table 8.1 continued)

Period	Time	Population Structure	Major City Functions	Urban Spatial Structure	Major Landmarks	System Evolvement of Urban Planning & Management	Urban Population	Urbanization Rate (%)
European Colonization Period	19th century–mid-20th century	Abundant European colonizers flooding into North Africa	Economic function	The dual-centre structure of the old Arab city and the colonial new city; The road network was a combination of square grids and circular radial structure	Church, theatre, public garden, food market	The European colonialists introduced Western urban planning concepts and institutional frameworks to North Africa. They focused on the planning of urban systems and implemented zoning plans.	12.806 million (1950)	26

| Independence Period | Mid-20th century–21st century | Abundant European colonizers retreating from North Africa; The proportion of Arabs increased significantly | Economic, cultural, religious and political functions | The urban spatial structure of major cities has evolved from a dual centre to a multi-centre structure | Martyrs monument, presidential statue, parliament, mosque | The government has formulated new urban development plans in an attempt to break racial the segregation, but has not included citizens in urban decision-making. | 100.776 50.5 million |

Source: The authors.

Second, at the level of abstract space, when different civilizations entered North Africa, they used their own language as the official language in the conquered region and changed the abstract spatial structure of these cities through religious and cultural outputs in order to achieve the goal of cultural assimilation. For example, Bourguiba Street in Tunis is known by local residents as Avenue Habib Bourguiba. Avenue is French, and Habib Bourguiba is the Arabic name of the first president of post-independent Tunisia. Both sides of the road retained the French style layout, and the Saint Vincent de Paul Cathedral has been preserved; but not far from the church stands the statue of Ibn Kaldoun, a famous medieval Arab Muslim scholar.

Third, as North Africa underwent the Islamization process after the Arabs entered the region in the 7th century, Islam plays an important role in contemporary urban development and urban life in the region. Today, preserving Islamic architectures and building new religious buildings are among the key tasks of urban planning and development in North Africa.

Fourth, as contemporary capital cities in the region have absorbed resources from all parts of the country, there has been a huge difference in the development speed between capital cities and small cities.

DISTRIBUTION AND CHALLENGES OF CHINA'S CURRENT BELT AND ROAD URBAN PLANNING AND INFRASTRUCTURE CONSTRUCTION IN NORTH AFRICA

According to the data of IntelTrak, the first visual analytic tool that maps Chinese global business developed by RWR Advisory Group, infrastructure, construction, transportation and real estate account for 69.6 per cent ($99,523,916,850 out of $142,989,416,850) of Chinese investment in Egypt, Libya, Tunisia, Algeria, and Morocco. However, there are a number of challenges that need to be addressed by Chinese enterprises when engaging in urban planning and infrastructure construction in North Africa.

First, how to strike a balance between the preservation of cultural heritage and urban development poses an important challenge for urban planning and infrastructure construction in North Africa. What makes the maintenance of continuity and compatibility in North Africa more complicated is that cities in this region contain mixed cultural heritages ranging from Roman relics to European cultural elements, due to entry of different civilizations into the region in history. As demonstrated in Table 8.1, districts constructed in different historical periods in the same cities may be characterized by completely different spatial structures and landmarks. For instance, the road width and building height in *medina* vary greatly from those in Avenue Habib Bourguiba in Tunis. Hence, when conducting urban planning and infrastructure projects in North African cities, it is important to ensure that new buildings are compatible with old ones in terms of the architectural standards, scales, styles, building facades, volume ratio and building backs in specific districts.

Second, as North Africa is characterized by cultural diversity, and as the architecture and infrastructure in the region has been influenced by various cultures, the region adopts diverse building construction standards and involve experts from various countries to participate in the construction of major projects. Consequently, when engaging in North African construction projects, an important difficulty for Chinese developers and engineers is to adapt to different construction standards and fit Chinese standards into them, as well as cooperate with experts who come from different countries and speak different languages. For instance, when cutting through the Gantas railway tunnel, a critical part of the railway between Oran and Algiers, the China Railway Construction Corporation Limited (CRCC) needed to adapt to a number of standards including the International Union of Railways (UIC) Standard, Euro Code, French National Standard, and Algerian design and technical standards (People Rail 2017). Meanwhile, the CRCC also faced language difficulties as it needed to cooperate with experts, engineers and skilled workers who speak French, Arabic and Algerian dialect (Darja) (*Sina News* 2017). To better adapt to the construction environment in North Africa, Chinese enterprises should hire more multilingual workers and professionals, enhance understanding of various construction standards, and balance between Chinese construction standards and other standards.

Third, as Islam dominates the demography in North Africa, and as religious architectures constitute important parts of the construction projects, Chinese enterprises need to adapt to and get accustomed to the specific construction requirements of religious architecture projects which have complex and strict demands for materials and styles. For instance, when China State Construction Engineering Corporation (CSCEC) constructed the Mohammadia Mega Mosque including a 265-meter-high minaret in Algiers, it faced a great number of technical difficulties, such as super high level formwork system, extra-long steel bar installation system, and adapting to high strength concrete pumps (*Huanqiu* 2017). To enlarge access to the North African market, Chinese enterprises needs to enhance understanding about the specific construction standards, materials and styles of religious architectures including vaultings, minarets and domes.

Fourth, many cities in North Africa face the problem of over urbanization. If planning efforts are not sufficient to cope with the influx of new inhabitants, rapidly increasing population density can lead to serious problems including widespread poverty. Take the case of Greater Cairo, one of the most over urbanized cities in North Africa, as an example. The city has a population of 14–15 million inhabitants, accounting for almost a quarter of Egypt's population of 67 million residents (Sims 2003, 3). Among Cairo's city dwellers, at least two-thirds (10.7 million) are currently living in slums (Sabry 2009, vii) which are featured by poor and unsanitary conditions without electricity, heating, sewage and healthcare system (*Middle East Eye* 2015). What is worse, the slum population has been growing faster than the city's population. Such a rapid expansion of slums in large cities exacerbates socio-economic disparities, and the harsh living conditions of slums facilitate the spread of disease. This situation calls for Chinese developers and engineers to help local governments reduce over urbanization by accelerating the urban planning and construction speed, promoting slum reconstruction and constructing satellite cities to distract populations from the metropolitan centres.

CONCLUSION

Overall, exploring the multiple historical and humanistic changes in North African cities and their imprints on the urban physical space and abstract space is of great significance to the development of transnational economic initiatives such as the BRI. When Chinese companies participate in local planning and construction, a problem that often occurs is that they do not understand the differences in spatial structure, scale, density, style, etc., in different regions, cities and neighbourhoods, which have led to a significant increase in late-stage costs. Therefore, regarding the urban infrastructure construction in North Africa, specific problems need to be specifically analysed, and the local history, religion and culture should be fully respected. It is thus necessary to handle and integrate local and functional architectures from different times and develop urban planning and development projects. Such an approach should keep in accordance with local features on the basis of protecting historical and cultural buildings, achieve organic integration between history and modernity, enhancing experience in constructing religious architectures, and help local cities overcome problems in urban development like over urbanization. By doing so, the integration process can enhance cultural integration and mutual complementation, reduce conflict friction and help investment-target countries achieve organic integration of urban multiculturalism, creating a balance between urban development and the preservation of cultural heritage.

REFERENCES

Brown, L. 1973. 'The Many Faces of Colonial Rule in French North Africa'. *Revue de l'Occident Musulman et de la Méditerranée* 13 (1): 171–191.
Depew, M., and D. Obbink. 2000. *Matrices of Genre: Authors, Canons, and Society.* Cambridge: Harvard University Press.
Dunn, J. 2011. *An Overview of the Cities and Towns of Ancient Egypt.* Touregypt.net http://www.touregypt.net/featurestories/cities.htm
Fage, J. 1978. *The Cambridge History of Africa c.500.B.C.–A.D.1050.* Cambridge: Cambridge University Press.
Findlay, A., and R. Paddison. 1986. Planning the Arab City: The Cases of Tunis and Rabat. *Progress in planning* 26: 1–82.
Graham, A. 1902. *Roman Africa: An Outline of the History of the Roman Occupation of North Africa.* London; New York and Bombay: Longmans, Green, and Co.
Guidobaldi, F. 2000. 'Architettura e Arredo Delle Domus Tardoantiche' [Architecture and Furniture of the Late Roman Domus]. In *Aurea Roma: Dalla città pagana alla città Cristiana* [Aurea Roma: From the Pagan City to the Christian City], edited by Serena Ensoli and Eugenio La Rocca. Rome: L'Erma di Bretschneider.
Ha, Q. 2010. *Middle East History 610–2000.* Tianjin: Tianjin People's Publisher.

Huanqiu. 2017, January 19. *The Highest Architecture in Africa is Constructed by A Chinese Enterprise*.
Kostof, S. 1999. *The City Assembled: The Elements of Urban from through History*. London: Thames and Hudson.
LeGates, R., and F. Stout. 1998. *Early Urban Planning*. London: Routledge.
Loyal, S. 2009. The French in Algeria, Algerians in France: Bourdieu, Colonialism and Migration. *The Sociological Review* 57 (3): 406–427.
McEvery, C., and R. Jones. 1978. *Atlas of World Population History*. Harmondsworth: Penguin Books Ltd.
McKenna, A. 2011. *The History of Northern Africa*. New York: Britannica Educational Publishing.
Middle East Eye. 2015, September 4. *Life in the Slums of Cairo*. https://www.middleeasteye.net/in-depth/features/cairo-part-world-slums-180211194
Naylor, P. 2015. *Historical Dictionary of Algeria*. Lanham: Rowman & Littlefield.
Nietzsche, F. 1998. *Twilight of the Idols*. New York: Oxford University Press.
Parragon. 2010. *Historical Atlas of the World*. Parragon Inc.
People Rail. 2017, November 1. 'Memo of Constructing Algeria's Longest Tunnel by the China Railway Construction Corporation Limited'. http://www.peoplerail.com/rail/show-456-355739-1.html
Sabry, S. 2009. 'Poverty Lines in Greater Cairo: Underestimating and Misrepresenting Poverty'. Working Paper for International Institute for Environment and Development. http://pubs.iied.org/pdfs/10572IIED.pdf
Saoud, R. 2004. 'The Impact of Islam on Urban Development in North Africa'. Foundation for Science Technology and Civilisation, Manchester, UK. http://www.muslimheritage.com/uploads/naurban.pdf
Scheidel, W. 2007. Roman Population Size: The Logic of the Debate. In *People, Land, and Politics: Demographic Developments and the Transformation of Roman Italy, 300 BC-AD 14*, edited by Luuk de Ligt and S. J. Northwood, 1–17. Leiden and Boston: Brill.
Silva, C. 2016. *Urban Planning in North Africa*. Oxon: Ashgate Publishing.
Sims, D. 2003. 'The Case of Cairo, Egypt'. *Understanding Slums: Case Studies for the Global Report on Human Settlements*. https://www.ucl.ac.uk/dpu-projects/Global_Report/pdfs/Cairo.pdf
Sina News. 2017, October 30. 'The Longest Tunnel of North Africa Known as "Disaster of Geoengineers" Was Established by a Chinese Enterprise'. http://news.sina.com.cn/o/2017-10-30/doc-ifynfrfn0465436.shtml
Tan, Z. 2005. *Urban Planning*. Beijing: Tsinghua University Press.

Chapter 9

Developing Effective Cross-Cultural Negotiations
The Case of the 'Belt and Road Initiative' for Turkey and China

Mustafa Gokhan Bitmis and Jack McGuire

The Belt and Road Initiative (BRI)—the name of which alludes to the historic Silk Roads dating back to the Han Dynasty (Hung and Chan 2019; Magri 2017)—is an extensive network of maritime and land routes for trade, communication and cultural exchanges, which connects China with countries based in Asia, the Middle East, Africa and Europe (Yu 2017). This initiative by China, which includes the Silk Road Economic Belt and the 21st Century Maritime Silk Road, was introduced with the aim to develop a globally oriented developmental strategy for the economic integration of China with the rest of the world. Furthermore, the high level of international political cooperation between BRI countries and governmental support needed in the BRI process may generate synergies between member countries and significantly decrease a BRI country's economic uncertainty and political risks, which in turn stimulates investment in this country (Du and Zhang 2018). Thus, the BRI does have aspirational objectives, such as the focus on mutual benefit and creating a 'win-win' scenario for all of its members.

Some countries such as India and Japan have doubts over this China-led initiative, as the initiative can potentially change the existing power dynamics and security architecture in the region, in which India and Japan have strategic interests (Baruah 2018). Although such countries are sceptical and have some doubts about the BRI with regards to transparency, trust, security concerns and conflicting strategic interests, many countries such as Italy—potentially the BRI's first G7 member country—have shown their intention of joining this project and helping to define the standards it should uphold. The BRI aims to connect more than 65 countries along the ancient Silk Roads through infrastructure projects. However, the BRI is not only concerned with infrastructure but also strives to promote policy coordination, enhance trade and financial integration and foster people-to-people bonds, emphasizing cooperation and 'togetherness' between China and the other countries involved in this initiative (Hu 2017). The list of member countries in the BRI accounts for 64 per cent of the world's population and 30 per cent of the world's GDP (Hu 2017). Such an initiative, which involves this number of countries that differ greatly with respect to social norms, cultural values and political orientation, requires a high level of cooperation, diplomacy, consensus and trust building between countries. In other words, the BRI requires the settlement of agreements between countries that may differ greatly to one another, but also in cases share similarities with, in terms of cultural background. For instance, many countries, such as Italy, Czech Republic, Pakistan, Spain, Indonesia, Argentina, Russia, Poland, Fiji, Vietnam, Turkey, and so on, attended a Joint Communique of the Leaders Roundtable of the Belt and Road Forum for International Cooperation in China in 2017. Collectively, these countries share vast differences as well as similarities. Therefore, underpinning the success of forming deals between these countries, for instance, at forums and platforms of this kind, will be the strategies that are used for negotiating them in a cross-cultural context.

It should be noted that although there are some similarities between belt and road countries, the BRI today should unite countries that may differ culturally from one another if the creation of economic and strategic partnerships will take place. Therefore, due to some cultural differences between BRI countries, cross-cultural negotiation is needed in order to reduce conflict and effectively manage future deals by promoting cooperation between the participating countries. One particularly important example of the effective cross-cultural negotiation in the BRI is the case of Turkey and China's negotiation strategies for BRI agreements.

Turkey has shown support for the BRI from its beginning and the presence of Turkey in the BRI is critical to its success. The reason for this is that Turkey holds a strategic geographical position, has close cultural ties with many BRI countries, and has a well-developed transportation network including railways, airports, seaports and so forth. For instance, Istanbul Airport, which is a key player in the global aviation sector, is expected to become one of the world's busiest airports. Turkey has also supported many grand investment projects (e.g. Republic of Turkey, Ministry of Transport and Infrastructure [MTI] 2018) These include the following:

- Edirne–Kars High Speed Railway that connects Turkey's east to west
- The Eurasia Tunnel: a road tunnel crossing underneath the Bosphorus
- Marmaray: a tube tunnel passing under the Bosphorus, connecting Europe and Asia
- Halkali–Istanbul–Gebze railway line, which is a part of the Marmaray project to connect Turkey's European and Asian rail networks
- BTK (Baku–Tbilisi–Kars): a regional railway line, which connects Turkey, Georgia and Azerbaijan

These investments will facilitate Turkey's integration into global trade networks. In March, 2019, an international train connected Asia and Europe via the Marmaray Tunnel, beneath the Bosporus strait in Instanbul, for the first time signifying the role it can play in connecting the East and West. Furthermore, Turkey is also becoming a key energy hub within the region. TurkStream, which is a natural gas pipeline project running from Russia to Turkey via the Black Sea, can contribute to the supply of gas to European countries (e.g. Gazprom, 2018)

Taken together, these projects position Turkey as a crucial member country for the BRI.

Moreover, due to its strategic geographical position between Asia and Europe, Turkey provides a cost-effective economic corridor to major markets, which China would like to access through the BRI. The transportation of goods from China to Europe through Turkey will take only around 15 days (Fasulo and Talbot 2017). In comparison to the northern corridor of BRI, which takes approximately 45–62 days (Fasulo and Talbot 2017), the route via Turkey presents a much quicker option. Therefore, Chinese policymakers want to cooperate with Turkish counterparts in order to ensure that Turkey remains a key partner through the development process of the BRI.

In addition to the benefits China would receive from Turkey's BRI participation, the BRI also has the potential to strengthen Turkey's regional and global position. The BRI provides new markets, trade routes and investment opportunities for Turkey and can aid with diversifying Turkey's trading partners (Fasulo and Talbot 2017). It might also provide a debt financing tool for infrastructure development projects in Turkey, which are currently mostly denominated by hard currencies (AIIB 2019). These factors can be considered as critical benefits that the BRI is expected to provide to Turkey. However, it is also fair to note that Turkey's involvement in the BRI justifiably warrants some concerns as well. This involvement comes with some concerns on increasing Turkey's trade deficit. Nonetheless, given the critical importance of Turkey and China's relationship in the BRI, the question is: How will China and Turkey effectively negotiate with one another and reach agreements that are acceptable and satisfying to both parties?

INTERCULTURAL NEGOTIATION AS A FOUNDATION FOR THE SUCCESS OF THE BRI

Cross-cultural negotiation is a strategic competency for organizations that will help negotiators from both sides to obtain joint gains from the BRI. Weiss (1993, 270) defines international business negotiations as 'the deliberate interaction of two or more social units (at least one of them a business entity), originating from different nations, that are attempting to define or redefine their interdependence in a business matter'. Negotiations, whether international or not, share some common characteristics (Hofstede and Usunier 2003). For instance, negotiations take place when two or more parties have conflicting interests, but also share a zone of mutual agreement from which they can resolve their differences (Ogliastri and Quintanilla 2016). Some characteristics may vary based on the national negotiating styles of each party. This includes, but is not limited to, reasons for trusting or distrusting a negotiating counterpart, tolerance for ambiguity during the negotiation process, and decision-making style of the negotiating partners (Hofstede and Usunier 2003). Similar to this view, Richardson and Rammal (2018) emphasize the critical role of local context (e.g., culture) in determining the success of international negotiations. In other words, global negotiations bring culture to the forefront due to the impact cultural factors have on these negotiations (Stahley 2006). In other words, culture becomes a priority. Adair and Brett (2005) also emphasize the importance of cultural elements during negotiation processes by examining negotiations between low and high context negotiators. Similarly, Brett, Gunia, and Teucher (2017) also underscore the importance of national cultural differences when dealing with negotiation strategies. A lack of understanding and awareness of the cultures involved in a negotiation process can lead to a failed negotiation in international negotiations (Groves, Feyerherm, and Gu 2015). According to Tse, Francis, and Walls (1994), executives may try to adopt behavioural patterns similar to that of the other party when dealing with a negotiator from a different culture in order to increase bargaining outcomes. Furthermore, international companies evaluate the host countries' culture when making their investment decisions. Specifically, Buckley et al. (2007) emphasize cultural proximity as one of the important determinants of China's outward direct investment. Taken together, awareness of the negotiators culture emerges as a highly influential factor when determining whether a negotiation will take place and if the outcome is likely to be a successful one.

As an important factor when negotiating with people from different nations', culture that is derived from one's social environment can be defined as 'the collective programming of the mind that distinguishes the members of one group or category of people from others'

(Hofstede, Hofstede, and Minkov 2010, 6). Consequently, culture can also be thought of as a 'system of collectively held values' (Hofstede 1980). Although some critiques regarding the explanatory power of the model exist (e.g., Brett et al. 2017), Hofstede's model is one that is generally accepted in culture and negotiation research. According to Hofstede's typology, the values that distinguish cultures from one another can be categorized into six groups (Hofstede's 6D model): power distance (PDI), individualism versus collectivism (IDV), masculinity versus femininity (MAS), uncertainty avoidance (UAI), long-term orientation (LTO), and indulgence versus restraint (IND; Coene and Jacobs 2017).

In this chapter, it will be argued that understanding these cultural dimensions is critical to effectively managing international negotiations that take place in the BRI, such as those that take place between China and Turkey. Designing the BRI strategies and policies through a culture-aware lens will provide unique opportunities towards increasing cooperation on investment, trade, finance, tourism and education. Additionally, it will also aid in satisfying both parties' priorities and sensitivities, which will ultimately result with better negotiated agreements between Turkey and China for joint gains.

Hofstede et al. (2010) describes these dimensions as follows:

- *PDI*: It refers to how power is distributed within a society and in interpersonal relationships. In other words, it is related to the way a country is organized and views authority. A high-PDI country places greater importance on hierarchy. In this case, the decision-making is centralized in society. A low-PDI country conversely places less importance on hierarchy, and decision-making is more evenly distributed across society.
- *IDV*: It refers to a person's self-image in a society, which is defined as 'I' or 'we'. People from collectivistic cultures, who emphasize the importance of interdependence and group harmony, bring to the bargaining table a different set of attitudes and values than people from individualistic cultures, which emphasize the importance of independence and individual rights (Tse et al. 1994). Individualistic societies tend to pay more attention to the 'success'

of a deal or the contract that was obtained, over developing and maintaining relationships. Contrary to this, developing and maintaining relationships comes first in collectivistic societies.
- *MAS*: It shows the extent to which social gender roles are distinct in a society. While social gender roles overlap substantially in a society of femininity, masculine societies are generally more distinct and tend to be more competitive than feminine ones as status in these societies is typically gained through obtaining success.
- *UAI*: People in a society with high UAI take steps to avoid uncertainty. They need rules, precision and formalization when structuring their life as they feel more threatened by unknown factors. On the contrary, people with a low UAI score tend to have a more relaxed attitude.
- *LTO*: This is related to a society's search for virtue. More specifically, long-term oriented societies value virtues that contribute towards long-term rewards such as perseverance and thrift. Conversely, short-term oriented societies value virtues related to the past and offer respect for tradition and preservation of 'face'. As a business mindset, long-term oriented people value, for instance, the gains 20 years from now while the short-term oriented ones value current year's profits.
- *IND*: Finally, a high IND score reveals a tendency for indulgence of basic and natural human drives related to enjoying life and having fun. On the other hand, a low score (restraint) reveals a conviction that such gratification needs to be suppressed by strict social norms. A country with a high indulgence score pays attention to the importance of leisure. According to Hofstede, indulgence also explains the norm of smiling. Indulgent societies like smiling whereas a big smile offered towards a stranger may not be well received in restrained societies, since they evaluate a stern face as a noble sign of seriousness (Coene and Jacobs 2017; Hofstede et al. 2010).

In order to have success in international negotiations, negotiators need to interpret correctly the meaning of the behaviour of their counterpart and having an insight into their counterpart's cultural values will aid with this interpretation tremendously (Hofstede and Usunier 2003).

Coene and Jacobs (2017) stress the importance of using Hofstede's cultural dimensions when dealing with international negotiations. As a tool to help with this interpretation process, they have clustered countries based on the scores each country receives across the six dimensions of Hofstede's 6D model. By clustering the countries in this way, it becomes easier to discern and identify the specific negotiating behaviours of each unique cluster. For instance, they emphasize that countries placed in the same cluster as China negotiate in terms of repeating cycles of negotiation and re-negotiation (Coene and Jacobs 2017). It may be a common issue when dealing with Chinese negotiators in BRI-related meetings to believe you have agreed on a deal and can move onto the next stage, when in fact no such deal was made in the eyes of your Chinese counterparts. As a result, you both go back to the drawing board to begin the negotiation process once again. Pye (1982) referred to this specific negotiation style of China's as 'continuous negotiation'. Moreover, Chinese negotiators are more sensitive to relational aspects of negotiations such as maintaining long-term relationships with their counterparts (Lee, Yang, and Graham 2006). In other words, the goal of a negotiation for Chinese negotiators is not a signed contract, but the creation of a relationship between two parties and the essence of the deal is the relationship itself (Salacuse 1998). On the other hand, building a strong relationship with counterparts is also an important factor for Turkish negotiators as well; however, they place a lot of importance on details and specific contract terms in negotiations (e.g., Metcalf et al. 2007). Thus, understanding such unique cultural codes between Turkey and China can smoothen the negotiating process and help Turkish and Chinese negotiators to better understand each other's priorities, leading to greater connectivity between Turkey and China in terms of policy coordination and implementation. For example, such an effective understanding on one another may lead to a memorandum of understanding (MOU) during the BRI negotiation process.

A CROSS-CULTURAL COMPARISON OF TURKEY AND CHINA

In the following section, we will elaborate further on the cultural differences and similarities between China and Turkey. First, Figure 9.1

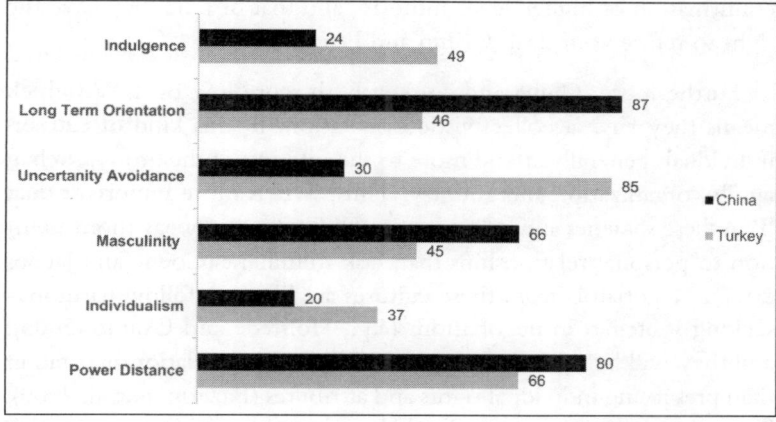

Figure 9.1 *Comparing Values for Turkey and China*
Source: Hofstede et al. (2010); ©Geert Hofstede B. V., quoted with permission.

provides the values for each dimension, through the lens of Hofstede's 6D model, with respect to both Turkey and China.

According to Figure 9.1, China and Turkey have both similarities and differences in terms of Hofstede's cultural dimensions. They both sit in the higher rankings of PDI, which means decision-making is generally centralized, individuals mostly rely on rules, and communication is indirect. Graham, Mintu, and Rodgers (1994) mention that cultures with high PDI can emphasize the importance of role relations in negotiations. It is also important to note that key negotiations have to be concluded by a top authority in high PDI cultures (Hofstede and Usunier 2003). According to the Griffin and Daggatt (1990), this situation results in a 'two bites at the apple' issue if the foreign negotiator (e.g., head of delegation) does not have authority to seal the deal and must send the deal to a final decision-maker, who is generally a higher level official, for approval. This situation can create an opportunity for the opposition to demand additional concessions, especially from the higher-level decision-maker, during this phase of the negotiation. While this can be a useful tactic, it should be kept in mind that such negotiators may not approve your deal before asking for the confirmation of higher-level authority and that or but? they have the right to refuse your deal (Griffin and Daggatt 1990).

Furthermore, China and Turkey both score low on IDV, which means they have a collectivistic orientation. In this kind of culture, individuals generally attend more to the interests of the group, such as family, organization and country. Thus, 'we' is more important than 'I' in these societies and collectivistic cultures generally pay more attention to personal relationships than task fulfilment (Coene and Jacobs 2017). Negotiators from these cultures are likely to follow harmony-seeking strategies in negotiations (e.g., Hofstede and Usunier 2003), and they will be more concerned with preserving relationships rather than preserving individual rights and attributes (Bazerman et al. 2000). Thus, time in these societies should be invested in building trust, which means that trust building will already have to take place in the pre-negotiation process of the BRI.

On the other hand, with a score of 66, China shows a masculine orientation that emphasizes 'success and competition'. Therefore, Chinese negotiators will probably sacrifice leisure arrangements to spend more time on working. However, compared to China, Turkey has a more feminine orientation, which indicates that some of the dominant values in this society are 'caring for others and quality of life'. Therefore, Turkish negotiators will probably be very sensitive and caring when it comes to dealing with people and environmental issues (e.g., supporting ecological sustainability), which the BRI's projects are expected to have positive implications for. For instance, in line with this cultural dimension, Turkey currently has an important role in hosting and caring for the largest refugee population in the world (World Bank 2015). Negotiations between the negotiators of two masculine cultures are usually more difficult than if at least one of the cultures is of feminine orientation (Hofstede and Usunier 2003). Therefore, Chinese and Turkish negotiators have an advantage when aiming to reach an agreement in BRI meetings that will result in joint gains.

Next, at a score of 30, China has a low score for UAI which shows that Chinese negotiators will be more comfortable with ambiguity. On the other hand, at a score of 85, Turkey scores high on this dimension. In other words, Turkish negotiators will have a negative attitude towards uncertainty, meaning that they will probably feel uncomfortable with unknown situations and unclear proposals during the BRI meetings. Thus, Chinese negotiators will need to use and communicate a clear message regarding the BRI in order to increase the zone of possible agreements (ZOPAs) with their Turkish counterparts. Turkey will be expecting a clear strategy and road map from their Chinese counterparts in the BRI, which is consistent with high UAI cultures.

Honour also can be considered an important element in the behaviour of Turkish negotiators. Research has shown that cultures in which honour plays an important element adopt a relatively more cooperative style of negotiation (Aslani et al. 2016). Chinese negotiators, on the other hand, are influenced by ideas rooted in Confucian values, such as moral cultivation and the importance of interpersonal relationships (e.g., Ghauri and Fang 2001; Warden and Chen 2009; Yan and Sorenson 2004;). Not surprisingly, China scores high on the LTO dimension and has a low score for indulgence, while Turkey reports the opposite trends for both dimensions (Turkey has a low LTO and a high indulgence score, when compared with China). Therefore, China has a pragmatic orientation, which means that Chinese negotiators will encourage thrift (e.g., availability of capital for the BRI's investment projects) and more easily adapt their behaviours and strategies based on the situation and context (e.g., Coene and Jacobs 2017). In addition to this, Chinese negotiators like perseverance and they will probably favour sustained efforts and policies (e.g., Hofstede et al. 2010) in the BRI meetings, which may not produce positive outcomes in the short run. In opposition to this, Turkish counterparts will pay more attention to time-honoured traditions and norms and they will be likely to favour decisions and policies that produce relatively quick results (e.g., Hofstede et al. 2010). Moreover, Turkish and Chinese negotiators should bear in mind that *the scripts* which are used in the BRI negotiation processes, in order to communicate with one another, should be complimentary so that both parties are able to obtain a result that is of the greatest mutual benefit. Thus, such a common script would enable them to easily perceive and decode culturally relevant information and adapt their negotiation behaviours accordingly during the various rounds of negotiation. Table 9.1 summarizes the similarities and

Table 9.1 Summary of the Similarities and Differences between Turkish and Chinese Negotiators Based on Hofstede's Cultural Dimensions

Dimensions	Prominent Similarity	Prominent Difference	Evaluation
Masculinity	–	Chinese negotiators are expected to have masculine orientation, and they probably exert competitive behaviours while Turkish counterparts will be emphasizing caring and cooperating behaviours.	Negotiators have an advantage as one of the party is of opposite orientation (e.g., masculine vs feminine).
Uncertainty Avoidance	–	Chinese negotiators are expected to have high tolerance for ambiguity, while Turkish counterparts probably will not prefer ambiguous and uncertain situations.	A clear strategy and road map needed to decrease uncertainty.
Indulgence	–	Chinese negotiators will likely exert more discipline while Turkish counterparts will prefer more personal freedom, and freely express their positive feelings during meetings.	A sensitive approach through positive and optimistic lens which emphasizes the importance of duty is needed to increase the possible zone of agreements.

(Table 9.1 continued)

(Table 9.1 continued)

Dimensions	Prominent Similarity	Prominent Difference	Evaluation
Long-Term Orientation	–	Chinese negotiators are very long-term oriented (e.g. Confucian values) and have a pragmatic culture while Turkish counterparts pay attention to time-honoured traditions and norms.	Chinese negotiators should come to the table with the deals that produce relatively quick results. Chinese negotiators will expect to build long term cooperation with their Turkish counterparts.
Power Distance	Chinese and Turkish negotiators place value on formal hierarchical structures Rank is critical for them.	–	Both negotiators can take the advantage of 'two bites at the apple' issue.
Individualism	Chinese and Turkish negotiators have collectivistic orientations.	–	Both negotiators pay attention to building trust and preserving relationships. Harmony-seeking strategies are needed for effective negotiations.

Source: The authors.

differences outlined between Turkish and Chinese negotiators, based on the aforementioned six key cultural dimensions.

In sum, Chinese and Turkish cultures are more similar in PDI and collectivism while they have differences in masculinity, UAI, indulgence and LTO. By evaluating the cultural similarities and differences between Turkey and China, a better understanding of how these countries should handle negotiations with each other during the BRI rounds is formed.

International business negotiations include three stages: pre-negotiation, negotiation and post-negotiation stages (e.g., Ghauri 2003). Such stages are affected by factors such as culture and strategy (Ghauri and Fang 2001). The next section of this chapter will analyse the BRI negotiation processes between Turkey and China by taking into consideration the cultural differences and similarities that exist between these two countries and the significance these will serve when going through these three critical stages of international business negotiations.

PRE-NEGOTIATION STAGE OF THE BRI

Before any steps are taken into the negotiation process itself, the first stage of international business negotiations relates to establishing early contacts and constructing diplomacy channels, which includes lobbying, presentations, informal discussion and trust building. By doing this, it enables negotiators to get to know each other better and understand their priorities (Ghauri and Fang 2001). First impressions and the nature of your first meeting is crucial as the quality of this contact is likely to determine the quality of the relationship you share in your future negotiations (e.g., Coene and Jacobs 2017). Lobbying channels, which includes visits to government authorities, effective presentations, advertising in national newspapers and business journals, and informal channels such as joining dinner events with the BRI negotiators, will contribute to the development of personal relationships which are vital for collectivistic cultures, as was previously touched upon. Doing so would enable the negotiators of these two countries to enhance the ZOPAs during the negotiation rounds (e.g., Ghauri and Fang 2001).

It can be observed that Turkish and Chinese officials have frequently visited each other in order to increase cooperation between their countries in the last decade. These kinds of visits are important in order to understand the priorities of each side for the pre-negotiation stage of the BRI. It should be noted that understanding the reciprocal needs of each side is a critical factor for the pre-negotiation stage. Initial

Sino-Turkish diplomatic relations were established in 1971 (Republic of Turkey, Ministry of Foreign Affairs [MFA] 2019a) and a high level of strategic orientation in their relationship has been observed following the year of 2010 (MFA 2019a), which is evident in the increasing frequency of visits made by both countries' leaders. As such, this has enabled a positive atmosphere in China–Turkey relationships. Furthermore, the year of 2018 was declared in China as Turkish Tourism Year in order to increase people-to-people exchanges between the two countries. It is apparent that both Turkey and China want to increase their economic and strategic relationships through the BRI by promoting their cooperation on trade, energy and infrastructure-led investment projects. China wants to use and relocate the excess of Chinese manufactured products and construction capacity to the belt and road countries, where there is a demand for such supplies, in order to stimulate and boost the Chinese economy (Bartosiewicz and Szterlik 2019; Yu 2017). Currently, China is Turkey's second largest trading partner globally, and the largest one based in East Asia (MFA 2019b). In 2017, Turkey's exports to China accounts for $2.9 billion but its imports amass to $23.3 billion, contributing to Turkey's trade deficit problem (Turkish Statistical Institute 2019). Thus, Chinese negotiators should come to the table with trade policies that are designed towards decreasing this trade asymmetry. This can be done by promoting BRI trade deals, which will have the potential to increase Turkey's exports to China. China may also want to contribute to the Turkish economy by increasing the level of foreign direct investment into Turkey through the BRI. For instance, China's participation in high-speed rail line projects in Turkey is a good sign that collaborations between the two countries are growing. By participating in these kind of investment projects, Chinese and Turkish policymakers can understand each other better in terms of culture and have an insight into the way each country does business.

Furthermore, Turkish negotiators will be expecting clear and unambiguous offerings from their Chinese counterparts in this stage of their BRI negotiations, as Turkey scores high on UAI. Additionally, presentation language is critical for the effective communication of expert groups in the BRI. A negotiating team of 4–5 person from one country may need to meet with a more crowded negotiating team from another country in which one interpreter may not be enough to help with the communication efficiently (Ghauri and Fang 2001). Thus, all presentation material and communication channels should be in Turkish, Chinese and another third language such as English to eliminate misunderstandings and to cross-reference the statements made in the meetings.

Once initial contact is made between the two parties (in the case of the BRI, this may constitute two member countries or two organizations from different countries), the next important step to be taken in the pre-negotiation stage is to begin establishing trust with one another. China and Turkey share some similarities with regards to how quickly one can build trust with other people. For example, in China, which is rooted in Confucian principles of mutual support, co-existence and cooperation (e.g., Chow and Ng 2004; Warden and Chen 2009), there is a popular expression that conveys this point very well, 'qiang da chu tou niao', which translates in English to as 'early birds get shot' (De Cremer, 2015). In this sense, one must only earn trust when he/she has proven him/herself worthy of it and those who trust others too early are destined to be punished for it. The default is mistrust and one must take care to ensure that they are patient enough to carefully build trust over time. Turkish people, as a collectivistic orientation society, are expected to build trust in a similar way. Once a connection has been made, it is expected that you take plenty of time getting to know each other first. In both cases, trust is established on a person to person basis and although building trust may take time for collectivistic cultures, they move fast once trust is built (Coene and Jacobs 2017). Ghauri and Fang (2001) state that when mutual trust between the business partners is high, the Chinese will negotiate as 'gentlemen', otherwise they will negotiate as 'strategists'. When they negotiate as 'gentlemen', they are far more likely to place greater weight on the concerns and values of their counterparts.

According to an adapted version of Lewicki and Bunker's (1996) staged model of trust building in organizations, there are five key stages to building trust across cultural boundaries (Saunders, Skinner, and Lewicki 2010). These stages are context, opening stance, early encounters, breakthrough or breakdown and consequences (Saunders et al., 2010). These stages can be understood in the following way:

- *Context*: First, the degree to which both parties are aware of each other's cultural patterns of thinking and conduct, including perhaps any cultural preconceptions (often times misconceptions) and their willingness to accommodate this will set the initial context from which trust can be built. In other words, the degree of cultural awareness both parties have with respect to each other will set the scene for the remaining trust building stages.
- *Opening stance*: Based on this initial context of cultural awareness (or lack thereof), each party will either convey an opening gesture of trust, active distrust or suspended judgement. As it was discussed earlier in the chapter, it is ordinary in Chinese culture to begin with distrust as a default and from there, trust must be earned. Therefore, one may expect that the opening stance taken by Chinese and Turkish negotiators would be one of suspended judgement or active distrust, which must be overcome.
- *Early encounters*: Next, as discussed before, early encounters and possible meetings should be arranged in an effort to establish mutual understanding and to take time to learn the counterparty's needs, priorities and values.
- *Breakthrough or breakdown*: Following these initial encounters, negotiators can either experience a breakthrough or a breakdown depending on their interest in their counterparty's offerings. For example, Turkish negotiators will probably expect an offer that will increase trade and financial cooperation, and the transfer of technology such as artificial intelligence and investment projects in Turkey as well. Thus, a possible breakthrough will be reached if Chinese negotiators satisfy their Turkish counterpart's expectations.
- *Consequences*: Finally, the last stage of the trust building model depicts the consequences that arise from either a breakthrough or a breakdown. In the case of a breakdown, one has failed to understand or accommodate for the cultural sensitivities of their counterpart. As a consequence, distrust is bred and will ensue unless trust repair efforts are initiated. On the other hand, if one experiences a breakthrough from their early encounters, understanding, acceptance and trust will be achieved.

Approaching trust building in this way promotes the likelihood of success when negotiating with a party of a different culture (Lewicki and Bunker 1996). Furthermore, developing trust will increase the probability of the signing of a MOU in the formation of a formal contract between countries in the BRI (e.g., Chen, 2016).

NEGOTIATION STAGE OF THE BRI

Formal negotiation starts when the two parties show a strong interest in 'further discussions', especially on task-related exchanges of information (Ghauri and Fang 2001). Chuah, Hoffmann, and Larner (2014) state that Chinese bargaining decisions are affected by some cultural values such as face (the positive public and self-image of a person), harmony (the Confucian avoidance of discord in social interactions) and the desire to win. Lin and Miller (2002) mention that Chinese negotiators generally use compromising approaches in their negotiating style. On the other hand, Turkish negotiators can be expected to focus on clear strategies, relationship stability, harmony, reliability, formality and hierarchy. Focusing on these cultural codes ensures that in your presentation of an agreement proposal you are optimizing the value you communicate to your counterparts (e.g., Coene and Jacobs 2017). The contributions offered by each party, management control (Ghauri and Fang 2001), and financial mechanisms (which will need to be regulated through the various BRI funding channels) are some of the important factors which should be addressed by Turkish and Chinese negotiators in the negotiation stage. It should be kept in mind that the Chinese style of dealing with details in negotiations is closely related to Chinese bureaucracy (Ghauri and Fang 2001), which may lead to the 'two bites at the apple' issue that was discussed earlier in the chapter and should be carefully considered and analysed by Turkish negotiating team of the BRI.

Another source of power between countries in international business negotiation is their BATNA, which means 'best alternative to a negotiated agreement' (e.g., Fisher, Ury, and Patton 1991). In other words, BATNA is related to what the negotiators will do if they do not reach an agreement. Negotiators can demand more concession from their counterpart(s) when they have a greater BATNA. For instance, China's BATNA regarding Turkey's middle corridor for the BRI is using the northern corridor to transfer goods from China to Europe. However, transferring goods by using this route is not economically desirable when compared with Turkey's middle corridor (e.g., Fasulo and Talbot 2017). Therefore, China has a poor BATNA in this case. Of course, it is clear that each country prefers the outcome that best fits in line with their BATNA during the BRI's negotiation processes; however, it is the attractiveness of each country's BATNA that ascertains whether a ZOPAs occurs (e.g., Fisher et al. 1991; Sebenius 2017).

In line with this discussion, Turkey and China signed a MOU on railroad cooperation with regard to Turkey's middle corridor at the G20 summit in Turkey in 2015 (Fasulo and Talbot 2017). Furthermore, Turkey attended the first OBOR international summit held in Beijing in 2017 which presidential leaders from each country attended. Ahead of this summit, some agreements on highway transportation and the reciprocal establishment of cultural centres in each country were signed. Following this, the second Belt & Road Industrial and Commercial Alliance (BRICA) Summit was held in Turkey in 2018. BRICA is a non-governmental and non-profit multilateral cooperation which facilities the promotion of industrial investment and trade cooperation among the BRI countries (Turkish Industry & Business Association [TUSIAD] 2018). All of these positive efforts towards the BRI ensure that Turkey's willingness and commitment to be included in this grand initiative was signalled to their Chinese counterparts. Moreover, the BRI not only promotes connectivity on trade and investment projects, but it also emphasizes the connectivity of people-to-people exchanges. Direct flights between China and Turkey can support the enhancement of these people-to-people exchanges. Educational bilateral agreements, which support cooperation between Turkey and China, should also be promoted in order to increase people to people exchanges. Doing so may enable greater connectivity between the two countries. In order to satisfy this aim, similar to Erasmus exchange programmes in Europe, new educational exchange programmes can be designed for the BRI countries as well.

Taken together, these positive efforts indicate that both parties understood the significance of their interactions during this negotiation stage. Both parties ensured that such kind of signals were harmonious with their joint BRI agenda and had taken measures to ensure that their intentions were being reciprocated.

POST-NEGOTIATION STAGE OF THE BRI

Implementation of agreements, monitoring and new rounds of negotiation occur at this stage. As we previously mentioned, in order to negotiate with the Chinese, it is sometimes required to progress through repeated cycles of negotiation, which is like a never-ending cycle of negotiation and renegotiation (e.g. Jang, Elfenbein, and Bottom 2018; Coene and Jacobs 2017). In other words, Turkish negotiators of the BRI should be ready to observe a continuous back and forth style of bargaining in the Chinese negotiating style. This is often likened to a 'ping-pong' metaphor due to its back and forth style (e.g., Ghauri and Fang 2001). Therefore, patience is a crucial and unique element when negotiating with Chinese negotiators at this stage (Ghauri and Fang 2001). The cycle of negotiations and renegotiations (continuous negotiations) should be anticipated by Turkish negotiators in the upcoming belt and road summits.

CONCLUDING REMARKS

The BRI involves member countries from a wide pool of social and cultural values. The success of the initiative depends on the extent to which these member countries cooperate with one another and see eye to eye on the agenda and objectives set out in the BRI. The BRI will induce substantial changes in the relationship between Beijing and Ankara. Thus, by taking the understanding of the cultural codes of Turkey and China as a case study, this chapter has endeavoured to explore the various steps that need to be taken in order to negotiate future deals regarding the BRI between these two countries more effectively. China and Turkey provide an interesting example as they share key similarities and differences with regards to their cultural patterns, and this is reflected somewhat in their political, economic and cultural relationships. By taking a cross-cultural approach to the BRI negotiations, smoother negotiation processes and greater connectivity to enhance policy coordination and implementation between two countries can be expected. Therefore, Chinese and Turkish authorities should employ culturally aware negotiators for their expert negotiating groups in the BRI. Such negotiators can use their cultural awareness sensitivities to cope with the cultural differences, manage them effectively and to take advantage of the cultural similarities, which will enable a bridging of the cultural gaps and a better attainment of joint mutual gains.

REFERENCES

Adair, W. L., and J. M. Brett. 2005. 'The Negotiation Dance: Time, Culture, and Behavioral Sequences in Negotiation. *Organization Science* 16 (1): 33–51.

AIIB. 2019. *Bridging Borders: Infrastructure to Connect Asia and Beyond*. Beijing, China: Author. https://www.aiib.org/en/news-events/asian-infrastructure-finance/common/base/download/AIIB-Asian-Infrastructure-Finance-2019-Report.pdf

Aslani, S., J. Ramirez–Marin, J. Brett, J. Yao, Z. Semnani–Azad, Z. X. Zhang ... and W. Adair. 2016. 'Dignity, Face, and Honor Cultures: A Study of Negotiation Strategy and Outcomes in Three Cultures. *Journal of Organizational Behavior* 37 (8): 1178–1201.

Bartosiewicz, A., and P. Szterlik. 2019. 'Łódź's Benefits from the One Belt One Road Initiative'. *International Journal of Logistics Research and Applications* 22 (1): 47–63.

Baruah, D. M. 2018. 'India's Answer to the Belt and Road: A Road Map for South Asia'. Working Paper, Carnegie Endowment for International Peace, Washington, DC, USA.

Bazerman, M. H., J. R. Curhan, D. A. Moore, and K. L. Valley. 2000. 'Negotiation'. *Annual Review of Psychology* 51 (1): 279–314.

Brett, J. M., B. C. Gunia, and B. M. Teucher. 2017. 'Culture and Negotiation Strategy: A Framework for Future Research'. *Academy of Management Perspectives* 31 (4): 288–308.

Buckley, P. J., J. Clegg, A. R. Cross, X. Liu, H. Voss, and P. Zheng. 2007. 'The Determinants of Chinese Outward Foreign Direct Investment'. *Journal of International Business Studies* 38 (4): 499–518.

Chen, H. 2016. 'China's "One Belt, One Road" Initiative and Its Implications for Sino-African Investment Relations'. *Transnational Corporations Review* 8 (3): 178–182.

Chow, H. S., and I. Ng. 2004. 'The Characteristics of Chinese Personal Ties (Guanxi): Evidence from Hong Kong'. *Organization Studies* 25 (7): 1075–1093.

Chuah, S. H., Hoffmann, R., and Larner, J. 2014. 'Chinese Values and Negotiation Behaviour: A bargaining Experiment'. *International Business Review* 23 (6): 1203-1211.

Coene, J. P., and M. Jacobs. 2017. *Negotiate Like a Local: 7 Mindsets to Increase Your Success Rate in International Business*. CreateSpace Independent Publishing Platform.

De Cremer, D. 2015. 'Understanding Trust, in China and the West'. *Harvard Business Review* 11.

Du, J., and Y. Zhang. 2018. 'Does One Belt One Road Initiative Promote Chinese Overseas Direct Investment?' *China Economic Review* 47: 189–205.

Fasulo, F., and V. Talbot. 2017. 'The MENA Region: Where the Belt Joins the Road'. In *China's Belt and Road: A Game Changer?* edited by Alessia Amighini. Milano, Italy: The Italian Institute for International Political Studies.

Fisher, R., W. Ury, and B. Patton. 1991. *Getting to Yes: Negotiating Agreement Without Giving In*. New York: Penguin.

Gazprom (2018). TurkStream: Gas exports to Turkey and Southern and Southeastern Europe. Retrieved from: http://www.gazprom.com/projects/turk-stream

Ghauri, P. N. 2003. 'A Framework for International Business Negotiations'. In *International Business Negotiations*, edited by P. N. Ghauri and J. C. Usunier, 3–23. Oxford: Pergamon Press.

Ghauri, P., and T. Fang. 2001. 'Negotiating with the Chinese: A Socio-Cultural Analysis'. *Journal of World Business* 36 (3): 303–325.

Graham, J. L., A. T. Mintu, and W. Rodgers. 1994. 'Explorations of Negotiation Behaviors in Ten Foreign Cultures Using a Model Developed in the United States'. *Management Science* 40 (1): 72–95.

Griffin, T. J., and W. R. Daggatt. 1990. *The Global Negotiator: Building Strong Business Relationships Anywhere in the World*. New York: Harper Business.

Groves, K. S., A. Feyerherm, and M. Gu. 2015. 'Examining Cultural Intelligence and Cross-Cultural Negotiation Effectiveness'. *Journal of Management Education* 39 (2): 209–243.

Hofstede, G. 1980. 'Culture and Organizations'. *International Studies of Management & Organization* 10 (4): 15–41.

Hofstede, G., and J. C. Usunier. 2003. 'Hofstede's Dimensions of Culture and their Influence on International Business Negotiations'. In *International Business Negotiations*, edited by P. N. Ghauri and J. C. Usunier, 137–153, second edition. Oxford: Pergamon Press.

Hofstede, G., G. J. Hofstede, and M. Minkov. 2010. *Cultures and Organizations: Software of the Mind*. Revised and expanded third edition. New York: McGraw-Hill.

Hu, R. W. 2017. 'China's "One Belt One Road" Strategy: Opportunity or Challenge for India?' *China Report* 53 (2): 107–124.

Hung, M., and T. Chan. 2019. 'The Belt and Road Initiative—The New Silk Road: A Research Agenda'. *Journal of Contemporary East Asia Studies* 7: 104–123. doi:10.1080/24761028.2019.1580407

Jang, D., H. A. Elfenbein, and W. P. Bottom. 2018. 'More than a Phase: Form and Features of a General Theory of Negotiation'. *Academy of Management Annals* 12 (1): 318–356.

Lee, K. H., G. Yang, and J. L. Graham. 2006. 'Tension and Trust in International Business Negotiations: American Executives Negotiating with Chinese Executives. *Journal of International Business Studies* 37 (5): 623–641.

Lewicki, R., and B. B. Bunker. 1996. 'Developing and Maintaining Trust in Work Relationships'. In *Trust in Organizations: Frontiers of Theory and Research*, edited by R. M. Kramer and T. R. Tyler, 114–139. Thousand Oaks, CA: SAGE Publishing.

Lin, X., and S. J. Miller. 2002. 'Negotiation Approaches: Direct and Indirect Effect of National Culture'. *International Marketing Review* 20 (3): 286–303.

Magri, P. 2017. 'Introduction'. In *China's Belt and Road: A Game Changer?* edited by Alessia Amighini. Milan, Italy: The Italian Institute for International Political Studies.

Metcalf, L. E., A. Bird, M. F. Peterson, M. Shankarmahesh, and T. R. Lituchy. 2007. 'Cultural Influences in Negotiations: A Four Country Comparative Analysis'. *International Journal of Cross-Cultural Management* 7 (2): 147–168.

Ogliastri, E., and C. Quintanilla. 2016. 'Building Cross-Cultural Negotiation Prototypes in Latin American Contexts from Foreign Executives' Perceptions'. *Journal of Business Research* 69 (2): 452–458.

Pye, L. 1982. *Chinese Commercial Negotiating Style*. Cambridge, MA: Oelgeschlager, Gunn and Hain.

Republic of Turkey, Ministry of Foreign Affairs (MFA). 2019a. *Relations between Turkey and China*. Retrieved from: http://www.mfa.gov.tr/relations-between-turkey-and-china.en.mfa

Republic of Turkey, Ministry of Foreign Affairs (MFA). 2019b. *Turkey-People's Republic of China Economic and Trade Relations*. Retrieved from: http://www.mfa.gov.tr/turkey_s-commercial-and-economic-relations-with-china.en.mfa

Republic of Turkey, Ministry of Transport and Infrastructure (MTI). 2018. Transportation and Communication Report of Istanbul. Retrieved from: http://www.uab.gov.tr/uploads/cities/istanbul/34-istanbul.pdf

Richardson, C., and H. G. Rammal. 2018. 'Religious Belief and International Business Negotiations: Does Faith Influence Negotiator Behaviour? *International Business Review* 27 (2): 401–409.

Salacuse, J. W. 1998. 'Ten Ways that Culture Affects Negotiating Style: Some Survey Results'. *Negotiation Journal* 14 (3): 221–240.

Saunders, M. N. K., D. Skinner, and R. Lewicki. 2010. 'Emerging Themes, Implications for Practice and Directions for Research'. In *Organisational Trust: A Cultural Perspective*, edited by M. N. K. Saunders, D. Skinner, N. Gillespie, G. Dietz, and R. Lewicki, 407–423. Cambridge: Cambridge University Press.

Sebenius, J. K. 2017. 'BATNAs in Negotiation: Common Errors and Three Kinds of "No"'. *Negotiation Journal* 33 (2): 89–99.

Stahley, S. 2006. 'Tuning the Harmony between Negotiation and Culture'. In *Cross Cultural Negotiation for U.S. Negotiators*, edited by Kristen Blankley. Ohio State University, Mortiz College of Law.

Tse, D. K., J. Francis, and J. Walls. 1994. 'Cultural Differences in Conducting Intra- and Inter-Cultural Negotiations: A Sino-Canadian Comparison'. *Journal of International Business Studies* 25 (3): 537–555.

Turkish Industry & Business Association (TUSIAD). 2018. 'BRICA Summit Gathered Countries Located on the Silk Road in Istanbul'. Retrieved from: https://tusiad.org/en/press-releases/item/10138-brica-summit-gathered-countries-located-on-the-silk-road-in-istanbul

Turkish Statistical Institute. 2019. 'Foreign Trade Statistics'. Retrieved from: http://www.tuik.gov.tr/PreTablo.do?alt_id=1046

Warden, C. A., and J. F. Chen. 2009. 'Chinese Negotiators' Subjective Variations in Intercultural Negotiations'. *Journal of Business Ethics* 88 (3): 529–537.

Weiss, S. E. 1993. 'Analysis of Complex Negotiations in International Business: The RBC Perspective'. *Organization Science* 4 (2): 269–300.

World Bank. 2015. *Turkey's Response to the Syrian Refugee Crisis and the Road Ahead.* Washington, DC: Author.

Yan, J., and R. L. Sorenson. 2004. 'The Influence of Confucian Ideology on Conflict in Chinese Family Business'. *International Journal of Cross-Cultural Management* 4 (1): 5–17.

Yu, H. 2017. 'Motivation behind China's "One Belt, One Road" Initiatives and Establishment of the Asian Infrastructure Investment Bank'. *Journal of Contemporary China* 26 (105): 353–368.

Chapter 10
China on the Arabian Sea
A Risk Assessment

Michael Tai

As part of the Belt and Road Initiative (BRI), the China–Pakistan Economic Corridor (CPEC) will upgrade Pakistan's infrastructure and deepen economic links with China. First proposed by Premier Li Keqiang on his visit to Pakistan in May 2013, the corridor connects Kashgar in China's Xinjiang province via a network of roads and railways to the port of Gwadar on the Arabian Sea giving China quick access to the Middle East and Africa. A total of 80 per cent of China's oil imports come through the Straits of Malacca (Panda 2015), and oil tankers from the Persian Gulf take 16–25 days to reach China's eastern coast, but with the CPEC, the journey overland from Gwadar will take just 48 hours. By bypassing the Straits of Malacca, the corridor cuts the shipping time from China to Europe from 45 days to 10 days. The $62 billion, 3,000 km economic corridor of roads, railways, pipelines and power stations will boost trade and development along the entire Eurasian Silk Road. As an outlet to the sea, it promises to open up the vast potential of landlocked Central Asia. Promising enormous benefits to Pakistan as well as China, the CPEC rests on a foundation of trust between the two neighbours but there are tangible risks.

SINO-PAKISTAN RELATIONS

Pakistan's relationship with China has been called a time tested, 'all weather' friendship. Pakistan recognized the PRC in 1951 and since settling their 523-km border in 1963, the two neighbours have had no major disputes. Dubbed the 'eighth wonder of the world', the Karakoram Highway which runs from Kashgar to Abbottabad, a distance of 1,300 km, is a symbol of Sino-Pakistan friendship. Both countries agree on most world issues and their stable relation has so far been immune to changes in government and international politics. Starting with Premier Zhou Enlai and President Ayub Khan in 1964, virtually every leader from each side has exchanged visits with their counterpart. China provided economic and military aid to Pakistan even when the country itself suffered deprivation in the 1960s and 1970s. China helped to build all three of Pakistan's nuclear power stations, and is said to have shared expertise on building atomic weapons (Kroenig 2010). Following the US arms embargo after the 1965 Indo-Pakistan war, China helped Pakistan develop its defence industry, making the country self-sufficient in tanks, artillery, aircraft weapons systems and munitions (Jalalzai 2003, 267). Other collaborative projects include a railway line between Peshawar and Lodhran, water and mineral exploration, and a space programme which launched Pakistan's first satellite. Chinese supported Pakistan built a reservoir of trust among the Pakistani political elite and people, who describe the friendship as 'higher than the mountains, deeper than the oceans…' (Xinhua 2015).

Trade and cultural exchanges, however, lag far behind defence cooperation. China and Pakistan signed a free trade agreement (FTA) in 2006, and bilateral trade grew to an estimated $13.8 billion in 2016 (up from $2.2 billion in 2005; Kamal and Malik 2017). However, the volume is modest compared to China's $102 billion trade with Malaysia, a country with less than one-sixth the population of Pakistan while Sino-Indian trade registered $71 billion the same year. Exports to China consists mostly of cotton and rice (Pakistan is the second largest supplier of rice to China after Vietnam since 2011) while imports include electrical equipment, high tech machinery, nuclear reactors, iron and steel, organic chemicals and synthetic fibres. More than half of Pakistan's import of electrical equipment and machinery comes from

China. The balance of trade is skewed in China's favour largely because Pakistan has a narrow export base. Furthermore, Pakistan's free trade advantages have been eroded by FTAs between China and other countries, especially ASEAN. There is also room for improvement in the area of social and cultural ties; Pakistan's film industry pales in comparison to Bollywood, and there are few cultural exports for Chinese consumers. Bilateral tourism and educational exchanges remain at a low level. Pakistan ranks 115th out of 137 countries in the World Economic Forum's 2017–2018 Global Competitiveness Report (GCR), and is the least competitive country in South Asia.[1]

THE RISKS

The CPEC project faces several important hurdles. First, Pakistan is short of energy. Parts of Karachi have no electricity for 12 hours a day, and, in recent years, power shortfalls have approached 50 per cent of national demand. This amounts to over 4.5 gigawatts, and, within a few years, Pakistan's power demand will exceed its installed capacity by nearly 10 gigawatts. Total demand will nearly double in the next 10 years, and quadruple in the next 60. In order to alleviate chronic power shortages, the CPEC will spend over $33 billion to boost capacity by 10 gigawatts by 2020 (Shah 2016). The shortfall is compounded by fast population growth and urbanization. The country's population has grown exponentially since 1947 to 191 million people, and is expected to top 300 million by 2050, making Pakistan the world's fourth most populous nation. About a third of the population is urban; by 2025, nearly half will live in cities. Population increase and urbanization will boost demand for energy.

The second hurdle is Baluchistan. Baluchistan accounts for nearly half the land mass of Pakistan but only 5 per cent of its population. The province is rich in natural resources, including oil, gas, copper and gold. Despite its mineral wealth, it is one of the poorest regions of Pakistan, and the majority of its people lives in woeful conditions with no access to electricity and clean drinking water. Since the mid-1970s,

---

[1] India ranks 40th, Bhutan 82nd, Sri Lanka 71st, Nepal 88th and Bangladesh 99th.

Baluchistan's share of the national GDP has fallen to 3 per cent. It has the lowest literacy rate and the highest poverty rate in the country; over half of Baluch households live below the poverty line (Webb and Wijeweera 2015). The lack of asset ownership and access to education and healthcare are the main drivers of poverty in Baluchistan (Naveed and Nazim 2012). Rising poverty and unemployment fuel militancy. Baluchistan gained independence from the British in 1947, three days before Pakistan, but seven months later Pakistan invaded and forced it to join Pakistan. Since then, the Baluchis have lived under Pakistani political domination, economic exploitation and cultural hegemony but are fighting back (Tatchell 2007). Separatist rebels have launched attacks on army convoys and coastal facilities near Gwadar. Islamabad has leased Gwadar to a Chinese state-owned company for 40 years, but the Baluchis say they were never consulted about the deal. The provincial government wants reassurances that Baluch social and economic concerns will be addressed, and that no foreign troops will be stationed at Gwadar (Baloch 2016). Taking over the operation of the port offers strategic advantages for China. First, oil and gas from Saudi Arabia and Iran can be transported via Gwadar to Xinjiang through pipelines. Second, Gwadar will provide a port of call for Chinese vessels albeit Beijing says it has no intention to use the port for naval purposes (Raman 2013). Three Chinese engineers were shot dead by Baluch insurgents in 2004. Two more were kidnapped, and one killed in a rescue attempt (Tang 2013, 228). The Pakistani army has promised to form a special brigade to protect Chinese construction crews. On the whole, however, Chinese enjoy much goodwill among the population and have not been deterred by the incidents.

The third challenge is Pakistan's internal instability (Rashid 2009). Its political institutions are not robust, and, since its independence in 1947, the country has been ruled alternately by civilian and military governments. Trust in politicians is low, and many see the army as the only guarantor of the state. There is little consensus in Pakistani society on fundamental questions such as the nature of the state and its relations with Islam (Fair 2011, 92). Entrenched vested interests engender political disparity between provinces, calling into question the legitimacy of the Punjabi-dominated federal government. At the same time, involvement with the American intervention in Afghanistan fosters ethnic and religious militancy (Fatemi 2011, 111). Pakistanis consider their political parties corrupt, incompetent and nepotistic. Many believe that electoral reforms under the military will produce clean and honest parties, but political parties reflect society and embody the contradictions of Pakistani society (Murtaza 2016). Pakistan ranked 147th out of 190 in the World Bank's *Ease of Doing Business 2017* survey which measures regulatory quality and efficiency. To capitalize on CPEC infrastructure and boost growth, Pakistan needs to improve governance and cut red tape. There is a clear need for institutional reform alongside physical infrastructure.

The fourth obstacle is Kashmir. The CPEC runs through Gilgit-Baltistan which is claimed by India. India has protested against the project saying that it crosses Indian-claimed territory. Present day Kashmir (officially called 'Jammu and Kashmir') consists of three sectors held separately by Pakistan, India and China. The Chinese sector is largely uninhabited, but Pakistan and India both lay claim to Kashmir in its entirety which is populated mainly by Muslims. The two South Asian neighbours have fought three wars over the territory (in 1947, 1965 and 1999). Pakistan-administered Gilgit-Baltistan and Azad Kashmir are autonomous states with sovereignty over internal affairs (defence and foreign policy are controlled by Islamabad). Islamabad has insisted all along that the two states have not been formally integrated into the country, but India claims it already has a legal right to the whole of Kashmir and dismisses any plans for a plebiscite. To provide legal cover for the CPEC, Pakistan is considering elevating the status of Gilgit-Baltistan to bring it closer to becoming a full-fledged province of Pakistan. China needs to carefully weigh the risks of building a road through disputed territory and of unilateral changes to the status quo (AFP 2016). Indians and Chinese alike have not forgotten the 1962 Sino-Indian Border Conflict which saw fierce fighting on the icy Himalayan slopes while the 2017 standoff at Doklam over the Chinese construction of a road through an area bordering Indian, Bhutan and China serves as a fresh reminder of the risk of a bloody confrontation which neither side wishes.

In the post-war era, China supported national liberation movements and backed Pakistan in the struggle for Kashmir, a Muslim-majority region under Indian rule (Tang 2013, 221). By the late 1970s, however, Beijing sought better ties with India in order to counter the Soviet Union. It wanted rapprochement with India without jeopardizing relations with Pakistan. The policy called for careful statecraft, and China went to great lengths to reassure Pakistan; before China's foreign minister's visit to India in 1981, Premier Zhao Ziyang travelled to Pakistan to promise President Zia ul-Haq that any improvement in Sino-Indian relations would not be at Pakistan's expense. Zhao told Zia that China wanted to improve its relationships throughout South Asia, and that the PRC planned to adopt a more neutral stance on South Asian affairs. Chinese leaders believed that warmer ties with India would moderate Indian attitudes towards Pakistan and foster peace on the subcontinent. Beijing chose not to intervene in Pakistan's favour in the 1999 Kargil War, and urged Islamabad to pull its troops back to the Line of Control (the provisional border since 1947). In addition to intractable South Asian political and security risks, the CPEC faces challenges on Chinese soil as well.

CHALLENGES ON THE CHINESE SIDE

The Chinese end of the Karakoram Highway opens into Xinjiang. This region was a protectorate of China as early as 60 BC, during the Han Dynasty (206 BC–220 AD). Historically, the province consisted of two distinct areas—Dzungaria in the north and the Tarim Basin in the south—which were populated by Indo-European peoples who practiced Buddhism before they were Islamized from the 8th century with the invasion by Turkic Muslims. The Xinjiang Uighur Autonomous Region of today is three times the size of France but has a population of only 22 million. Although only 4.3 per cent of the region is fit for human habitation, it comprises one-sixth of China's total territory, and contains large reserves of oil and gas (Goodman 2004). Bordering on eight of China's fourteen neighbours, the province has obvious strategic importance. In 1949, Xinjiang was inhabited mostly by Uighurs, Turkic people whose language resembles Uzbek. In the early years of the PRC, the government called for volunteers to develop frontier regions and strengthen border defences. Many PLA veterans answered the call to build towns, settlements and farms, and the population today is 45 per cent Uighur and 40 per cent Han Chinese. The Han Chinese are settled in the north while the Uighurs live mainly in the south. Minorities include Kazakh, Kyrgyz, Tajik, Hui, Mongols and Russians.

This once agricultural region has developed rapidly since 1949. Oil and petrochemicals now account for 60 per cent of its GDP, and the region has become an important pipeline route into Central Asia. The literacy rate rose from 10 per cent to 97 per cent while life expectancy went from 31 to 71 years (Lim and Ritzen 2015). Despite the impressive improvement in living standards, tensions between the Uighurs and the Han Chinese flared in 2009 resulting in fatalities. Violent incidents in recent years include bus bombings and attacks on police stations and government offices. Although suppression of religious freedom is often cited as the reason behind the unrest, the acrimony appears to stem from income disparity between Han Chinese and Uighurs. Their Confucian values, money management habits and entrepreneurial drive give the Han Chinese an edge. A tradition of resource pooling through family, friends and civic organizations provides capital to start businesses, and over time, they prosper (Ayyagari et al., 2010). To redress the economic imbalance, the government grants special privileges to minorities, such as exemption from the one-child policy, relaxed university admission standards, and representation quotas in local government—affirmative action, in short (Howell and Fan 2011). The government encourages intermarriage by offering annual cash payments of 10,000 yuan (£980) for Han-minority couples during the first five years of marriage, as well as housing, healthcare and education subsidies but the uptake has been slow (Wong 2014).

Much of the violence began after the Afghan War in the 1980s. Uighur men joined the mujahideen in Afghanistan and returned to China imbued with radical Muslim ideas. Many were trained in Pakistani *madrasas* which supplied fighters to the Afghan campaign. Better transport links with Pakistan could facilitate the spillover of Islamic radicalism into Xinjiang. While some militant groups stand ready to aid the Uighur cause, however, ordinary Pakistanis do not necessarily sympathize with Uighur separatists. Pakistani businessmen in Xinjiang often prefer to do business with or marry Han Chinese (Haider 2005). Even when Muslims share the same Sunni faith, this does not automatically translate into political, social or economic solidarity, any more than Irish do with Italian Catholics.

COMPETITION FROM OTHER ROUTES

Gwadar is not the only entry point into Central Asia from the Persian Gulf. Some 170 km further west on the Makran coast is the Iranian port of Chabahar which is being developed with Indian aid. The Indian government has earmarked $100 million to upgrade the port, which could service another north–south corridor into central Asia. Goods discharged at Chabahar will travel by rail to Mashhad on Iran's northern border, then onwards into Azerbaijan and southern Russia, and up the Volga into the Russian heartland. Some see Chabahar as India's answer to Gwadar but fears of a new 'great game' may be exaggerated. The British and the Russians once competed for supremacy in Central Asia, and some suggest that a new rivalry is brewing between India and China over the same territory. Geopolitical sensitivities between two Asian giants operating in the same space are unavoidable but that hardly warrants comparison with 19th-century European imperialists. India should take its rightful place in the region and contribute to its development, but the leaders understand that Sino–Iranian relations are almost as strong as Sino–Pakistan relations, and it would be futile to try to use Iran against China. The Chinese supported Iran during long years of Western sanctions, and are Iran's top customer for oil exports (AFP and AP 2016). Chinese oil companies already invest in Iran's energy sector, and the two countries have pledged deals worth $600 billion over the next 10 years (compared to the $62 billion for the CPEC), handily outstripping total Indian investments in Iran. Iran's relation with America remains fraught, and Teheran is unlikely to join an Indo-American nexus against China. President Trump's decision to withdraw from the Iran nuclear deal is only another reminder of American hostility and serves to push the Islamic republic further into Chinese arms. Teheran has joined the Asian Infrastructure Investment Bank (AIIB) and is keen to become a full member of the Shanghai Cooperation Organization.[2] Furthermore, the Chinese see the BRI as

---

[2] India and Pakistan became full members of the SCO in June 2017.

an inclusive vision where more connectivity is better than less. Nevertheless, unlike the CPEC with its comprehensive network of roads, railway and power stations, Chabahar is a standalone project which will improve logistics but is by no means of equal strategic import.

Concerns about potential incompatibility between the Eurasian Economic Union (EEU) and the BRI are equally misplaced. The former, a customs union of Russia, Belarus, Kazakhstan, Kyrgyzstan and Armenia, comprises a framework on tariffs, regulations and governance whereas the latter consists of physical infrastructure and transport networks aimed at boosting regional connectivity. The two spheres are complementary rather than mutually exclusive. In any case, EEU member states remain divided over the degree of political and economic integration. This division together with the fact that its two biggest economies, Russia and Kazakhstan, are sensitive to fluctuation in oil prices suggests that the future shape of the union remains uncertain. Moreover, the Silk Road has always has been not one but many routes connecting China across the Eurasian heartland to Europe. In Chinese, the word 'one' in 'One Belt, One Road' (一带一路) conveys unity rather than exclusivity, and the joining together of Eurasia in one community. The 'One Belt, One Road' initiative comprises multiple routes, including the northern Trans-Siberian rail link across Russia and a potential Arctic sea lane in the future. China's relations with Russia, the biggest of the three EEU states, is on a sound footing and has deepened in the wake of tensions between Russia and the West stemming from Nato's expansion into Russia's traditional backyard. Financing for the BRI will come mainly from the AIIB, the first Asia-based international development bank, independent of the West-dominated International Monetary Fund (IMF) and World Bank. The initiative anticipates wide participation by regional players, although many technology products such as hi-speed elevators, efficient heating and cooling systems, automatic controls, advanced sheet glass and metals used in tall buildings will come from giant American, European and Japanese firms.

Instability in Afghanistan, however, could have an impact on development projects in both Pakistan and Iran. Just as Gwadar is at risk from Baluch insurgency, Chabahar too faces unrest from Sunni groups. The borders are porous and while Pakistan combats Baluch insurgents crossing over from Afghanistan, Iran faces Baluch insurgents attacking from safe havens in Pakistan. Iran appears to have a better grip on its domestic affairs and Chabahar could start operating before Gwadar if pursued in earnest. No discussion of Sino-Pakistan partnership is complete, however, without reference to America's role in the region.

THE SINO-PAKISTAN-US TRIANGLE

Since its founding in 1947, Pakistan, in confrontation with India, has carefully managed relations with the United States of America and China. Pakistan mediated Henry Kissinger's secret 1971 visit to China, and, in the 1980s, Washington courted both Islamabad and Beijing to counter the Soviet intervention in Afghanistan. Pakistan plays a key role in America's war on terror, but US-Pakistan relations have been confused and ambivalent. The relations revolve primarily around security concerns with little attention paid to trade and cultural exchange. US-Pakistan relations are complicated by conflicting security interests and a deep vein of mistrust between American and Pakistani security forces. Although the Pakistani intelligence service worked closely with the CIA during the Soviet–Afghan War (1979–1989), it also provided support to the Afghan Taliban in the subsequent civil war against the Northern Alliance. The Northern Alliance was dominated by Tajiks whereas the Afghan Talibans are mainly Pashtuns, the largest ethnic group in Afghanistan. Pashtuns, however, are even more in number in Pakistan where they form the second largest community (15%) after the Punjabis (45%), and Islamabad cannot afford to alienate them. The borders between Iran, Afghanistan, Tibet and India were drawn by the British and Russians at the beginning of the 20th century, often in an arbitrary fashion, cutting across ethnic and sectarian lines. The mountainous Afghan–Pakistan border is porous, and relations among Pashtuns, Tajiks, Uzbeks, Hazaras and other tribal groups who populate the region are not easily understood by outsiders. While Pakistan readily accepted American support to drive communist invaders from Afghanistan, the prospect of joining hands with Western infidels to wage war on indigenous Muslim fighters is a different matter.

Meanwhile, America's relations with China oscillated often unpredictably over the course of the last one and half centuries. In the 20th century, America supported Chinese territorial integrity and opposed European and Japanese ambitions to carve China up. After the surprise attack on Pearl Harbor, the USA allied with China against Japan. The war ended with Japan's defeat but the outbreak of the Korean War in 1950, and the onset of the Cold War led American foreign policy to swing in the opposite direction; Washington quickly rearmed Japan to serve as an ally against China. In the 1950s, America stood against the Soviet Union and China until the Sino-Soviet split beginning in 1960. Thereafter Washington courted Beijing culminating in President Richard Nixon's historic visit to China in 1972. For the next two decades, Washington and Beijing collaborated against the Soviet Union; Washington lifted economic sanctions against China and welcomed it into the Western world order. With the fall of the Soviet Union in 1991, the pendulum swung again and China is deemed to be a dangerous threat.

THE CHINESE DILEMMA

In contrast to warm Sino-Pakistan ties, US-Pakistan relations are marked by mistrust and it is unlikely for Islamabad to side with Washington on virtually any issue concerning China, particularly on an infrastructure project promising to change the game for Pakistan's ailing economy. Notwithstanding the vagaries of Middle East politics, political trust between Pakistan and China is likely to endure but how will Pakistanis react if Chinese businesses, large and small, become a permanent fixture in the land as a result of the CPEC? Over the centuries, Chinese migrants ventured forth to different parts of the world including Southeast Asia, Australia, Europe and the Americas. Comprising mainly poor peasants and artisans, the migrants became known for their hardworking and entrepreneurial nature which enabled them to prosper. In the Philippines, Spanish colonial rulers welcomed them for the myriad services they provided efficiently and inexpensively, and for their role as middlemen (*compradors*) between Spaniards and the native population. By taking on manual and retail professions shunned by the Spaniards, the Chinese became indispensable and were soon perceived as a threat by the Spaniards who dealt with them with arbitrary taxation, corvée labour, periodic massacres and expulsions.

This dilemma typified the overseas Chinese experience wherever they went: Despite economic success, they lacked political clout and faced varying degrees of discrimination. The Chinese government offered no diplomatic support and left its subjects to the mercy of foreign rulers. In the USA, the Chinese Exclusion Act passed by Congress in 1882 banned Chinese labour immigration. The prohibition was extended to the Philippines when it became an American colony in 1898 and lifted only in 1943, but Chinese immigration to the USA remained negligible until the late 1960s. In the recent past, ethnic Chinese have suffered violence in Indonesia, Malaysia and Vietnam where they command important sectors of the economy. Living standards in China have risen, however, and those venturing abroad are no longer poor migrants but entrepreneurs and skilled professionals. Since 2000, China has become by far Africa's largest trade partner with over 10,000 Chinese firms of all sizes operating there, around 90 per cent of which are privately owned (Jayaram, Kassiri, and Irene 2017). Over a million Chinese now work in Africa, a sevenfold rise in less than two decades, stimulating economic growth with their business know-how, but there could be a backlash if they are seen to be gaining too much wealth as the experience of Southeast Asian Chinese has shown. With its swelling population, Pakistan is unlikely to welcome an influx of Chinese, but even sparsely populated areas such as Kazakhstan and the Russian Far East are wary of Chinese migrants. Businessmen will go wherever there is profit to be made but whether they will put down roots will depend on local conditions, especially law and order. As life in China continues to improve, its citizens may become less keen to settle in developing countries.

WHY TAKE THE RISK?

The CPEC promises to remake Pakistan by linking its fortunes more closely with that of China. It will drastically shorten the distance between China and the Middle East, Africa and Europe. Better connectivity promises to boost trade and development throughout the region and fundamentally reshape the global economic landscape. However, the project is fraught with risks. Pakistan faces a severe energy shortage exacerbated by rapid population growth and urbanization. Infrastructure building must take place in parallel with large investments in power generation. Meanwhile, uneven distribution of wealth and resources fuel provincial discontent and undermine nation-building. Political institutions are weak and the government is incapable of reining in disparate armed groups. The project faces tangible security challenges on three fronts: Baluch insurgents threaten to disrupt the project; India opposes road construction through Kashmir; and Islamic radicalism may spillover into Xinjiang bolstering Uighur separatist aspirations.

Why is China taking the risks? Some see the CPEC (and the BRI as a whole) as a way for China to offload excess industrial capacity; others suggest that it serves to counter US strategic containment. Chinese aid to developing countries can also be viewed in its historical context. It is rooted in the struggle for liberation from colonial rule. China emerged from a century of turmoil to become a socialist state in 1949 and set about to rebuild from the devastation of the war of resistance against Japan but soon suffered a US-led trade embargo which hindered reconstruction (Zhang 2001). Its own bid to accelerate industrialization during the Great Leap Forward (1958–1962) failed tragically leading to the loss of millions of lives through famine. When relations with its main ally, the Soviet Union, soured from the 1960s, the country became even more isolated but, despite shortages at home, continued to send aid to Africa, mainly in the form of agricultural and technical assistance. In the 1960s, Tanzania and Zambia proposed a rail link from the copper producing region of Zambia to the Tanzanian port of Dar-es-Salaam in order to bypass white-ruled Rhodesia. Neither the West nor the Soviet Union showed interest, but China took up the cause (Monson 2013). Over five years, some 30,000 Chinese technicians alongside 40,000 Tanzanians and Zambians built the Tanzam railway at a cost of $400 million (on a 30-year interest free loan), a massive outlay by 1970 standards. Climbing from sea level to a height of 1,800 meters before descending to 1,300 meters, it was considered the greatest engineering feat of its kind since the Second World War. Completed two years ahead of schedule, the project was an expression of Third World solidarity; the Africans called it the Great Uhuru Railway (*uhuru* being the Swahili word for freedom).

Since then, however, China has become an integral part of the world economy and the struggle against imperialism has evolved into a vision to build 'a community of common destiny'. President Xi Jinping points out that 'the world has increasingly grown into a community where one's destiny is interwoven with that of another'. Xi is not merely acknowledging the nature of today's interconnected world but also articulating a principle of sustainable development, and declared that '[China] will never threaten anyone, nor overthrow the existing international system... We will not seek to build up spheres of influence – China will always be a builder for world peace, a contributor to global development and an upholder of international order'.[3] It is all too easy to dismiss those words as empty rhetoric cloaking a new form of colonialism but China has no history of hegemony as Lord Charles Powell, foreign policy advisor to Margaret Thatcher and John Major, observes:

> Any intention on the part of China to rule the world would be completely contrary to its history. China has generally in the past disdained the rest of the world. It has felt self-sufficient. It hasn't needed the rest of the world and has had no great ambition to lead it.[4]

No one cast aspersions on the Marshall Plan to rebuild Europe. Whether the Chinese mean what they say only time will tell, but they deserve the benefit of the doubt. It is ironic that the very powers which subjugated the world by force of arms accuse China of colonial ambitions. Xi replied, 'China will never seek hegemony or expansion. Only those who are given to threatening others will perceive others as a threat'.[5] Chinese developmental experience, however, should not be applied uncritically, and Chinese officials admit they have much to learn about how to support other countries. Each country needs to work out its own developmental path but by putting in place basic infrastructure such as roads, railways, ports and power stations, the Chinese are helping to set the stage in Asia and Africa for manufacturing, without which no country has been known to move up the prosperity ladder (Chang 2002). As development takes on fresh urgency for poor countries buffeted by global warming, financial crisis or war, China's role will become even more pivotal.

---

[3] Xi Jinping's speech at the 2018 Boao Conference on Hainan Island.
[4] Remarks by Lord Charles Powell at the Oxford Union on 15 November 2012.
[5] Xi Jinping's closing speech to the National People's Congress on 20 March 2018.

REFERENCES

AFP and AP. 2016. 'Iran, China Discuss $600b Economic Deals as Xi Jinping Visits'. *The Times of Israel*, January 23.

AFP. 2016. 'Pakistan Mulls Elevating Status of Gilgit-Baltistan on Chinese Insistence'. *Dawn*, January 07.

Baloch, S. 2016. 'The Gwadar Deal'. *Int. News*. "Baloch Leader Demands Details of CPEC Project," *The Economic Times*, October 15, 2016.

Chang, H.-J. 2002. *Kicking Away the Ladder: Development Strategy in Historical Perspective*. Anthem Press.

David S. G. Goodman, *China's Campaign to "Open Up the West": National, Provincial and Local Perspectives* (Cambridge University Press, 2004).

Fair, C. C. 2011. 'Addressing Fundamental Challenges'. In *The Future of Pakistan*, edited by S. P. Cohen, 91–106. Brookings Institution Press.

Fatemi, T. 2011. 'Looking Ahead'. In *The Future of Pakistan*, edited by S. P. Cohen, 107–121. Brookings Institution Press.

Haider, Z. 2005. 'Sino-Pakistan Relations and Xinjiang's Uighurs: Politics, Trade, and Islam along the Karakoram Highway'. *Asian Survey* 45(4): 522–545.

Howell, A., and C. C. Fan. 2011. 'Migration and Inequality in Xinjiang: A Survey of Han and Uyghur Migrants in Urumqi'. *Eurasian Geography and Economics* 52: 119–139. doi:10.2747/1539-7216.52.1.119

Jalalzai, M. K. 2003. *The Foreign Policy of Pakistan : Kashmir, Afghanistan and Internal Security Threats (1947–2004)*. Lahore: Ariana Publications.

Jayaram, K., O. Kassiri, and S. Irene. 2017. *The Closest Look Yet at Chinese Economic Engagement in Africa*. McKinsey and Company.

Kamal, J., and M. H. Malik. 2017. 'Dynamics of Pakistan's Trade Balance with China'. Staff Notes, State Bank of Pakistan, Karachi.

Kroenig, M. 2010. 'Exporting the Bomb: Technology Transfer and the Spread of Nuclear Weapons'. Cornell studies in security affairs, Cornell University Press, Ithaca.

Lim, L. M., and Y. Ritzen. 2015. 'Interactive: China's Uighur Unrest'. Al Jazeera. http://www.aljazeera.com/indepth/interactive/2014/09/interactive-china-uighur-unrest-201492282424478793.html

Monson, J. 2013. 'Remembering Work on the Tazara Railway in Africa and China, 1965–2011: When "New Men" Grow Old'. *African Studies Review* 56: 45–64. doi:10.1017/asr.2013.5

Murtaza, N. 2016. 'Pakistani Political Parties and the Democratic Deficit'. *East Asia Forum* 20.

Naveed, A., and A. Nazim. 2012. 'Clustered Deprivation: District Profile of Poverty in Pakistan'. Sustainable Development Policy Institute, Islamabad, Pakistan.

Panda, A. 2015. 'Chinese State Firm Takes Control of Strategically Vital Gwadar Port'. *The Diplomat*, November 13.

Raman, B. 2013. 'Pakistan Inducts China into Balochistan to Counter India'. *Indian Strategic Studies* 1.

Rashid, A. 2009. *Descent into Chaos: The World's Most Unstable Region and the Threat to Global Security*. London: Allen Lane.
Shah, S. 2016. 'Chinese-Pakistani Project Tries to Overcome Jihadists, Droughts and Doubts'. *Wall Street Journal* 10.
Tang, C. 2013. 'Sino-Pakistan Border: Stability in an Unstable Region'. In *Beijing's Power and China's Borders: Twenty Neighbors in Asia*, edited by Bruce Elleman, Stephen Kotkin and Clive Schofield, 219–234. New York: M. E. Sharpe.
Tatchell, P. 2007. 'Pakistan Celebrates, Baluchistan Mourns'. *The Guardian*, August 15.
Webb, M., and A. Wijeweera. 2015. *The Political Economy of Conflict in South Asia*. London, UK: Palgrave Macmillan.
Wong, E. 2014. 'To Temper Unrest in Western China, Officials Offer Money for Intermarriage'. *The New York Times*, September 2.
Xinhua. 2015. 'Pakistanis Hail Ironclad Friendship with China Ahead of Xi's Visit'. http://en.people.cn/n/2015/0420/c90883-8880376.html
Zhang, S. G. 2001. *Economic Cold War: America's Embargo Against China and the Sino-Soviet Alliance, 1949–1963*. Stanford University Press.

PART IV

Managing the Business Dynamics of the Belt and Road Initiative

Chapter 11

Realizing the Potential of the Belt and Road Initiative
What Role for M&A?

Peter J. Williamson

INTRODUCTION

Investment in new infrastructure dominated the early discussion concerning how the Belt and Road Initiative (BRI) will be realized (Ritholtz 2018). Five years after the launch of the BRI, however, it seems that mergers and acquisitions (M&A) might also have an important role to play. While there has been limited cross-border M&A initiated by most countries along the BRI, China has become a very active player. China's M&A in economies related to the BRI increased 81 per cent in 2017 to a record high of $48.2 billion (E&Y 2018). This increase was despite an overall drop in Chinese outbound direct investment by 32 per cent from the previous year, in the face of a volatile global investment environment and tightened domestic regulation on cross-border investment (MOFCOM 2018). In a recent survey of executives, bankers and investors, some 18 per cent of respondents listed the BRI as the 'most important' driver of continued Asia-Pacific outbound M&A activity (FinanceAsia 2018).

M&A activity in ASEAN countries along the so called 'Maritime Silk Road', in particular, reached a new high, representing a quarter of total Chinese cross-border M&A in 2017. Among the BRI countries, Singapore attracted the most Chinese M&A, accounting for 58 per cent, followed by Mongolia (16.5%), United Arab Emirates (8%), Russia (4.2%), and South Korea at 3.8 per cent (Thomson Reuters 2017).

In terms of the distribution across industry sectors, Industrial companies accounted for the largest share of Chinese M&A along the BRI at 59 per cent, followed by transport and logistics (23%), materials (21%), energy and power (11%), financials (4%) and retailing at 3 per cent (Thomson Reuters 2018). As a result, for example, China now holds equity stakes in ports that clear approximately two-thirds of the world's container volume. The country has also acquired a number of warehousing and logistics operators along the BRI (Chamorro 2017). The ecommerce sector has also seen sizeable recent deals such as Alibaba Group's acquisition of the entire share capital of South Asian ecommerce platform Daraz Group in May 2018. Founded in Pakistan in 2012, Daraz operates online marketplaces in Pakistan, Bangladesh, Myanmar, Sri Lanka and Nepal (Reuters 2018).

The rich activities associated with M&A, especially in postacquisition integration, can contribute to the five main goals of the BRI, including policy coordination, facilities connectivity, unimpeded trade, financial integration and people-to-people bonds. For M&A to contribute to these goals, however, it requires a combination of good strategy, execution and perseverance. Many people open the champagne and toast the success of an acquisition when a deal is signed and sealed, but such celebrations are frequently premature. Numerous studies have shown that less than 50 per cent of acquisitions deliver the benefits promised in the years following their completion (Martin 2016). So with M&A along the BRI rising, it is opportune to ask what have we learned about Chinese cross-border acquisitions in the recent past that could help us understand which types of acquisitions and associated post-acquisition approaches might have the greater probability of contributing to the successful realization of the BRI.

LESSONS FROM CHINESE CROSS-BORDER M&A

In 2000, shortly before acceding to the World Trade Organization, the Chinese government came to the view that local companies would need to be globally competitive if they were to match growing rivalry from established multinationals in the home market as well as contributing to China's broader integration into the world economy. It announced a *zou chuqu* policy (which loosely translates as 'go global') that encouraged local companies to make acquisitions abroad. At that time, Chinese outbound M&A activity globally was negligible, running at less than $100 million per annum (Hanemann and Rosen 2012).

Since then, global Chinese outbound M&A has grown and developed through three broad phases. The first wave of overseas M&A deals, up until 2006, was aimed at growing sales in foreign markets. A second wave of acquisitions began in 2006 when the focus of acquisitions shifted to hard assets such as mineral deposits and oil and gas reserves—'resource seeking' acquisitions in the narrowest sense of the term (Williamson and Raman 2011). A third wave of acquisitions since around 2008 has seen the steady growth in acquisitions of 'industrial' companies abroad. These acquisitions are primarily aimed at capturing technology, know-how and sometimes brands (Williamson and Raman 2013).

The total value of Chinese outbound M&A peaked at an estimated $229 billion in 2016 (PwC 2017). This figure fell back to an estimated $125 billion in 2017. In part, this reflected a clampdown by the Chinese government. Since late 2016, Chinese companies investing over $300 million overseas have subsequently been required to report such deals to the National Development and Reform Commission (NDRC), which is empowered to cancel reported deals under certain circumstances. At the same time, there was an increasing pushback in the USA from the Committee on Foreign Investment in the United States (CFIUS), which became notably more risk-averse in 2017 under the Trump administration. Chinese investments into the semiconductor space as well as other sensitive technologies were heavily scrutinized, and reports of abandoned transactions because of 'unresolved national security concerns' identified by the government body increased (Zhang and Tsoi 2018). The deal value from Chinese firms investing in US assets dropped by 81 per cent from a record $56.7 billion in 2016 to $10.7 billion in 2017, while volume fell by 15 per cent. Not one deal with a US target featured in the top 10 Chinese outbound deals of 2017.

Against this background, it is particularly notable that M&A along the BRI has continued to growth rapidly. But few of the acquisitions associated with the BRI are sufficiently far advanced in the post-acquisition integration process to enable an assessment of their true impact. None the less, there are lessons to be drawn for the role of M&A in the BRI from the acquisitions that lie behind the increasing value and changing structure of Chinese M&A globally since 2000 that we have described above. The integration processes in many of these acquisitions are now mature enough to provide important pointers as to what kinds of acquisitions might contribute the realization of the BRI. This experience can also highlight the types of integration approaches and processes that are likely to be effective in enabling M&A deals along the BRI to deliver value for stakeholders.

To distil these potential lessons, we assembled a set of case studies involving one acquisition by each of five Chinese companies covering a wide span of industries: ChemChina (chemicals), Huawei (telecommunications equipment), Kingswood Printing Inks (printing ink), Beijing Automotive Industrial Company (automotive), and Industrial and Commercial Bank of China (ICBC; banking). Brief details of the nature and timing for each of these acquisition cases are provided in the Appendix 11.1. A total of 21 interviews were conducted by the author. Interviewees were encouraged to provide more details when their descriptions were brief or when novel strands of narrative emerged (Martin and Eisenhardt 2010; Strauss and Corbin 1990). Interviews generally lasted for 1–2 hours. Data collection stopped when theoretical saturation was reached (Strauss 1987).

Using these case study data, we then considered two specific questions. First, what were the key aspects of the nature of the post-acquisition process that contribute to success? Following Haspeslagh and Jemison (1990), this included an analysis of the degree to which the new owners retained management and staff; the amount and nature of new investments made in the acquired business; and the organizational and management interfaces between the acquirer and the acquired. The second aspect we analysed was the nature of potential new sources of competitive advantage that may have resulted from combining the existing resources and capabilities of the Chinese acquirer with those accessed through the acquisition.

Successful Acquisition Integration Processes

Gaining the benefits of a cross-border acquisition that offers the buyer the opportunity to access, internalize and subsequently exploit the strategic assets they acquire depends on its ability to design and manage a process of post-acquisition integration that enables these potential benefits to be realized (Bresman, Birkinshaw, and Nobel 1999; Haspeslagh and Jemison 1990; Jemison and Sitkin 1986; Kummer and Steger 2008). A considerable body of research suggests that it is difficult to achieve this integration successfully. Clashes between different organizational values and practices and 'us versus them' thinking among employees of the two organizations often undermines cooperation and thwarts knowledge transfer and learning (Cartwright and Cooper 1996; Nahavandi and Malekzadeh 1988; Schweiger 2002). Language and cultural barriers, constraints imposed by different legal systems and regulations can pose major obstacles to achieving the potential benefits to be gained by integrating the assets, particularly intangibles, acquired (Aguilera and Dencker 2004; Olie 1994; Shimizu et al. 2004; Vaara 2003). These difficulties are likely to be aggravated by the high psychic distance between China and Europe (Child, Ng, and Wong 2002) that magnifies Chinese firms 'liability of foreignness' (Zaheer 1995). Moreover, as latecomers to internationalization, most Chinese emerging market multinationals suffer from a shortage of management staff with extensive experience operating in foreign markets or undertaking acquisition integration (Williamson and Raman 2011).

In all of our successful case studies, Chinese acquirers took steps to retain the existing management and key staff (and hence the knowledge) of the companies they purchased. Despite some reservations among staff about Chinese ownership, the acquirers were also very largely successful in retaining and also motivating the management and staff of the acquired firms. One important reason was that acquisition by the Chinese company created new opportunities for the acquired companies by improving access to the China market, and hence their growth prospects—a fact that was widely recognized by their management and employees.

One of the keys to success we found in these case studies was the creation of a positive message that the new Chinese owners could enhance the prospects for the companies they acquired was reinforced by the actual investments in hiring new staff locally and improving facilities and equipment that were made within the first year of ownership (and in a number of cases, almost immediately). Both Huawei and Kingswood Brancher, for example, upgraded the R&D facilities in Europe and hired extra scientists and technologists. Subsequent to the acquisition Huawei, meanwhile, more than doubled the number of staff at the company it acquired; almost all of whom were local hires in the host country. In the case of the acquisition by ICBC, the Chinese acquirer increased the capital base on which to expand the business. In most cases, these investments took place in the home base of the acquired company (to expand its R&D or production capacity, for example).

The M&A literature also points to the critical role of interface structure and staffing in determining of the degree to which acquisitions are successfully integrated (Haspeslagh and Jemison 1990). In four of the five cases studied, the senior management of the Chinese acquirer headed up the integration team. The involvement of senior Chinese management enabled key decisions to be taken quickly without becoming bogged down in lengthy approval processes. It also meant that the leadership of the integration team was able to ensure the strategy of the using the acquisition to create competitive advantage remained at the forefront of decision-making. In the fifth case, Huawei–CIP (CIP stands for Centre for Integrated Photonics), this approach was taken even further, with senior management oversight being augmented by the appointment of a new research director to the acquired firm. This individual was a Chinese national who had earned his PhD overseas, with some years of experience working for an American company, who had also spent some years working for Huawei in China. He was, therefore, able to act as a bridge between the two organizations, helping to overcome differences in national and company culture and enterprise size between Huawei and CIP.

In all of the acquisition cases, new structures were also established through which to manage the interface between the Chinese acquirer and the acquired company in its home country. These included establishing joint committees both for strategy and particular functional and operational areas, joint product development teams, and processes to facilitate the rotation or transfer of staff, including rotation of Chinese engineers through the acquired company overseas (4 of 5 cases) and the transfer or secondment of foreign designers and engineers to China (2 cases). ChemChina went even further, establishing a new global business unit to manufacture and market Adisseo's nutritional additives for the animal feed sector. Senior management from the acquired company headed up this global business unit, with the result that they were also given responsibility for the Chinese operations in that product line.

Thus, while we observed some of the elements of 'light-touch' integration (Liu and Woywode 2013), we also found considerable evidence of successful integration initiatives that went much further. These included substantial additional investments in the acquired company, moves by the acquirer to strengthen its own absorptive capacity (Cohen and Levinthal 1990) by, for example, involving internationally experienced Chinese staff that can act as a bridge with headquarters, and the establishment of new structures and staff rotation mechanisms to promote knowledge transfer and the integration of complementary capabilities. Such proactive but carefully tailored integration approaches led to the acquisition creating additional value and new sources of competitive advantage.

The Resulting Competitive Advantages

Many commentators assume that cross-border M&A by Chinese companies is motivated by their desire simply to 'catch-up' with more experienced multinationals (Rui and Yip 2008). Our case study findings suggest that foreign M&A can also offer additional, and more exciting, opportunities by opening the way to the creation of new and distinctive competitive advantages.

The pre-requisite for cross-border M&A to create new types of advantage is the Chinese acquirers need to have built distinctive competitive advantages back at their home base. Compared with both their Chinese and international competitors, Huawei and Kingswood Brancher, for example, enjoyed superior capabilities in areas of product design (especially value engineering) and accelerated product development (Williamson and Yin 2014) as well as in manufacturing process innovation and the capability to reap scale economies through rapid scale-up. The two latter advantages were also enjoyed by ChemChina and Beijing Automotive Industry Holding Co (BAIC). Interviewees, for example, quoted benchmark data on product functionality and variety as well as comparisons of product development cycles and then time taken to commission and start up large-scale manufacturing lines to justify their claims. ICBC, meanwhile, pointed to the breadth and depth of its network in China and the speed with which innovative services and technologies had been introduced both at home and in other emerging markets as evidence of competitive advantage in customer relationship building and distribution.

The presence of these existing competitive advantages among Chinese acquirers is important because it opens the way for the possibility that the capabilities accessed through acquisitions along the BRI might allow new combinations of capabilities that, in turn, could generate novel and distinctive sources of competitive advantage. If this were the case, acquisitions in along the BRI might help Chinese firms go beyond the catch up postulated in existing literature (Deng 2009; Luo and Tung 2007; Rui and Yip 2008) to gain a competitive edge over established rivals in at least some areas.

In fact, our case studies find that rather than being only additive, the process of combining existing advantages with new capabilities acquired in overseas sometimes creates new sources of competitive advantage that are distinctive from those of established global competitors. We found that Chinese cross-border acquisitions do help the acquirers to catch up with global competitors (for example, ChemChina achieved minimum efficient scale in methionine and BAIC upgraded quality of its passenger cars to world-class standards). But we also found evidence of the creation of new and distinctive sources of competitive advantage as a result of successful as a result of acquisition integration. These included the development of innovative, environmentally friendly inks by Kingswood, innovations achieved by applying new photonics technologies to cost-efficient telecommunications equipment produced by large-scale manufacturing processes at Huawei, and processes to pioneer offshore trading of renminbi by ICBC. These innovations had the potential to provide competitive advantage relative to Chinese competitors (who generally lacked the capabilities available in overseas) as well as established multinationals and elsewhere (who lacked the ability to combine the strategic assets available overseas with the distinctive capabilities the acquirers had built up in China).

To leverage these new competitive advantages our successful case study companies invested in new capacity and capabilities. Huawei and Kingswood Brancher restructured and enhanced their product development processes, creating new projects and streams of activity to link their newly acquired R&D capabilities in Europe with product and process design capabilities in China to enable new technology to be commercialized and scaled up. Both also subsequently invested in specialized manufacturing capacity to produce the new products based on European technologies. ICBC created new teams in China to interface between Chinese customers and business units and the new trading team acquired from Standard Bank in London.

CONCLUSION

Over the past few years, M&A along the BRI led by Chinese firms has grown rapidly. Because of the multifaceted nature of the integration processes involved in creating value from an acquisition, this M&A activity has the potential to contribute to many of the five main goals of the BRI: policy coordination, facilities connectivity, unimpeded trade, financial integration and people-to-people bonds. The lessons from case studies of earlier, and therefore more mature, Chinese cross-border M&A suggest that M&A along the BRI can do more than simply promoting catch-up with their more established global competitors. Chinese companies can use these acquisitions to create new and distinctive sources of competitive advantage by melding the capabilities acquired overseas with existing sources of proprietary competitive advantage they have accumulated through operating in China. Our results suggest that, as a supplier of new and complementary capabilities, the acquired firm typically benefits from access to additional investment from the new Chinese owner. These investments reflect the fact that rather than wishing to restructure or downsize the acquired company, the strategy of Chinese acquirers usually means they wish to strengthen and expand the companies they acquire so as they can play an even greater role in contributing to the creation of future competitive advantages. At the same time, both the acquired company and its home country gain from the greater access to the massive Chinese market that their new parent can open up, resulting in increased exports and flows of goods and services to China.

To achieve these potential benefits and create value through M&A along the BRI, however, Chinese companies will need to overcome the many integration challenges prevalent in cross-border acquisitions. Success in their cross-border M&A strategy along the BRI can be achieved by focusing on initiatives to preserve and nurture the companies they acquire, often including investments to expand the acquired firms' capacities (including in the area of innovation), taking steps to enhance their own absorptive capacity, and setting up the right interfaces between the two companies, while limiting integration in other areas.

These lessons can be usefully applied to the growing volume and value of M&A along the BRI that has been foreshadowed for the near future. In March 2018, for example, state-backed PetroChina announced that it would step up its acquisition efforts in nations covered by President Xi Jinping's BRI and boost gas output to meet rising demand stemming from Beijing's war on pollution (Ng 2018). The international law firm Baker McKenzie forecast in a recent report that M&A would spread substantially into sectors that could benefit from the early investments that have established improved infrastructure, including the technology, manufacturing, real estate, logistics and warehousing industries (Marazzi 2017). Given the inherent risks M&A almost always necessarily involves, applying this learning from past experience is of paramount importance.

Appendix: Case Study Details

CHEMCHINA-ADISSEO

ChemChina is the largest basic chemical producer in China with business in six sectors: new chemical materials, basic chemical materials, oil processing, agrochemicals, rubber products and chemical equipment. It has 92 production and operation enterprises, and 24 scientific and research and design institutes.

In 2005, ChemChina acquired Franco-Belgian Adisseo for €400 million. Adisseo designs, manufactures and distributes nutritional additives for the animal feed sector. With 29 per cent global share, Adisseo was the second largest supplier of methionine used to boost animal growth.

KINGSWOOD BRANCHER

Suzhou Kingswood Printing Inks is a leading manufacturer of conventional printing inks in China. In June 2012, it acquired 100 per cent of the equity in Brancher Co. headquartered in Tremblay-les-Villages, France, and its Polish subsidiary, Brancher Central Europe Co. In addition to medium-scale manufacturing of inks, Brancher specialized in the development of UV inks, liquid inks, specialty inks for packaging and high added-value products.

ICBC-STANDARD BANK LONDON TRADING

ICBC is the world's most valuable and profitable bank with assets of over €1.4 trillion, 4.6 million corporate clients and over 200 million individual customers. Standard Bank is the largest bank in Africa. In 2008, ICBC purchased 20 per cent stake in South Africa's Standard Bank Group and also entered into long-term strategic partnership to develop joint business in China, Africa and other regions around the world in areas including trade financing, international settlement, investment funds, commodities, global markets and investment banking.

The case study used in this paper is the subsequent acquisition for €590 million of a 60 per cent share of Standard Bank PLC, Standard Bank's London-based entity that trades currencies, commodities, stocks and bonds that took place in early 2014.

HUAWEI-CIP

Huawei is a global leader in the design and manufacture of telecom network equipment, IT products and solutions, and smart devices are used in 170 countries and regions. With annual sales revenue of €31 billion in 2013, Huawei ranked 285th on the Global Fortune 500.

CIP, which stands for 'Centre for Integrated Photonics', traced its roots back to the 1960s when British Telecom, then the telecoms division of the British Post Office, began research into optical communications. Located in Martlesham Heath (British Telecom's main R&D hub), near Ipswich in the United Kingdom, CIP developed a distinguished research track record; it was awarded several hundred patents in photonics.

In July 2011, CIP entered into a strategic collaboration agreement with Huawei, cemented by the sale of 40 per cent interest in CIP's equity to Huawei. In January 2012, Huawei purchased the remaining 60 per cent stake and CIP became a wholly owned subsidiary.

BAIC–SAAB

BAIC is the fifth largest domestic Chinese automaker, owned by the Beijing state-owned Assets Management Co. BAIC's product offerings encompass many kinds of commercial vehicles, including agricultural machinery, construction machinery, light trucks and military vehicles. BAIC also manufactures and sells passenger cars under its own brands.

In December 2009, it acquired part of Saab Automobile from General Motors, comprising a package of technology, plant and the services of designers and engineers for €155 million. This included the intellectual property rights to three overall vehicle platforms, Saab 9–3 and Saab 9–5 technologies, two engine technologies and two transmission systems. The acquisition agreement allowed BAIC to produce and market the older Saab models, but not brand them as Saab.

REFERENCES

Aguilera, R. V., and J. Dencker. 1994. 'The Role of Human Resource Management in Cross-Border Mergers and Acquisitions'. *International Journal of Human Resource Management* 15 (8): 1357–1372.

Bresman, H., J. Birkinshaw, and R. Nobel. 1999. 'Knowledge Transfer in International Acquisitions'. *Journal of International Business Studies* 30 (3): 439–462.

Cartwright, S., and C. L. Cooper. 1996. *Managing Mergers, Acquisitions and Strategic Alliances: Integrating People and Cultures*. London: Butterworth-Heinemann.

Chamorro, D. 2017. 'Belt and Road: China's Strategy to Capture Supply Chains from Guangzhou to Greece'. *Forbes*, December 21.

Child, J., S. H. Ng, and C. Wong. 2002. 'Psychic Distance and Internationalization: Evidence from Hong Kong Firms'. *International Studies of Management and Organization* 30 (1): 36–54.

Cohen, W., and D. Levinthal. 1990. 'Absorptive Capacity: A New Perspective on Learning and Innovation'. *Administrative Science Quarterly* 35 (1): 128–152.

Deng, P. 2009. 'Why Do Chinese Firms Tend to Acquire Strategic Assets in International Expansion?' *Journal of World Business* 44 (1): 74–84.

E&Y. 2018. *China Go Abroad (7th Issue): Belt & Road: Exploring a Blueprint for Steady Growth in Overseas Investment*. Beijing: Ernst & Young, China.

FinanceAsia. 2018. 'Belt & Road Bolstering M&A Optimism'. FinanceAsia, January 3. https://www.financeasia.com/News/441910,belt–road-bolstering-ma-optimism-dealmakers.aspx

Hanemann, T., and M. Rosen. 2012. *China Invests in Europe: Patterns, Impacts and Policy Implications*. Washington, DC: Rhodium Group.

Haspeslagh, P., and D. Jemison. 1990. *Managing Acquisitions: Creating Value Through Corporate Renewal*. New York: Free Press.

Jemison, D. B., and S. B. Sitkin. 1986. Corporate Acquisitions: A Process Perspective. *Academy of Management Review* 11 (1): 145–163.

Kummer, C., and U. Steger. 2008. 'Why Merger and Acquisition (M&A) Waves Reoccur: The Vicious Circle From Pressure to Failure'. *Strategic Management Review* 2 (1): 44–63.

Liu, Y., and M. Woywode. 2013. 'Light-Touch Integration of Chinese Cross-Border M&A: The Influences of Culture and Absorptive Capacity'. *Thunderbird International Business Review* 55 (4): 469–483.

Luo, Y. D., and R. L. Tung. 2007. 'International Expansion of Emerging Market Enterprises: A Springboard Perspective'. *Journal of International Business Studies* 38 (4): 481–498.

Marazzi, M. 2017. 'Belt & Road: Opportunity & Risk—The Prospects and Perils of Building China's New Silk Road'. Baker & McKenzie International. https://www.bakermckenzie.com/-/media/files/insight/publications/2017/10/belt-road/baker_mckenzie_belt_road_report_2017.pdf?la=en

Martin, R. 2016. 'M&A: The One Thing You Need to Get Right'. *Harvard Business Review* 94 (4): 42–48.

Martin, J. A., and K. M. Eisenhardt. 2010. 'Rewiring: Cross-Business-Unit Collaborations in Multibusiness Organizations'. *Academy of Management Journal* 53 (2): 265–301.

MOFCOM. 2018. 'MOFCOM Department of Outward Investment and Economic Cooperation Comments on China's Outward Investment Cooperation in the First Quarter of 2018'. April 18. http://english.mofcom.gov.cn/article/newsrelease/policyreleasing/201804/20180402734717.shtml

Nahavandi, A., and A. R. Malekzadeh. 1988. 'Acculturation in Mergers and Acquisitions'. *Academy of Management Review* 13 (1): 79–90.

Ng, E. 2018. 'PetroChina seeks more 'Belt and Road' acquisitions, lifts gas output to feed China's war on air pollution'. *South China Morning Post*, March 23. https://www.scmp.com/business/companies/article/2138686/petrochina-seeks-more-belt-and-road-acquisitions-lifts-gas-output

Olie, R. 1994. 'Shades of Culture and Institutions in International Mergers'. *Organization Studies* 15 (3): 381–405.

PwC. 2017. 'M&A 2016 Review and 2017 Outlook'. https://www.pwccn.com/en/services/deals-m-and-a/publications/ma-2016-review-and-2017-outlook.html

Ritholtz, B. 2018. 'China's Belt & Road Global Infrastructure Plan'. *The Big Picture*, April 6. https://ritholtz.com/2018/04/chinas-belt-road-global-infrastructure-plan/

Reuters. 2018. 'Alibaba buys Rocket Internet's Pakistan ecommerce platform Daraz'. Reuters, May 8. https://uk.reuters.com/article/us-rocket-internet-divestiture-alibaba/alibaba-buys-rocket-internets-pakistan-ecommerce-platform-daraz-idUKKBN1I90N0

Rui, H., and G. S. Yip. 2008. 'Foreign Acquisitions by Chinese Firms: A Strategic Intent Perspective'. *Journal of World Business* 43 (2): 213–226.

Strauss, A. 1987. *Qualitative Analysis for Social Scientists*. New York: Cambridge University Press.

Strauss, A., and J. M. Corbin. 1990. *Basics of Qualitative Research: Techniques and Procedures for Developing Grounded Theory*. Newbury Park, CA: SAGE Publishing.

Schweiger, D. M. 2002. *M & A Integration: A Framework for Executives and Managers*. New York: McGraw-Hill.

Shimizu, K., M. A. Hitt, D. Vaidyanath, and V. Pisano. 2004. 'Theoretical Foundations of Cross-Border Mergers and Acquisitions: A Review of Current Research and Recommendations for the Future'. *Journal of International Management* 10 (3): 307–353.

Thomson Reuters. 2017. 'A Great Deal of Activity, Plenty of Risk: M&A in the Belt & Road'. Thomson Reuters, August 23. https://blogs.thomsonreuters.com/answerson/great-deal-activity-plenty-risk-ma-belt-road/

Vaara, E. 2003. 'Post-acquisition Integration as Sensemaking: Glimpses of Ambiguity, Confusion, Hypocrisy, and Politicization'. *Journal of Management Studies* 40 (4): 859–894.

Williamson, P. J., and A. P. Raman. 2011. 'How China Reset Its Acquisition Agenda'. *Harvard Business Review* 89 (4): 109–114.

Williamson, P. J. and A. P. Raman. 2013. 'Cross-Border M&A and Competitive Advantage of Chinese Multinationals'. In *The Competitive Advantages of Emerging Market Multinationals*, edited by P. Williamson, R. Ramamurti, A. Fleury, and M. Leme Fleury. Cambridge, UK: Cambridge University Press.

Williamson, P. J. and E. Yin. 2014. 'Accelerated Innovation: The New Challenge from China'. *MIT-Sloan Management Review* 55 (4): 27–34.

Zaheer, S. 1995. 'Overcoming the Liability of Foreignness'. *Academy of Management Journal* 38 (2): 341–363.

Zhang, Z. A., and V. Tsoi. 2018. 'Chinese Outbound M&A Set to Change Course in 2018'. *White & Case M&A Explorer*, March 7. http://mergers.whitecase.com/highlights/chinese-outbound-ma-set-to-change-course-in-2018#!

Chapter 12

Globalizing Innovation Ecosystem, Entrepreneurs and the Digital Silk Road

Mark J. Greeven

The Belt and Road Initiative (BRI) is not just the largest infrastructure project in modern times, involving over 60 countries on four continents with more than 60 per cent of the world's total population, one-third of global GDP, and a quarter of all goods the world moves between nations. The BRI will also encourage Chinese companies to compete internationally, adopt best practices, improve transparency and employ foreign workforces, that is, promote industrial restructuring. Moreover, it is an attempt to integrate Chinese innovation into global innovation ecosystems and leverage its digital innovation power to promote development and enterprise in countries along the BRI. The challenge, and key question of this chapter, is the extent to which Chinese companies can upgrade and innovate to compete internationally in countries along the BRI. Moreover, what does that mean for the countries involved in the BRI?

In this chapter, we will highlight China's innovativeness; summarize China's domestic innovation ecosystem; explore how China is globalizing the innovation ecosystem in terms of science, education, enterprise, standards and investment; discuss and compare innovative enterprise in countries along the BRI; highlight the comparative advantage of China's digital innovation and propose a third road, that is, the Digital Silk Road; lastly, we will discuss the opportunities and challenges of Chinese innovation and BRI. Specifically, the chapter will deal with the following questions:

- Is China innovative?
- Is China's innovation ecosystem mature enough to facilitate sustainable innovation?
- Is China's innovation ecosystem expanding into BRI countries?
- Who is innovating along the BRI?
- Why is the Digital Silk Road China's single most impressive opportunity for global innovation?
- What are the opportunities and challenges for innovation in countries along the BRI?

The chapter draws on insights from a decade-long research programme in Zhejiang University (2007–2017) that included interviews with hundreds of local Chinese entrepreneurs, investors as well as executives in large Chinese firms, focusing on the status and development of dynamic capability by local Chinese firms. Specifically, our research on Chinese digital business ecosystems and a proprietary database on their expansion activities are summarized by Greeven and Wei (2017). Our research on pioneering Chinese companies and hidden champions is summarized in another book, *Pioneers, Hidden Champions, Change Makers and Underdogs: Lessons from China's Innovators* (Greeven, Yip, and Wei 2019).

INNOVATIVE CHINA

Is China innovative? While Chinese companies have long had a reputation for imitation, they are now innovating, not only in process but also in product and technology (Fu 2015; Huang 2010; Yip and McKern 2016; Zeng and Williamson 2007). China's economic growth, expansion of markets and increasing consumer income are clear drivers of innovation, and competition is forcing Chinese innovators to accelerate (Breznitz and Murphree 2011; Williamson and Yin 2014). China has transformed from imitation to innovation in just a generation; an evolution going hand in hand with the development of China's entrepreneurial private sector (Nee and Opper 2012; Wu 2014). On the '50 Smartest Companies 2017' list, published by the *MIT Technology Review*, are now seven Chinese companies: iFlytek, Tencent, Face++, DJI, Alibaba, Ant Financial and Baidu. Moreover, Face++, a Chinese start-up valued at $2 billion, is considered one of the top firms in the list of '10 Breakthrough Technologies 2017' worldwide. The cover of *Wired* March 2017 issue showed a complete reversal on how the West is now viewing China's innovation capabilities. Placed beneath the face of Xiaomi founder Lei Jun is the headline 'It's Time to Copy China'. China's private entrepreneurs are fuelling innovation in China. Of course, innovation and entrepreneurial experiments are just that, experiments, and many of them will fail. Therefore, a mature innovation ecosystem is a necessary condition to foster innovation sustainably and in the long run.

CHINA'S MATURING INNOVATION ECOSYSTEM

Is China's innovation ecosystem mature enough to facilitate sustainable innovation? We should emphasize that China does not have one innovation ecosystem (Tylecote 2006). The national-level innovation ecosystem resembles the features of a developed market focusing on advanced technology. However, the regional innovation ecosystems are deeply embedded in local industries and markets, thereby having different strategic priorities and, in many provinces, related to agriculture and traditional technology fields. There are two important reasons for China's diverse innovation ecosystem. The first reason is that most things in China change very quickly and mostly in a positive direction, including policy, competition, markets and technologies. The second reason is the great regional diversity caused by geographic size and differences, by varying economic and institutional development. Having said that, China's innovation ecosystem is maturing and the following summarizes the key components: education, government, intellectual property rights (IPR), entrepreneurial ventures and venture capital. For excellent overviews of China's innovation ecosystem, we refer to Fu (2015) and Yip and McKern (2016).

In education, China depends on not just its own graduates but on returning graduates trained in developed markets. China has one of the world's largest percentages of university places devoted to STEM (Science, Technology, Engineering and Mathematics) subjects and the largest number in absolute terms of bachelors, masters and doctoral level graduates in STEM, totalling over 2.7 million students (National Bureau of Statistics of China 2017). Moreover, China attracts returnees—citizens who have received higher education from other countries. Since 1978, a total of 4 million students went abroad, of whom 2.8 million have graduated. Of the 2.8 million overseas graduates, 80 per cent have returned to China (National Bureau of Statistics of China 2017). These returnees form a critical and distinctive part of China's innovation ecosystem. Overall, this large group of Chinese students who return with overseas education, and the generation born and educated after 1980, have strong innovation skills and entrepreneurial mindsets.

Innovation for many years had high priority in the Chinese government's five-year plans and has now reached the top position in the list of priority focus areas in the latest five-year plan (2016–2020). This emphasis is made concrete in 22 strategic science and technology initiatives designated 'of strategic importance to China's modernization' as part of the plans of the Chinese Academy of Sciences (Pan 2016). While most other countries also have multifaceted structures to support S&T and innovation, China has the unique integrating mechanism of the Communist Party of China (CPC) and its single party government. In this way, the government could successfully implement large-scale national R&D programmes such as the Torch, 863 and 973 programmes starting in the 1990s. Much of the Chinese R&D funding is for large-scale projects aligned with national priorities and some critics argue that this, combined with state control and excessive centralization in universities and SOEs, inhibits inventiveness (Abrami, Kirby, and McFarlan 2014). Nevertheless, this does not mean that the private sector is not active in R&D. On the contrary, the private sector accounts for the majority of new patent applications—one outcome of R&D activity—after the 2000s (Huang 2010). Furthermore, with its centralization and determination, China has been able to force foreign companies to share technology with Chinese companies and research institutions. This transfer of technology can be viewed as part of the

Chinese innovation ecosystem. On the other hand, limited evidence indicates that foreign companies are not transferring new technologies to Chinese counterparts to the extent that might be expected from the extensive presence of their local R&D centres.

IPRs have been acknowledged in China since 1979. Its legal framework is built on three national laws and other legislation. However, in China, the law is one thing and implementation another. There are many deficiencies in the protection of IPR. Some multinationals hesitate to enter because of valid concerns about loss of intellectual property (IP). This concern applies even more when it comes to innovation or conducting R&D in China. But there is encouraging news for foreign MNCs on this front: the framework for IP protection in China is improving, and there are growing instances of firms that have successfully taken legal action. China's government is paying more attention to this issue and has made several recent announcements and taken several actions, including increasing the number of IP courts. Indeed, in 2016, there were more IPR lawsuits filed by Chinese companies against other Chinese than were filed by foreign companies.

Since early 2000, the Chinese government has fully endorsed and promoted private entrepreneurship, giving it equal status to the state sector, and preferential status since the latest Five-Year Plan. According to the *Global Entrepreneurship Monitor 2015 Global Report*, the Total Early-Age Entrepreneurial Activity of China is higher than India, Israel, United Kingdom and the USA. From 2010 to 2014, the number of start-ups in China doubled and reached 1.6 million which was almost twice the number of start-ups in the UK and India but lower than the 6.5 million per year in the USA. However, by 2016, China's entrepreneurial activity had increased to 5.4 million start-ups, according to Chinese national statistics. Start-ups in China are booming, especially in the high-tech sector due to market demand, industrial upgrading and government initiative. Besides the newly promoted university courses and the rise of incubators and science parks, we have seen a multitude of innovation competitions emerging. For instance, the China Innovation & Entrepreneurship Competition is one of the world's largest nation-wide competitions for new ventures, with 33 regional competitions across almost every province. This competition focuses on six fields: advanced manufacturing, mobile Internet, electronic information, new energy and environmental protection, new materials and biopharmaceuticals. Nationally, this competition alone attracted an estimated over 50,000 new ventures in 2016, up from 27,000 in 2015. Entrepreneurial ventures, the vehicles of innovation, are booming.

It is private venture capital, rather than public capital, that is fuelling new ventures. Private risk capital has seen an immense increase over the last decade, both in terms of number of deals and in total investment value. This ranges from angel investment to venture capital and private equity investments. Although the boundaries of these types of investments have been blurry for most of the time in China, we have seen in recent years a growing number of investors that focus on the early stage companies, and improving interest in angel investment by the affluent class. Moreover, since 2015, we have seen a strong influx of USD funds as compared to RMB funds investing in the market. In 2015, China's VC environment was thriving, with over 3,000 investors injecting over $17 billion into the market. However, China's private equity market lacks professional investors and investing organizations. Most of them follow market trends to invest, instead of relying on knowledge and experience to independently judge the value of a company. Professional investors and observers often refer negatively to a VC boom in China, where second-rate start-ups can relatively receive venture capital investment easily. While the overall flow of private capital to start-ups is good, it may have the side effect of 'spoiling the market', leaving less funds available for the better start-ups.

Concluding, China has rapidly built up a supportive innovation ecosystem. Three key elements are stronger in China than in other developing markets and have moved China far ahead of other developing markets' innovation performance. First is the strong, persistent and mostly successful support of a government taking a long-term view. Second is the role of fierce competition from a very large numbers of start-ups supported by abundant private capital. Third, an enormous, rapidly expanding and increasingly sophisticated domestic market. China's innovation ecosystem is also starting to globalize and this development will be discussed in the next section.

GLOBALIZING CHINA'S INNOVATION ECOSYSTEM TO BRI COUNTRIES

Is China's innovation ecosystem expanding into BRI countries? China introduced the 'Made in China 2025' plan in 2015 to help make China's manufacturing more competitive internationally. To enable companies to strengthen their innovative and technical capability, China aims to implement strategies such as collaborative innovation at the national and, increasingly, the international level. The BRI policy move in combination with the establishment of the Asian Infrastructure Investment Bank (AIIB) and the Silk Road Fund provides opportunities for companies to commercialize and test their innovations. Chapter 17 of the book discusses in great depth the financing of BRI, concluding that while BRI may strain China's financing capacity, much of it will be financially achievable. Although such policy moves cannot directly stimulate innovation in companies, together they do provide a clear direction. China has opted for globalizing its innovation ecosystem through the BRI, as discussed below.

In what follows, we do not intend to be exhaustive in terms of all the innovation-related initiatives in BRI, but provide a systematic analysis of the key components of the innovation ecosystem that China is exporting to the BRI countries. Five components of China's globalizing innovation ecosystem stand out: exporting technology systems, outward Chinese investment in innovation, the development of science along the Silk Road, financial innovations and higher education exchange.

Exporting Systems of Technology: Value Chains and Chinese Standards

The first component of China's globalizing innovation ecosystem is the export of technology or, rather, systems of technology and products. Specific technology fields that are included in the BRI are high-speed railway, electricity transmission systems, renewable energy, cloud computing, big data, artificial intelligence, Chinese global positioning systems, display technology, automotive, logistics automation technology, nuclear power, financial technology, augmented reality and virtual reality and mobile digital technology. To be clear, China has developed strong enterprises in these fields and there is a large group of newcomers with promising new technology suitable for global markets. Except for the well-known technology leaders such as Huawei, many smaller and lesser-known companies such as Geek+ (logistics automation), Malong (artificial intelligence and computer vision), Rejoin (visual aid products), Zongmu (advanced driver assistance system), KATVR (virtual reality solutions), Gago (big data), Mobvista (digital marketing) and many more are driving the technology frontiers, using their own IP from the start, and continuously launching new products.

However, China is not just exporting products; it is now exporting value chains. For instance, the high-speed railway project as part of the BRI aims to develop 26,000 km of tracks. This represents 22 per cent of global high-speed railway projects and 76 per cent of Chinese overseas railway projects. Expanding Chinese railways into BRI countries is an absolute priority. The future of rail on the New Silk Road is high speed; high-speed rail lines in Russia, India, Southeast Asia and Europe are currently in the works. However, it is not just about exporting trains or tracks but also about exporting a whole value chain. For instance, railway surveillance technology, railway telecommunications system, railway air-conditioning systems, cable line technology and other infrastructure required in the train stations, including power stations and enterprise resource planning for cargo management, among other things. One Chinese company in this ecosystem is iReal from Beijing (established in 1999) which focuses on railway safety and surveillance systems. Another good example is Dinghan Tech from Beijing (established in 2002) that produces train, station and track-related equipment such as power stations, air-conditioning, safety doors and cargo information system.

On the one hand, exporting a value chain and creating locally embedded value networks and ecosystems have the advantage of creating long-term competitive advantages for Chinese companies. On the other hand, except for a few sectors in which they have a strong technological advantage, such as nuclear power generation and high-speed train systems, Chinese companies face strong competition abroad. We should not forget that although the BRI was formally introduced in

2013, the plan was in the making for over a decade. While Chinese companies certainly will face strong competition abroad, they usually have longer experience in foreign markets, albeit under the radar, than typically thought.

Moreover, China is also exporting Chinese technology standards while selling products abroad. Developing countries in the Asian region are actively involved in standardization with various stakeholders involved in technology standardization for telecommunications and LED technology across developing countries in Asia (Van de Kaa and Greeven 2017). Within the Asian region, major differences between the countries in terms of local conditions and institutional environment make it difficult to develop one overall standard that can be applied to all the countries involved. Chinese standards that accompany products and technology exports may prove to be a dominant force in developing standards in BRI countries. For instance, large infrastructure and construction projects, such as the high-speed railways, involved multiple Chinese-developed standards. The most impressive example is the railway from Abuja to Kaduna in Nigeria. This is the first railway overseas that is built with Chinese technology standards. Initially the local government intended to buy a Chinese product, while emphasizing that it should not be lower than international standard. In the end, the contract specified it to be at the Chinese technological standard. Effectively, the Nigerians saw the Chinese standard as the world standard. Another example is China's audio–video coding standards for digital television. This standard is used in Laos, Sri Lanka and Cuba already. Lastly, China's champion telecommunication standard TD-LTE for 4th generation telecommunications equipment has 39 networks installed in BRI countries. During the process of internationalization of their home-developed standards, Chinese companies such as Huawei and ZTE gradually became global market leaders in equipment manufacturing, including technology and standards setting.

Outward Chinese Investment in Innovation

The second component of China's globalizing innovation ecosystem is outward Chinese direct investments in innovation, which could range from R&D to greenfield investment and acquisition of innovative companies. In recent years, Chinese outbound investments have been reaching all corners of both the developing and developed world. The year 2016 witnessed a 44 per cent year-on-year increase with a total of $170 billion invested in around 8,000 overseas projects. In terms of geographic locations for outward foreign direct investment to date, the majority is in Asia (74%), Latin America (8.6%), the USA (7.4%) and Europe (altogether only 4.9%). Many of the destinations are BRI countries.

When specifically looking at investments in R&D, we refer to the example of Europe. The 2015 EU Industrial R&D Investment Scoreboard ranked 2,500 global companies by R&D spending. Among the top 2,500 in 2014 (Hernández et al. 2015), there were 829 US companies, 608 EU companies, 360 Japanese companies and 703 others. Among the 'others' were 301 Chinese companies with average R&D intensity of 1.9 per cent, referring to R&D expense as a percentage of sales revenue. The Chinese companies (making China the 3rd largest country by number of companies in 2014) increased R&D investments by 23.6 per cent (the largest increase in the world), increasing total foreign R&D investment made in the EU to 5.9 per cent. For example, Baidu, Lenovo, Tencent, Huawei and ZTE had double-digit R&D and net sales growth in the EU. Among the top 50 international companies in the EU list, there was only one Chinese company, Huawei. However, the R&D investment of Huawei is comparable with that of developed market MNCs. Huawei was ranked 15 (up from 26 in 2013) on the EU list in 2014 and spent €5.4 billion on R&D, not far behind General Motors (ranked 11), which spent €6 billion.

One particularly active group of companies in cross-border investments, mergers and acquisitions comprises Baidu, Alibaba and Tencent (BAT). In the last five years, they jointly invested in over 40 companies in countries along the BRI. These countries include India, Israel, Singapore and Indonesia predominantly, with Israel being the second largest recipient of BAT investment after the United States. This chapter examines the role of cross-border merger and acquisitions in great depth. As we will discuss later, BAT play a pivotal role in laying out the Digital Silk Road, in collaboration with infrastructure providers such as Huawei, ZTE and China Mobile.

SCIENCE ALONG THE SILK ROAD: DECENTRALIZATION OF INITIATIVES

The third component of China's globalizing innovation ecosystem is its little noticed commitment to support science and engineering, including the creation of 50 new joint national laboratories. The BRI will include technical cooperation in fields including artificial intelligence, nanotechnology, quantum computing and smart cities. In September 2016, the government issued the 'Science and Technology Innovation Collaboration Plan' and during the International Summit on BRI in May 2017, President Xi emphasized explicitly the importance of innovation in the BRI with four specific actions: science and technology exchange, joint laboratory, science park collaboration and technology transfer.

There are several examples. Already in 2012, a China–Cambodia Joint Food Lab was set up in the field of food. Another example is a China–Mongolia Joint Lab for biopolymer research, set up in 2016. And in the field of renewable energy, the BRI includes a China–Egypt Renewable Joint Lab, also set up in 2016. In terms of science and talent exchange, the science and technology action plan calls for training 5,000 foreign scientists, engineers and managers as well as welcoming young scientists to China on short-term research visits. By 2017, over 200 young scientists from India, Pakistan, Bangladesh and Burma, among others, have come to China for scientific exchange. Moreover, 52 science parks have already been established in countries such as Thailand, Laos, Indonesia and Iran. Lastly, the BRI plan also includes the establishment of several China-based technology transfer centres. For instance, in Guanxi, there is a China–ASEAN technology transfer centre; in Yunnan, the China–South Asia technology transfer centre; in Ningxia, a technology transfer centre for Arab countries; in Jiangsu, a technology transfer centre for Central and Eastern European (CEE) countries. China's national strategy is implemented at the local level, and the central government has delegated part of the BRI task to the provinces. Moreover, the local provinces leverage their advantages, such as Ningxia's strong connection with the Muslim community and Jiangsu's existing presence of CEE companies.

Financial Innovations: The Case of the Sino-CEE Fund

The fourth component of China's globalizing innovation ecosystem is financial innovations. The case in point here is the financial arrangements for innovation in CEE under the BRI framework. China and CEE countries have established the '16 + 1' leaders' meeting. One of the innovative results of this is the Sino-CEE Fund cooperation platform to support the BRI as well as regional collaboration through financial innovation. The Sino-CEE Fund's target market is CEE countries as well as the rest of Europe and other regions where they have business relations. The target scale in future is €10 billion, and a credit fund of €50 billion is expected to be leveraged.

The main targets of investment are projects worthy of commercial development that reflect industrial collaboration and upgrading, and that can push forward regional development and economic growth. Bringing in capital to Central and Eastern Europe as well as Chinese partners will help the companies in this area to grow by developing competitive products and services for the Chinese market. CEE countries' investment in innovation accounts for 1.2 per cent of their GDP (China Europe International Business School [CEIBS] 2017), which is lower than the average percentage of the EU. Chinese companies aim to cooperate with companies in the CEE to work on R&D and innovation, especially in the fields of ecommerce, tourism service, digital technology and telemedicine. These are illustrations of the innovative ways of financing innovation in BRI countries, discussed in detail in Chapter 17.

Higher Education Exchange: Research, Engineering and Management

The fifth component of China's globalizing innovation ecosystem is exchange of education and talent with other countries in support of implementing the BRI. In 2015, China launched an international alliance of universities to back up its many BRI: The Universities Alliance of the New Silk Road (UASR). The UASR was launched on 22 May 2015, with about 100 universities from 22 countries. It is a new higher education platform to provide research and engineering support for the BRI. The UASR has since expanded to 132 universities across 32 countries in 5 continents. The Xi'an Jiaotong University (XJTU) is the hub for the UASR. XJTU has also set up a Collaborative Innovation Centre of Silk Road Economic Belt Research, backed by the Ministry of Foreign Affairs and the Chinese Academy of Social Sciences to develop into a 'world-class think tank' to provide policy advice to government on the Silk Road Economic Belt.

Another interesting development is the launch of the Economic Research Institute of Central and Eastern Europe (ERICEE). ERICEE is a joint initiative between China's leading business school, CEIBS, and the Sino-CEE Fund. It aims to leverage CEIBS' expertise on topics such as finance, international business and trade and carry out studies into economic, political, historical and cultural issues in Central and Eastern Europe, and generate support and policy suggestions for cooperation between China and the CEE. The collaboration between CEIBS and five schools in CEE will focus on research and teaching activities. CEIBS intends to collaborate with Corvinus Business School (CBS), at Corvinus University of Budapest, in Hungary, BMI Baltic Management Institute, in Lithuania, Kozminski University, in Poland, the Faculty of Economics, Ljubljana University, in Slovenia and the Faculty of Business Administration at the University of Economics Prague, in the Czech Republic.

In conclusion, China's innovation ecosystem is expanding steadily across the BRI countries. While the emphasis is often on infrastructure, construction and natural resources investments, in fact, we observe the exporting of leading Chinese technologies, outward Chinese investment in innovation, science collaboration initiatives, education programmes and exporting of Chinese technical standards. This is laying the groundwork for innovation in BRI countries, building up the necessary innovation infrastructure that will support the host country while at the same time enabling Chinese innovations to land and facilitate joint innovation initiatives between China and the BRI countries. A global 'Chinese' innovation ecosystem is emerging.

CHINESE ENTREPRENEURS ALONG THE BRI: ILLUSTRATIVE EXAMPLES

Who is innovating along the BRI? The private sector in many of the developing countries along the BRI is relatively nascent, and many firms lack the capacity or resources to implement properly the large construction projects proposed. New enterprise development along the New Silk Road will boom, but needs to be led by Chinese entrepreneurs. Utilizing Chinese firms will have benefits to both sides: utilize excess capacity of Chinese companies, bring in expertise, utilize the high technical capacity of firms, facilitate greater Chinese control of projects, create economic benefit for China and develop the capacity of domestic private sector firms. In what follows, we discuss several illustrative examples of Chinese entrepreneurs bringing innovation to the BRI countries.

Xiaomi (2010) is a Beijing-based consumer electronics giant with a market valuation of over $45 billion and 20 per cent overseas revenues in 2016. While Xiaomi's major market is still domestic, it has entered the Indian market and did so with reasonable success, achieving $1 billion sales revenue with 6.5 million mobile phone sales in 2016. Although a lawsuit by Ericsson in India in 2013 led to a temporary ban on Xiaomi's smartphones import, Xiaomi's second attempt in 2015–2016 was successful, and it is noteworthy that Ratan Tata of the Tata Group acquired a stake in Xiaomi after the initial success in India (Greeven and Wei 2017). Xiaomi is targeting other markets in BRI countries as well.

Huawei's internationalization started in 1997 by entering the largest emerging markets, such as Russia and Brazil. Besides successfully expanding into foreign markets in Africa and Asia, Huawei has rapidly built up a global innovation network with 54 per cent overseas revenues (Greeven et al. 2019). By 2017, Huawei has set up R&D centres in eight countries, each with a specific technology focus. For example, in India, the focus is on software research in its local Software R&D Centre. A third partner in the joint innovation centres is foreign governments. For instance, in 2016, Huawei initiated a new innovation centre with the Polish state-owned institute Poznan Supernetwork Computing Center. In Indonesia, Huawei has started to collaborate with the Indonesian government's Ministry of Telecommunications to build an ICT innovation centre.

Baidu, China's leading search, AI and data technology company, has established seven overseas branches in Brazil, India, Thailand, Indonesia, Japan, Egypt and the USA, and hired over 1,000 employees with a strategic focus on promoting mobile software tools to attract local users. Software tools such as DU Battery Saver, DU Speed Booster, ES File, Mobo Market, Simeji have been used in over 200 countries and regions, with about 260 million monthly active users. After accumulating a large amount of users of its software tools, and generating initial revenue, Baidu started to expand its businesses into other services.

Others, such as Alibaba and Tencent, are following an investment approach. Tencent especially stands out in overseas investments, with 28 per cent of its investments outside China, compared to Alibaba's 23 per cent and Baidu's 17 per cent. Israel is of particular interest to Alibaba. For instance, Alibaba invested in four Israeli companies, including QR code-generating software tool developer Visualead, ecommerce search venture Twiggle, Internet security service provider Thetaray and augmented reality company Infinity. It seems that Alibaba is exploring possible frontier technologies in Israel, whose companies are well known in China for innovativeness. China is investing in Israel's digital tech, electronics, agriculture, food, water, medtech and biotech industries. At the same time, ties between Israel and China embody significant growth potential for the Israeli economy. China is also involved in building infrastructures in Israel, such as digging the Carmel tunnels in Haifa, laying the light rail in Tel Aviv, and expanding the Ashdod and Haifa seaports. China is also encouraging the establishment of Israeli innovative enterprises in China. The establishment of a technological academic institute in Guangdong by an Israeli partner and financed by billionaire Li Ka-shing is an example of the role Chinese business people are playing in promoting bilateral relations.

In conclusion, Chinese entrepreneurs from a variety of industries are innovating in BRI countries. While some launch greenfield initiatives, others invest or just export products. In any case, the BRI helps to broaden the target geography for Chinese start-ups and incumbents alike, while deepening the ties between China and BRI countries. Not only Chinese enterprises see the potential of the BRI. For instance,

Siemens, the German high-tech giant has decided to join the BRI. In late March 2018, Siemens opened a special office in Beijing dedicated to the BRI. From this office will be organized all BRI projects in which Siemens participates, whether in China or in the other states along the New Silk Road.

THE THIRD ROAD: DIGITAL SILK ROAD

Why is the Digital Silk Road China's single most impressive opportunity for global innovation? Since the launch of BRI in 2013, Chinese President Xi has insisted that the New Silk Road would not be just about roads and railways but also include telecommunications, fibre and ecommerce. The March 2015 white paper articulating the vision for BRI called for growth in digital trade and the expansion of communications networks to develop a 'Digital Silk Road'.

'Beijing will lead the construction of the digital era equivalent of the World Trade Organisation (WTO), lay down the infrastructure of a "Digital Silk Road" through its One Belt, One Road initiative', said Wang Huiyao, founder and president of the Centre for China and Globalization (CCG). For instance, Alibaba's Jack Ma announced a partnership with the Malaysian government to establish the world's first 'digital free-trade zone' to reduce trade barriers in ecommerce: A first experiment of the digital era equivalent of the WTO. In 2016, China's digital economy, which consists of some 700 million Internet and mobile users, grew by nearly 20 per cent and contributed 27.2 trillion RMB (around $4 trillion) to the country's economy, according to a report released at the 2018 World Internet Conference (Xinhua 2018). China is the massive home base for starting a Digital Silk Road and can leverage an impressive, yet unsettling, domestic comparative advantage.

During the 2017 Wuzhen World Internet Conference, which featured most of the US, Chinese and Indian Internet giants, countries such as Saudi Arabia, Egypt, Turkey, Thailand, Laos and the United Arab Emirates formally committed to co-develop the Digital Silk Road with China. These six countries will expand broadband access, promote a digital transformation, encourage ecommerce cooperation as well as seek to encourage policymaking to create a transparent digital economy and promote cooperation in international standardization.

Initiatives are well under way with, for instance, Huawei delivering the cables for fibre optics, such as in Afghanistan recently, and BAT providing digital services. In particular, another infrastructure priority under the BRI is improving 'international communications connectivity' through 'the construction of cross-border optical cables and other communications trunk line networks'. State-owned enterprises in telecoms, including China Telecom, China Unicom and China Mobile, and also private companies such as Huawei, have already embarked on BRI-related projects. While providing such infrastructure, these firms encourage the adoption of China's Beidou satellite network as an alternative to GPS. ZTE and Huawei have expanded their efforts to supply 'smart city' projects in BRI nations such as Malaysia, Kenya and Germany. Two of China's ecommerce giants, Alibaba and JD.com, have already sought to link their global expansion to BRI. These companies are building warehouses in Russia, Central Asia and Southeast Asia.

However, it is not only ecommerce, communications networks and warehousing that China's digital giants export (Greeven and Wei, 2017). A true digital silk road is built on digital technology services, such as Alipay, Alibaba Cloud and WeChat. Besides expanding cross-border ecommerce and setting up overseas branches, Alibaba is also internationalizing its services such as Alibaba Cloud and Alipay. Initially, Alibaba Cloud opened a data centre in Hong Kong in 2014 and its first overseas data centre in Silicon Valley, to be followed by a joint venture YVOLV in Dubai with a local company Meraas, aiming to sell system integration services to companies and government organizations in the Middle East and North Africa. In June 2015, Alibaba Cloud launched its Marketplace Alliance Program, aiming to find global partners to build a cloud ecosystem and offer a one-stop cloud solution. By 2016, another five new data centres in Europe, Singapore, Australia, Japan and Middle East were established. Internationally, Alibaba is strongly competing with Amazon Web Services and Microsoft Azure Cloud Service.

Besides Alibaba Cloud, Alipay is one of the key successes of Alibaba's ecommerce business, the core of Alibaba's finance arm Ant

Financial, as well as the crucial glue of Alibaba's ecosystem. Alipay's international expansion is playing a significant role for Alibaba's ecosystem going global. In October 2013, Alipay started to support overseas shopping tax refunds in South Korea and expanded this service to Singapore and Europe in 2014. Now, it is available in over 150 countries and regions. Alipay has joined forces with One97 Communications, which oversees Paytm, India's largest mobile wallet provider, to fund payment services in the Indian ecommerce market.

WeChat, Tencent's flagship social communication tool, has eyed international markets since 2012. In Singapore, it collaborates with a local taxi-hailing app EasyTaxi to approach new users. In Indonesia, it has a joint venture with a large local media company PT Global Media and is already embedded in local Chinese communities. In South Africa, Tencent has a joint venture with Naspers (its biggest shareholder), promoting all kinds of services, including payment. In Europe, they cannot outcompete WhatsApp but nevertheless announced rapid user growth in Spain and Italy. By early 2018, there were reports of over 300 million overseas users for WeChat.

In 2016, a Digital Belt and Road Program (DBAR) was launched to strengthen the use of 'big data' among BRI members to better protect the environment. DBAR will analyse the evolution of ecosystems in Asia and in the rest of the world using satellite imagery. DBAR was initiated by the Chinese Academy of Sciences, which allocates €30 million to this programme for the next 5 years. In February 2018, this programme was further advanced with the creation of a Digital Belt and Road International Center of Excellence in Thailand. This centre is the result of cooperation between the National Research Council of Thailand (NRCT) and the Chinese Academy of Sciences.

Concluding, a digital power shift is under way and President Xi's BRI moves will make not only China thrive in the digital age but also a multitude of BRI countries. Here, we also have to raise a concern regarding the governance and monitoring of data in the Digital Silk Road. But, as China's domestic development has shown, there will be a lot of decentralization and experimentation.

OPPORTUNITIES AND CHALLENGES: PROMOTING CONNECTIVITY

What are the opportunities and challenges for innovation in countries along the BRI? The short answer is 'connectivity'. Connecting countries and stakeholders, jointly developing new business opportunities and developing a prosperous and healthy ecosystem is certainly an important prospect (cf. Chapter 2). It is, however, also a challenge to connect highly diverse cultures, business systems and local practices. Deep commitment and a mindset focusing on growth and collaboration, in combination with sufficiently long-term view, have the hope to overcome the challenges and exploit the opportunities. Considering that the BRI was written into China's constitution during the 19th CPC National Congress, it is unlikely that the BRI will be a short-term initiative (Shepard 2017). The opportunities and challenges that the BRI poses for Chinese innovation are therefore a significant direction and in line with the overall trends of China's global expansion.

Opportunities include the Digital Silk Road, fuelled by world-leading digital innovations from Chinese enterprises and their large home base of users. In particular, BRI countries can leverage China's experience and expertise in the Internet of Things, IT equipment, smartphones and digital technology. Second, there are significant opportunities in bridging developing and developed countries. Countries such as France, the Netherlands and Israel are already participating in the BRI. Lastly, the BRI provides opportunities for entrepreneurs, for not only Chinese but also the entrepreneurs from the BRI countries and beyond. The more private entrepreneurs take the lead in exporting innovations and building up a healthy global innovation ecosystem, the stronger the BRI will become in economic and technological impact. The potential is there, but it is up to entrepreneurs to take up on this challenge.

Challenges abound, as the other chapters in this book elaborate. While implementation of innovation projects and understanding of the widely diverse local markets is certainly a challenge, the biggest barrier for an innovative New Silk Road is talent. Managing and developing human capital for innovation is still a challenge for China and international talent development in particular is not one of its strengths currently. For BRI to have success in innovation and successfully expand the Digital Silk Road, a significant effort and commitment in international talent development is needed. So far, the importance of talent development for the BRI is more a footnote rather than a core principle.

CONCLUDING REMARKS

China's commitment to include innovation in the BRI includes an effort to 'export' an innovation ecosystem, not just products, projects and investments. Entrepreneurs are encouraged to explore and exploit opportunities and China is leveraging a strong domestic advantage: digital technology. Several insights stand out and warrant further research:

- China is expanding its innovation ecosystem across BRI countries and business ecosystems allow stakeholders to capture value from their initiatives. However, this also means building up a Chinese global innovation ecosystem, and economic influence, in over 60 countries.
- Entrepreneurship is a necessity and opportunity to ensure Chinese innovation will succeed along the BRI. China's domestic innovation power is derived from private entrepreneurs and so it will also need to be in the BRI. Much of the investment to date has been by state-owned enterprises, so there is a pressing need to encourage the private sector to participate. Most important will be to lead the private sector to those unknown but interesting BRI growth markets. Most of the Chinese private sector is just not aware of the potential. For instance, Pakistan has a population of over 200 million and is an early market in the making. Subsidies and fiscal policies may help but crucial will be information and opportunity recognition.
- The Digital Silk Road is one of the largest opportunities in BRI innovation for China and leverages a domestic comparative advantage in digital technology and application. It provides opportunities for not only BRI countries but also for MNCs to tap into significant local emerging markets. Yet, at the same time, there are concerns

of security, privacy and governance of data of more than 60 per cent of the world's population. How these will be addressed is important to the depth of involvement by participating countries. It will important to domestically raise the awareness of data security and privacy and improve alignment with global standards of compliance.

In conclusion, China, in collaboration with its partners and stakeholders, needs to orchestrate, rather than direct, initiatives to encourage innovative ways of working along the Belt and Road. China is rapidly emerging as an innovation nation and now faces the challenge of expanding its influence in innovation beyond its own borders in a manner that will bring lasting benefits to its neighbours.

REFERENCES

Abrami, R. M., W. C. Kirby, and F. W. McFarlan. 2014. 'Why China Can't Innovate'. *Harvard Business Review* 92 (3): 107–111.

Breznitz, Dan, and Michael Murphree. 2011. *Run of the Red Queen*. New Haven, CT: Yale University Press.

CEIBS. 2017. 'Jiang Jianqing: Financial Model Innovation under the BRI'. *CEIBS Alumni Magazine* 4, September 13. http://www.ceibs.edu/alumni-magazine/jiang-jianqing-financial-model-innovation-under-bri

Fu, Xiaolan. 2015. *China's Path to Innovation*. Cambridge, UK: Cambridge University Press.

Greeven, Mark J., and Wei. 2017. *Business Ecosystems in China: Alibaba and Competing Baidu, Tencent, Xiaomi and LeEco*. Routledge: Taylor & Francis Group.

Greeven, Mark J., George S. Yip, and Wei. 2019. *Pioneers, Hidden Champions, Change Makers and Underdogs: Lessons from China's Innovators*. Cambridge, MA: The MIT Press.

Hernández, H., F. Hervás, A. Tübke, A. Vezzani, M. Dosso, S. Amoroso ... and P. Gkotsis. 2015. *The EU Industrial R&D Investment Scoreboard*. Joint Research Centre: Institute for Prospective Technological Studies, European Commission, Luxembourg.

Huang, K. 2010. 'China's Innovation Landscape'. *Science* 329: 632–633.

National Bureau of Statistics of China. 2017. *China Statistical Yearbook 2017*. China Statistics Bureau. http://www.stats.gov.cn/tjsj/ndsj/2017/indexeh.htm

Nee, Victor, and Sonja Opper. 2012. *Capitalism from Below: Markets and Institutional Change in China*. Harvard University Press.

Pan, J. 2016. 'China's S&T Strategic Options'. Presentation given at Oxford Sino-UK Innovation and Development Forum, November 10.

Shepard, W. 2017. 'Why China Just Added the Belt and Road Initiative to Its Constitution'. *Forbes*, October 25.

Tylecote, A. 2006. 'Twin Innovation Systems, Intermediate Technology and Economic Development: History and Prospect for China'. *Innovation* 8 (1–2): 62–83.

Van de Kaa, G., and M. J. Greeven. 2017. 'LED Standardization in China and South East Asia: Stakeholders, Infrastructure and Institutional Regimes'. *Renewable & Sustainable Energy Reviews* 72: 863–870.

Williamson, P. J., and E. Yin. 2014. 'Accelerated Innovation: The New Challenge from China'. *MIT Sloan Management Review* 55 (4): 27–34.

Wu, Xiaobo. 2014. *Steering 30 Years: Chinese Companies 1978–2008* (In Chinese). China CITIC Press.

Xinhua. 2018. 'China's Digital Economy Reaches 27.2 Trillion Yuan: Report'. *Xinhua News*, November 9. http://en.ce.cn/Business/topnews/201811/09/t20181109_30746333.shtml

Yip, George S., and Bruce McKern. 2016. *China's Next Strategic Advantage: From Imitation to Innovation*. Cambridge, MA: The MIT Press.

Zeng, Ming, and Peter J. Williamson. 2007. *Dragons at Your Door: How Chinese Cost Innovation is Disrupting Global Competition*. Boston: Harvard Business School Press.

Chapter 13

'One Belt, One Road'
Risk Assessment and Chinese Investment

Chaowei Xiao and Chuchu Zhang

As many regions along the Belt and Road have long been struggling with terrorist attacks, crimes, wars and corruption, political risks pose important challenges for infrastructure projects and transnational investment. The chapter aims to contribute to the analysis and measurement of varying degree of political risks by identifying different types of political risks, mapping the spatial and temporal distribution of various political risks along the Silk Road Economic Belt and 21st Century Maritime Silk Road based upon the Global Database of Events, Language, and Tone (GDELT) data sets from October 2013 to May 2018. By adopting the bivariate Moran's I model to compare the distribution of political risks along the Belt and Road and that of the Chinese Belt and Road Initiative (BRI) investment and construction projects based upon the China Global Investment Tracker (CGIT) data, the chapter also generates the overall political risk profile of Chinese BRI projects. Our findings show that a particularly high percentage of Chinese BRI projects are distributed in regions with high political risks.

INTRODUCTION

In the context that the global economy experienced a slow recovery and that the international trade and investment landscape and rules for multilateral trade underwent important adjustments, the Chinese President Xi Jinping proposed the BRI in 2013. The BRI is set to open up new investment and trade opportunities, and reinvigorate flow of capital, goods and services between China and countries along the Belt and Road. In the past five years, over 88 countries and international non-governmental organizations (NGOs) have signed 103 documents for cooperation on the BRI (Xinhua 2018), and the initiative is expected to enter a new stage in 2019. However, as many regions along the Belt and Road have long been struggling with terrorist risks, crime, wars, corruption, etc., the sustainability of BRI is beset by potential political risks, and China has already experienced certain economic losses in Malaysia and Myanmar due to regional conflicts and alternation of political power. With this in mind, the chapter tries to identify different types of political risks faced by BRI, examine the potential costs they may bring to multinational enterprises, and map the risks along the Belt and Road. It is worth noting that today BRI has already developed into a broad initiative that is open to all nations and is not limited by geographic boundaries. However, this study focuses on the regions along the Belt and Road in the narrow sense, that is, the Silk Road Economic Belt and 21st Century Maritime Silk Road. Based upon the concept of the Silk Road Economic Belt and 21st Century Maritime Silk Road proposed by the official website of Xinhua Silk Road (2018), the chapter analyses 65 countries in East Asia, Southeast Asia, West Asia, South Asia, Central Asia and Central and East Europe.

The first contribution of this research is to provide a comprehensive assessment of the political risks along the Belt and Road including political instability, social unrest, lack of democracy and external conflict. Second, it uses big data sets and spatial statistical methods, which not only enable visualization of multifarious political risks at the micro-level scale but also provide a new quantitative analysis model to examine the political risk profile of China's BRI projects.

The remainder of this chapter proceeds as follows. A literature review on BRI and on political risk assessment is provided in the second section. The third section digs into the theories of political risks, identifies different political risk indicators and introduces the data sets that can be used to quantify these indicators. The fourth section elaborates the spatial statistical methods that are used in the study to analyse big data sets. In particular, the chapter adopts the method of kernel density estimation and bivariate Moran's I model. The fifth section presents the findings and provides a comparison between the distribution of the political risks along the Belt and Road and that of China's BRI investment and construction projects. Conclusions are given in the last section.

LITERATURE REVIEW

While there has been a remarkable increase of academic research on BRI in recent years dealing with topics ranging from motivations behind BRI (Huang 2016; Wang 2016; Yu 2017), Chinese foreign policy (Ferdinand 2016), impact on globalization (Jin 2016; Liu 2017), implications for countries and regions along BRI (Herrero and Xu 2017; Lim and Cheng 2015; Zeng 2017), to infrastructure connectivity (Fan and He 2016; Li 2018) and cultural exchange (Xing 2016; Zhao 2016), there has generally been a dearth of analyses of political risks along the Belt and Road, which have a great impact on the business environment and sustainability of BRI. The small number of publications devoted to it are limited in scope either due to their focus on specific countries (Ren and Niu 2015; Ren and Yi 2015) or due to their interest in a particular type of risk such as terrorism (Zhao et al., 2016).

Both business studies and political science research agrees that understanding political risks matters for investment and business. Studies of political risks have traditionally been dominated by qualitative methods and highly contextualized analysis (Ashley and Bonner 1987; Kennedy 1988; Kobrin 1979), and there lacks empirical information and quantitative measurement of specific risks. In recent years, more and more political risk scholars have attempted to combine qualitative and quantitative methods (Baek and Qian 2011; Jensen 2008). However, such studies are often problematic and fraught with pitfalls, as they heavily depend on rating indexes provided by rating agencies. On the one hand, rating indexes are mostly country-scale data and cannot reflect micro-level variations. On the other hand, as rating data of political risks rely largely on expert judgement, research based upon these data is often questioned for its objectivity.

The chapter aims to fill the gap in literature on BRI by providing a comprehensive evaluation of several political risk indicators along the Belt and Road. Also, the chapter tries to contribute to research on political risks by using big data sets and spatial statistical methods which not only enable micro-level and more objective analysis but also lead to effective visualization of political risks.

THEORY AND DATA

The chapter follows Root (1972), Brewers (1981) and Jodice (1984), and defines political risks as the probability of disruption of multinational enterprises' investment and operations by political forces or events. Political risks are divided by Robock (1971) into two categories: (a) macro political risks, meaning the probability of discontinuities of investment, trade and business that can have impact to all multinational enterprises and (b) micro political risks, referring to the probability of discontinuities that are selectively directed towards specific fields of business activity. This study focuses on macro political risks along the Belt and Road, aiming to analyse the probability of events that have the potential to affect profits or goals of multinational enterprises in general.

Academic scholars and rating agencies have introduced multifarious indicators to measure political risks. As is demonstrated in Table 13.1, we find that the most common indicators include regime type, political stability, social unrests, external conflicts, ethnic fragmentation and corruption. Considering the difficulty to quantify corruption, and the correlation between regime type and corruption, as in this example 'advanced democratic institutions eventually reduced corruption' (Sung 2004), as well as the correlation between ethnic fragmentation and political instability, as in 'areas with high levels of ethnic polarization encountered more terrorist attacks' (Python, Brandsch, and Tskhay 2017), this chapter excludes those two variables from the analysis. It focuses on the first four indicators and tries to quantify them with the help of big data.

Despite the frequent appearance of the term 'big data' in media reports, policy statements and academic papers, there is no straight hard

Table 13.1 *Indicators of Political Risks in Existing Literature*

Economist Intelligence Unit (EIU)	Baek and Qian	Robin et al.
Regime type	Democratic accountability	Political leadership
History of political instability	Government stability	Political terrorism
Proclivity to labour unrest	Internal conflicts	Civil war risks
A country's neighbourhood	External conflicts	External conflict
Ethnic fragmentation	Ethnic tensions	Racial and nationality tensions
Corruption	Corruption	Corruption in government
Trust in institutions	Military in politics	Military in politics
Status of minorities	Investment profile	Political party development
Level of social provision	Law and order	Quality of bureaucracy
Inequality	Religious tensions	Law and order tradition
State history	Socioeconomic Conditions	Organized religion in politics
	Bureaucracy quality	Economic expectations versus reality
		Economic planning failures

Source: Baek and Qian (2011), EIU (2009) and Robin, Liew, and Stevens (1996).

number that defines big data. In general, big data is considered to be a large amount of information that is generated automatically in the form of text, video, images, social media and information from sensor or machine-to-machine data (Beyer and Laney 2012). For social scientists, a vital obstacle to using big data is that the data accessible to them are often derive from mixed sources ranging from social media to digital sensors, which are not designed to produce valid and reliable data for academic analysis (Lazer 2015).

The data used for the analysis in this chapter have been acquired from the GDELT, created by Kalev Leetaru of Yahoo!, Georgetown University and other scholars. As a metadata (Bodas-Sagi and Labeaga 2016, 38), the GDELT Project collects information of events from 1979 to the present from the world's broadcast, print and web news in nearly every corner of every country in over 100 languages, and is one of the largest open-access spatio-temporal data sets in existence. The advantage of this database is not limited to its volume of data; it mainly collects its data from printed and web news rather than from completely different types of sources, which increases the data's reliability for social science research.

This study extracts and processes the data in GDELT, and gets the data of *assault, protest, coerce* and *fight* events in countries and regions along the Belt and Road from October 2013 to May 2018. We select data of this period because the BRI was not proposed until October 2013, and because another data we use in this study, CGIT, ends in May 2018. The data of *assault* refer to events that involve the use of unconventional forms of violence, which do not require high levels of organization, such as terrorist attacks and crimes. The data of *protest* refer to events that involve civilian demonstrations and other collective actions such as strikes, hunger strikes and rallies carried out as protests against enterprises or governments. The data of *coerce* includes events that involve repression against civilians, confiscation and destruction of property, restrictions on political freedoms. The data of *fight* contain events that involve the use of conventional force and acts of war, typically by organized armed groups.

As is demonstrated in Table 13.2, the four data variables respectively reflect political instability, social unrest, lack of democracy and external conflict, and bring different types of potential costs for the investment and operations of multinational enterprises.

To analyse the political risks of Chinese investment and construction in countries along the Belt and Road, we also employ the data of CGIT. The CGIT is the world's first and most comprehensive data

Table 13.2 *Data, Political Risk Indicators, and Potential Costs for Multinational Enterprises*

Data	Political Risk Indicator	Potential Costs for Multinational Enterprises
Assault	Political instability	Hiring private security; providing security training to employees and families; losing properties because of looting
Protest	Social unrest	Potential work and transport stoppages; losing man hours
Coerce	Lack of democracy	Government nationalization and confiscation actions; repudiation of contracts; increasing taxes and tariffs
Fight	External conflict	Losing contracts, rebuilding, loss of life

Source: The authors.

that tracks the global investment and construction of Chinese enterprises from January 2005 to May 2018. As a variable in the data is BRI, we select the data which are marked as BRI projects. It is worth noting that the CGIT only marks the geographic location of Chinese oversea investment projects at the national scale. Therefore, we search the geographic location of each of China's BRI investment projects from October 2013 to May 2018 at the local scale online, in order to examine the implications of the political risks along the Belt and Road on Chinese BRI investment and construction projects at the local scale.

METHOD

To visualize and analyse the political risks along the Belt and Road, this chapter combines the approach of kernel density and spatial overlay. In the first step, the chapter estimates kernel density of the distribution of each political risk to analyse the spatio-temporal patterns of *assault*, *protest*, *coerce* and *fight*. Next, it adopts the method of spatial overlay to conduct synthetic analysis of the four types of risks.

The kernel density calculates a magnitude-per-unit area from point or polyline features using a kernel function to fit a smoothly tapered surface to each point or polyline. It is a non-parametric method to estimate a variable's probability density function, based upon a finite data sample (Silverman 1986). The method has recently become a commonly applied spatial analysis tool to draw a density surface in a Geographic Information Systems (GIS)—a 'computer system that stores and links nongraphic attributes or geographically referenced data with graphic map features to allow a wide range of information processing and display operations' (Antenucci et al. 1991, 281)—environment.

The spatial overlay is one of the most fundamental GIS functions that aggregates data from one layer to another. By superimposing together multiple data sets which have the same spatial reference parameters such as the coordinate system, this method enables the identification of the spatial relationship between various political risks. The overlay creates a composite map of political risks by combining the data sets' geographic attributes.

The bivariate Moran's I is a model that helps evaluate whether one variable is spatially correlated to another variable. The model is not available in ArcGIS but can be computed in GeoDa.

EMPIRICAL RESULTS

In the first step, as is shown in Figure 13.1, the study uses scatter plot to map the incidents of *assault*, *protest*, *coerce* and *fight* respectively over the period of October 2013 to May 2018.

Next, as is demonstrated in Figure 13.2, the study adopts kernel density estimation by using the weighted overlay tool to multiply the incidents by the weights which were measured by GDELT database according to the incidents' impact on a country or region's safety and stability, and by aggregating points and calculate the Getis-Ord Gi★ statistic (hot spot analysis) for each bin. The Getis-Ord Gi★ statistic is calculated by the Hot Spot Analysis tool of ArcGIS, a cloud-based mapping and research platform. The resultant z-scores and p-values show where features with either high or low values cluster spatially. The Hot Spot Analysis tool examines each feature in the context of neighbouring features. Only if a feature has a high value and is

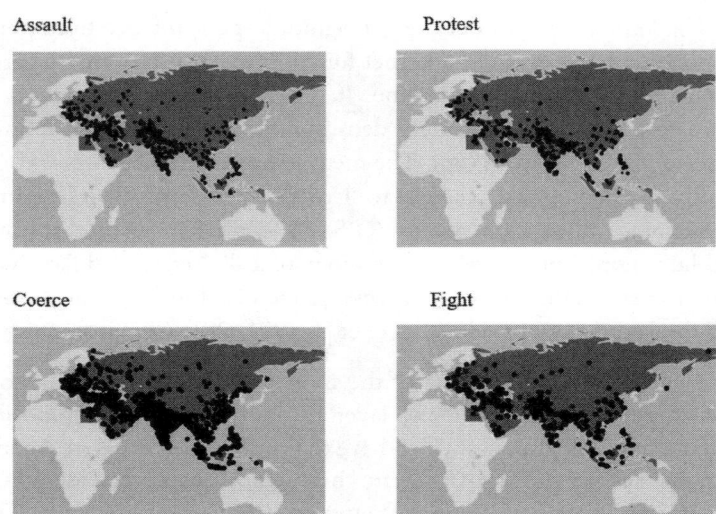

Figure 13.1 *Scatter Plot Map of* Assault, Protest, Coerce *and* Fight *(October 2013–May 2018)*

Source: The authors; data taken from GDELT.

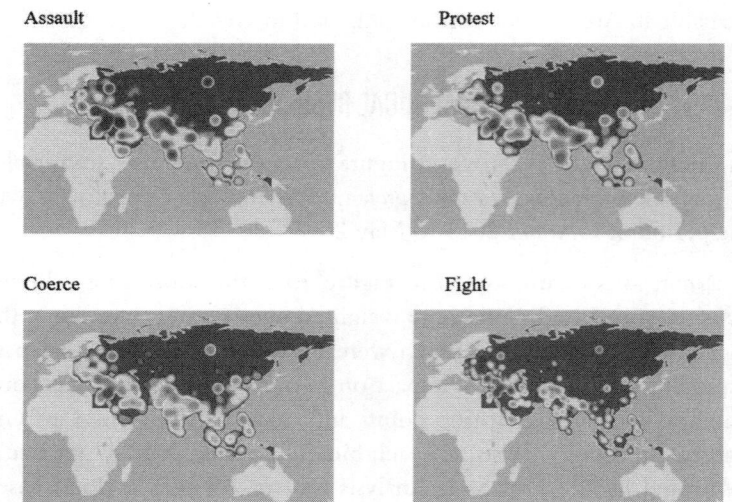

Figure 13.2 *Kernel Density Map of* Assault, Protest, Coerce *and* Fight *in October 2013–May 2018*

Source: The authors; data taken from GDELT.

surrounded by other features with high values, will it be marked as a statistically significant hot spot. The local sum for a feature and its neighbours is compared proportionally to the sum of all features. If there is a huge gap between the local sum and the expected local sum that does not result from random chance, then it produces the result of a statistically significant z-score.

The Getis-Ord local statistic is calculated as:

$$G_i^\star = \frac{\sum_{j=1}^n w_{i,j} x_j - \bar{X} \sum_{j=1}^n w_{i,j}}{s \sqrt{\frac{[n \sum_{j=1}^n w_{i,j}^2 - (\sum_{j=1}^n w_{i,j})^2]}{n-1}}}$$

Where x_j is the attribute value for feature j, $w_{i,j}$ is the spatial weight between feature i and j, n is equal to the total number of features and

$$\bar{X} = \frac{\sum_{j=1}^n x_j}{n}$$

$$S = \sqrt{\frac{\sum_{j=1}^n x_j^2}{n} - (\bar{X})^2}$$

The $G_i^\star$ statistics is a z-score so no further calculations are required.

In the map, the colour of dark black indicates a cluster of incidents and a strong impact on local safety. The aim of generating the kernel density map is to show the static distribution of the four types of incidents along the Belt and Road during October 2013 to May 2018. As demonstrated in Figure 13.1, unlike conventional wisdom which states that the most common political risks faced by multinational enterprises are political instability risks including those caused by terrorism and crime, the political risks that has the widest spatial influence along the Belt and Road are the risks of lack of democracy, followed by external conflict, political instability and social unrest.

A comparison of the kernel density estimation of the four types of incidents yields a couple of important findings that have significant implications for foreign investment along the Belt and Road.

First, it is worth noting that different countries and regions are beset with different types of incident. For instance, while the Metohija region suffered from more *assault* incidents, the Mindanao Island witnessed more *coerce* and *fight* incidents. This means that multinational enterprises need to pay close attention to potential costs caused by political instability when investing and operating in the Metohija, and to the costs caused by lack of democracy and external conflicts in the Mindanao Island. Another example is that while Jakarta suffered from more *coerce* incidents, Dhaka underwent more *protest* events. This indicates that multinational enterprises need to lay more emphasis on potential costs caused by lack of democracy in Jakarta and social unrest in Dhaka.

Second, we find that very different results can be yielded when we analyse political risks at different spatial scales. For instance, although few incidents occurred in Russia as a whole, the north part of the country, especially Moscow and the North Caucasus, appears to be highly instable and carries high political risks. To cite another example, although Saudi Arabia appears to be a country that has relatively high level of political risks, the Hejaz region has low political risks.

After visualizing and analysing different types of political risks along the Belt and Road, we examine the overall political risk profile of Chinese BRI investment and construction projects by comparing the geographic distribution of political risks along the Belt and Road, and that of Chinese BRI investment and construction. To do so, the study first adopts the spatial overlay method and generates Figure 13.3 based on the above-mentioned kernel density estimation of the *assault*, *protest*, *coerce* and *fight* incidents. The aim is to show the impact of the four types of risks along the Belt and Road in general.

In the next step, we adopt the CGIT data and use scatter plot to map the Chinese BRI investment and construction projects at a local scale, as shown in Figure 13.4. Based on Figure 13.4, we adopt kernel density estimation model to visualize the density of the Chinese BRI investment and construction, and generate Figure 13.5.

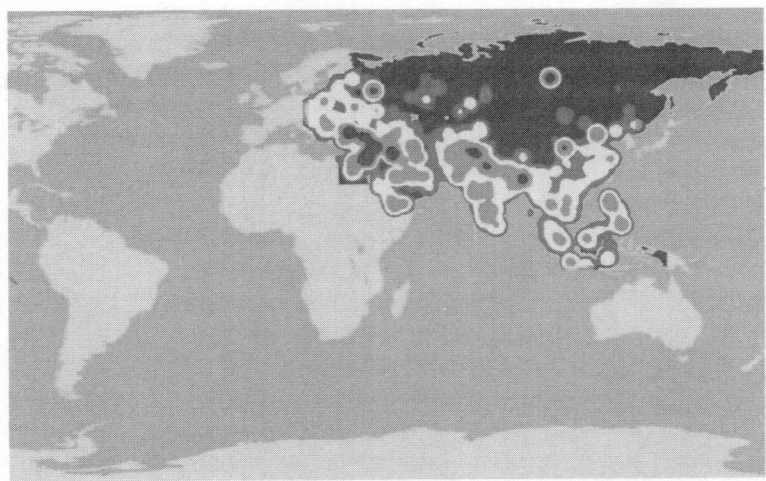

Figure 13.3 *Spatial Overlay Map of Assault, Protest, Coerce and Fight in October 2013–May 2018*

Source: The authors; data taken from GDELT.

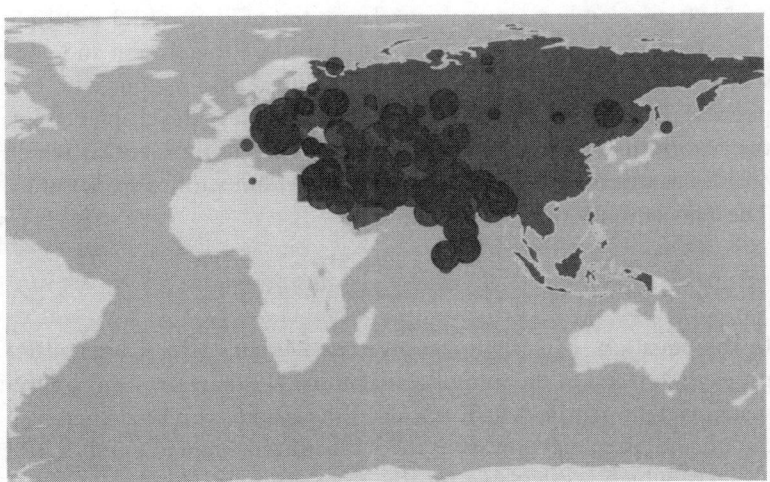

Figure 13.4 *Scatter Plot Map of Chinese BRI Investment and Construction Contracts (October 2013–May 2018)*

Source: The authors; data taken from CGIT.

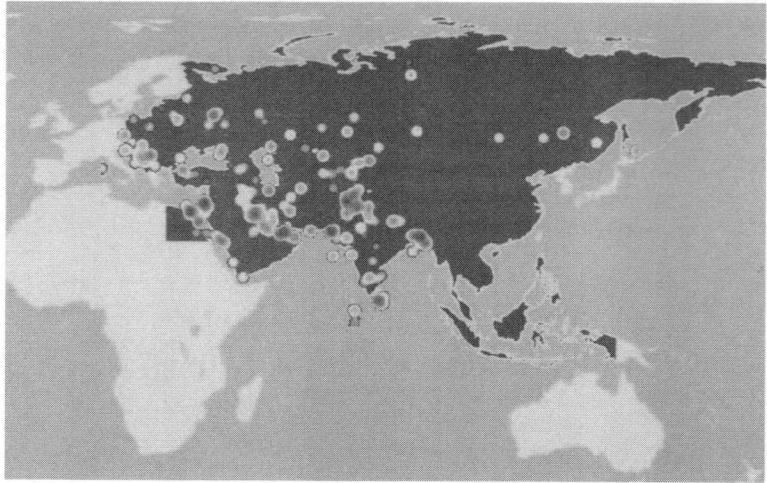

Figure 13.5 *Kernel Density Map of Chinese BRI Investment and Construction Contracts (October 2013–May 2018)*
Source: The authors; data taken from CGIT.

Next, we conduct a spatial correlation test of Figure 13.3 and 13.5. The aim is to examine whether China has more investment and construction projects in regions with high political risks regions with low political risks. To conduct the spatial correlation test, the chapter adopts the algorithm of local bivariate Moran's I by using GeoDa, which enables us to calculate spatial correlations within various spatial units. The calculation formula is as follows:

$$Il_{eu} = z^e \sum_{j=1}^{N} w_{ij} z_{ij}^u$$

In the equation, l_{eu} is the local bivariate Moran's I for China's BRI projects. N refers to the sum of spatial units. W_{ij} represents an N-by-N spatial weight matrix, which calculates the spatial correlation between the ith and jth spatial unit. z_j^u is the standardized value of China's BRI projects, which is calculated for the jth spatial unit.

The four possibilities generated by local bivariate Moran's I represent four type of local spatial correlations: Quadrant I, suggesting that the numbers of both political risks and Chinese BRI projects are large;

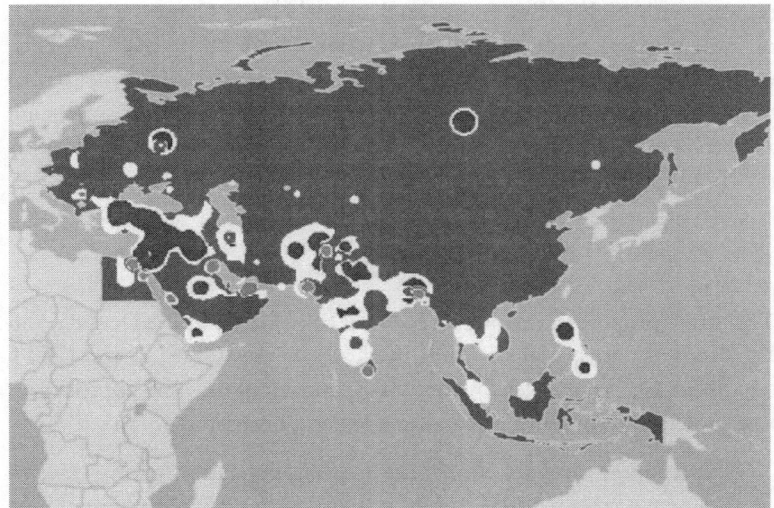

Figure 13.6 *Spatial Correlation between Kernel Density Map of Chinese BRI Investment and Construction Contracts and Spatial Overlay Map of Assault, Protest, Coerce and Fight (October 2013– May 2018)*
Source: The authors; data taken from GDELT and CGIT.

Quadrant II, indicating small numbers of political risks are surrounded by large numbers of Chinese BRI projects; Quadrant III, indicating large numbers of political risks are surrounded by small numbers of Chinese BRI projects; Quadrant IV, meaning that both political risks and Chinese BRI projects are small.

As Figure 13.6 demonstrates, Quadrant III and IV are not marked with any colour. The black colour marks Quadrant I, and the white colour marks Quadrant II. We find that China's BRI investment and construction projects cluster around both the regions with low political risks such as Kolkata, Zadar, Atyrau, Muscat and Alexandria, and regions with high political risks such as the North Caucasus, Baghdad, Basra, Aden, West Bank, Luzon, Mindanao Island. As there are more regions marked with the black we conclude that more China's BRI investment and construction projects are distributed in regions with high political risks than those with low political risks. This is partly because many regions with high political risks such as the North Caucasus have rich oil and mineral resources. Hence, when conducting BRI projects, Chinese multinational enterprises need to be invested and prepared to balance out the passive impacts of political risks and take measures such as purchasing customized insurance that covers the enterprises' interests on chosen territories to mitigate the potential political risks.

CONCLUSIONS

This study proposes a theoretical political risks analysis model based upon big data sets and spatial statistical methods. It uses GDELT and CGIT data from October 2013 to May 2018, and combines the approach of kernel density estimation, spatial overlay and bivariate Moran's I.

This chapter aims to contribute to the application of big data to social science research and public policy. Along with the emergence of the information-sensing Internet of things such as mobile devices, remote sensing, microphones and software logs, the so-called big data revolution not only has a great impact on natural science, but also on social science studies. Nonetheless, the use of big data in social science still faces huge challenges, given that 'the successful collection and rigorous analysis of this data require new skills, new collaborations, new research methods' (Metzler et al. 2016, 17). This research tries to contribute to this field in the specific context of a major economic development initiative. By adopting spatial statistical methods that are widely used in geography to analyse economic and political issues, the research suggests that interdisciplinary analysis is essential for social scientists to get the most meaningful conclusions out of big data sets.

Compared to traditional ways of analysing political risks, which largely rely on rating indexes and qualitative methods, the model proposed in this chapter allows micro-level risk examination. It leads to more effective visual analysis of the distribution of political risks, and makes the entire risk assessment process more reliable, reproducible and scalable. The proposed model can be further validated and improved by obtaining additional data on similar risks.

There are important policy implications that can be derived from this study. First, the chapter emphasizes the importance of distinguishing different types of political risks and adopting different policies to cope with each of them. For instance, while enterprises can reduce risks brought by political instability such as terrorist attacks and crimes through an increase of security personnel, risks caused by lack of democracy may only be addressed by intergovernmental negotiations. Second, the chapter considers that evaluation of political risks at exclusively the country level seems to be limited, given that a high-risk region may exist within a peaceful country. The mapping of political risks along the Belt and Road at a micro-level scale suggests the necessity for decision-makers to formulate investment and trade plans at the local level. This includes the prime mover in the BRI, China. As risk varies in nature and intensity across the participating countries, the actions China will need to take to reduce risk will have to be specific to each location. Third, the chapter indicates that a large proportion of Chinese BRI investment and construction projects are distributed in regions with high political risks. This means that Chinese multinational enterprises should take sophisticated measures to maximize their opportunities while mitigating potential costs caused by political risks.

REFERENCES

Ashley, David B., and Joseph J. Bonner. 1987. 'Political Risks in International Construction'. *Journal of Construction Engineering and Management* 113 (3): 447–467.

Baek, Kyeonghi, and Xingwan Qian. 2011. 'An Analysis on Political Risks and the Flow of Foreign Direct Investment in Developing and Industrialized Economies'. *Economics, Management, and Financial Markets* 6 (4): 60–91.

Beyer, M. A., and D. Laney. 2012. *The Importance of 'Big Data': A Definition*. Stamford, CT: Gartner.

Bodas-Sagi, D., and J. Labeaga. 2016. 'Using GDELT Data to Evaluate the Confidence on the Spanish Government Energy Policy'. *International Journal of Interactive Multimedia and Artificial Intelligence* 3 (6): 38–43.

Brewers, T. 1981. 'Political Risk Assessment for Foreign Direct Investment Decisions: Better Methods for Better Results'. *Columbia Journal of World Business* 16 (1): 5–12.

EIU. 2009. 'Political Instability Index: Vulnerability to Social and Political Unrest'. *The Economist*, March 19. http://viewswire.eiu.com/index.asp?layout=VWArticleVW3&article_id=874361472

Fan, Z., and H. He. 2016. 'The "Cut In" Strategy of the National Infrastructure Connectivity of the Belt and Road Countries'. *Forum of World Economics & Politics* 6: 129–142.

Ferdinand, P. 2016. 'Westward Ho: The China Dream and "One Belt, One Road": Chinese Foreign Policy under Xi Jinping'. *International Affairs* 92 (4): 941–957.

Herrero, A., and J. Xu. 2017. 'China's Belt and Road Initiative: Can Europe Expect Trade Gains?' *China and World Economy* 25 (6): 84–99.

Huang, Y. 2016. 'Understanding China's Belt & Road Initiative: Motivation, Framework and Assessment'. *China Economic Review* 240: 314–321.

Jensen, Nathan. 2008. 'Political Risk, Democratic Institutions, and Foreign Direct Investment'. *The Journal of Politics* 70 (4): 1040–1052.

Jin Bei. 2016. 'On the Era of Economic Globalization 3.0: Concurrently Discuss the Concept of Intercommunication of "One Belt One Road"'. *China Industrial Economics* 1: 5–20.

Jodice, D. A. 1984. 'Trends in Political Risk Assessment: Prospects for the Future'. In *International Political Risk Management*, edited by Fariborz Ghadar and Theodore H. Moran, 8–26. Ghadar and Associates: New Dimensions.

Kennedy, Charles R. 1988. 'Political Risk Management: A Portfolio Planning Model'. *Business Horizons* 31 (6): 26–33.

Kobrin, Stephen J. 1979. 'Political Risk: A Review and Reconsideration'. *Journal of International Business Studies* 10 (1): 67–80.

Li Nan. 2018. 'The Strategic Support of the Belt and Road: Infrastructure Connectivity Analysis'. *Enterprise Economy* 8: 170–174.

Lim, Alvin, and Cheng Hin. 2015. 'China's "Belt and Road" and Southeast Asia: Challenges and Prospects'. *Jati-Journal of Southeast Asian Studies* 20: 3–15.

Liu Weidong. 2017. *Inclusive Globalization: New Philosophy of China's Belt and Road Initiative*. Beijing: The Commercial Press.

Metzler, K., David A. Kim, Nick Allum, and Angella Denman. 2016. Who is Doing Computational Social Science? Trends in Big Data Research. *SAGE White Paper*. https://us.sagepub.com/sites/default/files/compsocsci.pdf

Python, A., Jürgen Brandsch, and Aliya Tskhay. 2017. 'Provoking Local Ethnic Violence—A Global Study on Ethnic Polarization and Terrorist Targeting'. *Political Geography* 58: 77–89.

Ren Lin, and Niu Heng. 2015. '"One Belt One Road" Investment Political Risk Study in Sri Lanka'. *Global Development Perspective* 15. 014.

Ren Lin, and Yi Lin Dian. 2015. '"One Belt One Road" Investment Political Risk Study in Israel'. *Global Development Perspective* 15. 011.

Robin, D., John M. Liew, and Ross L. Stevens. 1996. 'Political Risk in Emerging and Developed Markets'. *Financial Analysts Journal* 52 (3): 71–76.

Robock, S. H. 1971. 'Political Risk: Identification and Assessment'. *Columbia Journal of World Business* 6 (4): 6–20.

Root, F. R. 1972. 'Analyzing Political Risks in International Business'. In *Multinational Enterprise in Transition: Selected Readings and Essays*, edited by A. Kapoor and Philip Grub, 354–365. Detroit, Michigan: Darwin Press.

Silverman, B. W. 1986. *Density Estimation for Statistics and Data Analysis*. London: Chapman & Hall.

Sung, Hung-En. 2004. 'Democracy and Political Corruption: A Cross-National Comparison'. *Crime, Law and Social Change* 41 (2): 179–194

Wang, Y. 2016. 'Offensive for Defensive: The Belt and Road Initiative and China's New Grand Strategy'. *The Pacific Review* 29 (3): 455–463.

Xing Liju. 2016. 'The Humanistic Exchanges Beneficial to the "Belt and Road Initiative": Difficulties and Their Possible Solutions'. *International Studies* 6: 5–17.

Xinhua Silk Road. 2017. 'Which Countries Are Along the Belt and Road?' December 25.

Xinhua. 2018. 'China's Trade with Countries along One Belt and One Road Has Exceeded 5 Trillion US Dollars'. Xinhuanet, May 17.

Yu Hong. 2017. 'Motivation behind China's "One Belt, One Road" Initiatives and Establishment of the Asian Infrastructure Investment Bank'. *Journal of Contemporary China* 26 (105): 353–368.

Zeng Jinghan. 2017. 'Does Europe Matter? The Role of Europe in Chinese Narratives of "One Belt One Road" and "New Type of Great Power Relations"'. *Journal of Common Market Studies* 55 (5): 1162–1176.

Zhao Liqing. 2016. 'Research on the Realization Path of Cultural Exchanges under the Belt and Road Strategy'. *Academic Forum* 3 (4): 144–148.

Zhao Mingyan, S. Dong, Z. Wang, H. Cheng, F. Qin, Y. Li ... and F. Li. 2016. 'Assessment of Countries' Security Situation along the Belt and Road and Countermeasures'. *Bulletin of Chinese Academy of Sciences* 31 (6): 689–696.

Chapter 14

RMB Internationalization in Relation to the Belt and Road Initiative

Yimin Zhang and Qinli Zhu

INTRODUCTION

In this chapter, we will discuss how internationalization of the RMB requires some basic reform of China's monetary policy and how it is related to the Belt and Road Initiative (BRI). As China has become a capital-intensive economy, it is natural for the country to engage in outward capital investment, and this outward capital investment would help balance China's international payments as it would offset the country's trade surplus. This impact on the balance of payments also provides a complete cycle for the international flow of the RMB, a necessity for the internationalization of China's currency. The BRI provides an excellent opportunity for Chinese firms to make outward investments while promoting regional economic growth. Moreover, the internationalization of the RMB would significantly help firms in the BRI regions to manage currency risks and reduce financing costs.

In the literature on this topic, Wen and Xu (2015), Zhu (2015), Lin and Wang (2016), and Lian and Liu (2017) studied the future international financial system with RMB internationalization and BRI economic development. Zou et al. (2015) examined international trade relations between China and BRI countries, while Lu (2013), Bai, Wu, and Zhang (2016), and Tao and Gu (2016) studied the progress of RMB cross-border payments in international trade between China and BRI countries. These studies looked at different aspects of RMB internationalization and all agreed that the BRI is closely related to the progress of RMB internationalization.

Since China's accession to the WTO, the country has grown into one of the largest trading nations in the world. In 2015, the value of China's international trade, including both exports and imports, reached $4,400 billion, and Chinese exports made up 13.8 per cent of the world's total. In contrast, however, China's currency, the RMB, was only used for about 1 per cent of international trade. This posed a large exchange-rate risk for firms that use non-Chinese currency to do business with Chinese firms. In international investment and finance, there is also a similar situation: China has attracted a large amount of foreign investment, but most of this international investment into the country is conducted in non-Chinese currency. Apart from the exchange-rate risk, this would also create a foreign liability in China's international accounts, even though the funds from the foreign investment are converted into RMB when spent in China.

To manage the problem of exchange-rate risk when Chinese firms have increasingly been doing business in competitive global markets, it is natural that the Chinese currency, the RMB, should be more widely used in international trade and investment. While markets have a strong demand for internationalization of the RMB, there are some basic regulatory structures concerning the monetary policies that must be reformed before the RMB can become truly internationalized.

The basic requirements for internationalization of the RMB include ensuring that the monetary policy of China concerning supply of RMB is independent and effective, that interest rates and exchange rates are market based, and there should be a channel for international flow of the RMB. First, we look at China's money supply.

CHINA'S MONEY SUPPLY AND INTERNATIONAL BALANCE OF PAYMENTS

The money supply of China, in terms of the monetary base, expanded substantially during 2000–2016, as shown in Figure 14.1. In 2000, China's monetary base was RMB 1,465 billion, but, at the end of 2016, the monetary base had reached RMB 6,830 billion, with a growth of more than 360 per cent during the period. This growth can be explained by the expansion of the balance sheet of the People's Bank of China (PBC). From Table 14.1, we can see that the amount of monetary base is determined by three major assets held by the PBC: credits to Chinese financial institutions, credits to the Chinese government and the official reserve of foreign assets.

During 2000–2013, credits to Chinese financial institutions were rather stable at around RMB 2,000 million, and credits to the Chinese government were also stable at below RMB 300 million until 2003 and then below RMB 1,700 million since 2004. It is clear that the growth of monetary base in China has been largely driven by the country's official reserve of foreign assets. Indeed, the official reserve

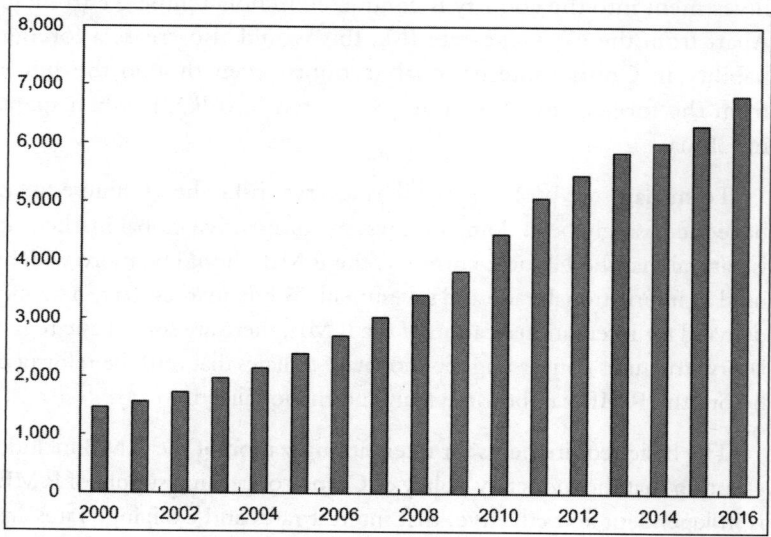

Figure 14.1 The Monetary Base of China (Billion RMB)
Source: PBC (2017).

Table 14.1 The Balance Sheet of the People's Bank of China (Billion RMB)

	Assets				Liabilities			
	Total	Foreign assets	Claims on government	Claims on financial institutions	Total	Monetary base	Deposit of government	Ratio of FX to Monetary base
2000	3,939.54	1,558.28	158.28	2,211.96	3,939.54	3,195.73	743.80	0.46
2001	4,254.06	1,986.04	282.13	1,985.89	4,254.06	3,395.78	858.28	0.56
2002	5,110.76	2,324.29	286.38	2,500.09	5,110.76	3,921.50	1,189.26	0.56
2003	6,200.41	3,114.18	290.10	2,796.12	6,200.41	4,683.01	1,517.40	0.64
2004	7,865.53	4,696.01	296.96	2,872.56	7,865.53	6,985.58	879.95	0.66
2005	10,367.60	6,333.92	289.24	3,744.44	10,367.60	8,454.12	1,913.48	0.74
2006	12,857.47	8,577.26	285.64	3,994.56	12,857.47	10,733.85	2,123.62	0.79
2007	16,913.98	12,482.52	1,631.77	2,799.69	16,913.98	13,585.66	3,328.32	0.85
2008	20,709.60	16,254.35	1,619.60	2,835.65	20,709.60	17,500.22	3,209.38	0.85
2009	22,753.50	18,533.30	1,566.20	2,654.00	22,753.50	18,604.92	4,148.58	0.94
2010	25,927.49	21,541.96	1,542.11	2,843.42	25,927.49	22,580.83	3,346.66	0.92
2011	28,098.00	23,790.00	1,540.00	2,768.03	28,098.00	24,797.70	3,299.95	0.94
2012	29,453.72	24,141.69	1,531.37	3,780.66	29,453.72	26,622.52	2,831.20	0.89

(Table 14.1 continued)

(Table 14.1 continued)

	Assets				Liabilities			Ratio of FX to Monetary base
	Total	Foreign assets	Claims on government	Claims on financial institutions	Total	Monetary base	Deposit of government	
2013	31,727.86	27,223.35	1,531.27	2,973.23	31,727.86	27,878.51	3,849.35	0.95
2014	33,824.88	27,862.29	1,531.27	4,431.32	33,824.88	30,061.50	3,763.38	0.90
2015	31,783.70	25,383.07	1,531.27	4,869.36	31,783.70	28,294.95	3,488.75	0.88
2016	34,371.16	22,979.58	1,527.41	9,864.17	34,371.16	30,947.96	3,423.20	0.71
2017	36,293.16	22,116.41	1,527.41	12,649.34	36,293.16	32,087.59	4,205.58	0.67

Source: PBC (2017)

has grown from around $200 billion at the end of 2000 to over $3,000 billion at the end of 2016, a growth of more than 1,400 per cent over 16 years. This fast accumulation in the official reserve has naturally caused substantial expansion of China's monetary base over the same period.

In essence, the money supply from the PBC is largely determined by a growth in the official reserve of foreign assets. Specifically, China will increase money supply whenever there is a large inflow of foreign capital, but will have a contraction of money supply whenever there is large capital outflow. Therefore, China does not really have an independent monetary policy. To sterilize the impact that an expansion of the official reserve has on the domestic money supply, the PBC raised the reserve ratio for China's commercial banks in an effort to control the amount of currency in circulation. The reserve ratio has been increased from 6 per cent in 2001 to 21 per cent in 2011 as shown in Figure 14.2. On the other hand, the regulation that the maximum loan-to-deposit ratio is 75 per cent in China implies that the reserve ratio cannot exceed 25 per cent. Hence, the use of the reserve ratio became less effective after 2011.

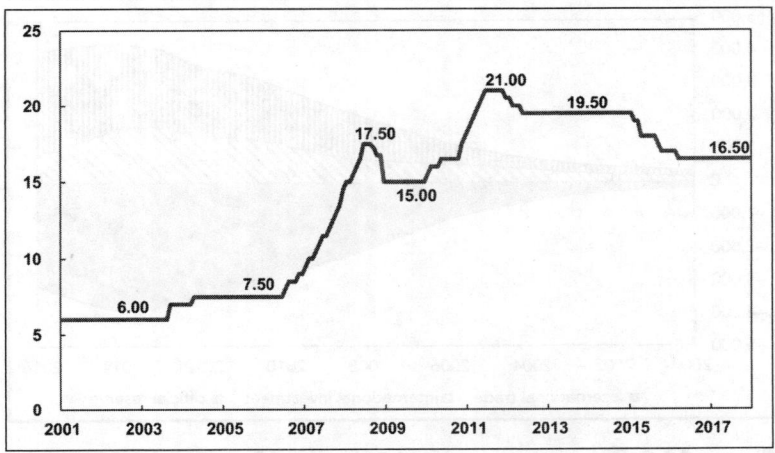

Figure 14.2 *China's Reserve Ratio (%)*
Source: PBC (2017).

CHINA'S INTERNATIONAL BALANCE OF PAYMENTS

Now we look at how China has accumulated such a large official reserve of foreign assets. It is well known that China has run a surplus in both its international trade and international investment accounts for many years. By the balance of payment identity:

$$C + K + \Delta R = 0$$

where C is change in the current account, K is change in the financial account, and ΔR is the change in official reserve. As a surplus in the current account is mainly attributed to a large surplus in international trade and a surplus in the financial account stems mainly from a large inflow of international investment, China has accumulated a substantial amount of official reserve. This is shown in Figure 14.3.

The large amount of official reserve has formed the major assets of the PBC, causing the monetary base of the RMB to expand accordingly. To maintain international balance of payments while controlling the level of official reserve, China must reverse its financial account

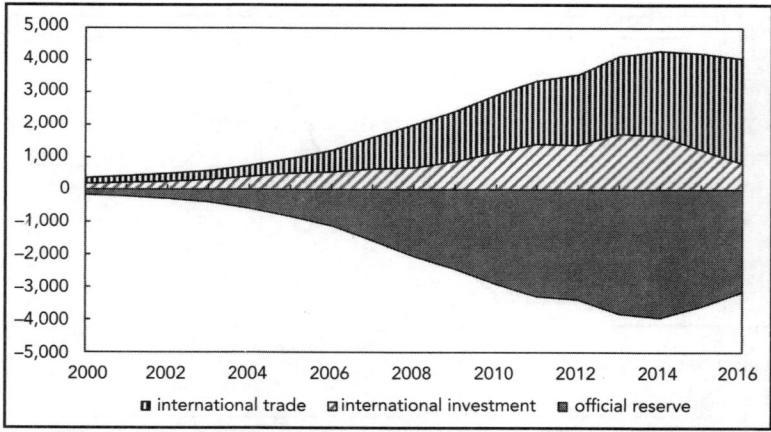

Figure 14.3 *China's International Balance of Payments (USD Billion)*
Source: PBC (2017).

from mainly inflow to mainly outflow. This implies that China must make large outward investment or allow the exchange rate to adjust.

On the equilibrium of domestic economy, there are two identities of national income, $Y = C + T + S$ and $Y = C + G + I + (X - M)$, which lead to $(G - T) + (I - S) + (X - M) = 0$. In these equations, Y is national income, C is consumption, T is taxation, S is savings, G is government expenditure, I is investment and $(X - M)$ is net export. Since the Chinese government did not run a significant fiscal deficit, $(G - T)$ has been small. The highest fiscal deficit was 3.79 per cent of GDP in 2016, but fiscal deficits in most of the years before 2015 were below 2.5 per cent of GDP.

Although China has maintained a sound national fiscal condition, there are often concerns in the financial markets about government debt at the provincial level. By September 2018, total debt outstanding for all the local governments in China amounted to RMB 18,259 billion, with an average interest rate of 3.5 per cent and average maturity of 4.6 years. While the amount of this debt was quite large (compared with the total GDP of RMB 82,712 billion in 2017), it was still within the limit set by the People's Congress of China.

On the other hand, China traditionally has a very high savings rate which is normally around 35–50 per cent of GDP, and Figure 14.4 shows the savings in China since 2000. Compared with Chinese domestic investment, which took around 35–40 per cent of GDP annually, the difference $(S - I)$ was around 5 per cent of GDP. Hence, by the above identity, China would run a surplus in net export. This is in contrast to the USA, as the savings rate in the USA (about 10–20 per cent of GDP) was normally lower than in China, which was largely due to the higher consumption rate (between 60–70 per cent of GDP) in the USA (US Bureau of Economic Analysis. July 30, 2015. Table 1.1.5 GDP, and Table 5.1 Saving and Investment). Thus, by the same economic identity, the USA would be more likely to run a trade deficit than China.

The savings in China were mostly converted into domestic investment; in addition, China also attracted a large amount of foreign investment for many years. Consequently, the continuous investment

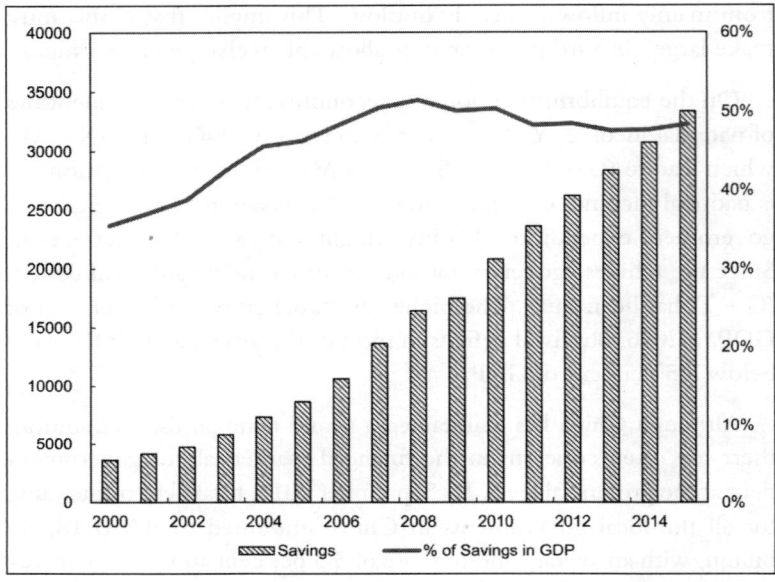

Figure 14.4 *National Savings in China (RMB Billion) and The Percentage of Savings in GDP*

Source: China National Bureau of Statistics. 2001–2017. 'Statistics Year Book of China: National Account, Table 3–11 GDP Composition'.

in fixed assets has led to a solid formation of productive capital in the Chinese economy year after year. Indeed, within 30 years, China has transformed from a relatively labour-intensive economy into a relatively capital-intensive one. This is evidenced by the increasing ratio of fixed capital per employee in China over time, as shown in Figure 14.5.

In the capital-intensive areas such as the manufacturing of high-speed rail equipment, railroad and highway construction, oil and gas tube construction, communication equipment manufacturing, communication network design and construction, power generation and transmission technology, China has achieved significant technological progress since 2000. Take the high-speed rail, for example, China has applied for more than 200 technical patents, about 70 per cent of worldwide patent applications in this area. China also has a cost advantage in high-speed rail construction. For a train speed of 350 km/hour, the construction cost of the railway is about $20 million per km, while

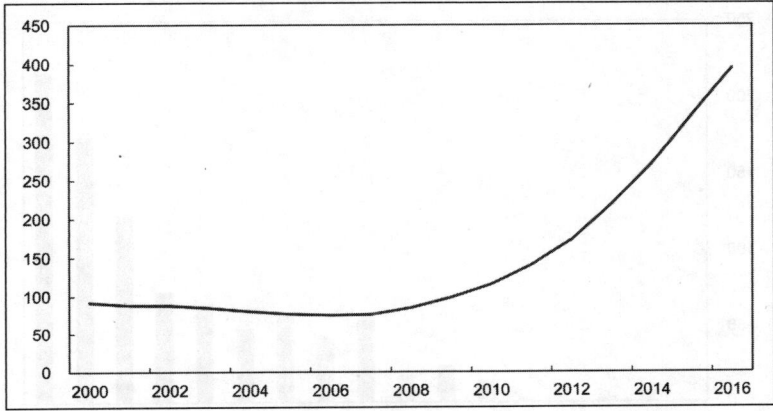

Figure 14.5 *The Capital Intensity of China: Fixed Capital (RMB 1000) per Employee*

Source: China National Bureau of Statistics. 2000–2017. 'Statistics Year Book of China: National Account, Table 10–1 Fixed Capital, and Table 4-3 Industrial Employment'.

for a train speed of 250 km/hour, the construction cost of the railway is only $12 million per km. These costs are much lower than the comparable worldwide high-speed rail construction cost which often costs more than $45 million per km (Sun 2016).

By the well-known theory of Comparative Advantage, China should now export capital or capital-intensive goods and services to countries that are at a lower stage of development, especially in infrastructure construction, in areas such as transportation, communication and the energy industry. Therefore, the large-scale FDI recently made by China along the BRI regions is a natural consequence of the country's economic transformation. Figure 14.6 shows the amount of outward FDI by Chinese companies since 2000.

In terms of RMB internationalization, trade surplus in China's current account would imply inflow of the RMB through international markets for goods and services. When China's financial account could be dominated by investment outflows, it would represent RMB outflow through international markets for capital. Consequently, trade surplus and net investment outflow would form a complete cycle of the RMB in international markets.

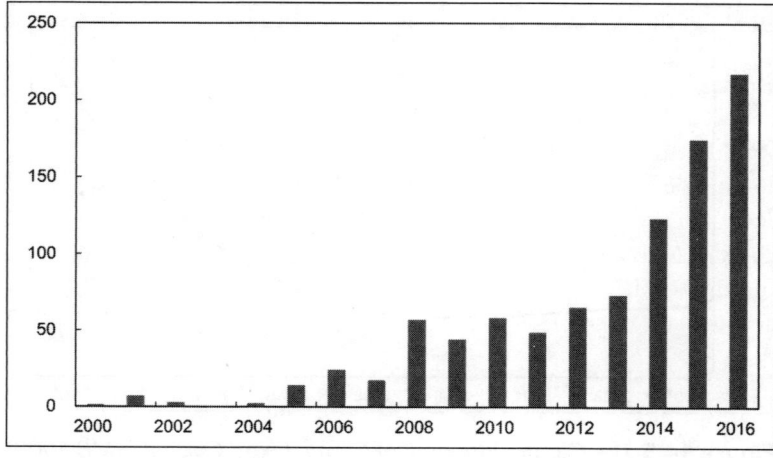

Figure 14.6 *The Outward FDI by China (USD Billion)*
Source: PBC (2017).

RMB INTERNATIONALIZATION WITH ONE BELT ONE ROAD

There are more than 60 countries along the BRI regions, with total population of 4.4 billion (63% of world population). Total GDP of BRI countries including China exceeds $23 trillion (29% of the world's GDP), and total trade value among BRI countries is about one-fourth of global figures. For current account, trade between China and BRI countries was $953.6 billion in 2016 (about 25% of China's total international trade). China is also the largest importing country along the BRI regions, running a trade surplus for most of the BRI countries. As local currencies of BRI countries are mostly not international currencies, it provides a good opportunity to use the RMB in these regions with growing economic cooperation between China and BRI countries.

In fact, as an example of comparative advantage at work, many BRI countries are commodity exporting while China is the largest commodity importing country. Thus, if commodities trade could be based on the RMB, it would help BRI countries to obtain stable exporting revenues and help reduce price fluctuations for China's importers. A related issue here is the currency risk among commodity exporters in BRI countries and importers in China. If trade were settled by dollars, exporters would have to face exchange rate risk between the dollar and their local currencies while Chinese importers would also face exchange rate risk between the dollar and the RMB. Thus, both exporters and importers would bear the costs of currency hedging. As the amount of trade in commodities between China and BRI countries is large, it would be more economical to convert indirect exchange (exporter's local currency—dollar–RMB) into direct exchange between the exporter's local currency and the RMB, thereby only one side, the exporter or importer, would bear the cost of currency hedging.

On the capital investment side, Asian Development Bank Institute (2010) estimated that the total demand for infrastructure investment would be worth as much as $26 trillion in Asia by 2030. Infrastructure projects require large amount of investment with long-term capital. However, in the BRI regions, many countries do not have advanced financial services, and so many small and medium companies face very high financial costs and find it difficult to obtain capital. As an important capital-intensive country, China can naturally provide financing to these countries and help them break the financial bottleneck. This way, capital outflow in the financial account from China can naturally form a closed cycle with trade surplus in the current account.

For BRI countries, this situation is similar to the early stages of China's economic reform. In the 1980s, after China launched its 'open-door'" policy and started the economic modernization programme, the country attracted foreign capital inflow in its financial account while it ran a trade deficit in its current account by importing modern production equipment, infrastructure and consumer goods that are capital intensive in their production. This way, advanced technology and modern management systems helped the Chinese economy to improve productive efficiency and Chinese consumers to improve their living standards. Now, China hopes BRI countries will develop their economies using a similar process of first investing in infrastructure and thereby improving productivity and raising living standards.

With the large demand for infrastructure investment in BRI regions, and China's comparative advantage in infrastructure areas such as railroad and highway construction, oil and gas tube construction, communication equipment manufacturing, communication network design and construction, power generation and transmission technology, Chinese companies obtained a large amount of investment projects. Thus, it would be more convenient for China to arrange official aid initiatives, commercial loans, FDI and infrastructure bonds from its financial account, and to solve financial problems for BRI countries. The annual financial statements of China Industrial and Commercial Bank, China Construction Bank, Bank of China and China Bank of Communication show that their foreign loans increased by 27 per cent, 31 per cent, 11 per cent and 18 per cent, respectively, in 2016. As Hong Kong and Macao are the most active regions for these bank loans, a considerable portion of these foreign loans would be denominated in RMB. In infrastructure financing, the situation is similar to the commodity trade, using RMB denominated debt would turn indirect exchange (local currency—dollar–RMB) into direct exchange between the local currency and the RMB, thereby reducing the cost of currency hedging.

In 2016, China's outward FDI to 53 BRI countries was $14.53 billion, about 8.5 per cent of China's total outward FDI. Chinese companies signed $126 billion worth of new construction contracts in 61 related countries, about 51.6 per cent of China's total new foreign construction projects in 2016 (China Ministry of Commerce Data Centre 2017). As China has better experience both in infrastructure investment and financing, the country will be better positioned to become a major organizer and financier in BRI countries for infrastructure projects. If 10 per cent of China's outward FDI and foreign loans could be denominated in the RMB, this would greatly promote RMB internationalization under the financial account.

Finally, China's cross-border e-commerce has grown by 20–30 per cent annually for a couple of years since 2014. In 2016, international trade through e-commerce was about RMB 6,300 billion, about 20 per cent of China's total international trade. In 2017, international trade through e-commerce may reach RMB 7,500 billion. In this area, Chinese e-commerce companies such as Alibaba and Alipay can become important channels for use of the RMB in international trade through e-commerce. Besides, as many BRI countries are located in transportation trunk roads, the international logistics flows resulting from international e-commerce can provide these countries with additional transportation revenue.

Based on past experience, an international currency should be carried by international banks. With internationalization of the RMB in progress, Chinese banks also offer their banking services internationally. By the end of 2016, nine Chinese banks had set up 18 subsidiaries, 35 branches and 9 representative offices in 26 BRI countries. During the same period, 54 foreign banks in 20 BRI countries had also set up subsidiaries in China. Commercial banks can play important roles in fund raising, resource allocation, package making, information exchange and risk assessment. Chinese commercial banks can also strengthen cooperation with foreign banks in RMB settlement, capital financing, asset pricing and market making, so as to serve companies investing in BRI regions better (Lian and Liu 2017).

INTERNATIONAL FINANCIAL COOPERATION IN BRI REGIONS

There are financial risks in the internationalization of the RMB. As BRI countries are mostly developing countries, their levels of economic development are relatively low, and the value of their currencies is unstable. This would cause credit risk and financial risk for companies investing in these countries. Finally, as economic construction in BRI countries requires long-term capital, while most capital inflows into BRI regions are short-term in nature, this would result in the risk of term mismatching. Although many of the loans from China's banks are long-term, these loans in fact created financial risks for banks that raised RMB funds from capital markets that are relatively short-term in China.

To manage these financial risks, international cooperation among different monetary authorities will play an important role. With this in mind, China's Banking Regulatory Commission had already signed memorandums of understanding with respective regulatory authorities in 28 BRI countries by 2017. That same year, the PBC also signed bilateral currency swap agreements with 35 central banks along BRI regions, and the total value of the swaps amounted to RMB 3,326 billion (PBC 2017). These bilateral currency swaps can help companies and financial institutions in the relevant countries or regions significantly reduce exchange rate risk and financial costs when doing business with Chinese companies. Yu (2010) and Zhang, Yu, and Yu (2017) used the gravitational model to gauge the effect of the currency-swap agreement on bilateral trade. Zhang et al. (2017) concluded that the currency-swap agreements signed between China and other countries significantly increased their bilateral trade; the larger the size of the currency swaps, the greater their role in promoting trade.

In October 2016, the RMB was officially added into the SDR basket. By the end of 2016, there were about 56 foreign central banks or monetary authorities that held RMB-denominated financial assets in China as part of their official reserves, and there were many banks from 129 foreign countries or regions that opened inter-bank accounts in China. There were over 1,900 financial institutions over the world that used the RMB as means of payment in 2016. Nevertheless, the amount of payments by the RMB was only 1.68 per cent of the world total, and ranked No. 6 in the world in 2016 (Wind Data 2017).

REFORM OF CHINA'S MONETARY POLICY

China has made significant progress in economic reform, transforming its economy from relatively labour intensive to relatively capital intensive. The large investment that China made into BRI countries has been made possible by China's economic transformation since the 1980s. Nevertheless, internationalization of the RMB lagged behind the outflow of Chinese capital. For international financial markets, dealing with the large amount of Chinese investment outflows in RMB would raise some critical issues, mainly because there are some conditions for an international currency that the RMB has not yet met. Basically, for the RMB to become an international currency, its interest rates and exchange rates against other major global currencies should be market based.

To make the RMB a truly international currency, the PBC started reforming its mechanism of money supply and the exchange rate system in 2013. Monetary reform started with changing the mechanism of setting interest rates. Prior to 2013, all interest rates in China were controlled by the PBC. Specifically, the PBC set the benchmark on the lending rates and deposit rates, while commercial banks were allowed to set their respective lending rates and deposit rates within a narrow band (ceiling and floor) around the benchmark rates. On 20 July 2013, the PBC first completely removed controls on lending rates, including the floor (0.7 times the benchmark lending rates set by the PBC) of the lending rates by financial institutions, the ceiling on the lending rates by rural credit cooperatives, and the controls on the interest rates for bill discounting.

Then, on 1 March 2014, the PBC removed the ceiling on small-value foreign exchange deposit rates in the China (Shanghai) Pilot Free-Trade Zone. In May 2015, the ceiling on the foreign exchange retail deposit rates was removed, and the ceiling on the interest rate for time deposits with maturities of more than one year (excluding one year) was removed in August. Finally, the ceiling on the deposit rates for all commercial banks and rural cooperative financial institutions was removed in October 2015, indicating that the removal of all controls on interest rates was completed. Since then, all interest rates have been market based.

After these reforms on interest rates, the PBC could use the interest rate as a pricing instrument through market mechanism to conduct monetary policy. The other instrument to conduct monetary policy is the reserve requirement, which is a quantitative instrument. However, use of the reserve ratio was limited by regulation on the loan-to-deposit ratio, which effectively set the lower limit for the amount of required reserve held by the commercial banks in China. On 24 June 2015, the limit set on loan-to-deposit ratio was removed, indicating that the PBC could begin using the quantitative instrument (the reserve ratio) more effectively.

While interest rates in the banking system are now market based, various financial markets are still heavily regulated. As financial markets are of critical importance to the Chinese economy, China still has a long way to go towards the development of a modern financial system including a banking system, money market and efficient securities market to support internationalization of the RMB.

RMB EXCHANGE RATE SYSTEM AND CROSS-BORDER RMB SETTLEMENT

Since 1994, China had kept the RMB on a fixed exchange rate vis-à-vis the US dollar. In 2005, China adopted a managed floating rate system, when the RMB began appreciating vis-à-vis the dollar until 2010. Then, at the end of 2014, China developed an RMB Index based on a basket of currencies, calculated by China's foreign currency trading centre, the China Foreign Exchange Trade System (CFETS). The CFETS basket consists of 13 major currencies traded in China's foreign currency trading centre, including USD, Euro, British Pound, Japanese Yen and others. The index is a weighted average of exchange rates between the RMB and currencies in the basket, with the weights calculated based on China's trading volumes with her major trading partner countries. In 2015, China pegged the RMB to the CFETS Index, making the RMB exchange rate on more flexible terms vis-à-vis the Dollar. Figure 14.7 shows the value of CFETS index.

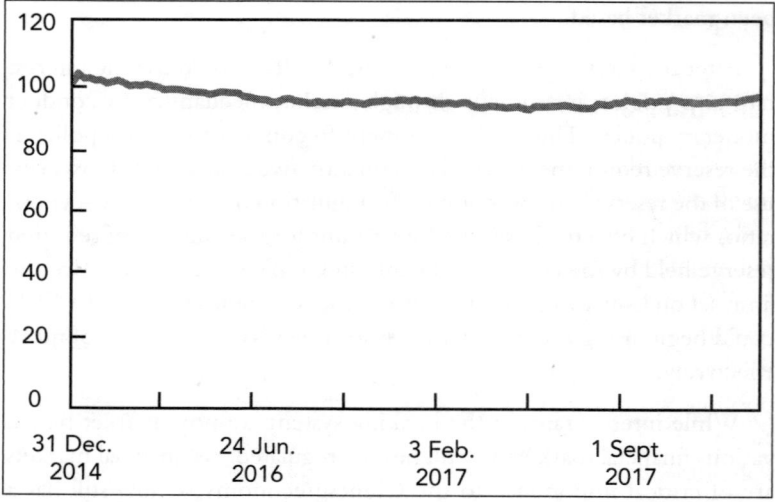

Figure 14.7 *The Value of CFETS Index (100 as on 31 December 2014)*
Source: China Foreign Exchange Trading System & National Interbank Funding Center.

In 2009, the PBC published 'Rules for RMB Settlement in Cross-Border Trade', and since then cross-border RMB settlement has grown rapidly in international trade settlement, international investment, currency swaps and offshore RMB market development. By the end of 2014, the RMB had become the world's 5th largest currency used in international transactions after the USD, Euro, British Pound and Japanese Yen, and the RMB's share in international transactions was 2.17 per cent in December 2014 (Wind Data 2015).

In October 2015, the RMB Cross-border Interbank Payment System (CIPS) started operation, providing currency settlement services for financial institutions and RMB offshore business. The CIPS uses the world standard code (ISO20022) and the code is convertible to the SWIFTMT code. At first, there were 19 Chinese and foreign banks listed as direct participants of the system, and there were 38 Chinese banks and 138 foreign banks across Asia, Europe, Oceania and Africa, listed as related participants. By the end of 2015, Chinese banks had made settlement for cross-border trade with RMB 72.3 billion which included RMB 63.9 billion in goods and RMB 8.4 billion in services and other current account transactions.

CROSS-BORDER RMB SETTLEMENT FOR INTERNATIONAL INVESTMENT

In 2011, with the reform of policies regulating China's international investments, RMB settlement could be used both for FDI into China and China's outward direct investment (ODI). Since 2012, with further policy reform, Chinese companies have been able to obtain offshore RMB loans and issue RMB bonds in Hong Kong (the 'DimSum' bond). In 2015, the PBC also raised the ceiling on cross-border RMB fund flows for multinationals via two-way cross-border RMB cash pooling and lowered the threshold for participation in business. The two-way cross-border RMB cash pooling means that multinational conglomerates, based on their operational and managerial needs, can make cross-border RMB fund flows to adjust surplus or shortage positions among their different non-financial member companies. These fund flows were treated as the internal financing activities of multinational conglomerates.

In fact, the PBC raised the cap on the net inflow of RMB funds and lowered multinationals' threshold for participation in business, thus making the RMB more easily available to multinationals. This was a big step for RMB internationalization. The two-way cross-border RMB cash pooling allows multinationals to more efficiently allocate their capital internationally and enhance their cash management efficiency while cutting financing costs. For a multinational conglomerate, one central company can select 1–3 banks with international settlement business to provide two-way cross-border RMB cash pooling services to the conglomerate.

Apart from giving multinationals more freedom in doing business in China, Chinese banks have also provided various financial products and services to their foreign clients. In the international settlement area, Chinese banks provide Letters of Credit, Funds transfer, Bank collections and Non-Resident Account (NRA) settlements. The NRA is a foreign currency account that a foreign institution can open with Chinese banks in mainland China. In the area of international finance, Chinese banks offer international Factoring, Letters of Guarantee, Standby Letters of Credit and Forfeiting services to their international clients

In 2014, with the development of an offshore market for the RMB, RMB settlement accounted for 23.6 per cent of China's total international transactions including current account, China's ODI and FDI into China. On the other hand, the regions involved in RMB settlement were also expanded. In 2013, RMB settlement was largely done in Hong Kong which alone accounted for 74 per cent of total RMB transactions. By the end of 2014, there were 189 countries involved in RMB transactions. There was one Chinese bank designated as the RMB settlement bank in each of the following cities: Singapore, London, Frankfurt, Seoul, Paris, Luxemburg and Toronto. With these settlement banks located in important international financial centres of the world, plus Hong Kong, Macao, and Taiwan, the global RMB settlement network has been gradually taking shape.

Tao and Gu (2016) believe that development of cross-border RMB settlement has a correlation to the RMB's interest rate reform. As the PBC removed controls, RMB interest rates have become more and more market based. Through the link between more flexible exchange rates and RMB interest rates, the international flow of funds could approach better equilibrium, which would more effectively promote RMB internationalization.

OPENING UP CHINA'S CAPITAL MARKETS

There are multiple channels for foreign investors to enter China's capital markets. First, the Qualified Foreign Institutional Investors (QFII) programme was launched in 2003. By the end of 2016, there were 270 foreign institutions obtaining QFII quotas totalling $81.5 billion, holding Chinese bonds valuing RMB 57.7 billion and Chinese stocks valuing RMB 412.1 billion. Then, the RMB Qualified Foreign Institutional Investors (RQFII) was launched in 2011. By the end of 2016, there were 170 foreign institutions from 17 countries/regions obtaining RQFII quotas totalling RMB 510.3 billion.

In 2013, the Chinese inter-bank bond market was open to foreign institutional investors. By the end of 2014, there were 14 QFII, 66 RQFII, 97 foreign banks and 11 foreign insurance companies participating in the Chinese inter-bank bond market. These foreign financial institutions contributed total trading volume of RMB 1.01 billion in 2014. In 2016, there were 349 foreign institutions holding Chinese bonds valuing RMB 714.2 billion, about 1.35 per cent of China's bond market, while total foreign investors including non-institutional investors were holding RMB financial assets of RMB 3,337 billion.

For foreign investors desirous of investing in RMB securities, the offshore centre of the RMB offers channels linking to the Chinese A-share stock market. Hong Kong, being the largest offshore centre for RMB securities, launched the 'Hu-Gang Tong' (direct link between Shanghai Stock Exchange and Hong Kong Stock Exchange) on 17 November 2014 and the 'Shen-Gang Tong' (direct link between Shenzhen Stock Exchange and Hong Kong Stock Exchange) on 5 December 2016. These direct links allow international investors in Hong Kong, through Hong Kong security dealers, to invest in designated A-share stocks in Shanghai or Shenzhen directly.

On 3 July 2017, 'Zhai-Quan Tong' (direct link of bond markets between the Chinese mainland and Hong Kong) was launched. This link sets up the necessary infrastructure to allow foreign institutional investors to invest in mainland China's domestic bond market via Hong

Kong. The bond market in China is already the third largest in the world, which has made it attractive to many overseas investors. According to PBC statistics, overseas capital of about RMB 346 billion flew into China's bond market in 2017, about one-third of this capital inflow being via 'Zhai-Quan Tong'. Total capital flowing into China's bond market in 2018 was estimated to have increased to around RMB 700 billion. As the bond market in China mainly saw the participation of Chinese banks, trading frequency was very low compared with the world's major bond markets. Therefore, the large inflow of foreign capital into the Chinese bond market can help improve the liquidity of the market

RMB OFFSHORE CENTRE

Some RMB offshore centres also provide RMB securities for international investors. London is an important RMB offshore centre, with its RMB transactions accounting for about one quarter of global RMB offshore transactions. On 8 April 2012, the City of London held an official ceremony to start RMB business, with HSBC issuing the first RMB bond worth RMB 2 billion to British and continental European investors. Then, on 21 November 2012, China Construction Bank issued an RMB bond of RMB 2 billion in London, which was the first RMB bond issued by a Chinese bank in London. In September 2014, China Development Bank also issued an RMB bond of RMB 2 billion in London. In addition, in October 2014, a Chinese sovereign bond of RMB 3 billion was issued in London.

On 22 October 2015, Agricultural Bank of China signed the 'Memorandum of Green Finance Cooperation' with London Stock Exchange (LSE) and issued a green bond denominated in RMB and worth $1 billion on the LSE. This was the first RMB green bond issued by an Asian issuer in the LSE. The proceeds of this green bond issue will be used in environmental-friendly projects such as clean energy, biomass power generation, urban waste and sewage disposal, etc. The listing of this green bond by Agricultural Bank of China on the LSE was a result of the '7th UK–China Economic and Financial Dialogue' held earlier that year, and reflected the cooperation of British and Chinese financial institutions in supporting environmental-friendly industries.

On 27 May 2015, Shanghai Stock Exchange, China Financial Futures Exchange, and Deutsche Borse jointly set up the China Europe International Exchange Ltd in Frankfurt, to offer offshore RMB securities and related derivative products. Thus, international investors can have RMB funds either held in overseas banks or invested in RMB-denominated bonds or securities on overseas security exchanges.

Li and Liu (2008) pointed out that the opening of the offshore RMB bond market would represent one important step in the internationalization of the RMB, and Lu (2013) discussed the effect of the expansion of RMB offshore centres on the transaction cost of the RMB as an international currency. Lu (2013) argued that the more a currency was in use, the lower would be its transaction cost and the better its liquidity, which in turn would cause more usage. Now, the offshore RMB market has developed into a rich financial market, providing various financial products to investors all over the world. RMB spot exchange, forward exchange, RMB loans, bonds, mutual funds and derivative products are actively traded in many offshore markets. According to the IMF (2006), by 30 June 2015, the value of total RMB international bonds was about $76 billion (about 0.4% of the world total). These RMB international bonds are traded in different offshore markets, such as the 'DimSum' bond in Hong Kong, 'BaoDao' bond in Taiwan, 'ShiCheng' bond in Singapore, 'KaiXuan' bond in France, 'GeDe' bond in Germany, 'ShenGen' bond in Luxemburg, and 'DaYang' bond in Sydney. In addition, Chinese banks made RMB loans of RMB 199 billion in overseas markets.

RMB INTERNATIONALIZATION AND THE BRI

With the growth of RMB offshore centres and offshore markets, more RMB banking services and investment products are available overseas. Thus, more RMB denominated assets are held by foreign monetary authorities and foreign financial institutions, and there are more RMB channels in operation that allow for investing in China's domestic capital markets. These advances made by RMB internationalization will greatly improve the efficiency of the international financial institutions and markets, which in turn can provide better financial services to firms doing international business in BRI regions. Hence, international trade or investment transactions can be more efficiently carried out by firms in BRI countries even if there are insufficient local financial facilities. Furthermore, internationalization of the RMB can also help firms to better manage currency risks that are inherent in international business.

On the other hand, firms doing international trade and investment in BRI regions will naturally demand better financial services, wider selection of RMB related financial products as well as larger and more flexible financing resources to international financial institutions and markets. All these various forms of market demand will push for deeper and wider internationalization of the RMB, which requires further reform of Chinese financial institutions and capital markets.

CONCLUSION

In this chapter, we discussed how the BRI requires internationalization of the RMB, which in turn requires some basic reform of China's monetary policy. The basic problem of China's monetary policy is caused by the imbalance of China's international payments, which is due to the country's lack of capital export. After 30 years of economic reform that began in the 1980s, China has gradually become a capital-intensive economy, and now it is natural for the country to make outward capital investment. This shows that China has successfully transformed herself from a capital-importing country into a capital-exporting country, and capital export coupled with trade surplus would result in balanced international payments for China. The balance of payments also provides a complete cycle for international flow of the RMB, a necessity for its internationalization.

In summary, the BRI provides an excellent opportunity for Chinese firms to make outward investments while promoting regional economic growth. Meanwhile, the internationalization of the RMB would significantly help firms along BRI regions to manage currency risks and reduce financing costs. Finally, firms doing international trade and investment in BRI regions will demand better financial services from relevant financial institutions and markets, which will require deeper and wider internationalization of the RMB and further reform of Chinese financial institutions and capital markets.

REFERENCES

Asian Development Bank Institute. 2010. 'Estimating Demand for Infrastructure in Energy, Transport, Telecommunications, Water and Sanitation in Asia and the Pacific: 2010–2020'. ADBI Working Paper Series No. 248, September 2010.
Bai Weidong, Wu Zhengkun, and Zhang Peiqin. 2016. 'The Analysis on the RMB Cross-Border Settlement under the OBOR Initiative'. *Xi Bu Jin Rong* 5: 55–59.
China Ministry of Commerce Data Centre. 2017. 'China's Outward Direct Investments'. Ministry of Commerce, PRC. http://data.mofcom.gov.cn
IMF. 2006. *World Economic Outlook*. Washington, DC: The Fund.
Li D., and Liu L. 2008. 'The RMB Internationalization: Econometric and Policy Analysis'. *Jin Rong Yan Jiu* 11: 1–16.
Lian P., and Liu J. 2017. 'The OBOR Initiative Opens New Space for the RMB Internationalization'. *Zhong Guo Zheng Quan Bao*, May 13.
Lin L., and Wang S. 2016. 'The Empirical Analysis on the RMB Internationalization under the OBOR Initiative'. *Guo Ji Jin Rong Yan Jiu* 2: 75–83.
Lu G. 2013. *The Progress and Problems of the RMB Settlement for Cross-Border Trading.* Zhejiang: Zhejiang University Press.
PBC. 2017. 'The Bilateral Currency Swaps between the People's Bank of China and Other Central Banks or Monetary Authorities'. www.pbc.gov.cn
Sun M. 2016. 'The Effects of the OBOR Initiative on the RMB internationalization'. *Jing Ji Yan Jiu Dao Kan* 17: 107–108.
Tao S., and Gu J. 2016. 'The Analysis on the RMB Interest Rate Reform and Cross-Border RMB Settlement'. *Cai Jing Li Lun Yu Shi Jian* 1: 11–18.
Wen X., and Xu X. 2015. 'The New era of the RMB Internationalization: The OBOR and the Future International Financial System'. *Ren Min Lun Tan – Xue Shu Qian Yan* 16: 61–71.
Wind Data. 2015. 'The Share of the RMB in Global Market Trading'. wind.com.cn
Wind Data. 2017. 'The RMB Bond in Offshore Markets'. wind.com.cn
Yu M. 2010. 'Trade, Democracy, and the Gravity Equation'. *Journal of Development Economics* 91 (2): 289–300.
Zhang F., Yu M., and Yu J. 2017. 'The Belt and Road Initiative and the Future of the RMB Internationalization'. *Ren Min Lun Tan – Xue Shu Qian Yan* 9: 28–45.
Zhu S. 2015. 'The Analysis on the International Financial Cooperation under the OBOR Initiative'. *Jin Rong Fa Zhan Ping Lun* 3: 83–91.
Zou J., Liu C., Yin G., and Tang Z. 2015. 'The International Trading and Its Economic Contribution among China and the OBOR Countries'. *Di Li Ke Xue Jin Zhan* 34 (5): 598–605.

Chapter 15

On the Leadership Challenges for China in the Belt and Road Initiative

David De Cremer

In 2013, president Xi Jinping first proposed the One Belt One Road (OBOR) Initiative (now called Belt and Road Initiative or BRI as the 'one' was, according to the Chinese government, subject to misinterpretation), with the aim of revitalizing transport and trade links along the ancient Silk Road Routes and boosting China's role on the international stage. This initiative represents a very significant event in terms of global leadership. Indeed, after years of the US being the global leader advocating values such as 'democracy', and 'freedom' as ethical standards, the world has arrived at a transient state in which geopolitical and business conflicts have surfaced. And, at this point of time, after having being cautious for many decades at the global level, China has set the step to launch the largest ever international collaboration initiative a single country has undertaken, with around 60 countries today participating in BRI.

The initiative has a primary focus on helping to solve a global infrastructure gap, at both the physical and digital level, and in doing so aid growth in developing countries while boosting trade and generating investor returns. The initial motivation underlying the BRI is clearly a domestic concern about slowing growth in China while at the same time also having an ambitious look on leadership by the desire to boost China's global influence. In a way, the BRI can be seen as a project that aims to recreate the powerful history of China. Indeed, it is the most significant and impactful project China has ever initiated, and has the potential to reshape the 21st century in terms of both domestic and foreign political and economic consequences. Because it is such a bold and ambitious project, the BRI will propel China to a more active leadership role in regional integration and the global economy. What are the leadership challenges that come along with BRI?

CHINA TAKING UP THE LEADERSHIP ROLE

As the second-largest economy in the world, China has made rapid strives to become a global superpower. To express this trend, the notion of 'the Chinese century' is a perfect example as it suggests that the 21st century will be geopolitically dominated by China. With the BRI, it seems that Beijing is ready to accept this leading role and influence global capitalism. Even more, with the BRI in place, China is rapidly enhancing both their hard and soft powers in the Asian and African regions. With this picture taking place, it is only logical that China has to take a role of responsibility where they consider the interests of all countries and regions involved to create the right kind of value. In other words, China is now obliged to demonstrate leadership, not only at the domestic level but even more so at the global level. It has taken up the role to lead the development of economic prosperity for many. Such a role does not come easy and requires many responsibilities and obligations while facing many challenges at the same time.

Leadership is usually thought of as 'a process of social influence through which the party being in the leadership role enlists and mobilizes the support and potential of other parties to help the attainment of a collective goal' (Chemers 1997). This means that as a leader of such an enormous, never seen before, economic initiative, China, in order to be effective, needs to show the abilities to connect with other countries by presenting a compelling and sustainable vision towards the future with the goal to create long-term value for all. According to path–goal theory (House 1971), the motivational effects of leadership are indeed derived from the impact leaders have on the other parties (also called followers) to ensure that those parties will contribute to the best of their efforts as improved participation will eventually lead to the desired reward of making BRI successful. Not an easy task at all. This is especially so, because most of the challenges that will occur would be situated at the global level. As such, China needs to demonstrate effective global leadership. Global leadership is thought of as a process where China will be able to influence the thinking and behaviours of other countries and communities to work together to fulfil the potential of the shared vision and values that come together in the BRI (Mendenhall et al. 2012).

In other words, China needs to ensure that the purpose it defines touches both the hearts and the minds of other countries, else the BRI will only be looked upon as Chinese and therefore not be able to inspire the rest of the world. This means that the leadership role China needs to take up is one where a reciprocal relationship is developed and China does not only influence but will also be influenced by the participating nations (Hollander 1992; Howell and Shamir 2005; also see De Cremer et al. 2009).

In 2017, state councillor Yang Jiechi pointed out that 'the initiative was proposed by China but it is not a one-man band. Rather, it is a symphony'. This statement suggests that China is aware of the fact that BRI needs to be a shared project if it wants to be successful. As such, China needs to take the lead to bring and inspire different countries to come together under the purpose of the BRI. At the same time, however, this statement can also be interpreted that China expects the participating countries to comply with the vision set out by China without too much hesitation as they expect the initiative to be flawless like a symphony. The remainder of this chapter wishes to examine the expectations and actions that accompany the leadership role that China has to take in the BRI by analysing their efforts in light of the two dominant drivers that characterize the kind of leadership needed to make BRI succeed, which are *vision* and *connection* (Figure 15.1).

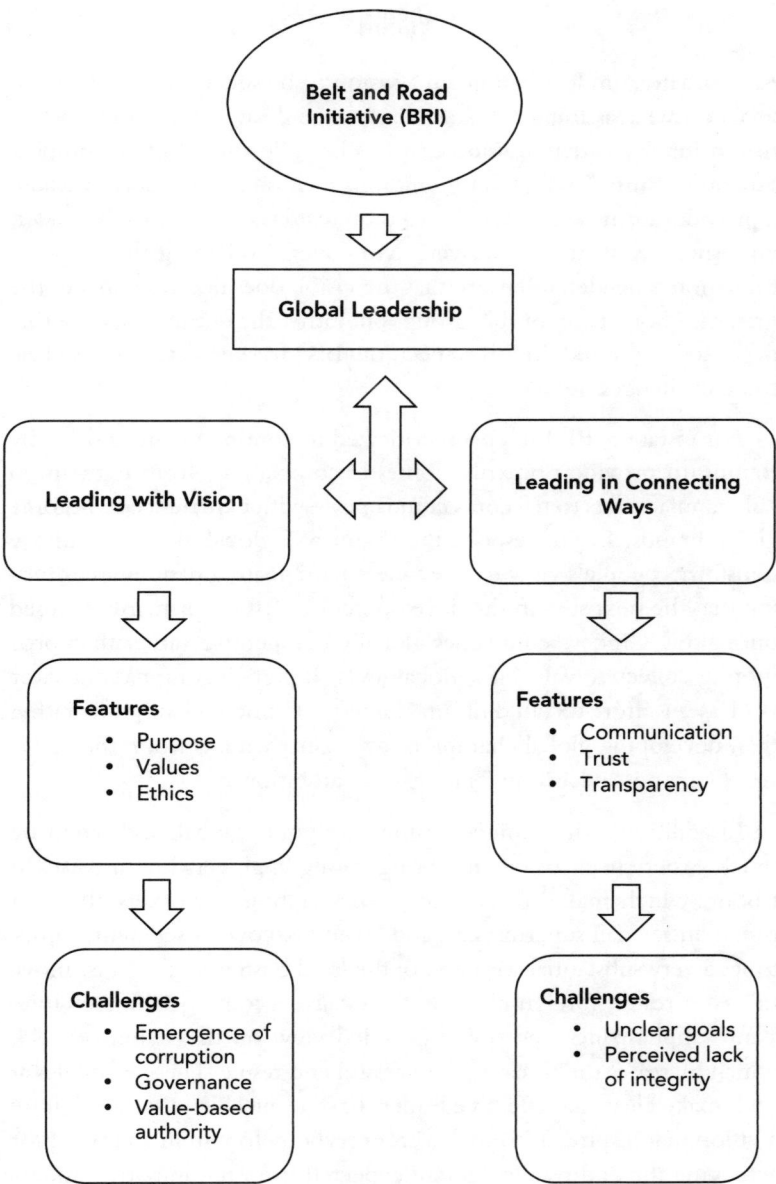

Figure 15.1 *Leading the Belt and Road Initiative by Means of Visionary and Connecting Leadership*

Source: The author.

VISION

Any initiative undertaken needs a vision to be successful as it helps to focus on what is important and need to be dealt with. An important reason for this is that a vision helps to be agile and adapt to complex situations (Burns 1978). Communicating a vision helps to adapt because it provides an answer to 'why' the vision matters, not only to the leader, but especially so to its followers. Moreover, explaining the 'why' of the vision is needed to ensure that the vision does not only further the interests of one party or sub-groups but rather the entire collective that needs to be inspired. In this respect, the BRI has been criticized to face some challenges.

For instance, BRI has been criticized to continue being a drive by Beijing to provide primarily domestic companies—from high-speed rail manufacturers to telecoms companies—with experience to become global brands. In this respect, the vision of a global initiative quickly transforms people's view to one where participating nations are thinking that the next step in the development of BRI is primarily focused on making Chinese companies globally competitive rather than promoting collective value at a global level. If participating nations view BRI as an effort to building up domestic Chinese champions rather than developing global champions everyone benefits from, then BRI will likely not succeed in its long-term ambitions.

In addition, with Chinese companies going global, and requiring much experience, it not only brings along engineers but also skilled labour, which makes that some of these Chinese workers also start restaurants, small supermarkets and 'even take over a segment, sometimes a very substantial segment, of the local businesses that they move to'. As a result, foreign cities are gradually becoming Chinese cities, again emphasizing a possible one-sided view on the vision of BRI, which increases the threat to a successful end result. These examples as such make clear that effective leaders have to be able to communicate a vision that inspires and empowers everybody to join in and work for achieving the end results that are expected from the initiative undertaken (Conger and Kanungo 1987; Kirkpatrick & Locke 1996): an initiative that needs to be shared by all.

An important element of a vision that makes impact entails the ability to link the present effort to the achievement of a future idea and hope, and, in this sense, leadership visions enable followers to connect with how the future of an initiative and all participating countries may look like (Berson et al. 2001; Shamir House, and Arthur 1993). Research has indeed shown that leaders with strong and meaningful visions are more effective as they positively influence the willingness of the other parties to participate, perform and provide support to the actions required to achieve the goals set out (e.g., Awamleh and Gardner 1999, Baum, Kirkpatrick, and Locke 1998, Shamir, Arthur, and House 1994). The way to deliver this message of hope to which all participating parties can connect entails effective communication. With respect to vision, research has shown that communication style (Awamleh and Gardner 1999), image-based rhetoric (Emrich et al. 2001; Naidoo and Lord 2008) and metaphors (Mio et al. 2005) that have a focus on followers (Den Hartog and Verburg 1997) matter.

In light of the BRI it is necessary to realize that these communication dimensions have significant effects on how the media responds (Bligh, Kohles, and Meindl 2004). So far, the rhetoric used to introduce the vision of BRI seems to have been successful, as attention is there worldwide. But is this rhetoric sufficient if it is not supported by reality? A study by Oxford University's Saïd Business School (Ansar et al. 2016) revealed that a large number of large infrastructure projects carried out by Chinese companies for other countries delivered few economic benefits to locals in the area and to the investors. In this sense, the actual results do not fit the rhetoric of the vision and this poses a threat to the credibility of the Belt and Road as an economic initiative that brings prosperity to all parties involved.

Of course, it is also important to realize that a vision makes sense only if we know the purpose and values underlying the message. So, what is the purpose and what are the values?

Purpose

Purpose is fundamentally tied up with leadership because it provides meaning to the vision (Bass 1985). That is, it makes clear why we want to pursue a vision and in doing this emphasizes that the leadership driving the initiative aims to achieve something significant that matters to individuals and societies (as it includes a moral component to the appeal; Kempster, Jackson and Conroy 2011). As we discussed in the Introduction of this book, BRI has set out five meaningful goals, of which one includes an explicit moral character relevant to the participating societies. Specifically, I refer to the fifth goal, representing the aim to 'create the world's largest platform for as social and cultural cooperation'. Xiang Zhaolun, vice-minister of the Ministry of Culture, noted the importance of promoting cultural ties across the BRI to promote common understanding, sharing and cooperation. The BRI strives for a reciprocal relationship where the values of each connecting culture are appreciated and made part of the economic initiative at play. This as well implies that Chinese can go to any country (as a tourist, businessperson, artist and individual) and learn from the other culture and vice versa.

Integrating the explicit aim of connecting people via their culture and underlying values is an important facet of making an initiative meaningful and rewarding to participating nations and is usually reciprocated by an enhanced motivation and extra effort on the part of the participating parties (Bass and Avolio 1990; Howell and Avolio 1993). It is therefore then also a possible threat if the BRI is perceived too much as China going to the world rather than China meeting the world and inviting the participating countries to participate also more in Chinese domestic society and economic system.

Values

With the BRI, global observers have noted that a change of guard seems to be happening. Indeed, despite the current US-China trade war, it has not escaped the attention of many that the USA is slowly retreating from its international leadership role (i.e., they do not want to play the world's policeman anymore). What made the USA the leading authority in the world? In their own words, it would have to do with the values that they wished to put out there. That is, the foundation of their international leadership was the championing of values such as liberalism. These values underscored the purpose of their actions and as such were used to legitimize their vision. Now China is moving gradually in this international leadership role; with the BRI being the primary display of this role, the values accompanying their vision need to be communicated clearly and adopted in consistent ways. China needs to be clear and specific about its values as will be the primary input into the question why others should follow their BRI.

From that perspective, China needs to develop a new coherent narrative with which other nations can identify and clear values are shown, an important one being generosity and openness—as those values are needed to make BRI succeed at a global level. Such a value-driven narrative will increase leadership legitimacy. Showing generosity by opening up its markets furthers, especially for low-income countries, and giving more international aid to emerging economies. Although China is already perceived as generous by several parties, the utilitarian tone used for most of the aid and support may undermine its sincerity and legitimacy as global leaders. For instance, China's international aid should not be seen as a way for China to export its overcapacity because otherwise that generosity still has a domestic focus and will not be perceived as sincere. It is this possible utilitarian perception that may cause challenges for international trade and business to continue as was demonstrated when premier Li Keqiang met with his European counterparts in Brussel on 1–2 June 2018, to exchange views on the increased protection measures against Chinese investments as they fear the focus of China on the domestic market only in their pursuit of initiatives like Belt and Road.

With the combination of having an inspiring vision that is supported by a clear purpose and its corresponding values, it becomes clear that vision-driven leaders need to be responsible ones. Responsible leadership requires leaders to be able to set goals that project the ethical values of the initiative that they pursue and make sense of those ethical values in the complex economic and political context. Making sense in this context implies being accountable for ensuring that ethics are part of any strategic decision-making process (e.g., investments, loans, exchange of labour, etc.). Below is outlined several of the ethical challenges that BRI has run into, which makes that the demand for ethical leadership is on the rise.

Ethics

Leadership aimed at transforming existing ways of working and implementing the necessary changes to achieve the end goals, need to be concerned with safeguarding that the conduct is done in normatively appropriate ways. For this reason, ethical leadership matters (e.g., Avey, Wernsing, and Palanski 2012; Chen and Hou 2016). The commonly accepted definition of ethical leadership is 'the demonstration of normatively appropriate conduct through personal actions and interpersonal relationships, and the promotion of such conduct to followers through two-way communication, reinforcement, and decision-making' (Brown, Treviño, and Harrison 2005, 120). In the BRI context, Chinese leadership is thus expected to deter the execution of the economic initiative from negative moral behaviour and such behaviour nevertheless emerges to take responsibility and take control of it.

That BRI could become subject of ethical transgression should not be a surprise because a precedent was for the Chinese government. Specifically, compare the strikingly similar plan rolled out by Japanese Prime Minister Keizo Obuchi in the 1990s, which also promised to provide work for Japan's recession-hit construction sector by building Japanese-funded infrastructure projects around Asia. This initiative was early on characterized by stories of wasted money and allegations of corruption. In a similar vein, Beijing now is facing similar allegations of corruption, which has motivated president Xi Jinping to address concerns about transparency, corruption and good governance in several speeches. 'We need to maintain that all cooperation is conducted under the sun and work together to combat corruption with zero tolerance', President Xi said in an address to the annual Belt and Road Forum for International Cooperation in Beijing on 26 April 2019. The awareness is very much there that if issues of ethics and governance are not adequately addressed, foreign firms will stay away from BRI.

The reason for this upsurge of speeches on this topic has been motivated by criticism that the BRI is indebting poorer nations and making them dependent on Beijing. In addition, legitimate concerns also exist over how the BRI is becoming what some have called a 'corruption bonanza' because of the Chinese practice of cultivating good relations or *guanxi* to get business done. For instance, in Kyrgyzstan, politicians were arrested in 2018 for corruption charges in light of BRI support for modernizing a thermal power plant in the capital. Claims also exist that in Sri Lanka, the Chinese construction fund was used to fund the election campaign of the former President Rajapaksa. Finally, in Malaysia, Prime Minister Najib Razak allowed China to have easy access to the country and in return Chinese money poured in to the development fund of 1Malaysia Development Berhad (which means limited; 1MDB) of which Najib used to be the chairman.

The response of Beijing to these corruption allegations has been firm with President Xi Jinping noting that China has the obligation to pursue high-standard cooperation. As a response, he pledged to 'adopt widely-accepted rules and standards, and encourage participating companies to follow general international rules and standards in product development, operations procurement, tendering and bidding'. As part of ethical leadership is to be accountable for wrongdoings of one's initiatives, Beijing is upgrading control over the BRI by providing clearer rules for state-owned enterprises (SOEs), making it more difficult to use the BRI brand for one's business, and building overseas auditing and anti-corruption mechanisms.

With these difficulties concerning ethics in sight, some have also argued that it is time to be humble in the pursuit of BRI. As is known to all, President Xi Jinping has made BRI his personal project and committed his heart and soul to it. In the first few years of the initiative, he was humble and hopeful; but in the recent years, criticism has surfaced on his somewhat hubris influenced style, which has been fuelled by him signing as president for life and the US-China trade war. Maybe it is time to take again a humble stand in order not to harm the reputation and survival of BRI as one of the biggest economic projects the world has ever seen. More precise, critics are saying that it may be wise again to follow former leader Deng Xiaoping's maxim—'China should hide its strengths and bide its time'—especially so when it comes down promoting acceptance of BRI. Humility is indeed seen as a counterweight to the ego and hubris pervasive in settings where financial and political concerns dominate and brings a moral foundation to the setting one works in (Cameron, Dutton, and Quinn 2003). In fact, according to Weick (2001, 93), it is clear that with the 'unpredictability and unknowability' organizations and societies face will require leaders of the 21st century to have 'more humility and less hubris' (Owens, Johnson, and Mitchell 2013, 1517).

CONNECTION

The effectiveness of any leader depends on what your followers (or in the BRI case, the participating countries) do. Do they provide support so the actions and decisions of the leader become legitimate or do they stay absent and undermine the legitimacy of your leadership position and thus also any initiative that you launch? The BRI is geographically structured along several land corridors, and the Maritime Silk Road, but it remains difficult for China to get all candidate nations assembled and participating fully in the initiative. This kind of inclusiveness is needed if one wants an initiative to succeed on the long-term and to ensure the participating nations join the initiator in leading the economic journey. Just as belongingness is an important human motive—people have an innate desire to be included in social relationships (Baumeister and Leary 1995)—so do effective leaders create a sense of inclusiveness among their followers (Nembhard and Edmondson 2006).

One important way to create a sense of inclusiveness when leading a project or initiative is to promote a feeling of participation that is facilitated and supported by the leadership in place (Edmondson 1999; Yukl 1998). Indeed, the concept of leader inclusiveness is defined as 'words and deeds by the leader or leaders that indicate an invitation and appreciation for others' contributions' (Nembhard and Edmondson 2006, 947). This type of leadership is categorized as a socialized leadership type, which are leaders who are oriented towards the common good and want to use everyone's potential to achieve the fulfilment of that goal. This kind of leadership is contrary to what has been called a personalized leadership type, which are leaders mainly concerned with exerting power and influence over others (Bass and Steidlmeier 1999; House and Howell 1992).

Communication

A first method to promote this sense of inclusiveness is to be a good communicator that binds people and nations together rather than keeping them on a distance. That is, the use of inclusive leader language is a first step towards mobilizing participating individuals, groups and nations (Steffens and Haslam 2013). So, how is the communication process working in the context of BRI? Is China succeeding into creating a BRI that is widely shared and endorsed?

In the process of communication, it is important that the initiator of the communication process is able to establish a platform that brings together the audience that needs to be targeted. This platform will allow making information available and let it travel around so it reaches everyone. In other words, the goal of the platform is to increase communication volume and value. In this respect, President Xi Jinping has communicated several times that BRI is a way for China to embrace an international presence like never before and to invite all nations to participate in this economic project. The message is clear: BRI is a 'philosophy' rather than a concrete message so it can be shared worldwide and adjusted where needed. The spirit may be out of the bottle, but communicating effectively on an international platform also means to be able to assess whether the message worked. In other words, you also included an element of control that enables you to review the effectiveness of the communication process. As China communicates a more abstract philosophical message, it has been noted that the country has adopted a 'no-strings attached' approach, which regretfully demonstrates a non-interventionist attitude. For instance, it is unclear for many observers how China is financing the BRI projects, and the extent to which they are able to manage security risks in BRI countries. Nothing is communicated about how this will work. This is not optimal because, as indicated earlier, this approach goes together with a lack of sense of accountability with the result that very little responsibility will be taken to make the collective movement grow and improve where needed. As a case in point, this lack of responsibility quickly surfaced in how Chinese SOEs showed a tendency to blur the lines between commercial and political factors, which makes them too optimistically relying on Beijing's support in case of a crisis.

In any communication process, a recipient is also present. For communication to be effective, the message needs to be clear and interpreted in ways that the communicator meant it. It is exactly this point that has received its fair share of criticism. That is, BRI has become such a popular buzzword that it proves very difficult to lock down criteria for how any given project would or could fit into the overall initiative. Specifically, according to critics, BRI remains a confusing concept, which has led to the saying, 'It means everything and nothing at the same time'. Put together, since Xi Jinping unveiled the initiative in 2013, the world is unsure about the specific parameters that are used to judge the eligibility of being a participating nation. In fact, in the early days, it was mentioned that any nation, company or organization anywhere is welcome to join BRI, even the USA (although the current US-China trade war has changed the public opinion on this point).

With communication that is unclear about concrete criteria, expectations and the shape the BRI wants to take, it is no surprise that the communication of the Chinese government is not succeeding turning BRI into an inclusive project. Indeed, because although the Chinese government emphasizes the collaborative efforts of BRI, it remains difficult to determine who is 'we' in this project. If a collaborative approach is being used to introduce BRI, but at the same time remains unclear about its collective parameters, the project will quickly be perceived as a more authority-driven structure with an unclear agenda, ultimately driving distrust rather than trust. This brings us to the next point of focus when it comes down to building connection with its followers, that is, the ability to build trust.

Trust

A reason why the lack of clarity in communication, by being unable to define the 'we' in the equation of BRI, may feed distrust rather than trust is because it creates concerns regarding the transparency of China's motives and ways of working (e.g., how projects are funded, who benefits, what agenda is pursued—domestic, regional or global?).

The presence of trust depends on several factors (e.g., Whitener 1997), and an important one concerns the presence of open communication or communication transparency. Although a number of different conceptualizations of transparency exists (e.g., Rogers 1987; Schnakenberg and Tomlinson 2016; Vogelgesang and Lester 2009; Walumbwa et al. 2008), most of these definitions contain a critical element of 'sharing relevant information' (Vogelgesang 2008, 43). In the context of BRI, communication transparency can therefore be seen as the extent to which relevant information about BRI (criteria, goals, financial flows and so forth) is shared among all participating nations (Vogelgesang and Crossley 2006). Furthermore, in the academic literature, transparency is conceptualized as a virtue that 'should' be encouraged (Murphy, Laczniak, and Wood 2007), and if communication is not transparent, intentions with respect to the integrity of the one communicating are coloured negatively, and, hence, trust suffers (Mayer, Davis, and Schoorman 1995).

Based on the above reasoning, it makes sense that if China does not improve communication transparency, a deficit in trust will emerge for the BRI and its further development will be slowed down by national counter blocs being formed. In this process, it is important to realize that taking leadership of a project such as BRI includes the awareness that no country can go alone in the modern world and therefore the primary task is to facilitate connection by installing trust. If this realization is clear, it also becomes clear who needs to initiate the trust. Research shows that trust is subjective in nature; therefore, it is said that trust is in the eye of the beholder (Mayer et al. 1995). Therefore, to be perceived as trustworthy in your leadership position, it is needed that the leader of the BRI makes the first step and shows risky behaviour by acting in ways that will serve the interests of the others first.

Research indeed demonstrates that those who are willing to promote common interests first will be met by positive reciprocity where the other parties give trust back (Pillutla, Malhotra, and Murnighan 2003). But, the main message is that in this process, China is destined to give trust first to receive trust from the other members in the BRI. How to do this? An example can be found in how Chinese SOEs can shape their foreign investment styles in countries where distrust is potentially high. First, try to avoid acquisitions that always receive much criticism in public debates. Instead, engage in greenfield investment which tends to attract less media hype. Second, when acquiring a local firm, allow for a more substantive role for local investors who are likely trusted by local stakeholders. This can be achieved by taking a lower equity stake. This way, China can make clear that they are serious in promoting local welfare and therefore are willing to contribute their fair share. As a result, possible perceptions of China only pursuing their own domestic agenda could be prevented.

FUTURE LEADERSHIP CHALLENGES

When the BRI was initiated in 2013, it was quickly followed up by criticisms that the building of infrastructure along the Belt and Silk roads was a hidden way for China to export their supplies (as the country recently also made the shift to a service-oriented economy). In other words, BRI would serve China's domestic manufacturing agenda. At the same time, Chinese President Xi Jinping always insisted that the BRI would not be just about roads and railways, and that this programme would also focus on innovations in telecommunications, fibre, e-commerce and so forth. Indeed, China has set ambitious innovation targets and promoted the country to a global innovation 'hub'. Despite the efforts to make innovation an important guideline in Chinese government strategies, for a long time Chinese companies have not been recognized for being good at it. As Frynas, Mol, and Mellahi (2018, 75) note, 'Innovative firms in China are said to excel at cost reduction, accelerated product development and networked production'. In the past, Chinese companies lagged behind in their focus on the right management approach that installs the leadership to create the right conditions to support creativity and management innovation. But times are changing. China has moved up the tech value chain quickly, demonstrated by successes like Huawei now being a world leader in telecom and communication technology.

As a result of innovation becoming a driving force behind the prosperity that can be found in China, also BRI made an important change in being transformed in what is now referred to as a digital Belt and Road. The introduction of a 'Digital BRI' was first proposed in July 2015 at the China-EU Digital Cooperation Roundtable in Brussels, and today it has become an important component of Beijing's strategy in BRI countries. The digital project will mainly consist of the construction of cross-border optical cables and mobile networks as well as the development of e-commerce between China and BRI countries. Obviously, this new form of BRI brings other challenges with it. One obvious challenge is the concern that Chinese cyber espionage will be linked to the BRI. This challenge demands that China shows strong and responsible leadership. How do you show leadership and win the hearts of followers in a digital era where digital platforms are the place to work on?

With respect to leading a digital BRI, it is important to stress that because of the open nature of platforms, China by definition has the responsibility to set the conditions for the rules of play (cf. De Cremer, Zhang, and De Schutter 2017). Indeed, digital platforms are recognized for the outreach and impact they can have; but to ensure that this happens in the intended and cooperative ways, it is necessary for platform leadership to be present to make clear the how and why they want this outreach. To conclude, a few suggestions can be given how to promote leadership in a digital era. First of all, the employment of a digital platform does not only require better compliance and regulation but also needs leadership actively engaged to deal with the concerns of the participating parties and at times to show their presence by intervening in service of these concerns. Second, as a platform makes use of integrated multiple channels, trust can only be fostered if the leading party (China) makes decisions in a consistent manner across these different channels. Third, working with a digital platform implies that collaboration is not simply a function of a direct relationship between the leading party (China) and other participants (nations) in the platform but also is a shared experience, where different parties will collaborate or will not be based on the input that the leading party provides via the different channels to the different parties.

REFERENCES

Ansar, A., B. Flyvbjerg, A. Budzier, and D. Lunn. 2016. 'Does Infrastructure Investment Lead to Economic Growth or Economic Fragility? Evidence from China'. *Oxford Review of Economic Policy* 32 (3): 360–390.

Avey, J. B., T. S. Wernsing, and M. E. Palanski. 2012. 'Exploring the Process of Ethical Leadership: The Mediating Role of Employee Voice and Psychological Ownership'. *Journal of Business Ethics* 107 (1): 21–34.

Awamleh, R., and W. L. Gardner. 1999. 'Perceptions of Leader Charisma and Effectiveness: The Effects of Vision Content, Delivery, and Organizational Performance'. *The Leadership Quarterly* 10 (3): 345–373.

Bass, B. J., and B. J. Avolio. 1990. *Transformational Leadership Development: Manual for the Multifactor Leadership Questionnaire*. Paola Alto, CA: Consulting Psychologist Press.

Bass, B. M. 1985. *Leadership and Performance beyond Expectations*. New York: Free Press.

Bass, B. M., and P. Steidlmeier. 1999. 'Ethics, Character, and Authentic Transformational Leadership Behaviour'. *The Leadership Quarterly* 10 (2): 181–217.

Baum, J. R., S. A. Kirkpatrick, and E. A. Locke. 1998. 'A Longitudinal Study of the Relation of Vision and Vision Communication to Venture Growth in Entrepreneurial Firms'. *Journal of Applied Psychology* 83 (1): 43–54.

Baumeister, R. F., and M. R. Leary. 1995. 'The Need to Belong: Desire for Interpersonal Attachments as a Fundamental Human Motivation'. *Psychological Bulletin* 117 (3): 497–529.

Berson, Y., B. Shamir, B. J. Avolio, and M. Popper. 2001. 'The Relationship between Vision Strength, Leadership Style, and Context'. *Leadership Quarterly* 12 (1): 53–73.

Bligh, M. C., J. C. Kohles, and J. R. Meindl. 2004. 'Charisma under Crisis: Presidential Leadership, Rhetoric, and Media Responses before and after the September 11th Terrorist Attacks'. *The Leadership Quarterly* 15 (2): 211–239.

Brown, M. E., L. K. Treviño, and D. A. Harrison. 2005. 'Ethical Leadership: A Social Learning Perspective for Construct Development and Testing'. *Organizational Behavior and Human Decision Processes* 97 (2): 117–134.

Burns, J. 1978. *Leadership*. New York: Harper & Row.

Cameron, K. S., J. E. Dutton, and R. E. Quinn. 2003. *Positive Organizational Scholarship: Foundations of a New Discipline*. San Francisco, CA: Berrett-Koehler.

Chemers, M. M. 1997. *An Integrative Theory of Leadership*. Mahwah, NJ: Lawrence, Erlbaum Associates.

Chen, A. S., and Y. Hou. 2016. 'The Effects of Ethical Leadership, Voice Behavior and Climates for Innovation on Creativity: A Moderated Mediation Examination'. *Leadership Quarterly* 27 (1): 1–13.

Conger, J. A., and R. N. Kanungo. 1987. 'Toward a Behavioral Theory of Charismatic Leadership in Organizational Settings'. *Academy of Management Journal* 12 (4): 637–647.

De Cremer, D., J. Zhang, and L. De Schutter. 2017. 'The Challenge of Responsible Leadership in Digital Platforms'. *The European Business Review* (July–August): 13–15.

De Cremer, D., D. M. Mayer, M. Van Dijke, B. C. Schouten, and M. Bardes. 2009. 'Self-Sacrificial Leadership Promoting Prosocial Behavior: The Moderating Role of Prevention Focus'. *Journal of Applied Psychology* 94 (4): 887–899.

Den Hartog, D. N., and R. M. Verburg. 1997. 'Charisma and Rhetoric: Communicative Techniques of International Business Leaders'. *Leadership Quarterly* 8 (4): 355–391.

Edmondson, A. 1999. 'Psychological Safety and Learning Behaviour in Work Teams'. *Administrative Science Quarterly* 44 (2): 350–383.

Emrich, C. G., H. H. Brower, J. J. Feldman, and H. Garland. 2001. 'Images in Words: Presidential Rhetoric, Charisma, and Greatness'. *Administrative Science Quarterly* 46 (3): 527–557.

Frynas, J. G., M. J. Mol, and K. Mellahi. 2018. 'Management Innovation in China: Haier's Rendanheyi'. *California Management Review* 61 (1): 71–93.

Hollander, E. P. 1992. 'The Essential Interdependence of Leadership and Followership'. *Current Directions in Psychological Science* 1 (2): 71–75.

House, R. J. 1971. 'A Path-Goal Theory of Leader Effectiveness'. *Administrative Science Quarterly* 16: 321–338.

House, R. J., and J. M. Howell. 1992. 'Personality and Charismatic Leadership'. *The Leadership Quarterly* 3 (2): 81–108.

Howell, J. M., and B. J. Avolio. 1993. 'Transformational Leadership Transactional Leadership, Locus of Control, and Support for Innovation: Key Predictors of Consolidated-Business-Unit-Performance'. *Journal of Applied Psychology* 78 (6): 891–902.

Howell, J. M., and B. Shamir. 2005. 'The Role of Followers in the Charismatic Leadership Process: Relationships and Their Consequences'. *Academy of Management Review* 30 (1): 96–112.

Kempster, S., B. Jackson, and M. Conroy. 2011. 'Leadership as Purpose: Exploring the Role of Purpose in Leadership Practice'. *Leadership* 7 (3): 317–334.

Kirkpatrick, S. A., and E. A. Locke. 1996. 'Direct and Indirect Effects of Three Core Charismatic Leadership Components on Performance and Attitudes'. *Journal of Applied Psychology* 81 (1): 36–51.

Mayer, R. C., J. H. Davis, and F. D. Schoorman. 1995. 'An Integrative Model of Organizational Trust'. *Academy of Management Review* 20 (3): 709–734.

Mendenhall, M. E., B. S. Reiche, A. Bird, and J. S. Osland. 2012. 'Defining the "Global" in Global Leadership'. *Journal of World Business* 47 (4): 493–503.

Mio, J. S., R. E. Riggio, S. Levin, and R. Reese. 2005. 'Presidential Leadership and Charisma: The Effects of Metaphor'. *The Leadership Quarterly* 16 (2): 287–294.

Murphy, P. E., G. R. Laczniak, and G. Wood. 2007. 'An Ethical Basis for Relationship Marketing: A Virtue Ethics Perspective. *European Journal of Marketing* 41 (1–2): 37–57.

Naidoo, L. J., and R. G. Lord. 2008. 'Speech Imagery and Perceptions of Charisma: The Mediating Role of Positive Affect'. *The Leadership Quarterly* 19 (3): 283–296.

Nembhard, I. M., & A. C. Edmondson. 2006. 'Making It Safe: The Effects of Leader Inclusiveness and Professional Status on Psychological Safety and Improvement Efforts in Health Care Teams'. *Journal of Organizational Behavior* 27 (7): 941–966.

Owens, B. P., M. D. Johnson, and T. R. Mitchell. 2013. 'Expressed Humility in Organizations: Implications of Performance, Teams and Leadership'. *Organization Science* 24 (5): 1517–1538.

Pillutla, M. M., D. Malhotra, and J. K. Murnighan. 2003. 'Attributions of Trust and the Calculus of Reciprocity'. *Journal of Experimental Social Psychology* 39 (5): 448–455.

Rogers, D. P. 1987. 'The Development of a Measure of Perceived Communication Openness'. *Journal of Business Communication* 24: 53–61.

Schnackenberg, A. K., and E. C. Tomlinson. 2016. 'Organizational Transparency: A New Perspective on Managing Trust in Organization-Stakeholder Relationships'. *Journal of Management* 31: 587–603.

Shamir, B., M. B. Arthur, and R. J. House. 1994. 'The Rhetoric of Charismatic Leadership: A Theoretical Extension, A Case Study, and Implications for Research'. *Leadership Quarterly* 5 (1): 25–42.

Shamir, B., R. J. House, and M. B. Arthur. 1993. 'The Motivational Effects of Charismatic Leadership: A Self-Concept Based Theory'. *Organization Science* 4 (4): 513–668.

Steffens, N. K., and S. A. Haslam. 2013. 'Power through "Us": Leaders' Use of We-Referencing Language Predicts Election Victory'. *PLos ONE* 8 (10): 1–6.

Vogelgesang, G. R. 2008. *How Leader Interactional Transparency can Impact Follower Psychological Safety and Role Engagement*. Unpublished Dissertation, University of Nebraska, Lincoln.

Vogelgesang, G. R., and C. D. Crossley. 2006. 'Toward an Understanding of Interactional Transparency'. *Gallup Leadership Summit*.

Vogelgesang, G. R., and P. B. Lester. 2009. 'How Leaders Can Get Results by Laying it on the Line'. *Organizational Dynamics* 38: 252–260.

Walumbwa, F. O., B. J. Avolio, W. L. Gardner, T. S. Wernsing, and S. J. Peterson. 2008. 'Authentic Leadership: Development and Validation of a Theory-based Measure'. *Journal of Management* 34: 89–126.

Weick, K. E. 2001. 'Leadership as the Legitimation of Doubt'. In *The Future of Leadership: Today's Top Leadership Thinkers Speak to Tomorrow's Leaders*, edited by W. Bennis, G. M. Spreitzer, and T. G. Cummings, 91–102. San Francisco, CA: Jossey-Bass.

Whitener, E. M. 1997. 'The Impact of Human Resource Activities on Employee Trust. *Human Resource Management Review* 7 (4): 389–404.

Yukl, G. 1998. *Leadership in Organizations*. Upper Saddle River, NJ: Prentice Hall.

Chapter 16

How Will the Belt and Road Initiative Be Financed?

Simon Taylor

INTRODUCTION AND CONCLUSIONS

This chapter considers the question of how China might pay for the Belt and Road Initiative (BRI). The second part of the chapter notes the difficulty of identifying what the bill actually is, given the lack of official clarity. We then consider in the third part the total bill in relation to China's ability to fund overseas investment, or to put it more bluntly, if China can afford it. We conclude that despite some deterioration in China's foreign exchange position and the probable worsening of its balance of payments, the answer is yes but not without limits. The fourth part examines the different ways in which China could potentially channel the finance, via instruments such as grants, debt and equity. It seems likely that most of the funding will be in the form of bank debt, much of it on 'soft' terms which amount to a large element of grant (or aid). Some will also come in the form of equity investments by Chinese state-owned enterprises (SOEs). Next, in the fifth part, we look at the organizations from which funding might come, across a wide range of institutions with varying degrees of association with the Chinese state. The sixth part looks at non-Chinese sources of finance that are available in principle for some BRI projects, mainly in infrastructure. The seventh part concludes the chapter.

DEFINITIONS AND THE PROBLEM OF QUANTIFICATION

Finance usually seeks to be a quantitative discipline but the question of financing the BRI is complicated by a lack of definite official amounts. The BRI scope is unclear with respect to both the scale of project and the time horizon for completing them. Media estimates range from $1 trillion to $8 trillion (Balding 2017; Hurley, Scott, and Gailyn 2018), but there is no official target.

Taking one extreme, $1 trillion of financing over 10 years would amount to $100 billion of Chinese funding, little more than a rounding error compared to the country's 2017 GDP of $12.9 trillion. At the other extreme, $8 trillion over five years would involve an annual financing of $1.6 trillion, a sum that would stretch even China.

The BRI was formally announced (as the One Belt One Road initiative) in 2013 and a leading group created in 2014. But some investment has already taken place, chiefly on projects that had been planned already, such as the China–Pakistan Economic Corridor, for which a memorandum of understanding was signed in 2013 and which was built on earlier Chinese infrastructure investments in Pakistan.[1] Other projects included under the BRI umbrella are the China–Mongolia–Russia Economic Corridor and the New Eurasian Continental Bridge.

Furthermore, to the extent that the BRI represents a long-term strategic commitment to a large region, it could continue over decades, changing its form according to the development needs of the region and Chinese state priorities.

It is not even necessary that all the funding come from China. The BRI is mainly a set of infrastructure investment projects, some of which could be funded by multilateral development banks (MDBs) or by other countries.

Lastly, many projects that either would have happened anyway or are only tangentially related to the core BRI goals may be included in

---

[1] CPEC Official website: http://cpec.gov.pk/faqs

BRI financial totals because the investing organizations (whether Chinese or foreign) may hope to seek political gain from supporting a state policy.

In sum, we have little idea of the totals, or timescales, but we can say with some confidence that the BRI probably involves a multitrillion-dollar programme of investments over at least a decade to come.

To give some sense of scale of spending, we can note that President Xi, in his speech to the Belt and Road Forum in Beijing in March 2017, stated that the recently created Asian Infrastructure Investment Bank (AIIB) had invested $1.7 billion and the equally new Silk Road Fund had invested $4 billion in the first four years of the BRI (Xi 2017).

The Chinese government's English-language website for the BRI states that for the whole of 2017, Chinese investors directly invested $14.4 billion in BRI countries (National Bureau of Statistics 2018).

While not trivial numbers, these are a very long way from the hundreds of billions of dollars that might seem to be needed annually to fulfil the grander interpretations of BRI's vision.

But the Chinese banks appear to have mobilized much larger sums. The executive vice president of the China Banking Association told reporters that by the end of 2016, the three largest Chinese commercial banks had committed $225 billion to BRI projects,[2] and the two major policy banks, Export–Import Bank of China (hereafter, Exim Bank) and China Development Bank (CDB), had committed $200 billion (Qinqin and Jia 2017).

A report by ICBC Standard Bank, a subsidiary of the largest Chinese bank, ICBC, estimated that the total BRI investments announced or under way as of early 2018 amounted to $750 billion, of which $330 billion was in transport and logistics (rail, road and ports) and $266 billion was in energy and utilities. About $50 billion was in Pakistan alone, reflecting the momentum behind the China–Pakistan Economic Corridor (ICBC Standard 2018).

---

[2] ICBC, Bank of China and China Construction Bank.

THE MACROECONOMIC ASPECT OF FINANCING

This section considers the question of the scale of BRI financing relative to the total Chinese international financial position, or if China can 'afford' the BRI. We assume that the BRI needs to be financed in foreign exchange, an assumption which is rather conservative given that much of the payment would be for Chinese resources that can be paid for in Chinese yuan.[3] This assumption therefore represents an upper bound on the impact on China's balance of payments position.

A flow of foreign exchange from one country to another can be in various forms (see the fourth section), but the overall impact on the balance of payments is the same. If a country is in balance and then makes major payments or investments abroad then, all else being equal, it has a net outflow of foreign exchange. If the country has a floating exchange rate (like most developed countries) then the exchange rate would tend to fall, reflecting a new demand for foreign currency relative to domestic currency. In the long term, the investments may generate a returning flow of foreign exchange to the country, thus pushing up the exchange rate; but here we assume that is some way off in the future.

The alternative arrangement is for a country to intervene in the foreign exchange markets and 'manage' its exchange rate. China has historically followed this policy, with varying levels of stringency. One indicator of the level of intervention is the size of a country's foreign exchange reserves. Compared with a market-based, non-interventionist approach, changes in the foreign reserves reflect intervention by the government (or central bank) in the market. Indeed, foreign reserves represent the result of taking foreign exchange out of the market by preventing resident firms from selling their earned foreign exchange in the open market. Instead, those firms are required to sell their foreign exchange to the central bank (in exchange for domestic currency), which invests the foreign exchange in suitable assets (such as US government bonds).

---

[3] Consider a contract for a Chinese construction company to build a bridge in Myanmar, using Chinese labour and imported materials from China. Most of the costs would arise in yuan and there would be relatively little foreign currency impact of the investment.

When the BRI was first launched, it was possible to argue that China could afford it by simply using part of its reserves, which were widely seen as far in excess of any operational need for policy intervention. With the reserves reaching $4 trillion in 2014, it was possible to argue that at least $1 trillion was 'surplus' and could be used for BRI funding.[4]

Whether running down the reserves was ever a policy goal is unclear. But with the reserves in 2017 around $1 trillion (about a quarter) below their peak, using them to fund a major foreign investment programme is now more difficult. Even $3 trillion is a large amount of reserves, but some (undisclosed) fraction of this is invested in illiquid assets by the People's Bank of China (PBC) and much of the remainder needs to be retained to fight off any future pressure on the yuan.

Nonetheless, China at the least has some flexibility in its ability to finance the BRI from its reserves. The other source of financing would be future balance of payments surpluses. China has historically run surpluses on its trade (exports and imports of goods and services) and sometimes on its capital account (net inflows of investment) as well. It was the combined high surpluses that fed the earlier rise in the reserves, which would otherwise have caused a rise in the yuan.

The International Monetary Fund (IMF) forecasts that China will run a small and declining balance of payments surplus in the next few years, from 1.4 per cent of GDP in 2017 to 0.4 per cent of GDP in 2022 (IMF 2017a). It also forecasts that the Chinese capital and financial account (net inflows and outflows of financing) will remain negative, even lower than in recent years, meaning that there will be more investment funds leaving China than entering it. This forecast includes some allowance for BRI financing, but it is unclear how much.

The net effect is that the IMF forecast that China's overall balance of payments will be a deficit, albeit a declining one, from 2018 to 2022. Unless the government chooses to leave the yuan value entirely to the

---

[4] Official website of State Administration of Foreign Exchange (SAFE): http://www.safe.gov.cn/wps/portal/english/Data/Forex

market (in which case the overall deficit would imply the yuan would depreciate), the logic is that China's foreign exchange reserves will fall further. On the IMF estimate, they would reach $2.7 trillion by the end of 2022, compared with a peak of $3.9 trillion at the end of 2014.

Outbound Foreign Direct Investment

Another trend in China's balance of payments that we need to consider is the increasing flow of Chinese outbound foreign direct investment (FDI). After two decades, when the flow was very heavily into China, many Chinese companies are now investing abroad, because they have reached a scale and international ambition that makes this sensible (You and Solomon 2015).

It is to be expected that as China has developed more internationally ambitious companies, this would be followed by greater FDI. In this respect, China is merely catching up with companies in the more advanced economies. We might therefore expect a trend increase in FDI, which would of course mean the Chinese balance of payments moving further away from its historic surplus pattern towards a deficit. Could this be a constraint on BRI-based investments? China can only afford so much overall foreign investing before the exchange rate is at risk.

A complicating factor is that even nominally privately owned companies are under the de facto control of the Chinese government. Some high-profile acquisitive Chinese companies were apparently reined in during 2017, whether for political reasons or because their foreign spending was risking a strain on the PBC's ability to maintain the yuan's value (Huang and Tang 2017). In 2017, overseas direct investment by Chinese investors was ¥810.8 billion, or $120 billion, down by 29.4 per cent over the previous year (National Bureau of Statistics 2018).

This implies that whereas in the USA, for example, total outbound FDI is the sum of many individual decentralized decisions, there is an element of central oversight in China which could, if necessary, curb some types of investment to make room for those seen as more essential to national policy, such as BRI.

Table 16.1 summarizes the IMF balance of payments forecast to 2023 and adds two estimates of BRI funding: a 'high' figure

Table 16.1 Possible Impact of BRI Financing on China's Overall Balance of Payments, 2018–2022 (Percentage of GDP)

Percentage of GDP	2017P	2018P	2019P	2020P	2021P	2022P
Current Account Balance (1)	1.4	1.3	1.2	0.9	0.7	0.4
Trade Balance	4.1	3.9	3.7	3.4	3.2	3.00
Services Balance	−2.3	−2.3	−2.3	−2.4	−2.4	−2.5
Other (Net)	−0.4	−0.3	−0.2	−0.1	−0.1	−0.1
Capital and Financial Balance (2)	−2.8	−1.6	−1.3	−1.1	−1.00	−0.8
Of Which: Net Foreign Direct Investment	0.8	−1.1	−1.1	−0.9	−0.7	−0.6
Overall Balance (1 + 2)	−1.4	−0.3	−0.1	−0.2	−0.3	−0.4
BRI: high Estimate	–	−5.8	−5.3	−4.9	−4.5	−4.2
Overall Balance Including BRI (High)	–	−6.1	−5.4	−5.1	−4.8	−4.6
BRI: Low Estimate	–	−2.9	−2.7	−2.5	−2.3	−2.1
Overall Balance Including BRI (Low)	–	−3.2	−2.8	−2.7	−2.6	−2.5

Source: IMF (2017a, Table 2) and author's estimates.
Note: P in the column heads stands for 'projected'.

of $800 billion a year (assuming a total of $8 trillion financed over 10 years) and a low figure of $400 billion a year (assuming a total of $4 trillion financed over 10 years). The IMF forecasts China's GDP to reach ¥121 trillion in 2022, which is about $19 trillion at the current exchange rate of ¥6.4 per dollar (during the writing of the chapter). The high BRI financing causes a significant annual deterioration in the balance of payments deficit from a forecast without BRI of 0.4 per cent of GDP in 2022 to a deficit including BRI funding of 4.6 per cent. An annual outflow on even the lower case would imply steady downward pressure on the yuan exchange rate.

The Stock of Debt

We also need to consider the stock of debt arising from cumulative investment. China's government debt at the end of 2017 was estimated by the IMF at ¥30.5 trillion, representing 47.5 per cent of GDP, a relatively comfortable level (IMF 2017a, Table 5). The IMF forecasts the narrow-level debt to rise to 65.5 per cent by 2023, still manageable by the standards of middle-income countries.

If we assume for illustration a cumulative BRI financing of $1 trillion by 2023, the government debt to GDP figure rises to 70 per cent. While $1 trillion is at the lower end of the scale, most of the financing will probably come from development banks and other institutions, which are linked to the state but have their own independent balance sheets; so most BRI financing will not show up as official state debt. On this scenario, the total state debt would be higher but still quite manageable with an additional $1 trillion of debt (see Table 16.2).

But the situation is more worrying if we consider the total impact of BRI financing on China's foreign debt, meaning debt owed to foreigners. For China to finance foreign investment in dollars beyond the dollar holdings it has in reserves and any additional net surplus earned from the balance of payments, it would need to finance this by borrowing abroad. Unless China can finance the bulk of BRI financing in its own currency, it needs to procure the foreign exchange to fund it. China could just buy dollars using yuan but that would put downward pressure on the yuan exchange rate. Even if China tries to use

Table 16.2 Chinese Government Debt with and without BRI Debt, 2016–2023P (USD Billion)

	2016	2017	2018P	2019P	2020P	2021P	2022P	2023P
China Government Debt	5,164	6,064	7,088	8,212	9,439	10,732	12,085	13,534
Add Estimated BRI Debt	100	200	300	400	500	600	800	1,000
Total	5,264	6,264	7,388	8,612	9,939	11,332	12,885	14,534
Percentage of GDP	45.2	49.4	53.4	57.1	60.6	63.8	67.2	70.3
Percentage of GDP (without BRI)	44.3	47.8	51.2	54.4	57.6	60.5	63.1	65.5

Source: Author's estimates based on IMF World Economic Outlook, April 2018.
Note: P in the column heads stands for 'projected'.

domestic yuan financing, some projects will probably require foreign capital goods that would need to be paid for in foreign currency.

Assuming that all the debt is in foreign currency, Table 16.3 considers crudely what the effect of low ($1 trillion) and high ($4 trillion) volumes of extra foreign debt would mean for the country's foreign debt position. At the end of 2017, China's total foreign debt was $1.7 trillion, of which only a small part was government debt, the balance being mainly of Chinese banks and companies. At 14.7 per cent, this was quite low by international standards.

Adding $1 trillion of BRI-related debt would put the figure up to 23 per cent, which remains manageable. But if we pick the higher case of $4 trillion, China's foreign debt to GDP would rise to around 50 per cent. Given that the IMF expects the country's overall balance of payments to be in a small negative position in the next few years, this scale of financing over say five years would mean a fairly radical shift in China's foreign liability position.

Table 16.3 *China's External (Foreign) Debt Relative to Estimated BRI Debt (USD Billion)*

Elements	2017
Gross Foreign Debt	1,711
Government Debt	169
Percentage of GDP	14.7
Add: BRI (Low Case)	1,000
Total, Including BRI Debt	2,711
Percentage of GDP	23.3
Add: BRI (High Case)	4,000
Total, Including BRI Debt	5,711
Percentage of GDP	49.0

Source: Author's estimates using SAFE data.
Note: Foreign exchange markets tend to focus on gross debt rather than amounts net of foreign assets. The risk of a large scale of BRI financing over a short period would be to make China's overall foreign debt position considerably more fragile.

Of course, in making BRI finance available, China will be acquiring foreign assets that would offset the debt. But most of the BRI countries are of relatively low credit quality, and much of the debt is likely to be on concessional terms (meaning some or all will be forgiven).

It is unlikely that the government would allow this to happen, which means that the higher case is unlikely to happen, or at least the higher BRI amount would take place over a much longer period. China government's ability to manage many of the moving parts of the balance of payments (including non-BRI FDI) means it should be able to calibrate BRI funding so as to avoid accelerating foreign debt. But, we see this as constraint on the speed of BRI financing.

We conclude that the larger estimates for BRI financing are implausible unless spread over much longer periods. China could probably accommodate $1 trillion of foreign outflows over a 10-year period without too much pressure on the balance of payments (meaning the exchange rate of the yuan) or on government debt. The government can use its control of other outflows such as SOE outward FDI to make 'room' for BRI. But, it is unlikely that anything like $8 trillion could be financed over the next decade without grave risk to China's external financial stability.

METHODS OF FINANCING: DEBT, EQUITY AND BANK LOANS

We now consider the different types of financing available for BRI. Whether sourced in China or from abroad, the options are grants, bank debt, bond debt and equity. It seems likely that most BRI investments would be infrastructure, which is typically financed with relatively large amounts of debt. These debts are usually lent by banks. But even for infrastructure, some equity funding is needed. Other BRI projects might be more equity financed.

Financing the BRI involves flow of funds from China to other countries. We will use a standard balance of payments classification to consider the different forms this financing can take, and then will consider the relative advantages to China and to the recipient governments (Table 16.4).

Table 16.4 Grants/Other Official Financing/Short- and Long-Term Debt/Portfolio and FDI Equity

Category	Type of Contract	Notes
Grants	Not repayable	Some part of debt may be de facto a grant
Debt:		
Bank	Fixed, repayable	One or a few lenders, private information
Bonds	Fixed, repayable	Many lenders, only public information
Equity:		
Portfolio	Contingent	Minority stake, no control
FDI	Contingent	Majority stake and/or control

Source: Author's analysis based on IMF Balance of Payments Manual (6th edition) https://www.imf.org/external/pubs/ft/bop/2007/pdf/bpm6.pdf

Grants

The first distinction is between whether the funds are in the form of a grant (a gift) or they require repayment. In the case of repayment, the funds may be in the form of debt (where the repayment terms are fixed in advance) or equity (where the payments depend on the success of the business venture concerned). An outright grant is usual in official development assistance (ODA), which is better known as foreign aid.

From a financial point of view, grants are simple: A direct and irrevocable transfer of resources from one country to another. Normally these funds would come from a state budget. Companies can give charitable donations, but these are not normally on a scale that is significant for a donor country and they are not necessarily connected to government policies. Not all ODA funds are pure grants. The criterion for defining funds as ODA (or equivalently 'concessional' financing) is that they have at least a 25 per cent grant component. If the grant component is less than 25 per cent, then the funds are termed other official financing (OOF), meaning the funds come from the state but the majority require some form of repayment, albeit possibly on concessional (or 'soft') terms (further explained in next paragraphs).

China gives both ODA and OOF. China's total official (state-sourced) finance to lower income countries in 2014 was $37.3 billion, which is greater than the US amount of $29.4 billion, but the majority was not ODA, of which the USA gave considerably more ($28.4 billion versus $6.9 billion).

Table 16.5 shows the countries that receive Chinese ODA and OOF. Since ODA is intended for the lowest-income countries, it's not surprising that most goes to African countries. OOF, which is a less well-defined form of state finance, is on a much larger scale, and the largest recipients are mostly BRI nations.

The line between grant and non-grant financing is blurred because a lot of debt is lent at 'concessional' rates (see the next section on debts). Also, a loan may be converted into a grant later, as reportedly has been

Table 16.5 Top 10 Countries Receiving Chinese ODA and OOF, 2000–2014 (USD Billion)

Official Development Assistance		Other Official Financing	
Country	Amount	Country	Amount
Cuba	6.7	**Russia**	36.6
Cote d'Ivoire	4	**Pakistan**	16.3
Ethiopia	3.7	Angola	3.7
Zimbabwe	3.6	**Laos**	3.6
Cameroon	3.4	Venezuela	10.8
Nigeria	3.1	**Turkmenistan**	10.1
Tanzania	3	Ecuador	9.7
Cambodia	3	Brazil	8.5
Sri Lanka	2.8	**Sri Lanka**	8.2
Ghana	2.5	**Kazakhstan**	6.7

Source: AidData (2018);
Note: Countries in boldface are BRI countries.

done by China for part of the CPEC financing for the construction of Gwadar Airport (Haider 2015).

Debt

Debt flows from one country to another represent a contract where the resources are expected to be repaid, usually on a fixed schedule and on fixed terms. For example, a loan may be for an amount of $100 million for 10 years with an annual interest payment of 5 per cent ($5 million). The interest rate is a matter of negotiation and policy. There is, in principle, a market rate of interest that reflects the creditworthiness (i.e., the estimated risk of default) of the borrower. But the actual interest rate may be lower than the market rate; in which case, the loan has an element of resource gift and is said to be 'concessional'.

Many very low-income countries have no practical access to international private financial markets owing to their very low creditworthiness; in which case, any loans they get will be either from states or from multilateral organizations. Since there is no benchmark market rate of interest, it is hard to estimate how much of the loan can be said to be concessional but some part almost certainly is.

Once again, the CPEC provides an example. Reportedly, part of the project lending by China was originally at 3 per cent, but, in 2015, the rate was cut to 1.6 per cent (Haider 2015). In 2015, the Government of Pakistan issued an international Eurobond at an interest rate of 8.25 per cent (Government of Pakistan 2015). A sovereign bond (i.e., a bond issued by a nation state) usually has the highest possible creditworthiness of any investment in the economy. Financing a project in the economy carries some additional risk (unless that project is guaranteed by the government). So, a private foreign investor financing infrastructure in Pakistan would reasonably require a premium of 8.25 per cent paid by the Government of Pakistan. For simplicity, if we round up the rate to 9 per cent, we can infer that, in providing a loan initially at 3 per cent, China was lending at a rate some six percentage points below the market rate (later increased further). In effect, most of the loan was concessional, that is, a grant.

Bank Loans versus Bonds

Debt comes in two forms, depending on the type of lender. The first is bank loans, where a single bank or a group of banks acting in a syndicate provide a loan. The second type is a bond, which is a security issued by the borrower that may be bought by one or more investors. Countries with an acceptable level of creditworthiness issue bonds in international markets, tapping global demand. Many lower income countries lack the financial credibility to issue bonds. However, they may still be able to borrow from banks.

A bank loan is essentially a bilateral contract and entails greater information sharing than with a bond deal, where the information is restricted to what can be put in the bond prospectus and openly shared. Banks may demand and get additional private and specific information from a borrower which allows them to judge whether to lend. They may also get legally binding promises known as covenants, which limit the freedom of action of the borrower in ways that raise the likelihood that they can and will repay the loans.

Loans can also be classified according to their maturity, meaning the number of years for repayment. Concessionary loans may be for much longer maturities (20–30 years) than more market-based loans, and this provides more time to the borrower to repay. Maturities can be extended by mutual agreement, something that is far more likely with concessional loans, which may even be written off if the lender decides.

Equity

Equity financing is a more variable and contingent form of financial contract. Only a corporation can issue equity shares; hence, this mechanism for financing government requires the state to set up a separate project company. A lot of infrastructure is funded through project companies, often called 'public–private partnerships' (World Bank 2018), which can receive equity financing from outside.

From the recipient's point of view, equity has the advantage that there is no fixed obligation to repay, unlike a debt, and it thus provides financial flexibility. On the other hand, if a company is very successful and pays large dividends, particularly to foreign investors, there may be controversy about the perceived fairness of such payments.

An important distinction in types of equity investing is between portfolio investing and FDI. Portfolio investing is equity investing for a minority share of a company, which leaves the investor as an essentially passive, part owner, without the ability to control or influence the company.

FDI represents investment that brings significant *de jure* or *de facto* control. If Volkswagen builds a new factory in China financed by its own equity, it will acquire significant operational control (possibly shared with a local partner under China's regulations limiting foreign ownership and control in certain industries). This is FDI and such an investment is more long term, if only because it is very hard to reverse at short notice due to the specific nature of the assets. FDI is therefore both more stable than portfolio investments and more likely to be associated with the transfer of skills and intellectual property to that country (Moran 2017).

Possible Sources of Equity

Banks usually don't provide equity finance, which requires both a different set of investment skills and a different type of repayment. Equity is normally not repaid, except in the rare case of an investment being sold or wound down, and the investor expects a return that compensates for the illiquidity of the invested capital. On the other hand, debt usually is repaid after a set number of years.

The practical sources of Chinese equity for BRI include Chinese SOEs, many of which are involved or plan to be involved in BRI projects. This can be done in two ways.

First, SOEs can own equity in a project, funded by a bank through a loan. The bank in this case is lending to the company, not the BRI nation, which reduces the bank risk somewhat.

Second, the SOE can invest in a project company, which is separately funded by a bank loan. In this case, the bank and SOE both are providing finance to the project and are bearing risks, although the risks are higher for the equity investor.

Since Chinese banks, whether commercial banks or policy banks, are owned and controlled by the state, the distinction may not matter, although each institution has a degree of independence in its goals and operations.

In the China–Pakistan Economic Corridor, most of the investments in the energy sector projects are by SOEs, but they are in turn funded by Chinese banks (IMF 2017b).

A second source of equity financing is the Silk Road Fund (discussed in the nest section), which was set up specifically to provide equity funding for BRI investments.

INSTITUTIONAL SOURCES OF BRI FINANCE IN CHINA

Financing can come from three segments of the economy: the public sector, the private corporate sector and the financial sector. The boundaries of public and private are not always clear in China (Lardy 2014). Although some companies are clearly SOEs, others may be privately owned but still amenable to state influence or direction.

Table 16.6 summarizes the domestic institutional options for BRI funding. The financial sector is overwhelmingly state owned, especially

Table 16.6 *Domestic Institutional Sources of BRI Funding*

Domestic Institutional Source	Comment
Government:	
Central	Direct funding unlikely, generally funded indirectly elsewhere
Provincial	May contribute to Chinese element of projects
State-Owned Enterprises	Main source of equity
Commercial Banks	Debt, mainly shorter term
Policy Banks:	
China Development Bank	Debt, mainly medium and long term
Export–Import Bank of China	Debt, mainly shorter term but some private equity

(Table 16.6 continued)

(Table 16.6 continued)

Domestic Institutional Source	Comment
Multilateral Banks in China:	
AIIB	Long-term debt, not exclusively BRI
New Development Bank	Long-term debt, only a fraction possibly for BRI
Other: Silk Road Fund	Equity fund dedicated to BRI

Source: Author's estimates.

the commercial bank sector. Additionally, there are some policy banks that are under direct state control. There is also a government fund specifically set up to finance BRI activities (known as Silk Road Fund).

We later consider the two multilateral (international) banks which are based in China and are clearly subject to Chinese government influence but not under direct control (the AIIB and New Development Bank [NDB]).

Commercial Banks

All of China's largest commercial banks (deposit-taking institutions) are majority owned by the national government. The great majority of medium and smaller banks are also owned by provincial and state governments or by state-owned financial institutions.

The very large banks are predominantly domestic, but, in recent years, they have expanded their foreign operations, mainly to help their Chinese corporate clients as they build an overseas presence. Whereas in other countries, it would be reasonable to see commercial banks as having different goals and responsibilities from development banks or export credit agencies (ECAs; see the following subsection); in China, the line is rather blurred. For example, the President of ICBC, which is the largest commercial bank in China (and in the world, at least by assets), said in September 2017 that the bank was already involved in 212 projects 'related to Belt and Road' with credit facilities exceeding $67 billion. He said that ICBC has a presence in 18 of the BRI countries and expects future funding to run to 'hundreds of billions' of dollars (Wright 2017).

Export-Import Bank of China

The Exim Bank is usually defined as an ECA, an organization that many countries have to promote their exports by providing finance and, in some cases, insurance, particularly when exporting to high-risk countries. Exim Bank's official description of its goal is 'supporting China's foreign trade, investment and international economic cooperation'.[5] It has provided a large part of the financing of the Chinese 'going global' programme. Reporting directly to the State Council, Exim Bank had around $300 billion of foreign loans outstanding at the end of 2016. Most of this was support for trade by Chinese companies, but the bank explicitly mentions that BRI support is part of its role.

ECAs are typically thought of as providing relatively short-term debt finance, with the loan being repaid once the exports have been fully paid for by the importer. But Exim Bank has been known to provide longer-term loans, more suitable for infrastructure investing, and also has reportedly put funds into private equity (meaning equity that is not quoted on stock markets and is often tied up for many years; Weinland 2018). So Exim Bank is more than just a conventional ECA and could make a significant contribution to BRI financing. Exim Bank is already active in BRI financing, an example being a loan for the construction in Pakistan of a liquefied natural gas pipeline, which will be built by a Chinese company (Rana 2016).

China Development Bank

Created in 1994 as a largely domestic development bank, CDB was in 2015 officially defined as a development finance institution, which encompasses a wider range of activities than the long-term lending, which is usually implied by the idea of a development bank. Reporting directly to the State Council, CDB's official mission is to provide 'medium- to long-term financing facilities that serve China's major long-term economic and social development strategies'.[6] For several years, CDB has been lending abroad in support of Chinese investments,

---

[5] Exim Bank's official website: http://english.eximbank.gov.cn/tm/en-TCN/index_618.html

[6] Corporate website of CDB: http://www.cdb.com.cn/English/gykh_512/khjj/

mainly in natural resources. It has grown rapidly, and its international loan portfolio of $278 billion (end of 2016) far exceeds that of the World Bank ($177 billion at the end of 2017), which is the 'official' global development bank.

With much of its traditional lending and expertise in railways, highways, electric power, public infrastructure and petroleum and petrochemicals (collectively making up about half of its lending), CDB is a major resource for BRI lending, both for funding and technical advice.

Silk Road Fund

President Xi announced in 2014 the setting up of a $40 billion Silk Road Fund for investing equity in BRI projects. The funding comes mainly from the State Administration of Foreign Exchange, the subsidiary of the PBC which manages the nation's foreign exchange reserves. The remainder comes from the Exim Bank and CDB (already mentioned) with 15 per cent also provided by China's sovereign wealth fund, the China Investment Corporation (CIC).[7]

Although $40 billion is relatively small if compared with the resources of CDB or Exim Bank—these two institutions are known mainly for debt funding—the Silk Road Fund will provide equity. Infrastructure projects such as roads and power stations are often funded with a high level (50–80%) of debt, so the equity is 'leveraged', meaning each dollar of equity can support 2–3 dollars of debt. So, the Silk Road Fund could in principle provide equity for projects with $80–$240 billion of total investment, and more if there is additional equity invested by Chinese companies.

Multilateral Financial Institutions Based in China

The AIIB and NDB are multilateral financial institutions where China has considerable influence but not full control. We consider each as a potential source of funding for the BRI.

---

[7] Official website of Silk Road Fund: http://www.silkroadfund.com.cn/enweb/23773/index.html

Asia Infrastructure Investment Bank

The AIIB is modelled on the World Bank in having international ownership by many nations, but with a de facto veto by the host country, China. The World Bank and IMF, both based in Washington DC, were set up in 1944 as multilateral institutions under the Bretton Woods Agreement. All three organizations have boards of directors with representatives from various country shareholders who make decisions by consensus where possible. But the articles of association and voting arrangements for the IMF and World Bank preserve a US veto. Whether this amounts to US control is of course arguable, but it means these organizations are unlikely to do anything that is clearly opposed by the US government.

In the same way, the AIIB gives China veto power but the government seems keen to emphasize the institution's freedom of action, while ensuring that it does nothing that is counter to Chinese interests.

There is a widespread consensus that Asia needs more infrastructure spending (Asian Development Bank [ADB] 2017). So a new organization set up to contribute to funding such infrastructure should be welcomed by the international community, which the AIIB was, with the notable exception of the USA, which refused to join the organization, unlike most other OECD countries. The other exception is Japan, widely perceived to have been discouraged by the USA from joining.

The AIIB will potentially compete with the existing ADB, based in Manila, of which the main shareholder is Japan. But given the demand for infrastructure funding that far exceeds the ADB's capacity, it is hard to argue that the AIIB is harmful. Indeed, the two plan to finance projects together (Reuters 2018).

The world of Asian infrastructure is not exactly the same as the universe of BRI countries, but there is a high degree of overlap, sufficient to expect that the AIIB can pursue its own mission while contributing to the funding of the BRI without any obvious conflict.

New Development Bank

The NDB, based in Shanghai, was set up in 2014 by the so-called BRICS countries (Brazil, Russia, India, China and South Africa). It is unclear quite what the purpose of the NDB is, given that the parent countries have relatively little in common.

The NDB's stated mission is to 'support infrastructure and sustainable development efforts in BRICS and other underserved, emerging economies'. This leaves open the possibility of lending to BRI nations. Other UN members may become members of the bank, but the founding nations' share must remain at least 55 per cent.[8]

The non-Chinese NDB countries may feel that the NDB should allocate its resources predominantly to them, given that China's needs are already well met and the BRI is at best tangential to their needs. From India's point of view, the BRI may appear outright hostile, particularly that part which centres on India's chief local rival, Pakistan.

FUNDING FROM MULTILATERAL BANKS OUTSIDE CHINA

The World Bank and ADB are also potential lenders to the BRI, so long as the projects meet their criteria. This is a mixture of economics and politics. In its early days, the World Bank was a major lender for infrastructure investment, initially to help the post-war reconstruction of Western Europe and Japan and later in developing countries. But in recent decades, the banks' mission has been changed, to reduce world poverty, not primarily to invest in infrastructure.

The World Bank's subsidiary, the International Finance Corporation (IFC), aims to promote economic development by helping private sector institutions to develop, including in relation to infrastructure, which makes it a more likely contributor to BRI projects, so long as they meet the IFC's economic criteria.

---

[8] NDB's official website: https://www.ndb.int/about-us/essence/mission-values/

The ADB is already investing in infrastructure, and has published research emphasizing the need for more investment across Asia (ADB 2017). So, it is somewhat obliged to support the principle of additional funding through the AIIB. The ADB's acknowledged expertise in this area is one reason why the two banks are initially planning to cooperate. But, as the AIIB builds its own team and eventually its own record of project execution, there is a possibility that it will decide to work more independently from the ADB.

From a borrower's point of view, having more competition among providers of finance should be welcome.

CONCLUSION

China has a range of institutional sources for funding the BRI, from commercial banks, policy banks to the dedicated Silk Road Fund. SOEs are likely to be heavily involved, typically with funding from Chinese banks. All of these organizations lie within the broad definition of the Chinese state, which gives the government more control over how and where the funds are allocated and perhaps a better ability to manage overall risks than a more decentralized approach.

As outlined above, the Chinese economy, already shifting towards a more outward investment model, cannot afford the higher estimates of BRI funding, at least not without alarming the financial markets and jeopardizing the yuan exchange rate. But it should be feasible for China to provide $3–4 hundred billion a year over the next decade without too much pressure on the balance of payments or government debt. Much will depend on when the investments start to show measurable returns. If it appears that the investment is productive and helps the Chinese economy, then the long-term financing will be much more sustainable. If, however, the returns are low or seen to serve mainly diplomatic objectives, the country's ability to fund major capital outflows will be limited.

China can therefore be expected to make as much use as possible or external sources of finance, including the AIIB and the existing MDBs, to increase the total funding and to spread the risk.

REFERENCES

ADB. 2017. *Meeting Asia's Infrastructure Needs*. Mandaluyong City, Philippines: ADB. https://www.adb.org/publications/asia-infrastructure-needs

AidData. 2018. 'China's Global Development Footprint'. Aiddata.org/china

Balding, C. 2017. *Can China Afford its Belt and Road? Bloomberg*, May17. https://www.bloomberg.com/opinion/articles/2017-05-17/can-china-afford-its-belt-and-road

Government of Pakistan. 2015. 'Euro-bond Analysis'. Ministry of Finance. (http://www.finance.gov.pk/euro_bond.html)

Haider, M. 2015. 'China Converts $230m Loan for Gwadar Airport into Grant'. *Geo TV*, September 23. https://www.geo.tv/latest/6270-china-converts-230m-loan-for-gwadar-airport-into-grant

Huang, Z., and H. Tang. 2017. *Why China Is Curbing Outbound Direct Investment*. Peterson Institute for International Economics, August 22. https://piie.com/blogs/china-economic-watch/why-china-curbing-outbound-direct-investment

Hurley, J., M. Scott, and P. Gailyn. 2018. *Examining the Debt Implications of the Belt and Road Initiative from a Policy Perspective*. CGD Policy Paper, Center for Global Development, Washington, DC. https://www.cgdev.org/publication/examining-debt-implications-belt-and-roadinitiative-policy-perspective

ICBC Standard. 2018. *BRI Thought Leadership*. An ICBCS B&R Interim Report. https://www.icbcstandardbank.com/CorporateSite/BRIThoughtLeadership

IMF. 2017a. *People's Republic of China: 2017 Article IV Consultation*. IMF Country Report No. 17/247, IMF, Washington, DC. https://www.imf.org/en/Publications/CR/Issues/2017/08/15/People-s-Republic-of-China-2017-Article-IV-Consultation-Press-Release-Staff-Report-and-45170

IMF. 2017b. *Pakistan: Twelfth and Final Review under the Extended Arrangement*. IMF Country Report No. 16/325, IMF, Washington, DC. http://www.imf.org/en/Publications/CR/Issues/2016/12/31/Pakistan-Twelfth-and-Final-Review-Under-the-Extended-Arrangement-Request-for-Waivers-of-44327

Lardy, N. 2014. *Markets over Mao: The Rise of Private Business in China*. New York: Columbia University Press.

Moran, T. 2017. 'Weighing up China's Investment in the United States'. *East Asia Forum*. http://www.eastasiaforum.org/2017/02/15/weighing-up-chinas-investment-in-the-united-states/

National Bureau of Statistics. 2018. 'Statistical Communiqué of China on 2017 National Economic and Social Development'. *Belt and Road Portal*. https://eng.yidaiyilu.gov.cn/qwyw/rdxw/49254.htm

Qinqin, P., and D. Jia. 2017. 'China State Banks Provide Over $400 Bln of Credits to Belt and Road Projects'. *Caixin*, May 12. https://www.caixinglobal.com/2017-05-12/101089361.html

Rana, S. 2016. '$8.2b Railtrack Upgrade Project Wins Go-ahead'. *The Express Tribune*, May 14. https://tribune.com.pk/story/1119229/8-2b-railtrack-upgrade-project-wins-go-ahead/

Reuters. 2018. 'ADB, China-Backed AIIB to Co-finance more Projects this Year'. *Reuters*, January 12. https://www.reuters.com/article/adb-asia-aiib/adb-china-backed-aiib-to-co-finance-more-projects-this-year-idUSL4N1P72UI

Weinland, D. 2018. 'China's ExIm Bank Commits $4bn in Push beyond Infrastructure'. *Financial Times*, January 23. https://www.ft.com/content/1092e1ca-ffef-11e7-9650-9c0ad2d7c5b5

World Bank. 2018. 'Public–Private Partnerships'. http://www.worldbank.org/en/topic/publicprivatepartnerships

Wright, C. 2017. 'Making Sense of Belt and Road: The Chinese Commercial Bank ICBC'. *Euromoney*, September 23. https://www.euromoney.com/article/b14t12brg3ynxd/making-sense-of-belt-and-road-the-chinese-commercial-bank-icbc

Xi, Jinping. 2017. 'Full Text of Opening Speech of Belt and Road Forum'. Xinhua, May 14. http://www.xinhuanet.com/english/2017-05/14/c_136282982.htm

You, Kefei., and Offiong H. Solomon. 2015. 'China's Outward Foreign Direct Investment and Domestic Investment: An Industrial Level Analysis'. *China Economic Review* 34: 249–260.

Chapter 17

Promoting the Belt and Road Initiative
A Strategic Marketing Approach

Eden Yin

THE BRI AS A 'MUST-SUCCEED' PROJECT FOR CHINA

Launched by China in 2013, the Belt and Road Initiative (BRI), previously branded as the One Belt One Road Initiative, now spans across 65 countries with $2 trillion planned investments under way by 2030, based on the American Enterprise Institute's estimate, ranging from highway and ports in Pakistan and Sri Lanka, to high-speed railways in Thailand and east Africa, and gas pipelines crossing central Asia. This makes it China's biggest foreign economic policy so far and arguably the largest overseas investment drive ever launched by a single country, dwarfing easily the once mighty Marshall Plan which only amounted to $130 billion in current dollars.

President Xi is the chief architect of this hugely ambitious plan. It was placed at such a strategic level as it is tied to China's much-touted aims of becoming a 'moderately well-off society' by 2020 and a 'strong, prosperous' one by the mid-century. Mr Xi seems to see the New Silk Road as a way of extending China's commercial tentacles and soft power. By financing around $150 billion of infrastructure spending a year in countries to China's south and west, Mr Xi hopes to create new markets for Chinese firms and new spheres of influence for his government. If the BRI succeeds, it integrates Asia and Europe as a single space, and China, not the USA, as its focal point. It will greatly enhance China's global influence. Hence, there is little wonder whether the BRI has become the most important feature of President Jinping Xi's foreign policy. It is not too much to say that he expects to be judged as a leader partly on how well he fulfils the BRI's goals. For China and Mr Xi, the BRI is the project of the century. Needless to say, for China and for President Xi, the BRI is a project that must succeed at almost any cost.

BRI UNFORTUNATELY ENCOUNTERING PROBLEMS

This initiative is of great strategic importance to China as it can extend the country's commercial interests and soft power in religions that are vital for its sustainable economic growth and national security. However, countries along the BRI may not share the same level of enthusiasm as the host country. Therefore, despite the lavishly organized Belt and Road Forum in May 2017, this project has been experiencing problems with some of the proposed deals failing already. For example, talks with Thailand over high-speed rail have stalled for the 3,000 km high-speed rail line from Kunming in the southwest to Singapore. The Thai government have said they would build only part of the project and would finance it themselves. There have been many other such failures. In Kara-Balta in Kyrgyzstan, Zhongda China Petrol, a state-owned company, built a big oil refinery, then found it could not buy enough crude oil to run it at more than 6 per cent of capacity. The Khorgos 'dry port' on the Kazakh-Chinese border is intended to be a hub for goods passing from China into Central Asia and Europe. China plans to invest $600 million in the project, building a vast complex of wholesale markets, train lines and cargo cranes. While the Chinese side of the border is surrounded by newly built tower blocks, the Kazakh side consists of a few semi-abandoned buildings. Silk routes are not always as appealing as they sound (*The Economist* 2017).

EFFECTIVE MARKETING AND PROMOTION AS AN APPROPRIATE SOLUTION

Some of the above-mentioned problems have resulted from factors well beyond Beijing's control, such as the outbreak of civil war in 2011 in Libya. In other cases, the problems occurred were due to worries about China's intention and criticism of China's approach. Countries related to the BRI worry that this project is largely self-serving and China plans to use the countries along the way to redirect its surplus savings and exporting its overproduction. More importantly, some of them may see this as a way for China to deepen its political hegemony across the region. The overweening behaviour of Chinese companies in some countries where they operate has further stoked fears in some places of an over-mighty China. Such negative perceptions of the BRI will continue to play a significant role in hindering the progress of this project which has the great potential to create win-win situation along the belt and the road. Given these doubts and worries, what will make the BRI really successful is not just rapid deployment of funds and infrastructure projects but also effective marketing and promotion of such a massive development project. In other words, the success of the BRI significantly relies on its successful marketing and promotion.

UNDERSTANDING THE STRATEGIC MARKETING FRAMEWORK

Successful marketing and promotion of a product, service, an organization, an ideology or an initiative can benefit greatly from an understanding and implementation of the strategic marketing planning framework, which is regularly used in the planning of new products and services in the context of commercial marketing (Kotler and Keller 2012). This framework enables strategic decision-makers to produce superior performance by creating three types of strategic fit between the organization and the customers or stakeholders: first, objective or goal fit, for example, the match or alignment between the objectives of the parties involved; second, value fit, for example, the alignment between the value that the organization offers and customers need; third, resource fit, for example, the fit between organizational capability and customer needs (Day 1994). These fits are essential for an organization to achieve desired outcomes.

The strategic marketing framework ensures the achievement of these fits through following a planning and implementation process which consists of the following components: first, situation analysis, aka 5Cs analysis, including customer analysis, competitor analysis, company analysis, collaborator analysis and context analysis; second, segmentation–targeting–positioning, referring to the selection of a particular segment of the overall market to focus on and the provision of more tailored value to best serve the needs of that segment; third, marketing mix strategies, aka the marketing 5Ps, including product strategy, promotion strategy, pricing strategy, place (distribution) strategy and people (service) strategy. This framework is illustrated in Figure 17.1.

The rationale of this framework is that achieving superior performance hinges on better satisfying customer needs, which in turn depends on a deep understanding of customer needs, competitors' offers, company's own strengths and weaknesses, collaborators' contribution, and context characteristics, for example, overall environment where organizations operate. Therefore, the strategic marketing framework starts with a situation analysis which provides decision-makers with a

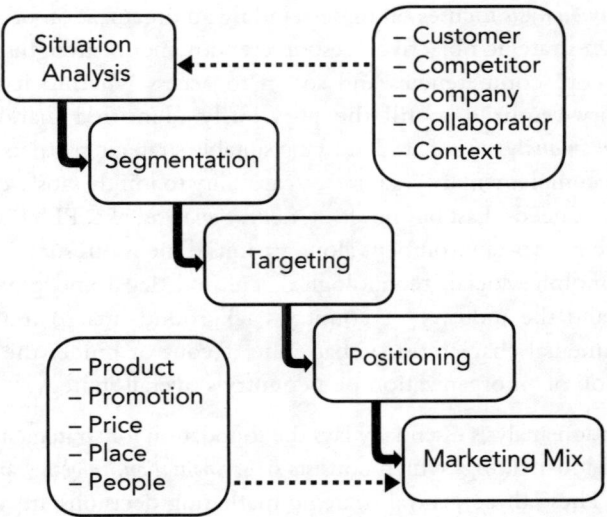

Figure 17.1 *Strategic Marketing Planning Framework*
Source: Strategic Marketing textbook by David W. Cravens, 6th edition, the McGraw-Hill Companies, Inc. 2000.

thorough understanding of the 5Cs, which represents the five key aspects of the market environment where their organization resides. The outcome of this 5Cs analysis is a clear identification of a *market gap* or gaps representing unmet needs in the overall marketspace, for example, the gap between what customer needs and what competitors offer. Moreover, it also demonstrates whether a 'company' or organization (in the context of BRI, a country such as China) possesses essential capabilities, skills or resources to tap into the market gap or unmet need.

Specifically, *customer analysis* first defines who customers are and investigates their overall goals and objectives, for example, job to be done, their needs or benefit sought, their wants, desires, aspirations, pain points or frustrations, consumption patterns, behavioural characteristics and so on. Namely, everything that helps decision-makers to better satisfy their needs to achieve their respective objectives. *Competitor analysis* defines the key competitors, analyse their offerings, corporate culture, core strengths and weaknesses and anticipate their strategic moves. This analysis enables decision-makers to identify the market gap and also effectively differentiate their own offers to achieve competitive advantage (MacMillan and McGrath 1997; Porter 1995). *Company analysis* focuses on understanding an organization or a country's own strategic objectives, resource endowment, strengths, weaknesses, core competencies and so on to access whether it has the capability required to fill the previously identified market gap. *Collaborator analysis* aims at identifying suitable strategic partners, which provide complementary resource or capability to jointly satisfy customers' unmet needs. Last but not least, *context analysis*, aka, PEST analysis, scans the macro-environment along various dimensions such as political, economic, social, technological, cultural, legal and physical to understand the industry or country background, macro-trends and environmental characteristics that either favour or hinder the implementation of an organization or a country's overall strategy.

Situation analysis essentially lays the foundation for strategic marketing decision-making, which consists of *segmentation*, *targeting* and *positioning*. These three central strategic marketing decisions are vital for achieving goal fit, value fit and resource fit which are the determinants for customer satisfaction and therefore superior organizational performance. Segmentation aims at dividing the overall market into segments that are homogenous within and heterogeneous across the most relevant and important criteria or segmentation variables. In most cases, such criteria are customer need or benefit sought. The purpose of segmentation is to help an organization identify and then concentrate on a particular segment or a set of segments in order to achieve the goal fit, value fit and resource fit. The process and act of identifying such a segment among all segments is targeting. In other words, since an organization has its own unique goal and capability, it is impossible for the organization to serve all segments equally well as every segment may have its own goal, need, want, aspiration and frustration. In order to best serve customers, an organization needs to identify the segment where it can serve the best, for example, achieving a strategic fit along the objective, value and resource dimensions. That is the rationale behind segmentation and targeting. After choosing the right segment(s), an organization needs to clearly define and then effectively communicate its goal, value proposition or product offered to the targeted segment or customers. It is the act of *positioning*, which is essentially the creation of an impression, image or concept in the mind of its customers by an organization about its goal, value proposition and resource endowment.

Once an organization has chosen its target and positioning strategy, it can then execute or implement such a positioning strategy by using its marketing tools or mix, that is, product, promotion, price, place (distribution) and people (service). *Product* strategy defines the product or service concept, its key benefits, primary point of differentiation and design aspects including the visual presentation, packaging and so on. *Promotion* strategy focuses on how to best communicate the product concept to the intended audience to achieve fast and wide adoption. Such a promotion strategy often includes a message strategy (e.g., what to say and how to say it) and a media strategy (e.g., where and when to say it). *Pricing* strategy is about how much an organization should charge its product or service. *Place* or distribution strategy concentrate on what distribution channels to use to most effectively make the product or service available to its intended audience. *People* strategy is about how to design a service strategy to further enhance the core benefit or value provided by the primary product and provide support to ensure a successful and pleasant overall consumption experience for the customers.

If an organization follows this planning and implementation process, it will most likely have a satisfied customer base and hence superior market performance.

ANALYSING 'CUSTOMER' OR 'BRI COUNTRIES' AS PAIN POINTS

As mentioned above, the BRI has not been as successful as Beijing had hoped despite its strong push. One of the key reasons for such a disappointing result is the lack of proper marketing planning and effective promotion of this initiative. The committee that is in charge of the BRI may have not considered this massive geo-economic project as a 'product' and see the countries involved as their 'customers'. That is why the effort up to date has failed to create the three much needed strategic fit (i.e., goal fit, value fit and resource fit) which are essential in driving the superior performance of any projects that involve a provider (or a seller) and a receiver (or a buyer). Even though the BRI can hardly be categorized as a pure commercial project, it has to be planned as such to achieve maximum effectiveness and results. Therefore, the strategic marketing framework and associated principles can provide tremendous value to the better planning and implementation of the BRI.

The starting point of such a planning process is customer analysis. To ensure success, one needs to thoroughly understand the short- and long-term objectives, needs, wants and especially the pain points of these countries covered by the BRI. Needless to say, many of the countries within the Belt and Road need better infrastructure and deeper international trade relationships, but a much deeper insight at a much granular level on their needs, worries and aspirations is needed to better motivate them to embrace the BRI plan. Moreover, besides focusing on the rational needs of the countries, one also needs to understand and satisfy their emotional needs. One such emotional need that plays a very prominent role in shaping the government or local attitude towards China's BRI project is the fear that an increasingly powerful China will become a threat to the sovereignty and national security of these countries.

Another important issue is to define 'customer'. Is it the government, the ruling parties, the intellectuals or the general public? Chinese firms are used to the 'top down' or the Chinese approach, that is, working with the government and political elites but ignoring other sections of the society. However, such a narrow approach is usually ineffective or even disastrous as evidenced by many high-profile failures experienced by Chinese firms overseas. Therefore, when understanding 'customer needs', one needs to take a much broader or holistic view on 'customers' and be as inclusive as possible. This is particularly important in countries where the public tends to hold negative or very mixed views towards China, such as the Central Asian and some of the Southeast Asian countries. Research indicates that China has been consistently perceived as a challenge in Central Asia (Peyrouse 2016). Widely engaging the public in the marketing and promotion of the BRI has become imperative.

ANALYSING 'COMPANY' OR CHINA'S STRENGTHS AND WEAKNESSES

Through 'customer analysis', market gap can be identified. The next task is to analyse China and Chinese companies' strengths and weaknesses to see whether China and its companies have the capabilities to fill these identified market gaps across the 65 BRI countries.

On the positive side, the BRI plays to China's strengths. The country has more savings than it can invest at home and experience with big infrastructure projects, especially high-speed rail. China's ability to build high-speed railways more cheaply than its competitors gave the technology a central place in the BRI. In fact, China intended to share its high-speed train technology worldwide. In many ways, the railway technology would become China's 'golden business card'. The total estimated value of 18 Chinese overseas high-speed rail schemes, including one completed (the Ankara–Istanbul service), five under way and twelve more announced amounts to $143 billion, which alone exceeds the total dollar amount of the legendary US-led Marshall Plan in today's value. So, as a 'company', China's strengths mostly lie in infrastructure-building capability and technologies, a very efficient national or government support system for the BRI once the country focuses on it as its national priority, speed of execution, availability of capital and loans, the physical proximity to a large number of BRI countries and most importantly, rising economic power that offers these countries tremendous growth potential. These Chinese advantages have certainly given China an upper hand in choreographing this massive Eurasia project, as they can be effective in filling in some of the main market gaps for those countries, such as the need for infrastructure.

But, at the same time, China and its companies also suffer from a number of weaknesses. First and foremost, China does not have a very positive image in some BRI countries. For example, in Central Asia, despite of the governments' positive tone towards China, there has been a rise in Sinophobia in these countries, especially in the intellectual circles, due to reasons such as fear of falling under Chinese economic domination, territorial dispute, competition for natural resources, dilution of identity and culture and so on. Moreover, there is a prevailing feeling of mistrust about China's possible hidden objectives (Peyrouse 2016). Second, China has limited experience in managing such a highly complex overseas operation, particularly when it concerns resolving border disputes (Pantucci 2015). Third, China and Chinese firms generally have limited knowledge and insights into the local markets and overall environment. These limitations will certainly hinder the progress of the BRI. Therefore, it is important for China to clearly and honestly identify all its strengths and weaknesses, and then assess the feasibility of filling the identified market gaps for the BRI countries, and more importantly, to create a strategic fit between its strengths and the 'customer needs' or market opportunities.

ANALYSING AND IDENTIFYING SUITABLE 'COLLABORATORS'

Inevitably, China will find itself incapable of satisfying such a diverse set of needs across all BRI countries due to its weaknesses or limitations. Therefore, working with the right collaborators becomes a critical factor for success. First of all, collaborating with the right partner in delivering these projects will reduce the fear and mistrust towards China and Chinese companies in some of the BRI countries. Second, working with more experienced collaborators can ensure higher standards and also provide Chinese firms with credibility, especially in the area of finance. Therefore, Chinese banks are asking international institutions, sovereign wealth funds, pension funds and so on to join them in lending to Belt and Road projects. Third, teaming up with internationally reputable collaborators also enables Chinese firms to learn and improve. Given these enormous benefits of working with international collaborators, China should be actively seeking out the most appropriate partners to work with.

Even though major Western companies such as GE, Caterpillar, Honeywell, ABB, Schneider Electric, Siemens and so on have already participated in various BRI projects (e.g., GE made sales of $2.3 billion in equipment orders from BRI projects in 2016, almost three times the total for the previous year; ABB did business with more than 400 Chinese enterprises in 2016 alone, helping them adjust for huge differences in construction and engineering standards across countries; Deutsche Bank has structured eight trade deals around it and has an agreement with the China Development Bank to fund several BRI schemes), the BRI is still dominated by Chinese firms. For example, 86 per cent of BRI projects have Chinese contractors, 27 per cent have local ones and only 18 percent have contractors of foreign origin, based on a database of open-source information collated by the Reconnecting Asia Project run by the Centre for Strategic and International Studies, a think tank in Washington, DC.

To ensure a fast and wide endorsement of these projects and their long-term success, China should be more open to partner with suitable foreign collaborators. While these projects are being built, local and global businesses, not just Chinese ones, should be involved. Hence, a critical task for the Chinese side is to thoroughly analyse all potential partnering countries and firms across industries and then choose the right ones that offer vital skills and credibility to partner with. For example, the China–Britain Business Council states that there will be real opportunities for British companies to work with Chinese partners in the Third World countries.

SEGMENTING 'CUSTOMERS' OR BRI COUNTRIES

China should segment the BRI countries based on certain criteria to develop tailored strategies for each cluster of countries that share similar characteristics. Besides the region- or country-level macro-segmentation, China should also segment all the stakeholders within a country, such as the entire population, all communities, tribes, NGOs and so on, as each of them may have different needs, pains, fears and aspirations. Stakeholders of similar needs can be grouped into segments and be served with a tailored strategy that is specifically designed to address their unique or idiosyncratic needs or problems. Only by segmenting the BRI countries along the three levels from macro to micro, one can fine-tune the strategies and value propositions to best serve the needs of each region, country and sector within a particular country. The key criteria for region- and country-level segmentation can be, for instance, attitude towards the BRI, attitude towards China, openness towards transformative innovation, ease of doing business, risk or stability level, size of the market and so on. Those for within country segmentation can be attitude towards BRI, attitude towards China, openness towards transformative innovation, and demographic variables such as income level, educational background, gender, age, ethnicity, family size and so on. Inevitably, segments at different levels may have conflicting needs or preferences. China will have to skilfully identify common interests across all segments and resolve these issues first. Once it can successfully satisfy a number of commonly shared needs, China will be able to establish a certain level of credibility in the minds of all major stakeholders. Such credibility will pave the way for further reconciliation.

TARGETING THE RIGHT SEGMENTS OR BRI COUNTRIES

After segmentation, the key strategic task is targeting. In the commercial context, companies often only target the segments where they can achieve a significant competitive advantage and ignore the rest of the markets. However, for BRI, China would need to work with all countries along the Belt and Road. In other words, it has to target every single region and sector within a country. In this case, the purpose of targeting is not to filter out less attractive segments, but to choose which region or sector within a country should be served first. In other words, targeting decision essentially creates a priority list that rank orders all regions and segments within each country for China and its companies to serve sequentially. As for better targeting decision, one should quantify the aforementioned criteria for segmentation and develop this rank order based on quantitative measures at both the country level and sector level within a country. The most relevant criteria for targeting should be the attitude towards the BRI, attitude towards China, feasibility of the projects involved and the social influence of a particular country or segment within a country. The reason why these criteria are more important is that the BRI can be considered as a 'new product' in the context of a marketing strategy. For the launch of any new product, it is vital to find the group of 'customers', that is, countries, or sectors within countries, which are more open minded or adaptive to such a new product. Targeting these more open-minded customers can ensure the fast adoption of such a new product at scale. This is particularly important in the case of the BRI as the early proof of concept provides later adopters with a powerful signal of quality and incentive to adopt.

Due to the slow start of this initiative, China needs to quickly demonstrate the positive impact of a particular project on the host country and implement the 'model projects' with 'early results, so that relevant countries can feel some real benefits' in President Xi's words in 2016. In its targeting decision, China should also give priority to countries or sectors within a country that can serve as an 'opinion leader' whose voice can significantly affect the behaviours of other countries or sectors within a country. These opinion leaders are often innovators or early adopters of any new product, service or idea and they can quickly start the adoption momentum and enable any new project to 'cross the chasm' (Moore 2014). For example, in a particular country, good candidates for opinion leaders are well-known media personalities, such as editors or journalists of major TV channels, magazines, newspapers or news sites, or alternatively cultural celebrities, such as famous writers, movie directors and university professors. Put simply, good candidates are anyone in the host country who can shape public opinions. So, it is vital to first target the countries and sectors of the population within these countries that can serve as key opinion leaders to speed up the adoption of BRI activities. In particular, China should target the most appropriate segments within the key countries' public instead of just the uppermost echelons of society in pushing this massive project forward to obtain wider support to ensure the feasibility and long-term sustainability of the initiative. For China, the most appropriate segments in host countries would be the ones that have significant market size, most active and vocal, and have either neutral or favourable attitude towards China and the initiative as well.

PROPERLY POSITIONING BRI'S VALUE PROPOSITION

Segmentation and targeting help decision-makers identify the most critical 'audience' to focus on. Positioning enables them to construct and communicate the value proposition to effectively encourage the early buy-in or adoption by these customers. In many ways, it is the core of any marketing and promotion strategies that can make or break a business. It is also an area that has not been adequately or effectively pursued by early effort in the BRI to date. In designing a powerful positioning strategy, a number of key principles have to be followed and they are discussed below.

Choosing a Proper Brand Name

Positioning is a key part of branding effort albeit not all. So, choosing a proper brand name is the first step in pursuing an effective positioning strategy. Unfortunately, from a branding perspective, the name China has chosen for this massive Eurasia project is not the most appealing one. Chinese officials originally named that policy 'One Belt, One Road', which is an effective brand name in Chinese. However, its English translation sounds ugly and also risks implying that it was all about one big Chinese plan. China wanted the venture to be seen as a cooperative one. So, they came up with the anodyne-sounding acronym translation, OBOR, which is rather odd and unlovely, especially when it is written in small letter 'obor', which is very similar to the English word 'odor'. At the same time, it has also produced a rather unfortunate acronym for the high-profile Belt and Road Forum: BARF.

In fact, the very meaning of 'One Belt, One Road' is also confusing as the road refers to ancient maritime routes between China and Europe, against the conventional definition of the Silk Road, while the belt describes the Silk Road's better-known trails overland. As a matter of fact, this initiative had a different and uncontroversial name, 'Silk Road Economic Belt', yet it appears to be an inadequate one when China expands the geographical scope for this initiative. The different names given to the project reflects China's struggle to make it sound palatable to foreigners. Chinese policymakers should have been more empathetic when they coined the English brand name for this initiative. It is likely that they have since realized this and have recently altered the name to BRI (Belt and Road Initiative).

Having a 'Customer Centric' View

Even though the BRI was initially motivated by concerns about the lack of adequate development in the west part of China, in particular Xinjiang where Uyghur minorities live, slowing domestic growth and a desire to boost China's global influence, it should have a global perspective by now. To ensure its long-term success and sustainability, this initiative should not be conceived and implemented as a self-centred domestic policy with geo-strategic consequences, but a foreign policy that acts as a stimulus for trade in a world struggling with middling economic growth and as a catalyst for fostering local prosperity and regional harmonization across the vast area it covers. This is especially important in regions or countries where anti-China sentiment in the public is gathering strength. For example, in Central Asia, the most vital region for the BRI, the 'Chinese question' is becoming increasingly central to political and intellectual debate. Research indicates that none of the experts surveyed believed that Chinese policy was fully compatible with Central Asian interests (Peyrouse 2016). Moreover, studies also reveal that 50 per cent of experts placed Russia as their country's number one partner, ahead of the USA and China, while none placed China first. Many Central Asian specialists also believe that China is trying to transform the economies of Central Asia to suit its own interests (Peyrouse 2016).

Given the current Sinophobe sentiment in many of the BRI countries, the key in promoting the BRI is not to position or present it as a 'China project', but a collaborative and multilateral project that involves all stakeholders along the way for mutual benefit and long-term gain. If the BRI is perceived as a vehicle for Beijing to export its own economic imbalances while buying regional leadership to increase its political influence abroad, as the title of a *Financial Times* article puts, 'China Encircles the World with One Belt, One Road Strategy' (2017), it will certainly create a backlash due to the Belt and Road countries' fear of being overwhelmed by an increasingly mighty and assertive China.

Developing a Clear, Comprehensive and Consistent Roadmap and Message

Five years have passed since its inception, yet the BRI still has not produced a clear roadmap or blueprint for all countries affected. First, the BRI puzzles many Western policymakers because it is amorphous. It has no official list of member countries, although the rough count is 65. Second, it is not clear what the overall objectives and priorities of this massive initiative are, how to achieve these objectives, what the milestones and deadlines would be and so on. In other words, there is no roadmap depicting a clear and comprehensive vision and game plan for this humongous project. Third, it is also quite vague who is in charge of the day-to-day operation and management and who should be involved and in what capacity. To hop on this huge bandwagon for either economic or political gains, two-thirds of China's provinces have emphasized the importance of the BRI for their development. Many big state-owned enterprises have a BRI department, if only in the hope of getting money for their projects. Since it is President Xi's personal project, it has become clear that in China if you want to get projects or programmes approved, you say it is BRI; so, everything becomes 'BRI', even including the joint China–France Hinkley Point nuclear project in Britain. The risk of the all-embracing nature of the BRI is it has become everything and nothing. This will further create confusion and frustration to all stakeholders involved. To successfully promote the BRI, it is crucial for China to develop a roadmap which is clear, comprehensive and consistent. It also has to be non-self-serving and long-term oriented to be appealing. In any case, the current catchy slogan such as 'mutual benefit, joint responsibility and shared destiny' promoted by Chinese official media is far from enough to induce rapid and massive adoption of various BRI projects in the countries affected. Obviously, producing such a roadmap is not without its challenges as the scope of this project is simply too vast to be planned with granular-level details and sufficient clarity. Moreover, China has many competing bureaucratic interests at stake in the BRI. Reconciling them would be tough if not impossible. Yet, a comprehensive roadmap for this initiative is absolutely essential to ensure its short- and long-term success.

DESIGNING AND EXECUTING EFFECTIVE 5PS

The last phase of the strategic marketing framework is the design and execution of the so-called marketing mix strategy, which consists of product strategy, promotion strategy, pricing strategy, place (distribution) strategy and people (service) strategy. Among the 5Ps, pricing, place and people strategies are less relevant in the context of BRI. So, the focus here is placed on product and promotion strategies.

Product Strategies for BRI

Product strategy in the context of the BRI refers to what projects should be offered to the host countries, how to deliver them and what the service components of these projects are to ensure its successful construction, ongoing maintenance and long-term functioning. Based on the needs, pain points and aspirations of BRI countries, a certain set of products should be chosen to satisfy these diverse needs. More importantly, China should provide a 'total solution' to the host countries instead of a set of disintegrated projects. In other words, China's best product strategy for BRI countries is to offer them a set of inter-related projects aiming at enhancing their industry capability and overall economy, holistically and optimally. This is the true driver for a thriving collaborative relationship and the eventual success of the BRI projects. This win-win product strategy will not be possible if the Chinese side has a self-serving motive behind the BRI. In parts of Asia, democratic politics have been challenging China's commonly used approach to deal making, cosying up to unsavoury regimes. For example, in 2011, Myanmar suspended work on a vastly Chinese-financed dam at Myitsone to popular acclaim. In Sri Lanka, the government elected in 2015 has been engaged in endless wrangling with China over the building of a Chinese-invested port in the hometown of the country's autocratic former President. China's product strategy should avoid employing these approaches or tactics. Moreover, another aspect of the product strategy is that China should not just offer projects but also the continuing management of them. Once built, these projects should be well utilized. Otherwise, the whole initiative will fail sooner or later.

Promotion Strategies for BRI

Promotion strategies should be guided by the positioning strategy discussed previously. It first focuses on producing a comprehensive and credible roadmap or white paper, and then the mass communication pursued on various mass media outlets such as TV, Radio, newspaper and the Internet. The message also has to be appealing, targeted and consistent over time. To win the hearts and minds of younger generations, China should also use social media platforms such as Facebook, Twitter and YouTube to connect with them at a deeper emotional level. This is an area that international ad and PR agencies can contribute to, as they are far more experienced in effectively communicating with culturally diverse audiences. As for what message should be conveyed to the locals, China needs to understand that they first need to communicate a respectable cultural and value system that represents China to various stakeholders in host countries to earn their genuine trust, before overtly promoting various BRI projects. Further thoughts along this line will be elaborated in the next section in discussing the David Livingstone movement.

In any case, the most effective communication is not in what one says, but what it does and the function it serves. For China—which is more commonly perceived by many BRI countries as a country that does not respect the locals and local culture, a country that cares less about the well-being of the local communities and hence does not contribute to their development—pursuing socially responsible acts such as building schools, providing educational scholarship and training for locals, improving the working and living conditions of the local employees and so on would be very powerful and far more effective in rectifying the negative view towards China, Chinese business and the BRI. In fact, doing the right thing for locals and the host country is in fact the core of a successful promotion strategy, besides focusing on establishing the cultural legitimacy for China and its enterprises. Therefore, China and its enterprises should have a hybrid communication strategy that emphasizes both the right message centred first on a cultural and value system and the right action that benefits the local communities and society at large.

LEARNING FROM THE 'DAVID LIVINGSTONE' APPROACH

As a wave of anti-globalization sentiment sweeps the developed world, China can present the BRI as the leading vehicle for increasing global trade and stimulate regional economic development and harmonization. However, despite all the efforts, it does not mean that China's plans will always be welcome in countries suspicious of its expanding reach. An effective marketing and promotional strategy for the BRI has become increasingly important. However, what need be marketed and promoted should not be some hollow and propaganda-sounding words. China should really understand what the true concerns many of the BRI countries have over the rise of China and its expansion into their own territories.

Research shows that in Central Asia, the widespread general view on China is that its authorities conceal their imperialist objectives when it pushes the BRI agenda. Moreover, Central Asian intellectuals also share the feeling that there exists a 'civilizational difference' between China and them, and falling into the Chinese sphere of cultural influence would mean the ethnic disappearance of Central Asian societies (Peyrouse 2016). These findings clearly indicate that the anti-China sentiment has a far deeper root and occurs at the cultural level. Even the most optimistic intellectuals who welcome China's presence in their countries in Central Asia turn out not to be Sinophiles on the cultural level. That is the root cause for increasingly prominent Sinophobe in Central Asia (Peyrouse 2016). Fighting the prejudice against China at the cultural level is extremely challenging, but an essential task to be done. Otherwise, the relationship between China and BRI countries, especially those in Central Asia, will remain intrinsically fragile, as will the BRI.

China should draw inspiration from how Britain managed to extend its influence far beyond its border in the 19th century. One of the key reasons for British successful global expansion is the expansion of its belief, ideology and religion, in one word, its culture. In other words, Britain pursued cultural expansion prior to its commercial expansion. One of the leading figures in the British cultural expansion was David Livingstone, the priest and medical doctor who had spent nearly 30 years in Africa for missionary work. Even though he had only managed to convert one person in Africa, his heroic story had inspired an entire generation of young missionaries, including Leader Stirling and Miss Annie Allen, venturing into every corner of the wild and dangerous Africa, which eventually gave rise to the endorsement of Christianity and British values in the region. The spread of the Christian belief and the British value system had paved the way for the commercial development of British establishment in the African continent. The endorsement of British commerce was much more straightforward and swift after Africa had a buy-in of British values and culture. The successful British presence and integration into the African continent followed naturally thereafter.

Needless to say, China should not even contemplate on the possibility of establishing an empire in modern times. But they certainly can learn from Britain in terms of successfully opening up new frontiers around the globe. The British approach can be labelled the 'David Livingstone approach', that is, 'cultural expansion proceeds commercial expansion'. China should draw inspiration from this particular British experience and first clearly define a genuine and inspirational cultural and value system and then communicate and promote it to the BRI countries. Before hundreds of China-backed business and infrastructure successfully enter their lands, an inspirational Chinese cultural and value system has to enter their hearts. That is what the BRI has been lacking so far. Chinese often say, 'business should only talk about business'. Even though it is one of the most popular and frequently used phrases in China, it actually does not make sense at all. There is no successful business in the world that can be achieved by only focusing on the business itself. The foundation of any successful business in any cultural context is always trust and respect. The David Livingstone model has certainly offered great insights into how a successful global business should be pursued.

Needless to say, China may not have the luxury of waiting for 30 years like the 19th-century Britain for its value system to be endorsed by the locals in various BRI-related countries due to the political, economic and financial pressure, but its unique political system and philosophical or cultural orientation such as long termism do produce the 'patient money' that enables China to even contemplate such a grand cultural and communication endeavour. If the Chinese government seriously considers such a cultural approach, strategically design and execute such a strategy, a decade's effort may well bear the much-needed fruit. Of course, it has to be a coordinated, integrated and almost simultaneous effort between the cultural and commercial fronts to achieve the maximum effect or impact. In the face of rising suspicion of many intellectuals and locals in member countries on China's ulterior motives of its BRI, China needs to stay away from all superficial cultural interactions or exchanges in the forms of movie, and music or dancing festivals or events, but concentrate its efforts in directly establishing dialogues with the local thought leaders and intellectuals by co-organizing forums, conferences, workshops, producing books, documentaries and YouTube videos, offering educational programmes or even university degrees for local youth, engaging influential bloggers, establishing meaningful links with local NGOs in advancing a mutually interesting agenda and so on.

The BRI is already beginning to challenge the notion of Europe and Asia existing side by side as different trading blocs. It is a serious long-term geo-economic strategy that will potentially shift the global economic centre of gravity. China needs to capitalize on this once-in-a-century opportunity and strive to be the driving engine for the collective prosperity of all the BRI countries. Effective marketing and promotion of this initiative is the first step.

REFERENCES

Day, G. S. 1994. 'The Capabilities of Market-Driven Organizations'. *Journal of Marketing* 58 (4): 37–52.
The Economist. 2017. *What is China's Belt and Road Initiative?* May, 15th, 2017.
Kotler, P., and K. L. Keller. 2012. *Marketing Management* (2nd European edition). Harlow: Prentice Hall/Pearson Education.
MacMillan, I. C., and R. G. McGrath. 1997. 'Discovering New Points of Differentiation'. *Harvard Business Review* 75 (4): 133–145.

Moore, G. 2014. *Cross the Chasm: Marketing and Selling Disruptive Products to Mainstream Customers*. New York: Harper Business.

Pantucci, Raffaello. 2015. Central Asia: The View from China, Report by European Union Institute for Security Studies, January, 2015.

Peyrouse, Sebastien. 2016. 'Discussing China: Sinophilia and Sinophobia in Central Asia'. *Journal of Eurasian Studies* 7: 14-23.

Porter, M. E. 1995. *Competitive Advantage: Creating and Sustaining Superior Performance* (revised edition). New York: Free Press.

Chapter 18

Central Asia and the Belt and Road Initiative

Richard Pomfret

CENTRAL ASIA AND THE BRI

In October 2013, President Xi Jinping gave a speech at Nazarbayev University in Astana (Kazakhstan) in which he announced the One Belt One Road project. This was part of a tour of Central Asia that ended with participation in the Shanghai Cooperation Organization summit in Dushanbe. Shortly afterwards, President Xi announced the creation of the Asian Infrastructure Investment Bank (AIIB) which would provide funding for the Belt and Road Initiative (BRI).

For Central Asia, Xi's tour marked the climax of rapid development of relations with China since the turn of the century. China had, from a low level of involvement in 2000, come to challenge Russia and the EU as Central Asia's leading economic partner. From cautious beginnings amid mutual suspicions in the 1990s, China became a major investor, not just in industrial activities but also building roads in Tajikistan and the Kyrgyz Republic, and most dramatically constructing pipelines across Central Asia for Kazakhstan's oil and Turkmenistan's natural gas. The gas pipeline built between 2006 and 2009 from Turkmenistan to China was especially important because it required cooperation with Uzbekistan and Kazakhstan as transit states, which proved China's reliability in delivering promised mega-projects (in contrast to Russia's failure to progress a new Caspian-coast gas pipeline from Turkmenistan through Kazakhstan to Russia) and illustrated the potential for win-win outcomes from cooperation.

The BRI announcement came at a propitious time for Central Asia. After a difficult transition from Soviet central planning during the 1990s, the regional economy had done well over the dozen years before President Xi's announcement. Since 2014, however, the Central Asian governments have acknowledged that the resource boom is over and that they need to diversify their economies. A key issue is whether BRI can be a handmaiden for diversification by alleviating the problems of being landlocked and providing a springboard for non-resource exports.

This chapter defines Central Asia as the five former Soviet republics that became independent in December 1991—Kazakhstan, the Kyrgyz Republic, Tajikistan, Turkmenistan and Uzbekistan. It focuses on rail connections in west from China that will pass through Central Asia to Europe or to the Middle East and North Africa and neglects other elements of BRI.

THE CENTRAL ASIAN COUNTRIES AND CHINA[1]

Following the Sino-Soviet split in the early 1960s, economic relations between China and Soviet Central Asia were practically non-existent. Roads were closed, apart from two that reopened in 1983. The first connecting railway was only completed in 1990, as relations thawed under Mikhail Gorbachev and Deng Xiaoping. Other border posts opened during the 1990s, including river ports, but they could be closed unilaterally at short notice. Air services began to operate between Urumqi and Central Asia.

In December 1991, the Soviet Union was dissolved and the five Central Asian countries became independent states. Soviet First Secretaries became country Presidents and devoted much of their time

---

[1] This section is based on Chapter 10.3 of Pomfret (2019).

to nation-building and cementing their own authority.[2] The governments were unprepared for independence, and in the early 1990s, faced the triple challenges of the collapse of Soviet supply chains, the sudden end of central planning and hyperinflation. Output fell, and poverty and inequality increased. The transition to different varieties of market-based economies lasted a decade, and pre-independence GDP levels were not regained until the early 2000s. Economic conditions only truly revived with the start of the resource boom at the very end of the 1990s.

Trade between Central Asia and China grew from a low base. In the 1990s and early 2000s, apart from minerals exported to China by Kazakhstan and occasional cotton deals with Uzbekistan, much of Central Asia's trade with China was unmonitored and small-scale, conducted by so-called shuttle traders importing manufactured goods from China. Even with the highest shuttle-trade estimates, trade with Central Asia accounted for under 1 per cent of China's total exports. Trade with China was no more than 5 per cent of Central Asian countries' total international trade. In the late 1990s, the shuttle trade became less attractive as Uzbekistan and Kazakhstan tightened their borders or monitored bazaars more closely, and the Kyrgyz Republic emerged as an entrepôt, importing goods from China and elsewhere, for sale to customers across Central Asia.

Political relations between Central Asian countries and China developed slowly after 1992. There was considerable mutual suspicion, as the Central Asian countries feared an influx of millions of Chinese and China feared Central Asian support for Uighur separatists. Border delimitation and demilitarization negotiations in the 1990s provided a basis for confidence building that was institutionalized in the Shanghai Five in 1996, and subsequently the Shanghai Cooperation Organization (SCO).

---

[2] The political transition was smooth in four of the countries. Tajikistan suffered a civil war from 1992 to 1997, but, by the end of the decade, President Rahmonov had established a super-presidential regime similar to those in other Central Asian countries.

China's economic influence in Central Asia increased rapidly in the 2000s, based on China's demand for energy and on Central Asian markets for Chinese manufactures (Table 18.1). Around 2002, China ceased to be energy self-sufficient, and became worried about energy security and vulnerability to choke points on maritime routes from the Middle East and other oil-producing regions. Investment in oil fields in Kazakhstan was accompanied by construction in stages between 2003 and 2009 of oil pipelines linking western Kazakhstan to Xinjiang. In 2005, the Chinese National Petroleum Corporation became owner

Table 18.1 *Central Asia's 10 Major Export and Import Markets, 2000 and 2010 (USD Billion)**

Exports			Imports		
Country/ Union	2000	2010	Country/ Union	2000	2010
EU	3.7 (23.8)	31.9 (37.7)	Russia	3.1 (27.2)	17.2 (27.3)
Russia	3.6 (23.3)	13.8 (16.4)	EU	2.2 (19.0)	11.1 (17.5)
China	0.7 (4.8)	12.4 (14.6)	China	0.3 (2.4)	6.8 (10.7)
Iran	0.5 (3.3)	4.0 (4.8)	USA	0.6 (5.1)	4.1 (6.6)
Turkey	0.4 (2.5)	2.7 (3.1)	Turkey	0.5 (4.6)	2.5 (4.0)
Switzerland	0.6 (4.1)	1.7 (2.0)	S. Korea	0.4 (3.8)	2.2 (3.5)
USA	0.2 (1.5)	1.1 (1.3)	Pakistan	0.2 (1.3)	1.9 (3.1)
Japan	0.1 (0.5)	0.6 (0.7)	Iran	0.2 (2.0)	1.8 (2.8)
S. Korea	0.1 (0.9)	0.4 (0.4)	Japan	0.3 (3.0)	0.9 (1.4)
India	0.1 (0.4)	0.3 (0.3)	India	0.1 (0.9)	0.8 (1.3)

Source: Mogilevskii (2012a, 30–31), based on data from COMTRADE and national statistical offices.
Notes: Totals include Afghanistan as well as the five Central Asian countries; numbers in parentheses are percentage shares.
*The substantial informal trade with China is not included in the source. The EU's position as Central Asia's largest export market was partly a statistical illusion because primary products like cotton or oil were often recorded as sold on European exchanges or to European companies, irrespective of their ultimate destination.

of PetroKazakhstan, Kazakhstan's largest independent oil producer. Even more dramatic was the pipeline agreement concluded with Turkmenistan in 2006 and completion of the gas pipeline through Uzbekistan and Kazakhstan by 2009. Thereafter China quickly became the dominant purchaser of Turkmenistan's natural gas.

The potential for increased trade between Central Asia and China was substantial, but realizing the potential depended upon a favourable trade environment and improved physical infrastructure. In 2001, China joined the WTO, which provided more predictable conditions for trade, and launched the Go West policy to stimulate economic development in Western China.[3] At that time, only the Kyrgyz Republic in Central Asia was a WTO member and it did not closely monitor imports from China, but Chinese-Kyrgyz trade was large and the Chinese goods were not destined solely, or even primarily, for Kyrgyz customers.[4] In 2004, China created a special zone on the Kazakhstan border to promote cross-border trade, and this was also a setting for substantial small-time unrecorded trade. Table 18.1 shows the rapid growth of recorded Chinese trade with Central Asia between 2000 and 2010, and the unrecorded trade was much larger with respect to imports from China than for any other entry in that table.

China's Go West policy bore fruit slowly. Improved connectivity within China encouraged Hewlett-Packard and Foxconn (assembler

---

[3] Officially called the Western Development Program, it covered the municipality of Chongqing, the provinces of Gansu, Guizhou, Qinghai, Shaanxi, Sichuan, and Yunnan, and the autonomous regions of Guangxi, Inner Mongolia, Ningxia, Tibet and Xinjiang.

[4] Recorded trade between the Kyrgyz Republic and China had stagnated after 1998, but the high values, relative to population or GDP, of Kyrgyz imports from China that appear in the Chinese trade data as early as 1997 (e.g., imports of $172 million in 1998 when total Central Asian imports from China were only $456 million) indicated a particular role for the Kyrgyz Republic. In 2008, China reported exports to the Kyrgyz Republic of $9,213 million, while the Kyrgyz statistics indicated imports of $728 million from China (Mogilevskii 2012b). World Bank (2009) analysis of 2008 mirror statistics found that the Kyrgyz Republic had 'excessive' imports and Uzbekistan 'under-imports', suggesting re-exports from the Kyrgyz Republic to neighbouring countries.

of Apple products) to invest $3 billion to build printer and laptop manufacturing bases in Chongqing, opening the prospect of Western China joining the boom in production along global value chains (GVCs). They and other exporters in Chongqing began searching for an alternative to the congested Yangtze River for export routes, and, after some experimental starts in 2010 and 2011 with individual trains, regular rail service between Chongqing and the German Rhine port of Duisburg was established in 2013; routes from other Chinese cities to Europe were also being explored. To electronics firms in Western China supplying EU markets (e.g., HP, Acer and Foxconn) and to EU firms shipping parts to their operations in China (e.g., Volkswagen, Audi and BMW), the Eurasian Land Bridge rail link through Kazakhstan, Russia, Belarus and Poland offered an attractive price/time option, faster than the sea route and at lower cost than air routes. This development is analysed in the next section.

In 2012, the Central Asian countries still imported more from Russia than from any other single country, but China had become by far the region's most important export destination (Table 18.2).[5] Formation of the customs union between Belarus, Kazakhstan and Russia after 2010 hurt China's exports by increasing Kazakhstan's external trade barriers and by cutting off part of the Kyrgyz Republic entrepôt trade (and potentially all of it after the Kyrgyz Republic's accession to the Eurasian Economic Union [EAEU] in 2015). However, the underlying complementarities are so strong that China's trade with Central Asia will continue to increase in the longer term, and it would be even more substantial if transport connections were better and trade costs lower.

In contrast to Russian and EU interaction with Central Asia, most of China's activities have been low key, at least until President Xi's September 2013 visit.[6] Pipelines and other investments are presented

---

[5] China was the most important export market for Kazakhstan, Turkmenistan and Uzbekistan largely because of oil and gas pipelines completed in 2009. Turkey was Tajikistan's largest export market. For the Kyrgyz Republic, it was Switzerland, primarily due to gold with unknown final destination.

[6] President Xi's visit was also contrasted with the fact that no US President has been to the Central Asia, despite visits to Afghanistan by Presidents G. W. Bush and Obama.

Table 18.2 Central Asian Countries' Exports to and Imports from Russia and China, 2012 (USD Million)

Country	Russian Federation			People's Republic of China		
	CA Exports to RF	CA Imports from RF	Total Trade	CA Exports to PRC	CA Imports from PRC	Total Trade
Kazakhstan	6,747	17,110	23,857	16,484	7,498	23,982
Kyrgyz Republic	219	1,785	2,004	61	1,210	1,271
Tajikistan	45	738	783	99	1,923	2,022
Turkmenistan	165	1,209	1,374	7,290	1,870	9,160
Uzbekistan	689	2,457	3,146	992	1,962	2,954

Source: ADBI (2014, 46–56), based on IMF's *Direction of Trade Statistics*.

as business arrangements, and the focus on roads contrasts with Russian involvement in controversial hydroelectricity projects. Politically, China presents itself as a good neighbour, with similar concerns to Central Asian governments, especially with respect to extremism and splittism.[7] In Central Asia, there are official concerns in Kazakhstan about pollution of rivers flowing west from China, and popular concerns about Chinese immigration, especially in Kazakhstan and the Kyrgyz Republic where numbers are larger.[8]

The speed with which China became a major economic partner for Central Asia between 2000 and 2013 is remarkable. Russia's response

---

[7] China's main concern is separatism in Xinjiang Autonomous Region, where the Turkic-speaking Islamic Uighurs have strong cultural affinities with Kazakhs and Kyrgyz. The implicit agreement with Central Asian governments is that, as long as they do not support Uighur separatism, China has only peaceful intentions.

[8] Laruelle and Peyrouse (2009, 56–60) discuss estimates. Violence against Chinese people seems to have been most common in the early 2000s, for example, in the Kyrgyz Republic, 19 Chinese businessmen were killed on 27 March 2003 and looting during the 2005 Tulip Revolution cost Chinese businesses 35 million dollars (Raballand and Andrésy 2007, 237).

has been ambivalent, with the creation of the EAEU placing a protectionist wall against Chinese trade in the region. On the other hand, initiation of the rail link from Chongqing to Duisburg required Russian cooperation, which appears to be willingly given, perhaps because with little effort, Russia benefits from large transit fees.

A NEW BELT OR OLD CLOTHES?

The rail land bridge between China and the EU flourished after the first trial runs. By the time President Xi gave his September 2013 speech proposing BRI, the Chongqing–Duisburg train was running on a thrice-weekly schedule. Other routes were being trialled, sometimes under pressure from local governments, for example, the Yiwu–Madrid or Chengdu–Łódź routes which would both establish regular services, but without influence from the central government.[9] When BRI was officially launched in Beijing at the May 2017 Belt and Road Forum for International Cooperation, China Railway Express, which coordinates all China Railways Corp's European services, showed connections from 27 Chinese cities to 11 European countries on its route map.

Given the prior development of the rail land bridge, what did the BRI have to add in creating overland rail connections between China and Europe? The maps accompanying reports in the Chinese media about BRI after President Xi's 2013 speech offer a clue to China's intentions. In contrast to the land bridge routes set up since 2011, which either went through Kazakhstan, Russia, Belarus and Poland or, less commonly, used Russia's Trans-Siberian Railway, the official Chinese maps showed a railway passing south of the Caspian Sea.

China's interest in the southern route is not just on paper. One week after the easing of UN sanctions on Iran in January 2016, President Xi visited Tehran. On 28 January, the first train left Yiwu for Tehran with 32 containers. It took 14 days due to a slightly

---

[9] Although some westbound routes and services have been subsidized by Chinese governments, the central government has committed to ending subsidies by 2020. Vinokurov et al. (2018) emphasizes the importance of local government subsidies for some routes.

circuitous route.[10] Although no train from China has yet gone beyond Tehran, the track for a south of the Caspian rail route to Europe via Iran and Turkey already exists, including a recently opened rail tunnel under the Bosporus. In September 2017, the first train to Tehran departed from Yinchuan, capital of Ningxia Autonomous Region, and a twice-weekly schedule for 2018 was announced. The departure point in a Muslim area of China suggested that the trans-Iranian route may not be just as an alternative passage to Europe but also a potential gateway to the Middle East and North Africa.

China's desire for multiple routes could come from two motives. Multiple routes enhance the range of transport options and reduce hold-up possibilities, which are always a danger along a single route passing through several countries. On the other hand, if the eventual intention is to cut transport times by constructing a high-speed rail line whose expense would justify only one route, then China may be trialling options to determine which route would have the better security/cost trade-off.

RESOURCE DEPENDENCE AND LIMITED DIVERSIFICATION IN CENTRAL ASIA

The Central Asian countries are at an important policy crossroads. Their economic performance in the 21st century has been driven by the resource boom: directly for exporters of oil, gas, gold, copper and other minerals, and indirectly for labour-exporting countries that receive large amount of remittances from citizens working in Russia.[11] The boom temporarily halted for the energy exporters in 2008–2009 but quickly resumed. The decline in energy prices in 2014 is widely

---

[10] The train went west across Kazakhstan to join the Kazakhstan–Turkmenistan–Iran rail line that had been opened in December 2014. The route avoided Uzbekistan, which was characterized by high transit costs, and sent a signal that such costs could mean missing out on the BRI. Following the death of President Karimov and his succession by Shavkat Mirziyoyev in September 2016, Uzbekistan appears to have embarked on a path of greater openness towards regional economic integration.

[11] By 2014, Tajikistan and the Kyrgyz Republic ranked first and second in the world for the ratio of remittances to GDP.

accepted as more permanent and hence requiring governments to promote economic diversification.

Individual countries have tried to promote economic diversification. In the 1990s, Uzbekistan and Turkmenistan aimed to diversify their manufacturing sectors by adopting import-substituting industrialization policies, with mixed results. Uzbekistan's car joint venture with Daewoo (with General Motors after Daewoo's bankruptcy) has survived, but its future is limited by the small size of the domestic market and the precarious nature of access to markets in the EAEU (Russia and Kazakhstan are the only exports markets, and these exports depend upon ad hoc agreements). Evidence on other ISI projects is scarce, but projects like the very large Turkmenbashi jeans factory in Turkmenistan involved substantial resource misallocation to the extent that the value of imports saved by producing jeans domestically was less than the export value of the cotton used in the jeans. Kazakhstan directed large amounts of oil revenues to promoting the agricultural sector, but this too has had limited success (Petrick and Pomfret 2018).

The most open Central Asian economy has been the Kyrgyz Republic, which in the first decade of the 21st century became the entrepôt for Central Asia.[12] Imported goods, mainly from China, were traded in huge bazaars outside Bishkek and Osh, where many of the customers were from neighbouring countries. Case studies of the Dordoi bazaar outside Bishkek estimate a workforce of 55,000 in what may have been the world's largest shopping mall by the number employed (Kaminski and Mitra 2010, 2012; World Bank 2009). Accommodation and food services were available, and efficient transport networks linked Dordoi to destinations in Uzbekistan, Kazakhstan and Russia.

Partly based on access to inputs at the bazaars and freer communications and upgraded roads, the Kyrgyz Republic saw the emergence of two international value chains in the 2000s. The textiles and clothing sector had collapsed in the 1990s, but a clothing industry re-emerged

---

[12] In May 1998, the Kyrgyz Republic became the first former Soviet republic to join the WTO, and its bound tariffs were low. It was also the most open Central Asian country in access to information, in contrast to the other Central Asian countries, which regulated access to internet sites and content in other media.

in the 2000s using materials largely imported from China and exporting to Kazakhstan and Russia, based on higher quality than clothing from Western China and lower prices than clothing manufactured in Eastern China. By 2010, the industry employed several hundred thousand people (Birkman et al. 2012; Jenish 2014; World Bank 2014). A second international value chain saw farmers in the north-western part of the country become major exporters of beans, a crop that did not feature in Kyrgyz national diets. The bean growers imported seeds and technology from Turkey, sorting and packing materials from China, and transport services from truckers who would otherwise return empty to Eastern Europe, Turkey or Russia. Beans-related activities provided employment to over 200,000 workers and significantly raised rural incomes in a previously relatively isolated part of the country (Tilekeyev 2013; Tilekeyev et al. 2018).

In the wider Central Asian context, these two examples of successful international value chains are small stuff. Moreover, even these examples came under threat after 2010 when Kazakhstan formed a customs union with Russia that would be broadened to the EAEU in 2015. The customs union increased the cost of transporting Chinese goods to the Kyrgyz Republic because the most direct routes passed through Kazakhstan. In 2015, in recognition that the country's current economic model was unsustainable, the Kyrgyz Republic joined the EAEU. Whether the EAEU has deepened fissures across Central Asia, with Kazakhstan and the Kyrgyz Republic inside the EAEU and Tajikistan, Turkmenistan and Uzbekistan outside, remains in dispute.[13]

PROSPECTS AND CHALLENGES OF THE BRI FOR CENTRAL ASIA

In Central Asia, participation in the China–EU rail land bridge has so far mainly involved Kazakhstan and has been low cost, low profile and low risk. Most land bridge trains pass through Kazakhstan. They do not stop to pick up or deliver freight, but this can still be useful as fees paid for travelling along already existing rail track do not involve large

---

[13] See, for example, Vinokurov (2017), Libman and Vinokurov (2018), Mogilevskii, Thurlov, and Yeh (2018) and Libman (2018).

costs to the transit country.[14] The land bridge runs on 20th century rail track and has required little investment beyond upgrading facilities for the change of gauge at the China–Kazakhstan border.[15]

The most controversial proposed investment is a rail link through the Kyrgyz Republic that would connect China's Western railhead at Kashgar to the eastern border of Uzbekistan and thence to existing track to Iran, that is, a shorter route from China to Southern Europe than a route north of the Caspian Sea. The terrain for the link, through very high mountains, is extremely difficult and cost estimates, depending on the precise route, range up to $6 billion. An issue for the Kyrgyz Republic is that the shortest route passes through a sparsely populated part of the country with little obvious economic benefit beyond transit fees, which may be insufficient to finance any debt incurred.[16]

Whether or not the Kyrgyz link is constructed, BRI is building on commercially viable China–EU rail freight services that will be available over alternative routes. One challenge for individual Central Asian countries is to decide whether they want to be on a main line and, if so, whether they are prepared to improve the soft infrastructure to make routes passing through their country competitive. The signs are that both Turkmenistan and Uzbekistan, which have been difficult transit countries since becoming independent in 1991, are now keen to participate actively in the regional trade network. For all Central

---

[14] The financial returns to the rail companies are commercially sensitive. However, Kazakhstan's rail company is reported to have earned over a billion dollars in transit fees in 2015 (see CAREC and CPMM 2015, 43).

[15] The container transfers at the change-of-gauge border are simple procedures: The incoming train and the outgoing train are lined up side by side, and a crane moves the containers from one to the other. At Khorgos, where the investment has been part of creation of a gateway special zone on the China–Kazakhstan border, the transfer for a 40-container train can be done in 47 minutes (Shepard 2016).

[16] The Kyrgyz Republic was one of eight countries that Hurley et al. (2018) identified to be vulnerable to debt dependence on China due to the high ratio of BRI construction costs to GDP. The Kyrgyz Republic's estimated annual GDP in 2017 was around $7 billion.

Asian countries, achieving the stated goal of economic diversification has become more pressing since the end of the resource boom in 2014.

The costs of international trade in Central Asia since the dissolution of the USSR have been high, although precise measurement is difficult. The four Central Asian countries covered in the World Bank's *Doing Business* database ranked between 77th and 166th out of 189 countries for overall ease of doing business in June 2014, but they were among the seven worst places in the world for ease of conducting international trade (Table 18.3). Turkmenistan was not covered but would have been lower than the other four Central Asian countries. In *Doing Business 2016*, which assessed performance in June 2015, the Central Asian countries had moved to higher ranks for overall ease of doing business and ease of international trade, and these positions were sustained in June 2016.

The *Doing Business* numbers may be poor guides to actual costs of international trade in Central Asia. The indicators have come under increasing scrutiny and the 'trading across border' component has been especially criticized for appearing to give concrete numbers for time

Table 18.3 Ease of Doing Business (June 2014, June 2015 and June 2016)

Country	Overall Ease[a, b]			Ease of International Trade[b]		
	June 2014	June 2015	June 2016	June 2014	June 2015	June 2016
Kazakhstan	77	41	35	185	122	119
Kyrgyz Republic	102	67	75	183	83	79
Tajikistan	166	132	128	188	132	144
Uzbekistan	141	87	87	189	159	165

Source: World Bank at www.doingbusiness.org
Notes: [a] overall rank based on unweighted average of scores in ten areas; [b] among 189 countries in 2014 and 2015, and 190 countries in 2016. Turkmenistan not included.

and cost.[17] They are especially poor for Central Asia, where the situation was not so bad as the June 2014 rankings imply, that is, placing Central Asia on par with the world's most desperate failed states. The apparent huge improvement in costs of international trade between 2014 and 2015 is also unbelievable, although the relative positions of the countries in June 2015 and in June 2016 are plausible and correspond to casual observation.

The Corridor Performance Measurement and Monitoring (CPMM) programme conducted by freight forwarders under the aegis of the CAREC secretariat (ADB 2014) produces the most convincing measures of high trade costs in Central Asia. For each trip, a reporter in a truck or on a train travelling along major corridors tracks the cost and time taken. The programme has been in operation since 2010, with between two and three thousand observations each year; the 2016 sample consisted of 2,756 trips, of which 70 per cent were by road, 26 per cent by rail, and 4 per cent multimodal. The CPMM indicators of cost and speed provide detailed information about the difficulties of conducting overland trade in Central Asia, and the large number of observations helps to address the uncertainty and variability of costs and time.

The overall picture is that, even when the physical infrastructure is good, journeys are slow and costly with especially long delays at border crossing posts (BCPs). Table 18.4 provides data for 12 road BCPs and 4 rail BCPs. CPMM (2015) identified the key problems for transport and transit to be lack of harmonized transit or BCP procedures with no best practice benchmark in the region, little effective inter-agency cooperation and absence of 'single window' BCPs, low adoption of risk-management

---

[17] The *Doing Business* methodology is based on asking informed people in national capitals about the cost in dollars and in time of shipping a container from the country's commercial centre, which may be appropriate for a country like Singapore but is less appropriate for the Central Asian countries where a small share of trade is by container and where there is a large variance between what an observer in the capital city may hear and what happens on the ground. Central Asian *Doing Business* estimates are mostly from respondents in consultancy firms, who refer to laws and regulations on the books rather than implementation on the ground or at the port. Pomfret (2019, Chapter 9.3) provides more details.

Table 18.4 Average Border Crossing Time in Hours, Inbound Traffic, Selected BCPs

	From–To	2010	2011	2012	2013	2014	2015	2016
		Road						
Khorgos	PRC/KAZ	16.0	12.7	17.3	11.2	6.8	5.8	3.3
Tazhen	UZB/KAZ	9.7	10.3	12.5	8.6	7.8	7.8	7.9
Konysbayeva	UZB/KAZ	8.2	8.7	7.8	6.8	7.5	7.5	7.6
Chaldovar	KAZ/KRG	36.9	5.1	4.9	6.6	6.5	6.5	5.2
Irkeshtam	PRC/KRG	4.5	12.0	9.9	7.2	6.1	5.2	5.7
Dusti	AFG/TAJ	8.7	5.4	4.6	5.3	5.8	5.8	4.0
Karamyk	KRG/TAJ	NA	3.9	3.6	1.9	2.3	4.7	2.8
Fotehobod	UZB/TAJ	8.0	4.8	4.4	5.1	6.6	7.1	7.0
Sarahs	IRN/TKM	6.4	6.5	10.5	8.8	6.1	6.1	6.2
Farap	UZB/TKM	8.6	7.8	8.5	6.6	7.3	7.1	7.5
Alat	TKM/UZB	3.7	5.3	5.8	4.6	5.3	5.4	5.4
Dautota	KAZ/UZB	3.9	4.8	12.8	6.1	5.8	5.9	6.1
		Rail						
Altynkol	PRC/KAZ	–	–	–	4.5	37.4	NA	54.0
Dostyk	PRC/KAZ	34.5	43.6	28.3	64.8	59.7	42.3	44.4
Farap	UZB/TKM	–	–	–	14.5	14.9	4.7	3.5
Keles	KAZ/UZB	–	–	–	4.9	0.8	5.7	3.5

Source: CPMM (2015, 42–43; 2016, 45).

techniques and persistent unofficial payments.[18] These problems reflect the poor soft infrastructure for international trade in Central Asia.

Improvements in the hard infrastructure (roads, railways, etc.) without improved soft infrastructure lead to only limited reduction in the time and money costs of international trade. In the early 2010s, delays became longer at many BCPs, apart from those between Russia and Kazakhstan, which were shortened after the establishment of the customs union; average border-crossing time for trucks leaving Kazakhstan for Russia fell from 7.7 hours in 2011 to 2.9 hours in 2012, while the average border-crossing time for trucks entering Kazakhstan from outside the customs union increased from 8.6 to 21.5 hours (CPMM 2012, 38–39). The longest delays were on the corridor with the highest volume of freight, the railway between China and Kazakhstan. At the border between China and Kazakhstan, the average time at the Chinese BCP (Alashankou) was 353 hours and at the Kazakhstani BCP (Dostyk) 54 hours in 2012.[19] The exception to the long delays in 2012 was the Chongqing–Duisburg train, which was subject to speedy gauge change and simplified border formalities. This last observation and the changes at the Kazakhstan–Russia border suggest that governments could facilitate trade when motivated, but the political will to do so for intra-Central-Asian trade has been lacking in the past years.

Arbitrary and capricious actions against traders appear to be becoming less common, although the CPMM project shows depressingly slow progress in increasing speeds and reducing border delays. Governments

---

[18] CPMM references in the text are to annual reports. The reports consistently find a 30–35 per cent chance that 'unofficial payments' are demanded at borders. Coulibaly and Thomsen (2016) provide examples of unofficial payments along the main Tajikistan–Kyrgyzstan–Kazakhstan route that were paid to avoid higher official fees, for example, for excessive axle load or breaking ecological rules, or to forestall a lengthy check, for example, paying officials not to open refrigerator doors on a truck.

[19] It is difficult to allocate the time to one BCP rather than the other because delays at one BCP lead to back-up of trains at the other, for example, delays entering Kazakhstan lead to back-up at the Chinese BCP. There is a suspicion that the 2012 data are influenced by the customs union's hard line towards goods entering from China (CPMM 2012, 21).

are beginning to undertake measures with the specific goal of trade facilitation (Pomfret 2019, Ch. 11.3). Starting from a 2013 initiative, the Presidents of China and Kazakhstan signed an agreement in May 2014 to introduce at the Bakhty/Bakhtu BCP, a fast-customs clearance green corridor for agricultural goods, after which the products (jam, beverages and sunflower seeds from Kazakhstan and apples, grapes, oranges, bell peppers and cucumbers from China) were passing through the green corridor in less than an hour. In 2015, the Kyrgyz Republic and Tajikistan announced that they would introduce green channels at BCPs with China; while across the Caspian, Azerbaijan announced similar plans. Although the initial steps are with respect to foodstuffs that may be perishable, the adjective 'green' is in the sense of green channels at airports, not in the sense of plants. Rapid clearance for pre-approved freight could be used to encourage manufacturers participating in international value chains.

The economics literature, although subject to many methodological caveats, consistently supports the hypothesis that improved infrastructure is positively related to increased trade, diversification and growth. The strongest evidence is for a market integration link, which is especially convincing in historical studies of the 19th-century agrarian economies of the Western USA or India. An important conclusion from more recent episodes is the importance of an infrastructure-growth link via labour movements, which promotes agglomeration benefits but has the potential to create losers as well as winners: The losers tend to be people stranded in depressed geographical regions, while the winners may be not only internal migrants to the big cities but also international migrants whose journeys are eased.

Many studies have found a significant positive relationship between infrastructure and international trade, typically using fairly general indicators of infrastructure, such as perceptions of port quality or the length of railways or paved roads. In this tradition, Portugal-Perez and Wilson (2012) used a gravity model to identify the impact on trade of indicators of hard infrastructure (physical infrastructure, and information and communications technology networks) and soft infrastructure (border and transport efficiency, and the business environment) in 101 countries over the period 2004–2007. Physical infrastructure and the business environment had the largest positive impact on bilateral trade flows; border efficiency and the business environment were more important at lower per capita GDP levels, and ICT and physical infrastructure increasingly important as per capita GDP increased. Portugal-Perez and Wilson (2012) also found less robust evidence of complementarity between hard and soft infrastructure, and weaker evidence that investment in physical infrastructure impacts more on GDP growth than on growth than on growth in GDP per capita.

A more recent literature emphasizes the complementarity between hard and soft infrastructure and their impact on the intensive and extensive margins of trade (i.e., whether infrastructure improvements stimulate greater levels of existing trade or trade diversification into new products) and on the nature of growth (e.g., whether favouring the rich or inclusive of poorer people). This is relevant to Central Asia, where high trade costs have not deterred exports with a strong comparative advantage, that is, primary products such as cotton, oil and gas, and minerals, but appear to have hampered diversification and been prohibitive for small and medium-sized enterprises. Reducing trade costs by improved hard and soft infrastructure can be expected to promote trade at the extensive margin and to stimulate inclusive growth.

More controversial, and more difficult to measure, are the magnitude of benefits, the determinants of benefits and their relation to costs. Influential analysis of the impact of improved infrastructure has been based on case studies. The difficulty is the representativeness of case studies, and also the endogeneity problem: Did infrastructure building stimulate trade and growth, or did it follow demand? The most cited studies focus on large-scale projects that had non-economic motives, such as the militarily driven railway programme in British India (Donaldson 2018), the US interstate highway programme, or nation-building exercises such as Canada's railway link to the Pacific or China's rail programme of the early 21st century. The principal gains in these studies are from market integration, which not only raises incomes but may also reduce price and income volatility by moderating demand–supply imbalances, for example, due to a poor harvest. Donaldson and Hornbeck (2016, 801) note that railways may have further benefits, such as enabling transport of perishable goods, facilitating access to inputs and participation in GVCs, stimulating technical transfer through the spread of ideas and increasing labour mobility. In rural areas, better transport can improve access to social services such as health and education, although that is typically associated with road rather than rail. These are all relevant to Central Asia.

In a more general context of any trade cost reducing shock, including improved transport infrastructure, Aghion et al. (2017) focus on two effects. The market expansion effect helps firms to cover fixed costs associated with innovating or exporting, which is positive for the firm and for the economy. The pro-competitive effect, that is, increased competition in the home market, is often unwelcome for firms, but positive for the economy as the least efficient firms are most likely to be culled, raising average productivity. This suggests that the effects of transport infrastructure improvements debated in terms of international change are also valid with respect to internal transport investment and domestic trade. It also implies that improved international connectivity is more important for smaller economies.

In sum, it is hard to forecast the economic impact of BRI on Central Asia, but the international evidence suggests that improved hard and soft infrastructure could promote desired economic diversification and generate inclusive growth. At the same time, BRI could exacerbate some less-desirable long-term economic development trends through migration, agglomeration and path-dependence effects. While soft infrastructure improvements tend to be low cost and win-win, hard infrastructure can be expensive, and many expensive projects have become symbols of poorly managed public spending. The potential for debt-dependence due to misguided spending is particularly acute for the smaller economies and, in the BRI context, is especially relevant to the Kyrgyz Republic.

CONCLUSIONS

The China–Europe Land Bridge and BRI could signal a new opportunity for Central Asia. Connectivity will be improved, especially if there are multiple routes, which may be stimulated by Iran's reintegration into the global economy and Turkey's rail tunnel under the Bosporus. The EAEU offers smoother travel between the

China–Kazakhstan border and the Belarus–Poland border and into Schengenlanden, while the BRI could speed up travel along a rail route south of the Caspian Sea and other spurs from and links between the main lines.[20] All Eurasian Land Bridge lines between China and Europe, except the Trans-Siberian, pass through Central Asia, and the key question is whether the domestic environment and soft infrastructure of trade can encourage more small- and medium-sized enterprises to follow the example of the Kyrgyz tailors and bean farmers by establishing or participating in GVCs.

The most likely outcome is that at least some of the Central Asian countries will seize the opportunity to generate economic diversification and inclusive growth in the 2020s. If Eurasian value chains displace regional value chains in East Asia and Europe, then successful GVC participants in Europe and Asia may find new opportunities in the larger Eurasian GVCs, rather than having to develop their own value chains or create integrated industries. As with most economic changes, there are potential losers from reduced transport costs as well as gainers. For example, reduced trade costs subject import-competing firms to greater competition. The policy challenge for Central Asian governments is to implement economic reforms to increase the ease of doing business and to improve the soft infrastructure of international trading without being distracted and obstructed by beneficiaries from the status quo.

REFERENCES

ADB. 2014. *Central Asia Regional Economic Cooperation Corridor Performance Measurement and Monitoring: A Forward-Looking Perspective*. Manila: ADB.

ADBI. 2014. *Connecting Central Asia and Economic Centers: Interim Report*. Tokyo: Asian Development Bank Institute.

Aghion, P., Antonin Bergeaud, Matthieu Lequien, and Marc J. Melitz. 2017. *The Impact of Exports on Innovation: Theory and Evidence* (No. w24600). National Bureau of Economic Research.

---

[20] The China–Pakistan Corridor component of the BRI could help Central Asian connectivity by providing a route to Pakistan and its ocean ports without transiting Afghanistan. However, the Karakoram Highway is a difficult road, especially in winter, and the rail link is a distant project.

Birkman, L., Maria Kaloshkina., Maliha Khan, Umar Shavurov, and Sarah Smallhouse. 2012. *Textile and Apparel Cluster in Kyrgyzstan*. Cambridge, MA: Harvard University Kennedy School and Harvard Business School.

CAREC and CCPMM. 2015. *Corridor Performance Measurement and Monitoring, Annual Report 2015*. Manila: ADB.

Coulibaly, S., and Lotte Thomsen. 2016. 'Connecting to Regional Markets? Transport, Logistics Services and International Transit Challenges for Central Asian Food-Processing Firms'. *Central Asian Survey* 35 (1): 16–25.

Donaldson, D. 2018. 'Railroads of the Raj: Estimating the Impact of Transportation Infrastructure'. *American Economic Review* 108 (4–5): 899–934.

Donaldson, D., and Richard Hornbeck. 2016. 'Railroads and American Economic Growth: A 'Market Access' Approach'. *Quarterly Journal of Economics* 131 (2): 799–858.

Dragneva-Lewers, R., and Kataryna Wolczuk. 2017. 'The Eurasian Economic Union: Deals, Rules and the Exercise of Power'. *Chatham House Research Paper*, Royal Institute of International Affairs, London.

Hurley, J., Scott Morris, and Gailyn Portelance. 2018. 'Examining the Debt Implications of the Belt and Road Initiative from a Policy Perspective'. *CGD Policy Paper 121*, Center for Global Development, Washington DC.

Jenish, N. 2014. 'Export-Driven SME Development in Kyrgyzstan: The Garment Manufacturing Sector'. Institute of Public Policy and Administration Working Paper No. 26, University of Central Asia, Bishkek.

Kaminski, B., and Saumya Mitra. 2010. *Skeins of Silk: Borderless Bazaars and Border Trade in Central Asia*. Washington, DC: World Bank.

Kaminski, B., and Saumya Mitra. 2012. *Borderless Bazaars and Regional Integration in Central Asia: Emerging Patterns of Trade and Cross-Border Cooperation*. Washington, DC: World Bank.

Laruelle, M., and Sébastien Peyrouse. 2009. *China as a Neighbor: Central Asian Perspectives and Strategies*. Washington, DC: Central Asia-Caucasus Institute Silk Road Studies Program.

Libman, A. 2018. 'Eurasian Economic Union: Between Perception and Reality'. *New Eastern Europe*, January 9. http://neweasterneurope.eu/2018/01/09/8767/

Libman, A., and Evgeny Vinokurov. 2018. 'Autocracies and Regional Integration: The Eurasian Case'. *Post-Communist Economies* 30 (3): 334–364.

Mogilevskii, R. 2012a. 'Trends and Patterns in Foreign Trade of Central Asian Countries'. Institute of Public Policy Working Paper No.1/2012, University of Central Asia, Bishkek.

Mogilevskii, R. 2012b. 'Re-export Activities in Kyrgyzstan: Issues and Prospects'. University of Central Asia Institute of Public Policy and Administration, Working Paper No. 9, Bishkek.

Mogilevskii, R., James Thurlov, and Adeline Yeh. 2018. 'Kyrgyzstan's Accession to the Eurasian Economic Union: Measuring Economy-Wide Impacts and Uncertainties'. *University of Central Asia Institute of Public Policy and Administration, Working Paper No. 44*, Bishkek.

Petrick, M., and Richard Pomfret. 2018. 'Agricultural and Rural Policies in Kazakhstan'. In *Handbook on International Food and Agricultural Policy Volume I: Policies for Agricultural Markets and Rural Economic Activity*, edited by T. Johnson and W. Meyers, 461–482. Singapore: World Scientific Publishing Company.

Pomfret, R. 2019. *The Central Asian Economies in the Twenty-first Century: Paving the New Silk Road*. Princeton, NJ: Princeton University Press.

Portugal-Perez, A., and John S. Wilson. 2012. 'Export Performance and Trade Facilitation Reform: Hard and soft infrastructure'. *World Development* 40 (7): 1295–1307.

Raballand, G., and Agnès Andrésy. 2007. 'Why Should Trade between Central Asia and China Continue to Expand?' *Asia Europe Journal* 5 (2): 235–252.

Shepard, W. 2016. 'Why the China–Europe "Silk Road" Rail Network is Growing Fast'. *Forbes*, January 28.

Tilekeyev, K. 2013. 'Productivity Implications of Participation in Export Activities: The Case of Farmers in Talas Oblast of Kyrgyzstan'. Institute of Public Policy and Administration Working Paper No. 17, University of Central Asia, Bishkek.

Tilekeyev, K., Roman Mogilevskii, Nazgul Abdrazakova, and Shoola Dzhumaeva. 2018. 'Production and Exports of Kidney Beans in the Kyrgyz Republic: Value Chain Analysis'. Institute of Public Policy and Administration Working Paper No. 43, University of Central Asia, Bishkek.

Vinokurov, E. 2017. 'Eurasian Economic Union: Current State and Preliminary Results'. *Russian Journal of Economics* 3 (1): 54–70.

Vinokurov, Evgeny, Vitaly Lobyrev, Andrey Tikhomirov, and Taras Tsukarev. 2018. *Silk Road Transport Corridors: Assessment of Trans-EAEU Freight Traffic Growth Potential* (Eurasian Development Bank Centre for Integration Studies Report 49). Saint Petersburg: EDB Centre for Integration Studies.

World Bank. 2009. *Bazaars and Trade Integration in Central Asia Regional Economic Cooperation (CAREC) Countries*. Washington, DC: World Bank. http://www.carecinstitute.org/uploads/events/2009/10th-TPCC/10thTPCC-Bazaars-Trade-Integration-Paper.pdf

World Bank. 2014. *Kyrgyz Republic—The Garment Sector: Impact of Joining the Customs Union and Options to Increase Competitiveness*. Washington, DC: World Bank. https://openknowledge.worldbank.org/handle/10986/21103

About the Editors and Contributors

EDITORS

David De Cremer is the provost chair and professor in management and organization at NUS Business School. Before moving to NUS, he was the KPMG endowed professor of management studies at the University of Cambridge (where he is now a fellow). He is a research affiliate at Yale Law School, Yale University (USA), and a fellow at the Hoover Institution, Stanford University. He is the founder of the LEAD platform (LEading Artificial intelligence & Digital management) and a scientific advisor to the companies Novartis (the Ethics-based Compliance Initiative), and KPMG (building trustworthy climates). He is a prolific author in the fields of management, behavioural economics and psychology and his research has received many international awards, including three early career awards and a mid-career award for his scientific contributions. In addition, he was elected as a member of the Royal Dutch Academy of Science, being named the most influential (behavioural) economist in the Netherlands (Top 40 of economists) and named one of the Top Thought Leaders in Trust by the organization Trust across America. He has consulted and taught many companies including, among others, KPMG, Barclays, Solvay, Novartis, HSBC, Mizuho, Microsoft, AB Inbev, and IBM. He is also a bestselling author, having sold over more than 1,000,000 copies of his latest book *Huawei: Leadership, Culture and Connectivity* (This book received the PwC best business book award in Russia). His work has been discussed in media such as, among others, the *Bloomberg News*, *The Economist*, *Forbes*, *The Financial Times*, *Harvard Business Review*, *The Economist Intelligence Unit*, *Wall Street Journal*, *CBS Money Watch*, *The Times*, *The Sunday Times*, *Daily Telegraph*, and *BBC*. He received his PhD from the University of Southampton, England, an MA from Cambridge University, and an MSc in social psychology, and BA in philosophy from the University of Leuven, Belgium. He was a (visiting) professor at New York University, Harvard University, China Europe International Business School (CEIBS) and London Business School (LBS) in the past.

Bruce McKern is currently an Adjunct Professor at the University of Technology Sydney and a member of the UTS Business School Advisory Board. In his early career as a chemical engineer, he worked with Dupont, Union Carbide and General Electric before completing a doctorate at Harvard University. His previous academic appointments include Director of the Stanford Sloan Master's Program at Stanford University's Graduate School of Business, Professor of International Business and Co-Director of the Centre on China Innovation at the China Europe International Business School in Shanghai, President of the Carnegie Bosch Institute and Professor of International Business at Carnegie Mellon University, Visiting Fellow at Stanford's Hoover Institution and Dean of two Australian business schools. During 2015 and 2016, he was also a Visiting Research Fellow working on innovation at INSEAD, the University of Oxford Technology and Management Centre for Development, and the Saïd Business School at the University of Oxford.

His research and publications have been in the fields of international business and innovation, and he is an authority on innovation in China. His most recent book is *China's Next Strategic Advantage: From Imitation to Innovation* (with George Yip), MIT Press, 2016. In addition to his current research on China's Belt and Road Initiative, he is co-editor of the *Oxford Handbook of China Innovation* (forthcoming in 2019). He is also author of numerous academic papers, Harvard and Stanford case studies and nine books, including 'China's Innovative Nation' in *Disruptive Asia*, Asia Society, 2017; 'Innovation in Emerging Markets: The Case of China' (with George Yip) in *International Journal of Emerging Markets*, 2014; and *Managing the Global Network Corporation* (2003). He is also an Editorial Board Member of *Management International Review*, Member of the International Advisory Committee of the Research Centre for Technological Innovation at Tsinghua University, Beijing; Adviser to the Maritime Silk Road Society in Hong Kong; and a Mentor for the CSIRO ON Prime Accelerator. Previously he was a Member of the US-Korea Business Council in Washington DC, the MIT Enterprise Forum in Pittsburgh, a Board Member of the Harmarville Rehabilitation Center and a Founding Member of the Global Trade Institute of Pennsylvania. He also comments in international media on issues of MNC strategy and China innovation, including *The Economist, Financial Times, Wall Street Journal, China Radio International, China Daily, South China Morning Post, The Conversation, Australian Financial Review*, RTS Switzerland; CGTV Washington DC, etc.

Jack McGuire is a Doctoral Student at the National University of Singapore Business School in the Department of Management and Organisation. Prior to this, he held the position of Experimental Lab Manager of the Cambridge Experimental and Behavioural Economics Group (CEBEG) and Research Assistant in the Department of Organisational Behaviour at Judge Business School, University of Cambridge. He has obtained an MA (SocSci) from the University of Glasgow, an MSc from University College London, and has also held research positions in the University of Tubingen and the University of Hong Kong. In addition to his time spent in academia, he has also worked in consultancy specializing in behavioural economics.

CONTRIBUTORS

Mustafa Gokhan Bitmis was a visiting post-doctoral researcher at Judge Business School, University of Cambridge in 2017–2019. His research was funded by the Scientific and Technological Research Council of Turkey. He has held academic appointments at the Universities of Baskent and Ankara HBV (Formerly known as Gazi) in Turkey. He received his PhD from Hacettepe University in 2014. Prior to joining the academia, he held various posts in automobile, insurance, cement and concrete industries.

Yann Duval is currently the Chief of Trade Policy and Facilitation at ESCAP, the regional branch of the United Nations Secretariat for Asia and the Pacific. Over the past 15 years, Dr Duval has conducted research and delivered technical assistance and advisory services on trade policy and facilitation throughout Asia and the Pacific, including on the WTO Trade Facilitation Agreement. He spearheaded the development of the Asia-Pacific Research and Training Network on Trade (ARTNeT) as well as the creation of the ESCAP–World Bank Trade Cost Database and the UN Global Survey on Trade Facilitation and Paperless Trade Implementation. Dr Duval was also instrumental in the development of the United Nations Network of Experts for Paperless Trade and Transport in Asia and the Pacific (UNNExT) and the negotiation of a new intergovernmental Framework Agreement on Facilitation of Cross-Border Paperless Trade in Asia and the Pacific, adopted as a UN treaty in 2016.

Mark J. Greeven is a Chinese-speaking Dutch professor of innovation and strategy at IMD Business School in Switzerland and former faculty at China's leading innovation institute at Zhejiang University. He is the author of *Pioneers, Hidden Champions, Changemakers, and Underdogs* (2019) and *Business Ecosystems in China* (2017).

Saite Lu is currently a final year PhD candidate at the Centre of Development Studies and Graduate Research Assistant at the Bennett Institute for Public Policy. Prior to coming to Cambridge, he was a Senior Economist/ODI Fellow in the Ministry of Finance and Economic Development in Sierra Leone. Upon completion of the fellowship, he continued to work as a macro-fiscal adviser for the Budget Strengthening Initiative (BSI), providing technical support to the governments of Sierra Leone and South Sudan. He also actively engaged in the research on microfinance in Bangladesh and multidimensional poverty measurement with the Oxford Poverty and Human Development Initiative. He has an MPhil in Economics from the University of Oxford and a BSc in Economics from the University of Ulster.

Dorinela (Dora) Munteanu is currently a PhD candidate in Applied Economics and Management in the field of International Entrepreneurship at Antwerp Management School and the University of Antwerp. She researches SMEs internationalization and the interactions between global macro-level trends and the micro-level entrepreneurial activities. She has been involved with research and education projects on China and Europe, such as the European project 'Understanding China' for European Chambers of Commerce and SMEs, the publication of a bi-annual report of Euro-China Investment Report and the analysis of the impact of the Belt and Road on the Antwerp regional ecosystem, Belgium. Dora Munteanu has also extensive practice experience in market research and advice regarding internationalization of SMEs in emerging economies of Central and Eastern Europe and in China. A native Romanian, she has studied sinology in Bucharest and Beijing, and obtained a management degree in Belgium, at the University of Antwerp.

Nikolay Murashkin is a Visiting Fellow at Griffith Asia Institute, Griffith University and Sessional Academic, School of Political Science and International Studies, University of Queensland. He earned his PhD from the University of Cambridge focusing on Japanese foreign policy in the New Silk Road region. Prior to his academic career, Nikolay completed a Master's degree at Sciences Po, Paris, and has worked as an analyst in a London-based bank on commodity finance transactions in Central Asia and Eastern Europe. He has been a Japan Foundation Fellow at Waseda University, Tokyo. He has published in a number of peer-reviewed journals and was the winner of the 1st prize of the Russian Association of Japanologists for the best academic paper by a junior scholar.

Richard Pomfret holds the Jean Monnet Chair on the Economics of European Integration at the Institute for International Trade and has been Professor of Economics at the University of Adelaide since 1992. From 1979 to 1991, he was a Professor of Economics at the Johns Hopkins University School of Advanced International Studies. He has acted as a consultant to the United Nations, World Bank, OECD, IMF and Asian Development Bank. He has published over a hundred articles and 20 books, including *The Economics of Regional Trading Arrangements* (2001), *The Central Asian Economies since Independence* (2006), *Regionalism in East Asia: Why has It Flourished Since 2000 and How Far will It Go?* (2011), *The Age of Equality: The Twentieth Century in Economic Perspective* (2011), *International Trade: Theory, Evidence and Policy* (2016) and *The Central Asian Economies in the Twenty-first Century: Paving a New Silk Road* (2019).

Zhu Qinli is currently a Research Assistant at the China Europe International Business School (CEIBS) in Shanghai. She obtained her Master of International Money, Finance and Investment degree from the University of Durham in 2007. Before joining the CEIBS, Ms Zhu worked as a consultant at a Dutch company for four years. Ms Zhu worked on the productivity and the impact of RMB exchange rate on industrial companies with Professor Zhang Yimin since she joined CEIBS in 2011. She is now working at the project of China RMB internationalization in relation to the One Belt and One Road.

Bala Ramasamy is Associate Dean and Professor of Economics at the China Europe International Business School (CEIBS), Shanghai, China. He researches in the areas of Foreign Direct Investment, International Trade and Economic Development, focusing mainly among Asian developing economies. His research has been published in the *Journal of Business Ethics*, *The World Economy*, *Journal of World Business*, *Journal of World Investment and Trade*, *Journal of Business Research*, among others.

Michael Tai is a professor of development studies at the Beijing Institute of Technology, and author of *US–China Relations in the 21st Century* and *China and Her Neighbours*. He is a frequent contributor to the South China Morning Post and has been a guest on BBC World Service. Michael spent a good part of his career in the media, steel and transportation sectors, and taught in Kyrgyzstan, Belarus, as well as the UK. He speaks fluent Chinese, French, German and Malay.

Simon Taylor, after completing his PhD in economics at the London School of Economics, spent 15 years working in the equity markets before joining Judge Business School's finance faculty in 2007 where he teaches international finance and infrastructure finance. He has published two books on the nuclear power industry and is a member of Cambridge University's Energy Policy Research Group. He has visited China many times and has been an honorary academic advisor to Minsheng Business Academy in Beijing and a visiting professor at Xiamen University. He is a Fellow of St. Catharine's College, Cambridge.

Chorthip Utoktham is a Consultant in the Trade and Investment Division of the United Nations Economic and Social Commission for Asia and the Pacific (ESCAP) in Bangkok. Her specialization includes gravity-related topics in inducing trade flows and trade costs reduction in enhancing trade facilitation.

Stefanie Weil is an Associate Professor and Academic Director at Antwerp Management School, University of Antwerp. At the same time, she also holds a position as Senior Associate visiting professor at Xi'an Jiaotong Liverpool University in Suzhou/China. Before starting her academic career in 2007, she worked as a managing director in various consulting companies in Germany, France and the UK. Prior to her current posts, she also was a research fellow at the Brussels Institute for Contemporary China Studies (BICCS) and Head of Business department and Associate Dean at the Vesalius College/Free University Brussels. She also worked as a research follow at Tong Ji University in Shanghai. She is specialized in international political economy and China's foreign policies. She has published on comparative politics across China, European Union and the United States, lobbying in China and comparative Western Chinese political concepts.

Peter J. Williamson is a Professor of International Management at Judge Business School and Fellow of Jesus College, University of Cambridge. He divides his time between research and consulting on global strategy, M&A, and business ecosystem innovation and serving as non-executive director of several companies spanning financial services through to green energy. He has held professorships at London Business School, Harvard Business School and INSEAD (in Singapore). Formerly with Merrill Lynch and the Boston Consulting Group, he earned his PhD in Business Economics from Harvard University. Peter has been visiting China since 1983 and has authored two of Asia's bestselling business books *Dragons at Your Door: How Chinese Cost Innovation is Disrupting Global Competition* and *Winning in Asia*.

Chaowei Xiao is Assistant Professot at The National Academy of Development and Strategy, Renmin University, China. He receives his PhD at the Department of Land Economy, University of Cambridge, UK. He is editor of *Urban Planning International*. His research interests are big data analysis, spatial statistics, urban development, and Belt and Road Initiative. His articles have appeared in *Environment and Planning A: Economy and Space*, *Sustainability*, *Pacific Focus*, and *Urban Planning International*.

Matthew Yeung is an Associate Professor of Research Methods at the Institute of International Business and Governance of the Open

University of Hong Kong, HKSAR. His research interest focuses on applied statistical methods, foreign direct investment, consumer sentiment and big data analysis. Dr Yeung's research has been published in the *Journal of Business Ethics*, *The World Economy*, *Journal of World Business*, *Journal of World Investment and Trade*, *Journal of Business Research*, among others.

Yimin Zhang is a professor at the China Europe International Business School (CEIBS) in Shanghai. HE obtained his PhD from University of British Columbia in 1989. After two years of post-doctoral research at the University of British Columbia, he worked at the Faculty of Business, University of New Brunswick in Canada from 1991 to 1997, then moved to Hong Kong in 1997 to work at City University of Hong Kong until 2004 before Joining CEIBS. Dr Zhang's research interests include industrial economics, productivity and impact of RMB exchange rate on industrial companies. Dr Zhang's publications appeared in *Journal of Public Economics*, *Journal of Business Economic Statistics*, *Review of Economics and Statistics*, *Journal of Transport Economics and Policy*, *Journal of Urban Economics*, *Journal of Comparative Economics*, *China Economics Review* and *Review of Pacific Basin Financial Markets and Policies*, among others.

Eden Yin is a senior lecturer in marketing at the Judge Business School, University of Cambridge. He has obtained his PhD from the Marshall School of Business, University of Southern California. Eden's research centres on the branding strategies, innovation and internationalization strategies of Chinese firms. His work has been published at top academic journals such as *Marketing Science*, *Journal of Marketing Research*, and practitioners' journals such as *Sloan Management Review*, *Ivey Business Journal* and a few others. He teaches MBA, EMBA and executive programmes at the Judge Business School and a few other universities.

Chuchu Zhang is an Associate Professor at School of International Relations and Public Affairs, Fudan University, China. She receives her PhD in Politics and International Studies, University of Cambridge, UK. Her research interests are Middle Eastern politics, China–Middle

East relations, and terrorism. Her articles have appeared in *Environment and Planning A: Economy and Space, Sustainability, Pacific Focus, Chinese Political Science Review,* and *Journal of Middle Eastern and Islamic Studies.*

Ying Zhang holds backgrounds of economics, management, and industrial engineering, and has been actively contributing as a scholar, educator, advisor, TEDx Speaker, business developer, and a social entrepreneur. At Rotterdam School of Management, Erasmus University in the Netherlands, she is an Associate Professor of Entrepreneurship and Innovation, and an Associate Dean for China Business and Relations. In 2019, she has been recognized as one of the Top 30 Thinkers under Radar by Thinkers50.com, and one of the 'Top 40 Business School Professor Under 40' by Poets and Quants in 2015. Dr Zhang received her PhD from Eindhoven University of Technology, the Netherlands.

Index

1Malaysia Development Berhad (1MDB), 309
2+2 talks between Russia and Japan, 111
21st Century Maritime Silk Road, Indonesia, 111, 179, 258
7th UK–China Economic and Financial Dialogue, 296

Abe Shinzō, 113, 123
African Development Bank, 52
AidData database, 140
Algerian design and technical standards, 175
Alibaba, 238, 250, 251
Alibaba Cloud, 252
Alipay, 252
Amazon Web Services, 252
American Enterprise Institute (AEI), 46, 48, 50
Ant Financial, 238, 253
APEC, 107
ASEAN, 106, 111, 205
    China–FTA for the Indochina Corridor, 106
    -Japan Development Fund, 114
    M&A activity in, 222
Asia Infrastructure Investment Bank (AIIB), 339
Asian developing countries, need to invest in infrastructure, 27, 50
Asian Development Bank (ADB), 27, 50, 52
Asian Development Bank (ADB), 123
Asian Development Bank Institute, 287

Asian financial crisis (1997), 69, 76, 84, 118
Asian Infrastructure Investment Bank (AIIB), 10, 62, 81, 107, 112, 151, 210, 365
audio–video coding standards for digital television, 244
Aung San Suu Kyi, 125

Baidu, 238, 245
Baidu, Alibaba and Tencent (BAT), 245
balance sheet of People's Bank of China, 279
Bangladesh–China–India–Myanmar Economic Corridor (BCIM), 93, 108
Bank of China, 288
BaoDao bond, Taiwan, 297
BATNA, 196
Bay of Bengal Initiative for Multi-Sectoral Technical and Economic Cooperation (BIMSTEC), 106
behavioural discrimination, 13
Beijing Automotive Industry Holding Co (BAIC), 228, 232
Beijing Consensus, 70
Belt & Road Industrial and Commercial Alliance (BRICA) Summit in 2018, Turkey, 197
Belt and Road Forum (BARF), 356
Belt and Road Forum for International Cooperation
2017, 180, 372
2019, 308

Index | 397

Belt and Road Initiative (BRI), 36, 138, 145, *See also* Chinese Marshall Plan
  academic-driven analysis of, 6
  acceptance and operationalisation of AIIB, 11
  aims and objectives of, 3, 93
  analysis of company or strengths and weakness of China, 352
  and David Livingstone approach, 363
  and improvement in transport corridor, 107
  and singularity, 13
  balance of payments, impact on, 325
  capacity to finance, 28
  challenges and obstacles in, 53
  changes in exports of economies and corridors, 100
  collaborators, analysis and identification of, 353
  corridors, analysis of, 97
  criticism of, 4
  cross-continent platform, 11
  customer or BRI countries, pain points for analysis, 351
  debt with and without, 327
  dilemma in investment, 56
  domestic institutional source for funding, 335
  estimation of infrastructure investment, 51
  external foreign debt, 328
  financing, methods of, 335
  funded by multilateral development banks, 320
  ideas from Chinese perspective, 83
  institutional source for financing, 340
  intercultural negotiation as foundation for success of, 186
  investment estimation, 321
  issues in projects and reasons for it, 24
  macroeconomic aspect of financing, 324
  marketing and promotion as solution for problems, 346
  multilateral banks funding from outside, 341
  narrative, ideas and interest of, 75
  OFDI and construction in countries of, 50
  opportunities for Chinese firms for outward investments, 276
  outward foreign direct investment, 48
  paradox in, 15
  positioning value proposition, 359
  problems faced by, 345
  product strategies for, 360
  promotion strategies for, 361
  propositions of, 20
  provide stimulus to external trade, 28
  quanitification, definition and problem of, 321
  results of corridors analysis, 101
  revival of Silk Road through, 4
  segmentation of customers and countries, 354
  strategic marketing framework, 350
  strategy to claim world leader in international system, 61
  targeting rights segments or countries, 356
  tool with Chinese characteristics, 84
  unveiled in 2013, 63
  vision document of, 92
  Xi Jinping personal and authority on, 5
Belt and Road Initiative (BRI), 10, 153, 180
BMI Baltic Management Institute, Lithuania, 248
border crossing posts (BCPs), 378
Bretton Woods system, 68, 69
Brexit, 76

business process analyses of trade procedures (BPA), 104

capital intensity of China, 285
capital-intensive economy, 276
Central Asian countries and China, relationship between
   in trade, 367
   New Silk Road railway, 373
   political relations, 367
   prospects and challenges of BRI in Central Asia, 383
   resource dependence and limited diversification in Central Asia, 375
   rising economic influence of China, 372
Central Asian Regional Economic Cooperation programme (CAREC), 115
Centre for China and Globalization (CCG), 251
Chabahar Port project, 125, 210
ChemChina, 224, 227
Chen Xiaoming, 37
China Bank of Communication, 288
China Banking Association, 321
China Construction Bank, 288
China Development Bank (CDB), 338
China Europe International Business School (CEIBS), 248
China Europe International Exchange Ltd., 297
China Financial Futures Exchange, 297
China Foreign Exchange Trade System (CFETS), 292
China Global Investment Tracker (CGIT), 258, 263
China Harbour Engineering Company, 144
China Industrial and Commercial Bank, 288
China National Petroleum Corp (CNPC), 143

China State Construction Engineering Corporation (CSCEC), 176
China–Central Asia–West Asia Economic Corridor (CAWA), 93, 108
China–Indochina Peninsula (ICP), 108
China–Mongolia–Russia Economic Corridor (CMR), 93, 108, 320
China–Pakistan Economic Corridor (CPEC), 93, 108, 207, 215, 332
   and US-Pakistan relations, 214
   challenges from Pakistan and Chinese side, 210
   competition from other routes, 212
   reasons for China to take risks, 216
   upgrade infrastructure of Pakistan, 203
China–Pakistan FTA for the CP corridor, 106
Chinese Academy of Sciences, 253
Chinese Academy of Social Sciences, 248
Chinese Marshall Plan, 3
Chinese National Petroleum Corporation, 369
Chinese outbound M&A
   acquisition integration process, 227
   competitive advantages of, 229
   phases of, 223
   potential benefits, 230
   rise in value, 224
   role in BRI, 225
clusters
   emerging, 46
   frontier, 46
collaborator analysis, 348
Commonwealth of Independent States (CIS), 106
company analysis, 348
competitor analysis, 348
context analysis, 348
Corridor Performance Measurement and Monitoring (CPMM) programme, 378

Index | 399

corruption bonanza, 308
Corvinus Business School (CBS), 248
cross-cultural negotiation, 182

data of fight, 263
data of protest, definition of, 263
DaYang bond, Sydney, 297
Deng Xiaoping, 309
Deutsche Bank, 353
Deutsche Borse, 297
Development Assistance Committee (DAC), 139
Digital Belt and Road Program (DBAR), 253
Digital Silk Road, 254, 255
Digital Silk Road, 253
DimSum bond, Hong Kong, 297
Dinghan Tech, 243
DJI, 238
doing dusiness (DB) methodology, 378

East Asian Summit (2017), 126
Economic and Technological Development Zone (ETDZ), 36
economic opportunism, 4
Economic Research Institute of Central and Eastern Europe (ERICEE), 248
equality, causes after World Wars, 12
ESCAP Framework Agreement on Facilitation of Cross-border Paperless Trade in Asia and the Pacific (2016), 106
Eurasian Development Bank (EDB), 119
Eurasian Economic Community (EAEC) for Central Asia, 106
Eurasian Economic Union (EAEU), 130, 211, 212, 374
Eurasian Silk Road, 203
Euro Code, 175
European Bank for Reconstruction and Development, 52

European Union TRACECA programme, 128
EXIM Bank, 152
Export Processing Zone (EPZ), 36
Export–Import (EXIM) Bank of China, 140
Export–Import Bank of China (Exim), 337

Face++, 238
Faculty of Business Administration at University of Economics Prague, Czech Republic, 248
Faculty of Economics, Ljubljana University (FELU), Slovenia, 248
finances for infrastructure investment, 141
foreign engagement, 41
free trade agreements (FTAs), 106
Free Trade Zones (FTZs), 41
French National Standard, 175
Fukuda Takeo, 114

G20, 69, 84
Gago (big data), 243
GATT, 68
GeDe bond, Germany, 297
Geek+ (logistics automation), 243
Geographic Information Systems (GIS), 265
Global Database of Events, Language, and Tone (GDELT), 263
Global Entrepreneurship Monitor 2015 Global Report, 240
global financial crisis of 2008, 70, 84
Go West policy of China, 369, 370
gravity modelling method, 95
Great Leap Forward (1958-1962), 215
Greater Bay Area (GBA) (original Pan Pearl Rive Delta or 9+2 plan), 45
Greater East Asia Co-Prosperity Sphere, 114
Greater Mekong Subregion (GMS) programme, 115

gross expenditure on R&D (GERD), in China, 33
Gross National Income (GNI), 152
Gwadar Port, 203, 210

Han Dynasty (206 BCE–220 CE), 4
Heavily Indebted Poor Countries (HIPC), 146
High-Tech Industrial Development Zone (HIDZ), 36
Hofstede's 6D Model, 184, 186, 187
Hong Kong Stock Exchange, 295
Huawei, 243, 244, 245, 249, 252
Hu-Gang Tong, 295

ideas
  cognitive, 73
  definition of, 71
  influenced through media, 73
  normative, 73
  rooted within society, 73
iFlytek, 238
individualism versus collectivism (IDV), 184
Indo-China Peninsula corridor, 107
Indochina Peninsula Economic Corridor (IP), 93
Indo-Pakistan war of 1965, 204
indulgence versus restraint (IND), 184, 185
Inept Systematic Intelligence (ISI), 15
innovation ecosystem, 34
innovative China, 238
innovative maturing ecosystem, of China
  Chinese entrepreneurs along BRI, case studies, 251
  expansion into BRI countries, 244
  higher education exchange, 248
  in education, 240
  intellectual property rights (IPR), 241
  opportunities and challenges in promoting connectivity, 255

outward direct investments in innovation, 246
private venture capital, 241
Sino-CEE Fund, case study, 247
support for science and engineering, 247
intellectual property rights (IPRs), 241
Inter-American Development Bank, 52
interest group, 71
International Bank for Reconstruction and Development (IBRD), 52
international business negotiations, definition of, 182
International Finance Corporation, 52
International Monetary Fund (IMF), 63, 66, 68, 69, 115, 211
  forecasts on China's balance of payments surplus, 324
International Union of Railways (UIC) Standard, 175
iReal, 243
Islamic Development Bank, 115

Jack Ma, 251
Japan
  approach towards BRI, 128
  rejection of Russia ADB membership bid, 123
  vs Asian infrastructure, 117
Japan–China Economic Association, 127
JD.com, 252
Jing-jin-ji initiative for Beijing-Tianjin-Hebei region, 44
Juncker, Claude, 4

KaiXuan bond, France, 297
Karakoram Highway, 384
KATVR (virtual reality solutions), 243
Keizo Obuchi, 308
Khan, Ayub, 204
Kissinger, Henry, 212
Korean War of 1950, 213
Kozminski University, Poland, 248

leadership role and BRI
  and challenges in future, 315
  connection with followers, 314
  vision, importance of, 309
LED technology, 244
Lenovo, 245
Li Keqiang, 126, 203, 307
liberal international system, China's
  leadership in, 70
logistics (or trade facilitation) corridor,
  103
long-term orientation (LTO), 184, 185
lower-middle income countries
  (LMICs), 150

Made in China 2025 plan, 34, 37
Malong (artificial intelligence and
  computer vision), 243
Maritime Silk Road, 53, 126, 145,
  222, 310
Marx, Karl, 75
masculinity versus femininity (MAS),
  184, 185
Microsoft Azure Cloud Service, 252
Ministry of Commerce (MOFCOM),
  China, 47, 50
MIT Technology Review, 238
Mobvista (digital marketing), 243
monetary base of China, 278
Multilateral Debt Relief Initiative
  (MDRI), 146

Nakasone Yasuhiro, 114
National Intellectual Property
  Administration (CNIPA)
  (formerly the State Intellectual
  Property Office), 33
National Research Council of
  Thailand (NRCT), 253
national savings, in China, 284
natural resources in Africa, Chinese
  investment in, 142
New Asian Industries Development
  Plan (New AID), 114

New Development Bank (NDB), 151,
  340
New Eurasia Land Bridge Economic
  Corridor (NELB), 93, 108
New Eurasian Continental Bridge,
  320
Nixon, Richard, 213
North Africa
  and ancient Egypt and Carthage
    period, 159
  and Belt and Road Initiative,
    distribution and challenges due
    to, 176
  and European colonial period, 164
  and Roman and Byzantine periods,
    161
  city distribution after independence,
    168
  city distribution during Arabian and
    Ottoman empire, 163
  evolution of cities in, 158
  evolvement of urban spatial
    structure and function in, 169
  urbanization problem due to, 176
Northern Alliance, 212

official development assistance (ODA),
  139, 140, 147, 152, 330
official finance by sector in African
  countries, 142
One Belt One Road (OBOR)
  Initiative, 9, 14, 27, 300, 344,
  See also Belt and Road Initiative
  (BRI)
One97 Communications, 253
Other Official Finance (OOF), 139,
  141
outward FDI (OFDI) by Chinese
  firms, 36, 286

Patent Cooperation Treaty (PCT)
  process, 34
Paytm, 253
people strategy, 349

PetroChina, 230
polarized world, composition after world war II, 12
policy approach adopted by China, 32
political risks
  definition of, 261
  types of, 261
potential political risks along BRI
  and potential costs for multinational enterprises, 264
  indicators of, 262
  methodology to analyse, 265
  results of case study, 272
poverty in China, challenges and priority, 31
power distance (PDI), 184
pricing strategy, 349
private entrepreneurship, 240
private venture capital, 241
product strategy, 349

Qualified Foreign Institutional Investors (QFII) programme (2003), 295

Razak, Najib, 309
regional integration, 46
regional trade agreement (RTA), 95
regional trade agreements (RTAs), 106
Rejoin (visual-aid products), 243
reserve ratio of China, 281
RMB international bonds, 297
RMB internationalization, 277
  and BRI countries, 298
  and BRI countries, 289
  and international balance of payments, 285
  and money supply, 281
  and role of international finance cooperation, 290
  cross-border settlement for international investment, 295
  exchange rate system, 293
  financial risks involved in, 290
  monetary policy, reforms in, 291
  offshore centres, 297
  opening of capital markets, 296
RMB Qualified Foreign Institutional Investors (RQFII) (2011), 295
Russia, engagement with BRI, 131

Shanghai Cooperation Organization (SCO), 210, 365, 367
Shanghai FTZ, 37
Shanghai Lingang Industrial Area, 40
Shanghai Stock Exchange, 295, 297
Shen-Gang Tong, 295
ShenGen bond, Luxemburg, 297
Shenzhen Stock Exchange, 295
ShiCheng bond, Singapore, 297
Silicon Valley (US), 41
Silk Road Economic Belt (SREB), 4, 9, 14, 80, 126, 129, 248, 258, 259, 356
Silk Road Fund, 338, 341
singularity, 13
Sino-Pakistan relations, 205
Sino-Pakistan-US triangle, 213
situation analysis, 348
South Asian Association for Regional Cooperation (SAARC), 106
South Asian FTA (SAFTA), 106
South Sudan, Chinese investment in, 146
Soviet Union, 12
Soviet-Afghan War (1979–1989), 212
strategic marketing decision-making, 348
Sub-Sahara Africa (SSA), 137
  gross debt in, 146
  Mamamah Airport in Sierra Leone case st, 150
Sub-Sahara Africa (SSA), Chinese investment in infrastructure of commercial loans by China, 146

Tanaka Kakuei, 114
Taylor, Simon, 28, 55

Tencent, 238, 245, 250, 253
Total Early-Age Entrepreneurial Activity of China, 240
trade facilitation, 93
trade war between US and China, 309
Trans-Pacific Partnership (TPP), 10
Trump, Donald, 126
Turkey and China
  BRI negotiators, similarities and differences between, 192
  cross-cultural comparison between, 189
Turkey support and presence in BRI
  benefits for China, 182
  formal negotiation stage, 197
  post-negotiation stage, 198
  pre-negotiation stage, 196
  reasons for, 181
Turkmenistan–Afghanistan–Pakistan–India gas pipeline project, 120
Twiggle, 250

UN Global Survey on Trade Facilitation and Paperless Trade Implementation, 106
UN Sustainable Development Goals (SDGs), 138
uncertainty avoidance (UAI), 184, 185
United Nation Economic and Social Commission for Asia and the Pacific (ESCAP), 107
United Nations (UN), 66, 74
United Nations Development Programme, 115
Universities Alliance of the New Silk Road (UASR), 248
upper-middle income countries (UMICs), 150
US-China relations, 62

Waigaoqiao FTZ, 37
Wang Huiyao, 251
Wang Yi, 127
WeChat, 253
WhatsApp, 253
World Bank, 68, 69, 74, 115
  Doing Business in 2014, 378
World Economic Forum, 34
World Economic Forum Enabling Trade Index (ETI), 95
World Trade Organization (WTO), 66, 74, 223, 251
  China's accession to, 277
Wuzhen World Internet Conference (2017), 251

Xi Jinping, 3, 5, 9, 34, 62, 111, 230, 253, 259, 300, 308, 321, 345, 366
  idea of Chinese dream, 78
  voice of emerging powers in global governance system, 64
Xi'an Jiaotong University (XJTU), 248
Xiang Zhaolun, 306
Xiaomi smartphones, 249
Xinhua Silk Road, 259
Yang Jiechi, 302
Yangtze River Delta (YRD) cluster, 46

Zhai-Quan Tong, 295
Zhejiang University, 237
Zhou Enlai, 204
zone of possible agreement (ZOPA), 197
Zongmu (Advanced Driver Assistance System), 243
zou chuqu policy ('Go Global'), 223
ZTE, 244, 245, 252